Guyana and Belize
country studies

Federal Research Division
Library of Congress
Edited by
Tim Merrill
Research Completed
January 1992

On the cover: Linden Forbes Burnham, first prime minister of independent Guyana, and George Cadle Price, first prime minister of independent Belize

Second Edition, First Printing, 1993.

Library of Congress Cataloging-in-Publication Data

Guyana and Belize : country studies / Federal Research Division, Library of Congress ; edited by Tim L. Merrill. — 2d ed.
p. cm. — (Area handbook series, ISSN 1057-5294) (DA pam ; 550-82)
"Supersedes the 1969 edition of Area Handbook for Guyana, coauthored by William B. Mitchell, et. al."—T.p. verso.
"Research completed January 1992."
Includes bibliographical references (pp. 345-369) and index.
ISBN 0-8444-0778-X
1. Guyana 2. Belize. I. Merrill, Tim L., 1949- .
II. Library of Congress. Federal Research Division. III. Area handbook for Guyana. IV. Area handbook for Belize. V. Series. VI. Series: DA pam ; 550-82.
F2368.G88 1993
988.1—dc20 93-10956
CIP

Headquarters, Department of the Army
DA Pam 550-82

For sale by the Superintendent of Documents, U.S. Government Printing Office
Washington, D.C. 20402

Foreword

This volume is one in a continuing series of books prepared by the Federal Research Division of the Library of Congress under the Country Studies/Area Handbook Program sponsored by the Department of Army. The last page of this book lists the other published studies.

Most books in the series deal with a particular foreign country, describing and analyzing its political, economic, social, and national security systems and institutions, and examining the interrelationships of those systems and the ways they are shaped by cultural factors. Each study is written by a multidisciplinary team of social scientists. The authors seek to provide a basic understanding of the observed society, striving for a dynamic rather than a static portrayal. Particular attention is devoted to the people who make up the society, their origins, dominant beliefs and values, their common interests and the issues on which they are divided, the nature and extent of their involvement with national institutions, and their attitudes toward each other and toward their social system and political order.

The books represent the analysis of the authors and should not be construed as an expression of an official United States government position, policy, or decision. The authors have sought to adhere to accepted standards of scholarly objectivity. Corrections, additions, and suggestions for changes from readers will be welcomed for use in future editions.

Louis R. Mortimer
Chief
Federal Research Division
Library of Congress
Washington, D.C. 20540

Acknowledgments

The authors would like to acknowledge the contributions of William B. Mitchell, William A. Bibbiani, Carole E. DuPre, Diane Fairbank, Janice H. Hopper, Ransford W. Palmer, Theodore L. Stoddard, and Robert L. Wood, who wrote the 1969 first edition of *Guyana: A Country Study*. The present volume incorporates portions of their work.

The authors are grateful to individuals in various government agencies and private institutions who gave of their time, research materials, and expertise in the production of this book. These individuals include Ralph K. Benesch, who oversees the Country Studies—Area Handbook Program for the Department of the Army. None of these individuals, however, is in any way responsible for the work of the authors.

The authors also would like to thank those people on the staff of the Federal Research Division who contributed directly to the preparation of the manuscript. They include Sandra W. Meditz, who reviewed drafts, provided valuable advice on all aspects of production, and conducted liaison with the sponsoring agency; Marilyn L. Majeska, who reviewed editing and managed production; Andrea T. Merrill, who edited figures and tables; and Barbara Edgerton and Izella Watson, who did the word processing. In addition, thanks go to Vincent Ercolano and Richard Kollodge, who edited chapters; Catherine Schwartzstein, who performed the final prepublication editorial review; Joan C. Cook, who compiled the index; and Malinda B. Neale and Linda Peterson of the Library of Congress Printing and Processing Section, who performed the phototypesetting, under the supervision of Peggy Pixley.

Thanks also go to David P. Cabitto of the Federal Research Division, who provided valuable graphics support and who, along with the firm of Greenhorne and O'Mara, prepared the maps; and to Wayne Horne, who did the cover art and chapter illustrations. Finally, the authors acknowledge the generosity of the individuals and the public and private agencies who allowed their photographs to be used in this study.

Contents

Page

Foreword iii

Acknowledgments v

Preface xv

Introduction xvii

Guyana: Country Profile xxix

Chapter 1. Guyana: Historical Setting 1
Scott B. MacDonald

THE EARLY YEARS 4
THE COMING OF THE EUROPEANS 6
TRANSITION TO BRITISH RULE 7
THE EARLY BRITISH COLONY AND THE LABOR PROBLEM 9
ORIGINS OF THE BORDER DISPUTE WITH VENEZUELA 10
POLITICAL AND SOCIAL AWAKENINGS 11
- Nineteenth-Century British Guiana 11
- Political and Social Changes in the 1900s 13
- The Development of Political Parties 15

PREINDEPENDENCE GOVERNMENT, 1953-66 18
- The PPP's First Government, 1953 18
- The Interim Government, 1953-57 19
- The Second PPP Government, 1957-61, and Racial Politics 19
- PPP Reelection and Debacle 21

INDEPENDENCE AND THE BURNHAM ERA 22
- Burnham in Power 23
- The Cooperative Republic 24
- From Burnham to Hoyte 27

Chapter 2. Guyana: The Society and Its Environment 29
Frederick J. Conway

GEOGRAPHY 31
- Terrain 31
- Hydrology 34

Climate 34
POPULATION 35
Demographic Profile 35
Ethnic Composition 37
Population Distribution and Settlement Patterns 37
Urban Population 38
Emigration 38
ETHNIC GROUPS 40
Afro-Guyanese 40
Indo-Guyanese 41
Portuguese and Chinese 41
Amerindians 42
Development of Ethnic Identity 43
Ideologies of Race and Class 44
FAMILY AND KINSHIP STRUCTURE 44
Afro-Guyanese Patterns 44
Indo-Guyanese Patterns 46
RELIGION 47
Christianity 48
Hinduism 48
Islam 49
Obeah and Amerindian Practices 50
Cults 50
Religion and Politics 51
EDUCATION 52
Education Policy and the Teaching Profession 54
Primary Schools 55
Secondary Schools 55
Institutions of Higher Education 56
Attitudes Toward Education 58
HEALTH AND WELFARE 60
Food and Diet 60
Health 60
Health and Welfare Services 61

Chapter 3. Guyana: The Economy 65
Brian D. McFeeters

GROWTH AND STRUCTURE OF THE ECONOMY 68
History 68
Structure 74
Parallel Economy 75
Infrastructure 77
GOVERNMENT POLICY 78

The Economic Recovery Program ... 78
Results of the Economic Recovery Program ... 81
LABOR ... 82
AGRICULTURE ... 84
Sugar ... 84
Rice ... 86
Forestry ... 86
Fisheries ... 88
Livestock ... 88
MINING ... 89
Aluminum ... 89
Gold and Diamonds ... 91
INDUSTRY ... 92
Energy Supply ... 92
Manufacturing ... 93
SERVICES ... 94
Banking ... 94
Transportation ... 96
Communications ... 97
EXTERNAL ECONOMIC RELATIONS ... 97
Foreign Trade ... 97
Foreign Debt ... 99
Balance of Payments ... 101
Foreign Investment ... 102
Foreign Aid ... 104
Regional Integration ... 104

Chapter 4. Guyana: Government and Politics ... 107
Georges A. Fauriol

CONSTITUTIONAL BACKGROUND ... 109
Preindependence Constitutions ... 109
Independence Constitution ... 111
Constitution of 1980 ... 112
GOVERNMENT INSTITUTIONS ... 113
Executive ... 113
Legislature ... 115
Judiciary ... 115
Other National Institutions ... 116
Local Government ... 117
Civil Service ... 118
POLITICAL DYNAMICS ... 118
Electoral Process ... 118
Political Parties ... 119
Interest Groups ... 120

FOREIGN RELATIONS 123
Relations with the United States 123
Relations with Venezuela 125
Relations with Brazil 127
Relations with Suriname 127
Relations with Britain 128
Relations with the Commonwealth Caribbean 128
Relations with Communist Countries 129

Chapter 5. Guyana: National Security 131
Christopher S. Simmons

THE ARMED FORCES 133
Mission, Organization, and Capabilities 136
Involvement in Political Affairs 137
THE SECURITY FORCES 140
Mission and Organization 140
Human Rights Violations 143
THE COURTS AND THE PENAL SYSTEM 144
BORDER DISPUTES 145
Guyana-Venezuela Dispute 145
Guyana-Suriname Dispute 147

Belize: Country Profile 151

Chapter 6. Belize: Historical Setting 155
O. Nigel Bolland

ANCIENT MAYAN CIVILIZATION 157
PRE-COLUMBIAN MAYAN SOCIETIES AND THE CONQUEST 161
THE EMERGENCE OF THE BRITISH SETTLEMENT . . . 163
Colonial Rivalry Between Spain and Britain 163
Beginnings of Self-Government and the Plantocracy 164
Slavery in the Settlement, 1794–1838 166
Emigration of the Garifuna 169
THE EARLY COLONY 169
Constitutional Developments, 1850–62 169
Mayan Emigration and Conflict 170
Formal Establishment of the Colony, 1862–71 172
COLONIAL STAGNATION AND CRISIS 172
The Colonial Order, 1871–1931 172
The Genesis of Modern Politics, 1931–54 174
DECOLONIZATION AND THE BORDER DISPUTE WITH GUATEMALA 181

Chapter 7. Belize: The Society and Its Environment 187
Charles C. Rutheiser

GEOGRAPHY 189
Boundaries, Area, and Relative Size 189
Geology 191
Physical Features 191
Natural Resources 192
Climate 192
POPULATION AND SETTLEMENT PATTERNS 193
Size, Growth, and Distribution 193
Migration 195
THE CULTURAL DIVERSITY OF BELIZEAN SOCIETY 196
Ethnicity 196
Language 200
Religion 201
Cultural Pluralism and Ethnic Diversity 202
STRUCTURE OF BELIZEAN SOCIETY 204
The Upper Sector 204
The Middle Sector 206
The Lower Sector 208
Social Dynamics 210
EDUCATION 211
School System 213
Patterns of Access and Performance 215
STANDARD OF LIVING 217
Food and Diet 217
Health and Welfare 218

Chapter 8. Belize: The Economy 221
Uwe Bott

GROWTH AND STRUCTURE OF THE ECONOMY 223
The Colonial Economy 223
The Small Economy 225
Economic History 226
Growth During 1980–85 227
Growth after 1985 229
Peripheral Factors 229
GOVERNMENT POLICY 230
Economic Diversification 230
Balance of Payments 231
Investments 231

Fiscal Performance 233
External Debt 233
LABOR 234
FOREIGN ECONOMIC RELATIONS 235
AGRICULTURE 236
Sugar 236
Citrus 237
Bananas 238
Other Crops 239
FISHING AND FORESTRY 240
INDUSTRY 240
Mining and Energy 240
Manufacturing 241
Construction 241
TOURISM 242
OTHER SERVICES 243
Transportation and Telecommunications 243
Banking and Finance 244
ECONOMIC PROSPECTS 245

Chapter 9. Belize: Government and Politics 247
Steven R. Harper

CONSTITUTIONAL BACKGROUND 249
Constitutional and Political Structures prior to Independence 249
Constitution of 1981 253
GOVERNMENT INSTITUTIONS 255
Executive 255
Legislature 258
Judiciary 261
Public Service 262
Local Government 263
POLITICAL DYNAMICS 264
Electoral Procedures 264
Electoral Process since Independence 266
Political Parties 269
Interest Groups 274
Mass Communications 279
FOREIGN RELATIONS 280
Relations with the United States 280
Relations with Guatemala 282
Relations with Other Latin American and Caribbean Countries 284

Relations with Britain 285
Relations with Other Countries 286

Chapter 10. Belize: National Security 289
Melinda W. Cooke

BELIZE'S MILITARY HISTORY AND STRATEGIC SETTING 292
THE BELIZE DEFENCE FORCE 296
Personnel and Training 296
Organization and Equipment 298
Defense Spending 299
Foreign Military Relations 300
PUBLIC ORDER AND INTERNAL SECURITY 301
Crime 302
The Belize National Police 303
The Criminal Justice System 305

Appendix A. Tables 309

Appendix B. The Commonwealth of Nations ... 319
Deborah Cinchon

Appendix C. The Caribbean Community and Common Market 327
Jeffrey Taylor

Appendix D. Caribbean Basin Initiative 337
Daniel Seyler

Bibliography 345

Glossary 371

Index 377

List of Figures

1 Guyana: Administrative Divisions, 1991 xxviii
2 Guyana: Topography and Drainage 32
3 Guyana: Estimated Population by Age and Sex, 1985 ... 36
4 Guyana: Gross Domestic Product (GDP) by Sector of Origin, 1989 76
5 Guyana: Transportation System, 1991 98
6 Guyana: Organization of the Government, 1991 114
7 Guyana: Border Disputes, 1991 126
8 Guyana: Military Ranks and Insignia, 1991 138
9 Belize: Administrative Divisions, 1991 150

10 Belize: Mayan Settlements, A.D. 700–1700 160
11 Belize: Topography and Drainage 190
12 Belize: Estimated Population by Age and Sex, 1986 194
13 Belize: Gross Domestic Product (GDP) by Sector of Origin, 1987 232
14 Belize: Transportation System, 1991 244
15 Belize: Organization of the Government, 1991 256
A Organization of the Caribbean Community and Common Market (Caricom), 1992 330

Preface

Like its predecessor, this study is an attempt to examine objectively and concisely the dominant historical, social, economic, political, and military aspects of contemporary Guyana and Belize. Sources of information included scholarly books, journals, monographs, official reports of governments and international organizations, and numerous periodicals. Chapter bibliographies appear at the end of the book; brief comments on sources recommended for further reading appear at the end of each chapter. To the extent possible, place-names follow the system adopted by the United States Board on Geographic Names. Measurements are given in the metric system; a conversion table is provided to assist readers unfamiliar with metric measurements (see table 1, Appendix A). A glossary is also included.

The body of the text reflects information available as of January 1992. Certain other portions of the text, however, have been updated. The Introduction discusses significant events that have occurred since the completion of research; the Country Profile includes updated information as available; several figures and tables are based on information in more recently published sources; and the Bibliography lists recently published sources thought to be particularly helpful to the reader.

Introduction

GUYANA AND BELIZE belie their geographic location. Although both are located on the mainland of the Americas, they more closely resemble the English-speaking islands of the Caribbean than they do their Latin American neighbors. Christopher Columbus passed near the coasts of both countries, but later Spanish explorers and settlers ignored the areas because they lacked the mineral riches that brought the Spanish to the New World. The wealth of both areas would prove to be not gold but agriculture. By the end of the eighteenth century, the indigenous populations of both regions had been greatly reduced or driven to remote areas, and the coastal lands held growing populations of British or Dutch plantation owners. Plantation work was labor intensive, and initially African slaves, then other ethnic groups, were imported to work the land. As the colonies expanded economically, Britain claimed formal sovereignty, but title to each colony remained contested.

The twentieth century saw a shift in political power from the old plantocracy to a new nonwhite middle class, a rising self-consciousness among the various ethnic groups, and a slow evolution toward independence. Formal ties to Britain eventually were broken, but, like their anglophone Caribbean neighbors, Guyana and Belize today still strongly bear the mark of their colonial heritage. They retain their British institutions, their use of the English language, their economies based on agriculture, and their societies composed of a complex ethnic mix often divided along racial lines.

Unlike the great civilizations of Middle America that left monuments and records for archaeologists to decipher, the early societies in Guyana were relatively simple, nomadic cultures that left few traces. Early Spanish records and linguistic studies of the Caribbean reveal only a broad outline of pre-Columbian events. We do know that several centuries before the arrival of the Europeans, the Arawak moved north from Brazil to settle and farm the area along the northeast coast of South America before expanding farther north onto the Caribbean islands. Shortly before the arrival of the Europeans, the aggressive, warlike Carib pushed into the area and largely destroyed Arawak society.

Because of the warlike Carib and the region's apparent lack of gold or silver, the Spanish ignored the northeastern coast of South America. Settlement by Europeans would wait until 1616, when a group of Dutch arrived to establish a trading post. The Dutch soon realized the agricultural potential of the swampy coastal land

and aggressively set out to drain the coast, using a vast system of seawalls, dikes, and canals. What had been swampy wasteland decades before, soon turned into thriving sugar plantations.

The development of agriculture brought rapid change to the colony. Because the plantation economy needed labor, the Dutch imported African slaves for the task. The growing economy also attracted the attention of the British, and British settlers from neighboring Caribbean islands poured into the three Dutch colonies established along the coast. By the late 1700s, the new British settlers effectively controlled the colonies. Formal control by Britain would come in 1814, when most Dutch colonies were ceded to Britain after the Napoleonic wars.

In 1838 Britain completed the abolition of slavery throughout the British Empire, and the problem of obtaining cheap and plentiful labor arose anew. The planters first sought to attract Portuguese, then Chinese, workers, but both groups soon left plantation work. Concerned that the decline in labor would ruin the sugar-based economy, the planters finally contracted laborers from India to work the sugar fields. Large numbers of indentured workers poured into British Guiana in the late 1800s. Although theoretically free to return after their contract period had expired, most East Indians remained, adding a new ethnic group to the colony's mélange of Africans, Europeans, and Amerindians.

The twentieth century saw a rising consciousness among the country's ethnic groups and a struggle for political power between the new, disenfranchised, nonwhite middle class and the old plantocracy. Economic changes gave momentum to the growing call for political changes. The country saw rice production, dominated by the Indo-Guyanese (descendants of East Indians), and bauxite mining, dominated by the Afro-Guyanese (descendants of Africans), grow in importance, whereas sugar growing, controlled by the European plantation owners, declined. The British colonial administration responded to demands for reform by establishing universal suffrage in 1950 and allowing the formation of political parties.

The People's Progressive Party (PPP), the country's first political party, quickly became a formidable force. The PPP was formed by two men who would dominate Guyanese politics for decades to come: Cheddi Jagan, a Marxist Indo-Guyanese, and Linden Forbes Burnham, an Afro-Guyanese with leftist political ideas. A new constitution allowing considerable self-rule was promulgated in 1953; in elections that year, the PPP, headed by Jagan, won a majority of seats in the new legislature. The new administration immediately sought legislation giving the labor unions expanded power. This legislation and the administration's leftist rhetoric frightened the British colonial authorities, who suspended the new government after only four months.

Conflict with the British was not the only problem facing the PPP. Personal rivalries between Jagan and Burnham and growing conflict between the Indo-Guyanese and the Afro-Guyanese widened into an open split. In 1957 Burnham and most of the Afro-Guyanese left the PPP and formed the rival People's National Congress (PNC). The two parties shared left-wing ideologies; the differences between them were largely based on ethnicity.

The British promulgated a new constitution in 1957. Elections in that year and in 1961 resulted in more PPP victories. Under the new constitution, considerable power resided in the hands of the governor, who was appointed by the British. The PPP administration headed by Jagan was therefore unable to implement most of its radical policy initiatives. The Marxist rhetoric, however, intensified.

Convinced that independence under a PPP administration would result in a communist takeover, the British authorities permitted and even encouraged a destabilization campaign by the opposition PNC. Antigovernment demonstrations and riots increased, and in 1963 mobs destroyed parts of Georgetown, the capital. When labor unrest paralyzed the economy, British troops were called in to restore order. In the midst of the unrest, the government scheduled new elections in 1964.

Voting along ethnic lines again gave the PPP the largest number of seats in the legislature. But the rival PNC, by allying itself with a small business-oriented party, was able to form a coalition government. Jagan had to be forcibly removed as prime minister, and in December 1964 Burnham assumed the post. Under the new administration, events stabilized, and independence was set for May 26, 1966.

The independent Guyana inherited by the PNC was one of the least-populated and least-developed countries in South America. Located on the northeast coast of the continent just north of the equator, the Idaho-sized country is wedged among Venezuela, Brazil, and Suriname (former Dutch Guiana). More than 90 percent of the population lives within five or six kilometers of the sea. This coastal plain, constituting only 5 percent of the country's total area, was originally low swampland but was transformed by the Dutch into the country's most productive agricultural land. Inland from the coastal plain lies the white-sand belt, site of most of Guyana's mineral wealth of bauxite, gold, and diamonds. Farther inland are the interior highlands, consisting of largely uninhabited mountains and savannahs.

Guyana's ethnic mix at independence, still the same in 1993, consisted primarily of Indo-Guyanese—about half the population—and Afro-Guyanese—slightly more than 40 percent of the total. Smaller numbers of Amerindians, Asians, and Europeans completed Guyana's ethnic mélange. More than two-thirds of the population was Christian, with significant Hindu and Muslim minorities. Established by the British, the school system has resulted in high literacy rates (more than 90 percent).

The small military, the Guyana Defence Force, existed primarily as a deterrent to Venezuela's territorial claim. Venezuela's claim to the western three-fifths of Guyana, a dispute that dated from the colonial era, was thought to have been settled by arbitration in 1899. When later evidence showed that one of the judges had been influenced to vote against Venezuela, that country declared the arbitration settlement invalid and in the 1960s aggressively pursued its territorial claim on western Guyana. This border dispute was to flare periodically after Guyana's independence.

The first years of PNC administration after independence saw Prime Minister Burnham vigorously establishing control over Guyana's political and economic life. The 1968 elections were won by the PNC, despite charges of widespread fraud and coercion of voters. As the government's control over the country's political institutions increased, Burnham began nationalizing industries and financial institutions. In 1970 Guyana was declared a "cooperative republic," and government control of all economic activity increased. The 1973 elections were considered the most undemocratic in Guyana's history, and by 1974 all organs of the state had become agencies of the ruling PNC.

In the late 1970s, a number of events increased opposition to the Burnham regime. The economy, which had grown immediately after independence, began to contract because of nationalization. In addition, in 1978 negative international attention was focused on Guyana when more than 900 members of the People's Temple of Christ led by Jim Jones committed mass murder and suicide at their community in western Guyana. As opposition to the government increased, the government responded by violence against opposition members and meetings. The authoritarian nature of the Burnham government caused the loss of both foreign and domestic supporters.

A new constitution was promulgated in 1980, shifting power from the prime minister to the new post of executive president, but the political and economic situation continued to decline. Government programs had been financed by increasing the foreign debt, but in the early 1980s, most foreign banks and lending organizations refused further loans. The quality of life deteriorated: blackouts were frequent, and shortages of rice and sugar, Guyana's two largest crops, appeared. In 1985 in the midst of this turbulence, Burnham died while undergoing throat surgery.

Vice President Hugh Desmond Hoyte became the country's new executive president. He had two stated goals: to secure political power and revitalize the economy. Establishing political control was easy. The PNC chose Hoyte as its new leader, and in the 1985 elections the PNC claimed more than 79 percent of the vote. Economic growth, however, would require concessions to foreign lenders. Hoyte therefore began to restructure the economy. An economic recovery plan was negotiated with the International Monetary Fund (see Glossary) and the World Bank (see Glossary), allowing for new loans in exchange for free-market reforms and reversal of the Burnham administration's nationalization policies. To win favor with Western governments and financial institutions, Hoyte also moderated the previous administration's leftist tilt in international relations.

The results of economic reform were slow to appear, but by 1990 the economy began to grow again. The last legitimate date for new elections was December 1990. Sensing, however, that the PNC might be able to win a fair election (and thus regain a measure of international respect) if the economy continued to improve, the government invoked a clause in the constitution allowing elections to be postponed a year. Seeing a chance for an honest election, a group of Guyanese civic leaders created the Elections Assistance Board (EAB) to monitor the upcoming elections. The EAB appealed to the Carter Center in Atlanta for international support in its effort.

Despite threats and intimidation, in July 1991 the EAB conducted a door-to-door survey to verify voter lists. When the lists were shown to be grossly inaccurate, the Hoyte administration, under pressure from the EAB and the international community, declared a state of emergency and agreed to postpone the elections until October 1992 and implement a series of reforms suggested by the Carter Center. The reforms included appointment of a new election commissioner and agreement that the ballots be counted at polling centers in view of poll watchers instead of being taken to government centers and army bases for tallying.

The election date was finally set for October 5, 1992. Hoyte based the PNC campaign on the improving economy, which he credited to his free-market reforms. The PPP, still headed by Jagan after forty-two years, renounced its past Marxist policies and embraced elements of a free-market economy. In a reversal of decades of racial politics, Jagan attempted to downplay the country's ethnic polarization by naming an Afro-Guyanese, Sam Hinds, as his running mate.

Monitored by an international team of observers headed by former United States President Jimmy Carter, election results gave an alliance of the PPP, the smaller Working People's Alliance (WPA), and the United Force (UF) 54 percent of the vote, and the PNC, 45 percent. These results translated into thirty-two seats in the National Assembly for the PPP, thirty-one seats for the PNC, and one apiece for the WPA and the UF. Foreign observers certified the elections as "free, fair, and transparent." The PNC conceded defeat on October 7 and, after twenty-eight years, stepped down from power. Following brief consultations, the PPP formed a coalition government with the WPA and the UF (named the PPP-Civic coalition) and named Jagan executive president.

Two days of rioting and looting in Georgetown and Linden in eastern Guyana followed announcement of the election results. By the time the army and police restored order, two demonstrators had been killed and more than 200 injured. Many analysts attributed the violence to the fear that a PPP government would mean fewer economic benefits for the Afro-Guyanese population. Former President Carter, however, stated that the violence was localized and the looting unrelated to the voting.

In a radio broadcast on October 13, Jagan outlined the direction of the new government. He stated his intention to build a political consensus that cut across ethnic lines and to continue the privatization policies of his predecessor. Analysts speculated that the new administration would have difficulty in getting measures approved by the National Assembly and would face strong opposition from the PNC-dominated military and civil service. Election observers noted also the need to lower racial tension in a society that some characterized as one of the most racially divided they had witnessed. The motto on the Guyanese coat of arms proudly proclaims, "One people, one nation, one destiny." In 1993, however, this motto remained a distant goal.

The history of preindependence Belize parallels in many ways the history of Guyana. Unlike the pre-Columbian inhabitants of Guyana, however, the Maya in Belize left majestic ruins of their civilization. Remains of the earliest settlers of the area date back at least to 2500 B.C. By 250 A.D. the classic period of Maya culture had begun; this period of city-building lasted for more than 700 years. During this time, the Maya built large ceremonial centers, practiced large-scale agriculture using irrigation, and developed writing and a sophisticated calendar. Around the tenth century, evidence suggests that the great cities were abandoned, perhaps because of increased warfare among the city-states, revolt of the peasants against the priestly class, overexploitation of the environment, or a combination of these and other factors. Even though the great ceremonial centers were left to decay, the Maya continued to inhabit the region until the arrival of the Europeans.

The first European settlers in the area were not Spanish but English. Although Christopher Columbus passed through the area on his fourth voyage to the Americas in 1502, Spanish explorers and settlers ignored the region because it lacked gold. English pirates roaming the Caribbean in the seventeenth century began establishing small camps near the Belize River to cut logwood, from which a black dye was extracted. Logwood extraction proved more profitable than piracy, and the English settlements on the Caribbean coast grew.

The Spanish sent expeditions throughout the eighteenth century to dislodge the British settlers. The British were repeatedly forced to evacuate but returned shortly after each attack. Several treaties in the late 1700s recognized the British settlers' right to extract logwood but confirmed Spanish sovereignty over the region, a concession that later would lead to a territorial dispute.

The colony continued to grow throughout the nineteenth century. Logwood extraction was replaced by mahogany cutting as the settlement's principal economic activity, and slaves were introduced to increase production. By the time emancipation was completed in 1838, the settlement had evolved into a plantation society with a small number of European landowners and a large population of slaves from Africa.

In the nineteenth century, the colony was also a magnet for dispossessed groups throughout the region. The Garifuna (see Glossary), an Afro-indigenous people descended from the Carib Indians and slaves of the Eastern Caribbean, found refuge in the area in the early 1800s. In the mid- and late 1800s, large numbers of Maya, many of whom had intermarried with or become culturally assimilated to the Spanish-speaking population of Central America, fled fighting in the Yucatán or forced labor in Guatemala and settled in the colony.

The nineteenth century also saw the development of formal government. As early as 1765, a common law system for the settlers was formalized, and a superintendent was named in 1794. A rudimentary legislature began meeting in the early 1800s, and in 1854 the British produced a constitution and formally established the colony of British Honduras in 1862. Political power in the colony remained firmly in the hands of the old settler elite, however; blacks working the plantations were disenfranchised, and smaller populations of smallholder Garifuna and Maya lived on the periphery of society.

The early 1900s were a period of political and social change. Nonwhite groups, particularly an emerging black middle class, began to agitate for the vote and political power. Mahogany production slowed, and the colony began to depend on sugar for revenue. Additional immigrants from neighboring Spanish-speaking countries drifted in and settled among the rural Maya. Creoles (see Glossary), as the English-speaking blacks called themselves, began to participate in colonial politics.

The Great Depression of the 1930s greatly accelerated the pace of change. Mahogany exports virtually collapsed, and the colonial officials responded with measures designed primarily to protect the interests of the plantation owners. As a result, widespread labor disturbances broke out. Pressured by persistent labor unrest, the government eventually legalized trade unions in 1941. The unions soon broadened their demands to include political reform, and in 1950 the first and most durable political party, the People's United Party (PUP), was formed with strong backing from the labor movement. Universal suffrage was granted to literate adults in 1954, and by the 1960s the colony was being prepared for independence.

The final obstacle to independence proved to be not internal problems or resistance from the colonial power, but an unresolved territorial claim over all of Belize by neighboring Guatemala. The dispute dated to treaties signed in the 1700s, in which Britain agreed to Spanish sovereignty over the region. Guatemala later claimed it had inherited Spanish sovereignty over Belize. Although negotiations over the issue had occurred periodically for more than a century, the matter of sovereignty became a particularly important issue for Guatemala in the 1960s and 1970s, when it realized Britain might grant independence to Belize.

Guatemala's demand for annexation of Belize was largely fought in the international arena. Realizing that Belize's small defense force of 700 was no match for Guatemala's army, the British stationed a garrison force to deter any aggression. Belize sought support for sovereignty from the United Nations, the Nonaligned Movement, the Commonwealth of Nations, and the Organization of American States. First, individual states and then the international organizations themselves came to support Belize's cause. By 1980 Guatemala was completely without international support for its territorial claim, and the British granted Belize independence in 1981.

Belize at independence was a small country whose economy depended on one crop. Unlike many other newly emerging nations, however, Belize was underpopulated in the early 1990s. The country, approximately the size of Massachusetts, consists largely of tropical forest, flat in the north and with a low range of mountains in the south. Belize has traditionally depended on one crop (forest products in the 1700s and 1800s; sugar in the mid-1900s) for its economic livelihood. A collapse in the price of sugar in the 1980s forced the government to diversify the economy. The growth of tourism and increased citrus and banana production in the 1990s made the economy less vulnerable to the price swings of a single commodity.

Ethnic diversity characterized Belizean society. The two largest groups were the Creoles, an English-speaking group either partly or wholly of African descent, and Mestizos (see Glossary), the Hispanic descendants of immigrants from neighboring Spanish-speaking countries or Hispanicized indigenous groups. Smaller groups included the Garifuna and the various Maya peoples. The 1980 census showed the population to be about 40 percent Creole and 33 percent Mestizo. A considerable influx of people from Central America shifted these percentages, however, so that the 1991 census showed the Mestizos to be the larger group, a change that distanced the country from the anglophone Caribbean and made it increasingly resemble its Hispanic neighbors on the isthmus of Central America.

The British legacy included a parliamentary democracy based on the British model, a government headed by the British monarch but governed by a prime minister named by the lower house of the bicameral legislature, and an independent judiciary. The constitutional safeguards for citizens' rights were respected, and the two elections since independence had seen power alternate between the country's two political parties with an absence of irregularities or political violence. The last election in 1989 saw George Cadle Price, leader of the PUP, regain the position of prime minister, a post he had held at the time of independence.

In 1993 Belize faced a number of challenges. The nation endeavored to meet the needs of a growing population with only limited resources. The makeup of the population itself was changing as Belizeans became more like their Central American neighbors and less like the English-speaking Caribbean. Most analysts agreed, however, that as the twentieth century drew to a close, Belize seemed well-positioned to deal successfully with the economic and social changes confronting it.

March 3, 1993

* * *

In the months following completion of research and writing of this book, significant political developments occurred in Belize. On May 13, 1993, the British government, saying that it felt its military presence in Belize was no longer necessary because resolution of Guatemala's long-standing territorial claim seemed imminent, announced that it would remove most of its troops from Belize within a year. On June 1, buoyed by overwhelming victories in by-elections for the Belize City Council and for a vacated parliamentary seat, Prime Minister George Price called for the governor general to dissolve the National Assembly on June 30 and hold general elections the following day, fifteen months before the mandate of his People's United Party (PUP) was due to expire. The main opposition party, the United Democratic Party (UDP) headed by Manuel Esquivel, and the newly formed National Alliance for Belizean Rights headed by veteran UDP politician Philip Goldson announced they would participate in the election. The PUP was confident of victory because the economy was growing and the opposition appeared disorganized. The PUP also claimed that recently passed legislation giving Guatemala access to the Caribbean through Belizean territorial waters had finally settled the dispute with Guatemala.

Events in neighboring Guatemala, however, came to dominate the issues in the Belizean election. On June 2, the Guatemalan military removed President Jorge Serrano Elías, who had earlier accepted Belize's right to exist and established diplomatic relations with Belize. Later in June, the Guatemalan military announced plans to impeach Serrano in absentia for his accord with Belize.

In its election campaign, the UDP seized on many Belizeans' fears of renewed Guatemalan territorial claims, the consequence of the British troop withdrawal, and resentment by Creoles over the growing hispanicization of the country. Esquivel accused Price's administration of making too many concessions to Guatemala to obtain a settlement to the dispute and promised to suspend the legislation granting Guatemala access to the Caribbean. The UDP also charged that the PUP had not fought hard enough to keep the British garrison in Belize and promised to reopen talks to maintain a British presence if it were brought to power. In addition, the UDP accused the PUP of having allowed too many Spanish-speaking refugees into Belize (the 1991 census revealed that for the first time there were more Mestizos than Creoles in the country) and then catering to the Spanish-speaking vote.

These campaign charges, along with attacks on the PUP as being corrupt and secretly planning to devalue the Belizean dollar, resulted in a surprise victory for the UDP on July 1. Although the

PUP won a slim majority of the total votes cast, the UDP won sixteen of the twenty-nine seats in the National Assembly. The UDP victory for several seats was razor-thin (six of the seats were won with a majority of five or fewer votes), and several recounts were held. Results of the sixteen-seat victory for the UDP were confirmed, however, and on July 5, Manuel Esquivel was sworn in as Belize's new prime minister.

July 12, 1993 — Tim L. Merrill

Figure 1. Guyana: Administrative Divisions, 1991

Guyana: Country Profile

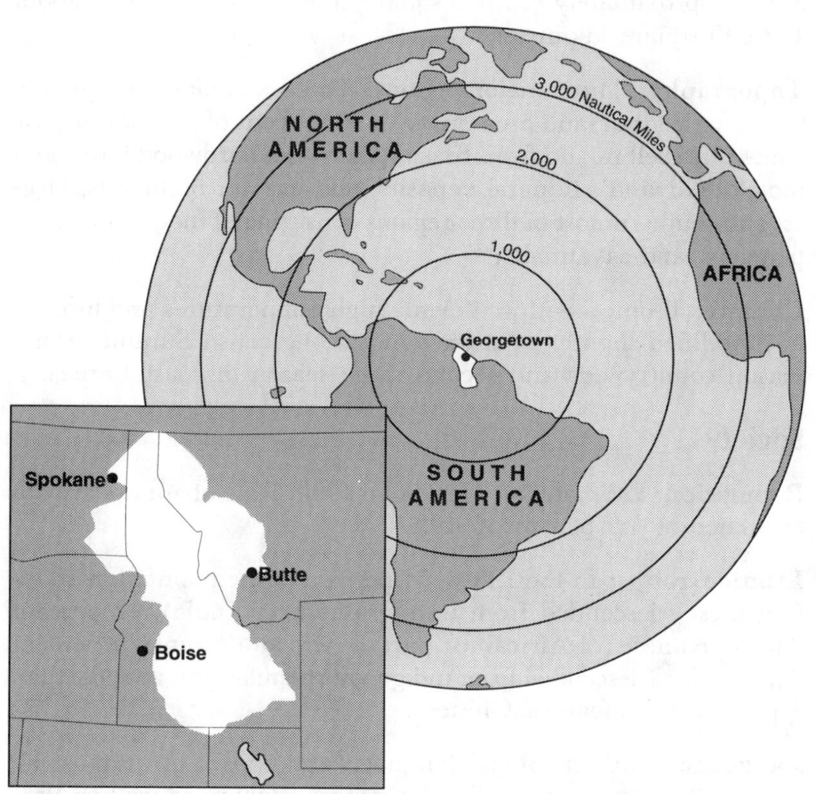

Country

Formal Name: Cooperative Republic of Guyana.

Short Form: Guyana.

Term for Citizens: Guyanese.

Capital: Georgetown.

Independence: May 26, 1966, from Britain.

NOTE—The Country Profile contains updated information as available.

Geography

Size: Approximately 215,000 square kilometers. Land area about 197,000 square kilometers.

Topography: Three major regions: the coastal plain comprising only 5 percent of land area but with 90 percent of population; the white sand belt inland from coastal plain with hardwood forest and most of Guyana's mineral deposits; and interior highlands, largest and southernmost of three regions consisting of mountains, high plateaus, and savannahs.

Climate: Tropical with uniformly high temperatures and humidity, modified slightly by trade winds along coast. Summer rainy season countrywide and second rainy season in coastal areas.

Society

Population: Estimated at 764,000 in 1990. Rate of annual growth estimated at 1.9 percent in 1990s.

Ethnic Groups: In the 1980s, 51 percent of the population Indo-Guyanese (descended from immigrants from India), 42 percent Afro-Guyanese (of African or partial African descent), 4 percent Amerindian (descended from indigenous population), and less than 3 percent European or Chinese.

Language: English official language and spoken by almost all Guyanese. Some Amerindian languages spoken, as well as Portuguese near Brazilian border.

Religion: In 1990 about 52 percent of population Christian, 34 percent Hindu, and 9 percent Muslim. Christians primarily Afro-Guyanese; Hindus and Muslims primarily Indo-Guyanese. Two-thirds of Christians Protestant, one-third Roman Catholic.

Education and Literacy: Approximately 96 percent of adult population considered literate in the 1990s. Public education system included two years of preschool, six years of basic education (compulsory), five years of secondary education, four years of university education, and several master's degree programs. One university—University of Guyana.

Health: Malnutrition increased in 1980s. Malaria most serious disease. Medical facilities and potable water inadequate, especially in rural areas. In 1988 infant mortality rate 43.9 per 1,000 live births; life expectancy sixty-six years.

Economy

Gross Domestic Product (GDP): In 1990 US$275 million, or US$369 per capita, one of lowest in the Western Hemisphere.

Agriculture: Most important sector of economy, accounting for 30 percent of GDP in 1989. Sugar and rice most important crops.

Mining: One of largest bauxite reserves in the world. Nationalization of the industry and labor disputes have hampered mining operations and refining of bauxite into alumina; in 1991 Guyana exported only small amounts of unprocessed bauxite ore. Unknown reserves of gold and diamonds.

Manufacturing: Small sector consisting of food processing, mineral processing, textiles, ceramics, and pharmaceuticals.

Exports: US$204 million in 1990. Major commodities: sugar, bauxite, shrimp, rice, and gold.

Imports: US$250 million in 1990. Primarily fuel, machinery, and consumer goods.

Debt: US$1.96 billion (Dec. 1990)

Currency: Guyanese dollar (G$) divided into 100 cents. G$ repeatedly devalued in 1980s; official exchange rate dropped from US$1 = G$4.252 in 1985 to US$1 = G$10 in 1987. In April 1989, official exchange rate US$1 = G$33. As of December 1992, official rate US$1 = G$125, with adjustments made weekly.

Fiscal Year: Calendar year.

Transportation and Communications

Railroads: None.

Roads: 7,200 kilometers total in 1993; about 700 kilometers paved, 5,000 kilometers gravel, and rest earthen.

Inland waterways: Only lower reaches of Berbice, Demerara, and Essequibo rivers navigable.

Ports: Georgetown only significant port. New Amsterdam in east minor port.

Airports: Timehri, south of Georgetown, Guyana's only international airport.

Communications: Underdeveloped network with only 27,000 telephones in 1983, or 3.3 per 100 inhabitants. Rudimentary broadcast facilities with three television stations, three AM radio, and three FM radio stations in 1993.

Government and Politics

Government: Parliamentary-style government based on modified British model. Head of state executive president chosen by fifty-three-member unicameral National Assembly. Judicial system based on English common law.

Politics: Two major parties whose constituents predominantly from one of Guyana's two largest ethnic groups. The People's National Congress (PNC), headed by Hugh Desmond Hoyte, largely Afro-Guyanese; the People's Progressive Party (PPP), headed by Cheddi Jagan, mostly Indo-Guyanese. The PNC held power from independence in 1966 until 1992 by manipulation of electoral process and racial politics. The PPP assumed power in October 1992 elections.

International Organizations: Member of United Nations and its specialized agencies, Nonaligned Movement, Commonwealth of Nations, Organization of American States, and Caribbean Community and Common Market.

National Security

Armed Forces: In 1991 armed forces included 1,700-member Guyanese Defence Force (GDF), unified service with ground, naval, and air elements; 2,000-member National Guard Service, reserve unit; and two paramilitary organizations: 2,000-member Peoples's Militia and 1,500-member Guyana National Service.

Army: Ground forces organized into two infantry battalions, one guard battalion, one Special Forces battalion, one support weapons battalion, one artillery battery, and one engineer company.

Maritime Corps: Naval element of GDF consisted of four patrol craft and 100 personnel based in Georgetown and New Amsterdam.

Air Command: Air element of GDF consisted of 200 personnel with five aircraft and five helicopters based at Timehri Airport.

Equipment: Most weaponry supplied by Britain, the Soviet Union, and the United States. Some naval craft acquired from North Korea.

Defense Budget: US$5.5 million in 1989, about 6 percent of GDP.

Internal Security Forces: National police, the Guyana Police Force, with about 5,000 members.

Chapter 1. Guyana: Historical Setting

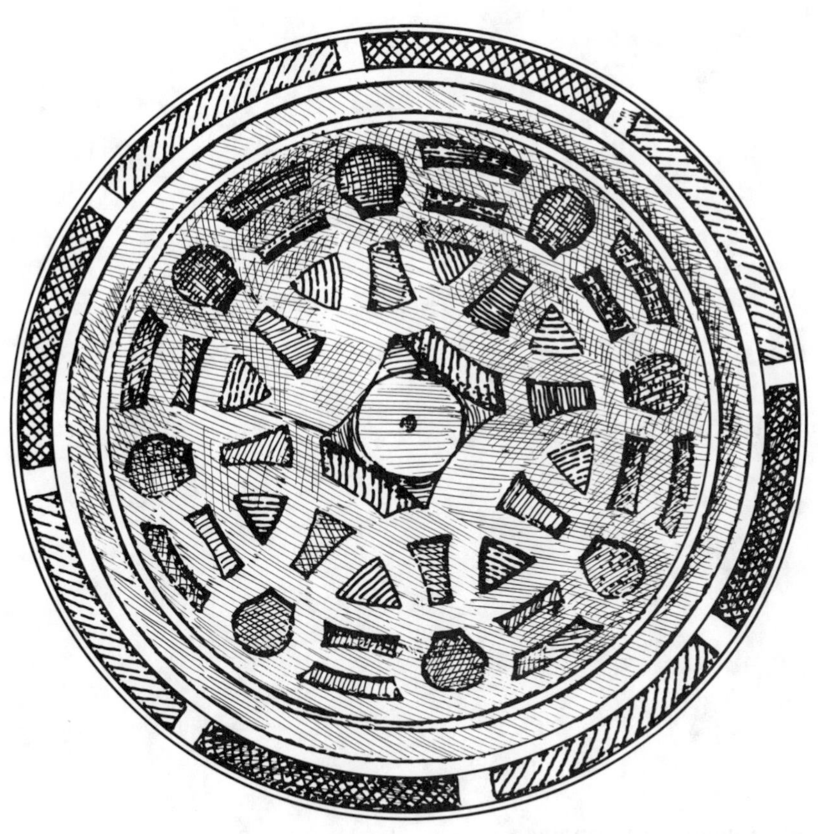

Amerindian wood carving

MORE THAN TWENTY-FIVE YEARS after gaining independence, Guyana retained the clear imprint of its colonial past. Sighted by Columbus during his third voyage, the area was virtually ignored by later Spanish explorers and conquistadors. The first European settlers were the Dutch, who established a trading post in 1616. The native Carib and Awarak peoples were killed by disease or conflict over the land or forced into the interior. The Dutch, realizing the agricultural potential of the swampy coast, drained the land with a network of dikes and canals. In the 1700s, the three Dutch colonies in present-day Guyana grew and prospered with plantation economies based on sugarcane and slave labor. Increasing numbers of British settlers were also drawn to the area in the second half of the eighteenth century. Dutch rule ended in 1814 when the colonies were awarded to Britain following the Napoleonic wars.

Much of British rule in the 1800s was simply a continuation of the policies of the Dutch. Consolidated into one colony—British Guiana—in 1831, the sugar-based economy continued to expand, and when emancipation was completed in 1838 other ethnic groups, most notably from India, were imported to work the plantations. The 1900s saw an increased political awareness of the varied ethnic groups and a slow transfer of political power from the old plantocracy and colonial administration to the Afro-Guyanese and the Indo-Guyanese. Amid growing polarization between these two groups, self-government was granted in the 1950s. Political conflict between the Afro-Guyanese and the Indo-Guyanese, sometimes marked with violence, caused the British to delay independence until 1966. Since independence, two characteristics have dominated Guyanese society and politics: the presence of strong political personalities (Cheddi Jagan, Linden Forbes Burnham, and Hugh Desmond Hoyte) and ethnic and racial divisions based on mutual suspicion and manipulation by these strong personalities.

Ideology played a large part in the newly independent country's approach to economic development. The initial selection of a Marxist-Leninist economic system was motivated by a desire to break with the capitalist past. But authoritarian rule by one dominant political personality and continued ethnic tension undermined the crafting of a coherent or pragmatic development strategy. Independent Guyana's history under its first prime minister,

Forbes Burnham, is one of political confrontation and prolonged economic decline. Desmond Hoyte's tenure appeared to represent a departure from the economic and authoritarian policies of his predecessor, but in 1991 it was unclear if the historical patterns of personal political dominance and ethnic tension could be changed.

The Early Years

The first humans to reach Guyana belonged to the group of peoples that crossed into North America from Asia perhaps as much as 35,000 years ago. These first inhabitants were nomads who slowly spread south into Central America and South America. Although great civilizations later arose in the Americas, the structure of Amerindian society in the Guianas remained relatively simple. At the time of Christopher Columbus's voyages, Guyana's inhabitants were divided into two groups, the Arawak along the coast and the Carib in the interior. One of the legacies of the indigenous peoples was the word *Guiana,* often used to describe the region encompassing modern Guyana as well as Suriname (former Dutch Guiana) and French Guiana. The word, which means "land of waters," is highly appropriate, considering the area's multitude of rivers and streams.

Historians speculate that the Arawak and Carib originated in the South American hinterland and migrated northward, first to the present-day Guianas and then to the Caribbean islands. The peaceful Arawak, mainly cultivators, hunters, and fishermen, migrated to the Caribbean islands before the Carib and settled throughout the region. The tranquility of Arawak society was disrupted by the arrival of the bellicose Carib from the South American interior. Carib warlike behavior and violent movement north made an impact still discussed today. By the end of the fifteenth century, the Carib had displaced the Arawak throughout the islands of the Lesser Antilles (see Glossary). The Carib settlement of the Lesser Antilles also affected Guyana's future development. The Spanish explorers and settlers who came after Columbus found that the Arawak proved easier to conquer than the Carib, who fought hard to maintain their freedom. This fierce resistance, along with a lack of gold in the Lesser Antilles, contributed to the Spanish emphasis on conquest and settlement of the Greater Antilles and the mainland. Only a weak Spanish effort was made at consolidating Spain's authority in the Lesser Antilles (with the arguable exception of Trinidad) and the Guianas.

Kaieteur Falls on the Potaro River. Its 226-meter perpendicular drop is one of the world's most spectacular.
Courtesy Embassy of Guyana, Washington

The Coming of the Europeans

Although Columbus sighted the Guyanese coast in 1498, during his third voyage to the Americas, the Dutch were the first Europeans to settle what is now Guyana. The Netherlands had obtained independence from Spain in the late 1500s and by the early 1600s had emerged as a major commercial power, trading with the fledgling English and French colonies in the Lesser Antilles. In 1616 the Dutch established the first European settlement in the area of Guyana, a trading post twenty-five kilometers upstream from the mouth of the Essequibo River. Other settlements followed, usually a few kilometers inland on the larger rivers. The initial purpose of the Dutch settlements was trade with the indigenous people. The Dutch aim soon changed to acquisition of territory as other European powers gained colonies elsewhere in the Caribbean. Although Guyana was claimed by the Spanish, who sent periodic patrols through the region, the Dutch gained control over the region early in the seventeenth century. Dutch sovereignty was officially recognized with the signing of the Treaty of Munster in 1648.

In 1621 the government of the Netherlands gave the newly formed Dutch West India Company complete control over the trading post on the Essequibo. This Dutch commercial concern administered the colony, known as Essequibo, for more than 170 years. The company established a second colony, on the Berbice River southeast of Essequibo, in 1627. Although under the general jurisdiction of this private group, the settlement, named Berbice, was governed separately. Demerara, situated between Essequibo and Berbice, was settled in 1741 and emerged in 1773 as a separate colony under direct control of the Dutch West India Company.

Although the Dutch colonizers initially were motivated by the prospect of trade in the Caribbean, their possessions became significant producers of crops. The growing importance of agriculture was indicated by the export of 15,000 kilograms of tobacco from Essequibo in 1623. But as the agricultural productivity of the Dutch colonies increased, a labor shortage emerged. The indigenous populations were poorly adapted for work on plantations, and many people died from diseases introduced by the Europeans. The Dutch West India Company turned to the importation of African slaves, who rapidly became a key element in the colonial economy. By the 1660s, the slave population numbered about 2,500; the number of indigenous people was estimated at 50,000, most of whom had retreated into the vast hinterland. Although African slaves were considered an essential element of the colonial economy, their working conditions were brutal. The mortality rate was high, and the dismal conditions led to more than half a dozen slave rebellions.

The most famous slave uprising began in February 1763. On two plantations on the Canje River in Berbice, slaves rebelled, taking control of the region. As plantation after plantation fell to the slaves, the European population fled; eventually only half of the whites who had lived in the colony remained. Led by Cuffy (now the national hero of Guyana), the rebels came to number about 3,000 and threatened European control over the Guianas. The insurgents were defeated with the assistance of troops from neighboring French and British colonies and from Europe.

One of the most significant Dutch legacies in Guyana was the method of land management. Settlement and agriculture initially were limited to a belt of land extending 50 to 150 kilometers upriver. The marshy coast flooded at high tide and did not appear conducive to European settlement. The prospect of large profits for tropical agricultural products, especially sugar, led to the reclamation of coastal lands in the second half of the 1700s. The Dutch were eminently suited to this task, having originated the polder system, a technique by which a tract of usable land is created by damming and then draining a water-covered area. Using this system, the Dutch created a coastal plain that remains one of Guyana's most productive plantation areas.

The polder system entailed the use of a front dam, or facade, along the shorefront. This dam was supported by a back dam of the same length and two connecting side dams, which formed a rectangular tract of land known as a polder. The dams kept the salt water out, and fresh water was managed by a network of canals that provided drainage, irrigation, and a system of transportation. The labor for the "polderization" of Guyana's coast was provided by the Dutch colony's African slaves.

Transition to British Rule

Eager to attract more settlers, in 1746 the Dutch authorities opened the area near the Demerara River to British immigrants. British plantation owners in the Lesser Antilles had been plagued by poor soil and erosion, and many were lured to the Dutch colonies by richer soils and the promise of landownership. The influx of British citizens was so great that by 1760 the English constituted a majority of the population of Demerara. By 1786 the internal affairs of this Dutch colony were effectively under British control.

As economic growth accelerated in Demerara and Essequibo, strains began to appear in the relations between the planters and the Dutch West India Company. Administrative reforms during the early 1770s had greatly increased the cost of government. The company periodically sought to raise taxes to cover these expenditures and thereby provoked the resistance of the planters. In 1781 a war broke out between the Netherlands and Britain, which resulted in the British occupation of Berbice, Essequibo, and Demerara. Some months later, France, allied with the Netherlands, seized control of the colonies. The French governed for two years, during which they constructed a new town, Longchamps, at the mouth of the Demerara River. When the Dutch regained power in 1784, they moved their colonial capital to Longchamps, which they renamed Stabroeck. The capital eventually would become known as Georgetown (see fig. 1).

The return of Dutch rule reignited the conflict between the planters of Essequibo and Demerara and the Dutch West India Company. Disturbed by plans for an increase in the slave tax and a reduction in their representation on the colony's judicial and policy councils, the colonists petitioned the Dutch government to consider their grievances. In response, a special committee was appointed, which proceeded to draw up a report called the Concept Plan of Redress. This document called for far-reaching constitutional reforms and later became the basis of the British governmental structure. The plan proposed a decision-making body to be known as the Court of Policy. The judiciary was to consist of two courts of justice, one serving Demerara and the other, Essequibo. The membership of the Court of Policy and of the courts of justice would consist of company officials and planters who owned more than twenty-five slaves. The Dutch commission that was assigned the responsibility of implementing this new system of government returned to the Netherlands with extremely unfavorable reports concerning the Dutch West India Company's administration. The company's charter therefore was allowed to expire in 1792, and the Concept Plan of Redress was put into effect in Demerara and Essequibo. Renamed the United Colony of Demerara and Essequibo, the area then came under the direct control of the Dutch government. Berbice maintained its status as a separate colony.

The catalyst for formal British takeover was the French Revolution and the resulting Napoleonic Wars. In 1795 the French occupied the Netherlands. The British declared war on France and in 1796 launched an expeditionary force from Barbados to occupy the Dutch colonies. The British takeover was bloodless, and local Dutch administration of the colony was left relatively uninterrupted under the constitution provided by the Concept Plan of Redress.

Both Berbice and the United Colony of Demerara and Essequibo were under British control from 1796 to 1802. By means of the Treaty of Amiens, both were returned to Dutch control. Peace was short-lived, however. War between Britain and France resumed in less than a year, and the United Colony and Berbice were seized once more by British troops. At the London Convention of 1814, both colonies were formally ceded to Britain. In 1831 Berbice and the United Colony of Demerara and Essequibo were unified as British Guiana. The colony would remain under British control until independence in 1966.

The Early British Colony and the Labor Problem

Political, economic, and social life in the 1800s was dominated by a European planter class. Although the smallest group in terms of numbers, members of the plantocracy had links to British commercial interests in London and often enjoyed close ties to the governor, who was appointed by the monarch. The plantocracy also controlled exports and the working conditions of the majority of the population. The next social stratum consisted of a small number of freed slaves, many of mixed African and European heritage, in addition to some Portuguese merchants. At the lowest level of society was the majority, the African slaves who lived and worked in the countryside, where the plantations were located. Unconnected to colonial life, small groups of Amerindians lived in the hinterland.

Colonial life was changed radically by the demise of slavery. Although the international slave trade was abolished in the British Empire in 1807, slavery itself continued. However, the momentum for abolition remained, and by 1838 total emancipation had been effected. The end of slavery had several ramifications. Most significantly, many former slaves rapidly departed the plantations. Some ex-slaves moved to towns and villages, feeling that field labor was degrading and inconsistent with freedom, but others pooled their resources to purchase the abandoned estates of their former masters and created village communities. Establishing small settlements provided the new Afro-Guyanese communities an opportunity to grow and sell food, an extension of a practice under which slaves had been allowed to keep the money that came from the sale of any surplus produce. The emergence of an independent-minded Afro-Guyanese peasant class, however, threatened the planters' political power, inasmuch as the planters no longer held a near-monopoly on the colony's economic activity.

Emancipation also resulted in the introduction of new ethnic and cultural groups into British Guiana. The departure of the Afro-Guyanese from the sugar plantations soon led to labor shortages.

After unsuccessful attempts throughout the 1800s to attract Portuguese workers from Madeira, the estate owners were again left with an inadequate supply of labor. The Portuguese had not taken to plantation work and soon moved into other parts of the economy, especially retail business, where they became competitors with the new Afro-Guyanese middle class. Some 14,000 Chinese came to the colony between 1853 and 1912. Like their Portuguese predecessors, the Chinese forsook the plantations for the retail trades and soon became assimilated into society.

Concerned about the plantations' shrinking labor pool and the potential decline of the sugar sector, British authorities, like their counterparts in Dutch Guiana, began to contract for the services of poorly paid indentured workers from India. The East Indians, as this group was known locally, signed on for a certain number of years, after which, in theory, they would return to India with their savings from working in the sugar fields. The introduction of indentured East Indian workers alleviated the labor shortage and added another group to Guyana's ethnic mix.

Origins of the Border Dispute with Venezuela

When Britain gained formal control over what is now Guyana in 1814, it also became involved in one of Latin America's most persistent border disputes. At the London Convention of 1814, the Dutch surrendered the United Colony of Demerara and Essequibo and Berbice to the British. Although Spain still claimed the region, the Spanish did not contest the treaty because they were preoccupied with their own colonies' struggles for independence. In 1835 the British government asked German explorer Robert Hermann Schomburgk to map British Guiana and mark its boundaries. As ordered by the British authorities, Schomburgk began British Guiana's western boundary with Venezuela at the mouth of the Orinoco River. A map of the British colony was published in 1840. Venezuela protested, claiming the entire area west of the Essequibo River. Negotiations between Britain and Venezuela over the boundary began, but the two nations could reach no compromise. In 1850 both agreed not to occupy the disputed zone.

The discovery of gold in the contested area in the late 1850s reignited the dispute. British settlers moved into the region, and the British Guiana Mining Company was formed to mine the deposits. Over the years, Venezuela made repeated protests and proposed arbitration, but the British government was uninterested. Venezuela finally broke diplomatic relations with Britain in 1887 and appealed to the United States for help. The British at first rebuffed the United States government's suggestion of arbitration, but when President

Grover Cleveland threatened to intervene according to the Monroe Doctrine, Britain agreed to let an international tribunal arbitrate the boundary in 1897.

For two years, the tribunal consisting of two Britons, two Americans, and a Russian studied the case. Their three-to-two decision, handed down in 1899, awarded 94 percent of the disputed territory to British Guiana. Venezuela received only the mouth of the Orinoco River and a short stretch of the Atlantic coastline just to the east. Although Venezuela was unhappy with the decision, a commission surveyed a new border in accordance with the award, and both sides accepted the boundary in 1905. The issue was considered settled for the next half-century (see Relations with Venezuela, ch. 4; Guyana-Venezuela Dispute, ch. 5).

Political and Social Awakenings

Nineteenth-Century British Guiana

The constitution of the British colony favored the white planters. Planter political power was based in the Court of Policy and the two courts of justice, established in the late 1700s under Dutch rule. The Court of Policy had both legislative and administrative functions and was composed of the governor, three colonial officials, and four colonists, with the governor presiding. The courts of justice resolved judicial matters, such as licensing and civil service appointments, which were brought before them by petition.

The Court of Policy and the courts of justice, controlled by the plantation owners, constituted the center of power in British Guiana. The colonists who sat on the Court of Policy and the courts of justice were appointed by the governor from a list of nominees submitted by two electoral colleges. In turn, the seven members of each College of Electors were elected for life by those planters possessing twenty-five or more slaves. Though their power was restricted to nominating colonists to fill vacancies on the three major governmental councils, these electoral colleges provided a setting for political agitation by the planters.

Raising and disbursing revenue were the responsibility of the Combined Court, which included members of the Court of Policy and six additional financial representatives appointed by the College of Electors. In 1855 the Combined Court also assumed responsibility for setting the salaries of all government officials. This duty made the Combined Court a center of intrigues resulting in periodic clashes between the governor and the planters.

Other Guianese began to demand a more representative political system in the 1800s. By the late 1880s, pressure from the new

Afro-Guyanese middle class was building for constitutional reform. In particular, there were calls to convert the Court of Policy into an assembly with ten elected members, to ease voter qualifications, and to abolish the College of Electors. Reforms were resisted by the planters, led by Henry K. Davson, owner of a large plantations. In London the planters had allies in the West India Committee and also in the West India Association of Glasgow, both presided over by proprietors with major interests in British Guiana.

Constitutional revisions in 1891 incorporated some of the changes demanded by the reformers. The planters lost political influence with the abolition of the College of Electors and the relaxation of voter qualifications. At the same time, the Court of Policy was enlarged to sixteen members; eight of these were to be elected members whose power would be balanced by that of eight appointed members. The Combined Court also continued, consisting, as previously, of the Court of Policy and six financial representatives who were now elected. To ensure that there would be no shift of power to elected officials, the governor remained the head of the Court of Policy; the executive duties of the Court of Policy were transferred to a new Executive Council, which the governor and planters dominated. The 1891 revisions were a great disappointment to the colony's reformers. As a result of the election of 1892, the membership of the new Combined Court was almost identical to that of the previous one.

The next three decades saw additional, although minor, political changes. In 1897 the secret ballot was introduced. A reform in 1909 expanded the limited British Guiana electorate, and for the first time, Afro-Guyanese constituted a majority of the eligible voters.

Political changes were accompanied by social change and jockeying by various ethnic groups for increased power. The British and Dutch planters refused to accept the Portuguese as equals and sought to maintain their status as aliens with no rights in the colony, especially voting rights. The political tensions led the Portuguese to establish the Reform Association. After the anti-Portuguese riots of 1889, the Portuguese recognized the need to work with other disenfranchised elements of society, in particular the Afro-Guyanese. By the turn of the century, organizations including the Reform Association and the Reform Club began to demand greater participation in the colony's affairs. These organizations were largely the instruments of a small but articulate emerging middle class. Although the new middle class sympathized with the working class, the middle-class political groups were hardly representative of a national political or social movement. Indeed, working-class grievances were usually expressed in the form of riots.

Political and Social Changes in the 1900s

The 1905 Ruimveldt Riots rocked British Guiana. The severity of these outbursts reflected the workers' widespread dissatification with their standard of living. The uprising began in late November 1905 when the Georgetown stevedores went on strike, demanding higher wages. The strike grew confrontational, and other workers struck in sympathy, creating the country's first urban-rural worker alliance. On November 30, crowds of people took to the streets of Georgetown, and by December 1, 1905, now referred to as Black Friday, the situation had spun out of control. At the Plantation Ruimveldt, close to Georgetown, a large crowd of porters refused to disperse when ordered to do so by a police patrol and a detachment of artillery. The colonial authorities opened fire, and four workers were seriously injured.

Word of the shootings spread rapidly throughout Georgetown, and hostile crowds began roaming the city, taking over a number of buildings. By the end of the day, seven people were dead and seventeen badly injured. In a panic, the British administration called for help. Britain sent troops, who finally quelled the uprising. Although the stevedores' strike failed, the riots had planted the seeds of what would become an organized trade union movement.

Even though World War I was fought far beyond the borders of British Guiana, the war altered society. The Afro-Guyanese who joined the British military became the nucleus of an elite Afro-Guyanese community upon their return. World War I also led to the end of East Indian indentured service. British concerns over political stability in India and criticism by Indian nationalists that the program was a form of human bondage caused the British government to outlaw indentured labor in 1917.

In the closing years of World War I, the colony's first trade union was formed. The British Guiana Labour Union (BGLU) was established in 1917 under the leadership of H.N. Critchlow. Formed in the face of widespread business opposition, the BGLU at first mostly represented Afro-Guyanese dockworkers. Its membership stood around 13,000 by 1920, and it was granted legal status in 1921 under the Trades Union Ordinance. Although recognition of other unions would not come until 1939, the BGLU was an indication that the working class was becoming politically aware and more concerned with its rights.

After World War I, new economic interest groups began to clash with the Combined Court. The country's economy had come to depend less on sugar and more on rice and bauxite, and producers of these new commodities resented the sugar planters' continued domination of the Combined Court. Meanwhile, the planters were feeling the effects of lower sugar prices and wanted the Combined Court to provide the necessary funds for new drainage and irrigation programs.

To stop the bickering and resultant legislative paralysis, in 1928 the British Colonial Office announced a new constitution that would make British Guiana a crown colony (see Glossary) under tight control of a governor appointed by the Colonial Office. The Combined Court and the Court of Policy were replaced by a Legislative Council with a majority of appointed members. To middle-class and working-class political activists, this new constitution represented a step backward and a victory for the planters. Influence over the governor, rather than the promotion of a particular public policy, became the most important issue in any political campaign.

The Great Depression of the 1930s brought economic hardship to all segments of society. All of the colony's major exports—sugar, rice and bauxite—were affected by low prices, and unemployment soared. As in the past, the working class found itself lacking a political voice during a time of worsening economic conditions. By the mid-1930s, British Guiana and the whole British Caribbean were marked by labor unrest and violent demonstrations. In the aftermath of riots throughout the British West Indies, a royal commission under Lord Moyne was established to determine the reasons for the riots and to make recommendations.

In British Guiana, the Moyne Commission questioned a wide range of people, including trade unionists, Afro-Guyanese professionals, and representatives of the Indo-Guyanese community. The commission pointed out the deep division between the country's two largest ethnic groups, the Afro-Guyanese and the Indo-Guyanese. The largest group, the Indo-Guyanese, consisted primarily of rural rice producers or merchants; they had retained the country's traditional culture and did not participate in national politics. The Afro-Guyanese were largely urban workers or bauxite miners; they had adopted European culture and dominated national politics. To increase representation of the majority of the population in British Guiana, the Moyne Commission called for increased democratization of government as well as economic and social reforms.

The Moyne Commission report in 1938 was a turning point in British Guiana. It urged extending the franchise to women and persons not owning land and encouraged the emerging trade union movement. Unfortunately, many of the Moyne Commission's

The Umana Yana Benab, a traditional meeting place built by the Waiwai, Georgetown
Courtesy Embassy of Guyana, Washington

recommendations were not immediately implemented because of the outbreak of the World War II.

With the fighting far away, the period of World War II in British Guiana was marked by continuing political reform and improvements to the national infrastructure. The reform-minded governor, Sir Gordon Lethem, reduced property qualifications for officeholding and voting, and made elective members a majority on the Legislative Council in 1943. Under the aegis of the Lend-Lease Act of 1941, a modern air base (now Timehri Airport) was constructed by United States troops. By the end of World War II, British Guiana's political system had been widened to encompass more elements of society, and the economy's foundations had been strengthened by increased demand for bauxite.

The Development of Political Parties

The immediate postwar period witnessed the founding of Guyana's major political parties, the People's Progressive Party (PPP) and the People's National Congress (PNC). These years also saw the beginning of a long and acrimonious struggle between the country's two dominant political personalities—Cheddi Jagan and Linden Forbes Burnham.

The end of World War II began a period of worldwide decolonization. In British Guiana, political awareness and demands for independence grew in all segments of society. At the same time, the struggle for political ascendancy between Burnham, the "Man on Horseback" of the Afro-Guyanese, and Jagan, the hero of the Indo-Guyanese masses, left a legacy of racially polarized politics that remained in place in the 1990s.

Jagan had been born in British Guiana in 1918. His parents were immigrants from India. His father was a driver, a position considered to be on the lowest rung of the middle stratum of Guianese society. Jagan's childhood gave him a lasting insight into rural poverty. Despite their poor background, the senior Jagan sent his son to Queen's College in Georgetown. After his education there, Jagan went to the United States to study dentistry, graduating from Northwestern University in Evanston, Illinois, in 1942.

Jagan returned to British Guiana in October 1943 and was soon joined by his American wife, the former Janet Rosenberg, who was to play a significant role in her new country's political development. Although Jagan established his own dentistry clinic, he was soon enmeshed in politics. After a number of unsuccessful forays into Guiana's political life, Jagan became treasurer of the Manpower Citizens' Association (MPCA) in 1945. The MPCA represented the colony's sugar workers, many of whom were Indo-Guyanese. Jagan's tenure was brief, as he clashed repeatedly with the more moderate union leadership over policy issues. Despite his departure from the MPCA a year after joining, the position allowed Jagan to meet other union leaders in British Guiana and throughout the English-speaking Caribbean.

The springboard for Jagan's political career was the Political Affairs Committee (PAC), formed in 1946 as a discussion group. The new organization published the *PAC Bulletin* to promote its Marxist ideology and ideas of liberation and decolonization. The PAC's outspoken criticism of the colony's poor living standards attracted followers as well as detractors.

In the November 1947 general elections, the PAC put forward several members as independent candidates. The PAC's major competitor was the newly formed Labour Party, which, under J.B. Singh, won six of fourteen seats contested. Jagan won a seat and briefly joined the Labour Party. But he had difficulties with his new party's center-right ideology and soon left its ranks. The Labour Party's support of the policies of the British governor and its inability to create a grass-roots base gradually stripped it of liberal supporters throughout the country. The Labour Party's lack of a clear-cut reform agenda left a vacuum, which Jagan rapidly moved to fill. Turmoil on the colony's sugar plantations gave him an opportunity to achieve national standing. After the June 16, 1948, police shootings of five Indo-Guyanese workers at Enmore, close to Georgetown, the PAC and the Guiana Industrial Workers' Union (GIWU) organized a large and peaceful demonstration, which clearly enhanced Jagan's standing with the Indo-Guyanese population.

Jagan's next major step was the founding of the People's Progressive Party (PPP) in January 1950. Using the PAC as a foundation, Jagan created from it a new party that drew support from both the Afro-Guyanese and Indo-Guyanese communities. To increase support among the Afro-Guyanese, Forbes Burnham was brought into the party.

Born in 1923, Burnham was the sole son in a family that had three children. His father was headmaster of Kitty Methodist Primary School, which was located just outside Georgetown. As part of the colony's educated class, young Burnham was exposed to political viewpoints at an early age. He did exceedingly well in school and went to London to obtain a law degree. Although not exposed to childhood poverty as was Jagan, Burnham was acutely aware of racial discrimination.

The social strata of the urban Afro-Guyanese community of the 1930s and 1940s included a mulatto or "coloured" elite, a black professional middle class, and, at the bottom, the black working class. Unemployment in the 1930s was high. When war broke out in 1939, many Afro-Guyanese joined the military, hoping to gain new job skills and escape poverty. When they returned home from the war, however, jobs were still scarce and discrimination was still a part of life. By the time of Burnham's arrival on the political stage in the late 1940s, the Afro-Guyanese community was ready for a leader.

The PPP's initial leadership was multiethnic and left of center, but hardly revolutionary. Jagan became the leader of the PPP's parliamentary group, and Burnham assumed the responsibilities of party chairman. Other key party members included Janet Jagan and Ashton Chase, both PAC veterans. The new party's first victory came in the 1950 municipal elections, in which Janet Jagan won a seat. Cheddi Jagan and Burnham failed to win seats, but Burnham's campaign made a favorable impression on many urban Afro-Guyanese.

From its first victory in the 1950 municipal election, the PPP gathered momentum. However, the party's often strident anticapitalist and socialist message made the British government uneasy. Colonial officials showed their displeasure with the PPP in

1952 when, on a regional tour, the Jagans were designated prohibited immigrants in Trinidad and Grenada.

A British commission in 1950 recommended universal adult suffrage and the adoption of a ministerial system for British Guiana. The commission also recommended that power be concentrated in the executive branch, that is, the office of the governor. These reforms presented British Guiana's parties with an opportunity to participate in national elections and form a government, but maintained power in the hands of the British-appointed chief executive. This arrangement rankled the PPP, which saw it as an attempt to curtail the party's political power.

Preindependence Government, 1953–66

The PPP's First Government, 1953

Once the new constitution was adopted, elections were set for 1953. The PPP's coalition of lower-class Afro-Guyanese and rural Indo-Guyanese workers, together with elements of both ethnic groups' middle sectors, made for a formidable constituency. Conservatives branded the PPP as communist, but the party campaigned on a center-left platform and appealed to a growing nationalism. The other major party participating in the election, the National Democratic Party (NDP), was a spin-off of the League of Coloured People and was largely an Afro-Guyanese middle-class organization, sprinkled with middle-class Portuguese and Indo-Guyanese. The NDP, together with the poorly organized United Farmers and Workers Party and the United National Party, was soundly defeated by the PPP. Final results gave the PPP eighteen of twenty-four seats compared with the NDP's two seats and four seats for independents.

The PPP's first administration was brief. The legislature opened on May 30, 1953. Already suspicious of Jagan and the PPP's radicalism, conservative forces in the business community were further distressed by the new administration's program of expanding the role of the state in the economy and society. The PPP also sought to implement its reform program at a rapid pace, which brought the party into confrontation with the governor and with high-ranking civil servants who preferred more gradual change. The issue of civil service appointments also threatened the PPP, in this case from within. Following the 1953 victory, these appointments became an issue between the predominantly Indo-Guyanese supporters of Jagan and the largely Afro-Guyanese backers of Burnham. Burnham threatened to split the party if he were not made sole leader of the PPP. A compromise was reached by which members of what had become Burnham's faction received ministerial appointments.

The PPP's introduction of the Labour Relations Act provoked a confrontation with the British. This law ostensibly was aimed at reducing intraunion rivalries, but would have favored the GIWU, which was closely aligned with the ruling party. The opposition charged that the PPP was seeking to gain control over the colony's economic and social life and was moving to stifle the opposition. The day the act was introduced to the legislature, the GIWU went on strike in support of the proposed law. The British government interpreted this intermingling of party politics and labor unionism as a direct challenge to the constitution and the authority of the governor. The day after the act was passed, on October 9, 1953, London suspended the colony's constitution and, under pretext of quelling disturbances, sent in troops.

The Interim Government, 1953–57

Following the suspension of the constitution, British Guiana was governed by an interim administration consisting of small group of conservative politicians, businessmen, and civil servants that lasted until 1957. Order in the colonial government masked a growing rift in the country's main political party as the personal conflict between the PPP's Jagan and Burnham widened into a bitter dispute. In 1955 Jagan and Burnham formed rival wings of the PPP. Support for each leader was largely, but not totally, along ethnic lines. J.B. Lachmansingh, a leading Indo-Guyanese and head of the GIWU, supported Burnham, whereas Jagan retained the loyalty of a number of leading Afro-Guyanese radicals, such as Sydney King. Burnham's wing of the PPP moved to the right, leaving Jagan's wing on the left, where he was regarded with considerable apprehension by Western governments and the colony's conservative business groups.

The Second PPP Government, 1957-61, and Racial Politics

The 1957 elections held under a new constitution demonstrated the extent of the growing ethnic division within the Guianese electorate. The revised constitution provided limited self-government, primarily through the Legislative Council. Of the council's twenty-four delegates, fifteen were elected, six were nominated, and the remaining three were to be ex officio members from the interim administration. The two wings of the PPP launched vigorous campaigns, each attempting to prove that it was the legitimate heir to the original party. Despite denials of such motivation, both factions made a strong appeal to their respective ethnic constituencies.

The 1957 elections were convincingly won by Jagan's PPP faction. Although his group had a secure parliamentary majority, its support was drawn more and more from the Indo-Guyanese community. The faction's main planks were increasingly identified as Indo-Guyanese: more rice land, improved union representation in the sugar industry, and improved business opportunities and more government posts for Indo-Guyanese. The PPP had abrogated its claim to being a multiracial party.

Jagan's veto of British Guiana's participation in the West Indies Federation resulted in the complete loss of Afro-Guyanese support. In the late 1950s, the British Caribbean colonies had been actively negotiating establishment of a West Indies Federation. The PPP had pledged to work for the eventual political union of British Guiana with the Caribbean territories. The Indo-Guyanese, who constituted a majority in Guyana, were apprehensive of becoming part of a federation in which they would be outnumbered by people of African descent. Jagan's veto of the federation caused his party to lose all significant Afro-Guyanese support.

Burnham learned an important lesson from the 1957 elections. He could not win if supported only by the lower-class, urban Afro-Guyanese. He needed middle-class allies, especially those Afro-Guyanese who backed the moderate United Democratic Party. From 1957 onward, Burnham worked to create a balance between maintaining the backing of the more radical Afro-Guyanese lower classes and gaining the support of the more capitalist middle class. Clearly, Burnham's stated preference for socialism would not bind those two groups together against Jagan, an avowed Marxist. The answer was something more basic—race. Burnham's appeals to race proved highly successful in bridging the schism that divided the Afro-Guyanese along class lines. This strategy convinced the powerful Afro-Guyanese middle class to accept a leader who was more of a radical than they would have preferred to support. At the same time, it neutralized the objections of the black working class to entering an alliance with those representing the more moderate interests of the middle classes. Burnham's move toward the right was accomplished with the merger of his PPP faction and the United Democratic Party into a new organization, the People's National Congress (PNC).

Following the 1957 elections, Jagan rapidly consolidated his hold on the Indo-Guyanese community. Though candid in expressing his admiration for Josef Stalin, Mao Zedong, and, later, Fidel Castro Ruz, Jagan in power asserted that the PPP's Marxist-Leninist principles must be adapted to Guyana's own particular circumstances. Jagan advocated nationalization of foreign holdings, especially in the sugar industry. British fears of a communist takeover, however, caused the British governor to hold Jagan's more radical policy initiatives in check.

PPP Reelection and Debacle

The 1961 elections were a bitter contest between the PPP, the PNC, and the United Force (UF), a conservative party representing big business, the Roman Catholic Church, and Amerindian, Chinese, and Portuguese voters. These elections were held under yet another new constitution that marked a return to the degree of self-government that existed briefly in 1953. It introduced a bicameral system boasting a wholly elected thirty-five-member Legislative Assembly and a thirteen-member Senate to be appointed by the governor. The post of prime minister was created and was to be filled by the majority party in the Legislative Assembly. With the strong support of the Indo-Guyanese population, the PPP again won by a substantial margin, gaining twenty seats in the Legislative Assembly, compared with eleven seats for the PNC and four for the UF. Jagan was named prime minister.

Jagan's administration became increasingly friendly with communist and leftist regimes; for instance, Jagan refused to observe the United States embargo on communist Cuba. After discussions between Jagan and Cuban revolutionary Ernesto "Che" Guevara in 1960 and 1961, Cuba offered British Guiana loans and equipment. In addition, the Jagan administration signed trade agreements with Hungary and the German Democratic Republic (East Germany).

From 1961 to 1964, Jagan was confronted with a destabilization campaign conducted by the PNC and UF. Riots and demonstrations against the PPP administration were frequent, and during disturbances in 1962 and 1963 mobs destroyed part of Georgetown.

Labor violence also increased during the early 1960s. To counter the MPCA with its link to Burnham, the PPP formed the Guianese Agricultural Workers Union. This new union's political mandate was to organize the Indo-Guyanese sugarcane fieldworkers. The MPCA immediately responded with a one-day strike to emphasize its continued control over the sugar workers.

The PPP government responded to the strike in March 1964 by publishing a new Labour Relations Bill almost identical to the 1953 legislation that had resulted in British intervention. Regarded as a power play for control over a key labor sector, introduction of the proposed law prompted protests and rallies throughout the capital. Riots broke out on April 5; they were followed on April 18 by a general strike. By May 9, the governor was compelled to declare a state of emergency. Nevertheless, the strike and violence continued until July 7, when the Labour Relations Bill was allowed to lapse without being enacted. To bring an end to the disorder, the government agreed to consult with union representatives before introducing similar bills. These disturbances exacerbated tension and animosity between the two major ethnic communities and made a reconciliation between Jagan and Burnham an impossibility.

Jagan's term had not yet ended when another round of labor unrest rocked the colony. The pro-PPP GIWU, which had become an umbrella group of all labor organizations, called on sugar workers to strike in January 1964. To dramatize their case, Jagan led a march by sugar workers from the interior to Georgetown. This demonstration ignited outbursts of violence that soon escalated beyond the control of the authorities. On May 22, the governor finally declared another state of emergency. The situation continued to worsen, and in June the governor assumed full powers, rushed in British troops to restore order, and proclaimed a moratorium on all political activity. By the end of the turmoil, 160 people were dead and more than 1,000 homes had been destroyed.

In an effort to quell the turmoil, the country's political parties asked the British goverment to modify the constitution to provide for more proportional representation. The colonial secretary proposed a fifty-three-member unicameral legislature. Despite opposition from the ruling PPP, all reforms were implemented and new elections set for October 1964.

As Jagan feared, the PPP lost the general elections of 1964. The politics of *apan jhaat,* Hindi for "vote for your own kind," were becoming entrenched in British Guiana. The PPP won 46 percent of the vote and twenty-four seats, which made it the majority party. However, the PNC, which won 40 percent of the vote and twenty-two seats, and the UF, which won 11 percent of the vote and seven seats, formed a coalition. The socialist PNC and unabashedly capitalist UF had joined forces to keep the PPP out of office for another term. Jagan called the election fraudulent and refused to resign as prime minister. The constitution was amended to allow the governor to remove Jagan from office. Burnham became prime minister on December 14, 1964.

Independence and the Burnham Era

Burnham in Power

In the first year under Burnham, conditions in the colony began to stabilize. The new coalition administration broke diplomatic ties with Cuba and implemented policies that favored local investors

Saint George's Anglican Church in Georgetown, built in 1889, is one of the tallest wooden buildings in the world.
Courtesy Embassy of Guyana, Washington

and foreign industry. The colony applied the renewed flow of Western aid to further development of its infrastructure. A constitutional conference was held in London; the conference set May 26, 1966, as the date for the colony's independence. By the time independence was achieved, the country was enjoying economic growth and relative domestic peace.

The newly independent Guyana at first sought to improve relations with its neighbors. For instance, in December 1965 the country had become a charter member of the Caribbean Free Trade Association (Carifta). Relations with Venezuela were not so placid, however. In 1962 Venezuela had announced that it was rejecting the 1899 boundary and would renew its claim to all of Guyana west of the Essequibo River. In 1966 Venezuela seized the Guyanese half of Ankoko Island, in the Cuyuni River, and two years later claimed a strip of sea along Guyana's western coast.

Another challenge to the newly independent government came at the beginning of January 1969, with the Rupununi Rebellion. In the Rupununi region in southwest Guyana, along the Venezuelan border, white settlers and Amerindians rebelled against the central government. Several Guyanese policemen in the area were killed, and spokesmen for the rebels declared the area independent and asked for Venezuelan aid. Troops arrived from Georgetown within days, and the rebellion was quickly put down. Although the rebellion was not a large affair, it exposed underlying tensions in the new state and the Amerindians' marginalized role in the country's political and social life.

The Cooperative Republic

The 1968 elections allowed the PNC to rule without the UF. The PNC won thirty seats, the PPP nineteen seats, and the UF four seats. However, many observers claimed the elections were marred by manipulation and coercion by the PNC. The PPP and UF were part of Guyana's political landscape but were ignored as Burnham began to convert the machinery of state into an instrument of the PNC.

After the 1968 elections, Burnham's policies became more leftist as he announced he would lead Guyana to socialism. He consolidated his dominance of domestic policies through gerrymandering, manipulation of the balloting process, and politicalization of the civil service. A few Indo-Guyanese were coopted into the PNC, but the ruling party was unquestionably the embodiment of the Afro-Guyanese political will. Although the Afro-Guyanese middle class was uneasy with Burnham's leftist leanings, the PNC remained a shield against Indo-Guyanese dominance. The support of the Afro-Guyanese community allowed the PNC to bring the economy under control and to begin organizing the country into cooperatives.

On February 23, 1970, Guyana declared itself a "cooperative republic" and cut all ties to the British monarchy. The governor general was replaced as head of state by a ceremonial president. Relations with Cuba were improved, and Guyana became a force in the Nonaligned Movement. In August 1972, Burnham hosted the Conference of Foreign Ministers of Nonaligned Countries in Georgetown. He used this opportunity to address the evils of imperialism and the need to support African liberation movements in southern Africa. Burnham also let Cuban troops use Guyana as a transit point on their way to the war in Angola in the mid-1970s.

In the early 1970s, electoral fraud became blatant in Guyana. PNC victories always included overseas voters, who consistently and overwhelmingly voted for the ruling party. The police and military intimidated the Indo-Guyanese. The army was accused of tampering with ballot boxes.

Considered a low point in the democratic process, the 1973 elections were followed by an amendment to the constitution that abolished legal appeals to the Privy Council in London. After consolidating power on the legal and electoral fronts, Burnham turned to mobilizing the masses for what was to be Guyana's cultural revolution. A program of national service was introduced that placed an emphasis on self-reliance, loosely defined as Guyana's population feeding, clothing, and housing itself without outside help.

Government authoritarianism increased in 1974 when Burnham advanced the "paramountcy of the party." All organs of the state would be considered agencies of the ruling PNC and subject to its control. The state and the PNC became interchangeable; PNC objectives were now public policy.

Burnham's consolidation of power in Guyana was not total; opposition groups were tolerated within limits. For instance, in 1973 the Working People's Alliance (WPA) was founded. Opposed to Burnham's authoritarianism, the WPA was a multiethnic combination of politicians and intellectuals that advocated racial harmony, free elections, and democratic socialism. Although the WPA did not become an official political party until 1979, it evolved as an alternative to Burnham's PNC and Jagan's PPP.

Jagan's political career continued to decline in the 1970s. Outmaneuvered on the parliamentary front, the PPP leader tried another tactic. In April 1975, the PPP ended its boycott of parliament with Jagan stating that the PPP's policy would change from noncooperation and civil resistance to critical support of the Burnham regime. Soon after, Jagan appeared on the same platform with Prime Minister Burnham at the celebration of ten years of Guyanese independence, on May 26, 1976.

Despite Jagan's conciliatory move, Burnham had no intention of sharing power and continued to secure his position. When overtures intended to bring about new elections and PPP participation in the government were brushed aside, the largely Indo-Guyanese sugar work force went on a bitter strike. The strike was broken, and sugar production declined steeply from 1976 to 1977. The PNC postponed the 1978 elections, opting instead for a referendum to be held in July 1978, proposing to keep the incumbent assembly in power.

The July 1978 national referendum was poorly received. Although the PNC government proudly proclaimed that 71 percent of eligible voters participated and that 97 percent approved the referendum, other estimates put turnout at 10 to 14 percent. The low turnout was caused in large part by a boycott led by the PPP, WPA, and other opposition forces.

Burnham's control over Guyana began to weaken when the Jonestown massacre brought unwanted international attention. In the 1970s, Jim Jones, leader of the People's Temple of Christ, moved more than 1,000 of his followers from San Francisco to Jonestown, a utopian agricultural community near Port Kaituma in western Guyana. The People's Temple of Christ was regarded by members of the Guyanese government as a model agricultural community that shared its vision of settling the hinterland and its view of cooperative socialism. The fact that the People's Temple was well-equipped with openly flaunted weapons hinted that the community had the approval of members of the PNC's inner circle. Complaints of abuse by leaders of the cult prompted United States congressman Leo Ryan to fly to Guyana to investigate. The San Francisco-area representative was shot and killed by members of the People's Temple as he was boarding an airplane at Port Kaituma to return to Georgetown. Fearing further publicity, Jones and more than 900 of his followers died in a massive communal murder and suicide. The November 1978 Jonestown massacre suddenly put the Burnham government under intense foreign scrutiny, especially from the United States. Investigations into the massacre led to allegations that the Guyanese government had links to the fanatical cult (see Cults, ch. 2).

Although the bloody memory of Jonestown faded, Guyanese politics experienced a violent year in 1979. Some of this violence was directed against the WPA, which had emerged as a vocal critic of the state and of Burnham in particular. One of the party's leaders, Walter Rodney, and several professors at the University of Guyana were arrested on arson charges. The professors were soon released, and Rodney was granted bail. WPA leaders then organized the alliance into Guyana's most vocal opposition party.

As 1979 wore on, the level of violence continued to escalate. In October Minister of Education Vincent Teekah was mysteriously shot to death. The following year, Rodney was killed by a car bomb. The PNC government quickly accused Rodney of being a terrorist who had died at the hands of his own bomb and charged his brother Donald with being an accomplice. Later investigation implicated the Guyanese government, however. Rodney was a well-known leftist, and the circumstances of his death damaged Burnham's image with many leaders and intellectuals in less-developed countries who earlier had been willing to overlook the authoritarian nature of his government.

A new constitution was promulgated in 1980 (see Constitution of 1980, ch. 4). The old ceremonial post of president was abolished, and the head of government became the executive president, chosen, as the former position of prime minister had been, by the majority party in the National Assembly. Burnham automatically became Guyana's first executive president and promised elections later in the year. In elections held on December 15, 1980, the PNC claimed 77 percent of the vote and forty-one seats of the popularly elected seats, plus the ten chosen by the regional councils. The PPP and UF won ten and two seats, respectively. The WPA refused to participate in an electoral contest it regarded as fraudulent. Opposition claims of electoral fraud were upheld by a team of international observers headed by Britain's Lord Avebury.

The economic crisis facing Guyana in the early 1980s deepened considerably, accompanied by the rapid deterioration of public services, infrastructure, and overall quality of life. Blackouts occurred almost daily, and water services were increasingly unsatisfactory. The litany of Guyana's decline included shortages of rice and sugar (both produced in the country), cooking oil, and kerosene. While the formal economy sank, the black market economy in Guyana thrived.

In the midst of this turbulent period, Burnham underwent surgery for a throat ailment. On August 6, 1985, while in the care of Cuban doctors, Guyana's first and only leader since independence unexpectedly died. An epoch had abruptly ended. Guyana was suddenly in the post-Burnham era.

From Burnham to Hoyte

Despite concerns that the country was about to fall into a period of political instability, the transfer of power went smoothly. Vice President Desmond Hoyte became the new executive president and leader of the PNC. His initial tasks were threefold: to secure authority within the PNC and national government, to take the PNC through the December 1985 elections, and to revitalize the stagnant economy.

Hoyte's first two goals were easily accomplished. The new leader took advantage of factionalism within the PNC to quietly consolidate his authority. The December 1985 elections gave the PNC 79 percent of the vote and forty-two of the fifty-three directly elected seats. Eight of the remaining eleven seats went to the PPP, two went to the UF, and one to the WPA. Charging fraud, the opposition boycotted the December 1986 municipal elections. With no opponents, the PNC won all ninety-one seats in local government.

Revitalizing the economy proved more difficult. As a first step, Hoyte gradually moved to embrace the private sector, recognizing that state control of the economy had failed. Hoyte's administration lifted all curbs on foreign activity and ownership in 1988.

Although the Hoyte government did not completely abandon the authoritarianism of the Burnham regime, it did make certain political reforms. Hoyte abolished overseas voting and the provisions for widespread proxy and postal voting. Independent newspapers were given greater freedom, and political harassment abated considerably.

In September 1988, Hoyte visited the United States and became the first Guyanese head of state to meet with his United States counterpart. By October 1988, Hoyte felt strong enough to make public his break with the policies of the Burnham administration. In a nationally televised address on October 11, he focused Guyana's economic and foreign policies on the West, linking Guyana's future economic development to regional economies and noting that the strengthening of Guyana's relations with the United States was "imperative." While these objectives were in contrast to the policies of the past two decades, it was unclear what the long-term political and economic results would be.

* * *

Several good books are available on Guyanese history. For the region's early history, see Michel Deveze's *Antilles, Guyanes, La Mer des Caraïbes de 1492 à 1789,* and Vere T. Daly's *The Making of Guyana.* Walter Rodney's *A History of the Guyanese Working People, 1881–1905* is excellent on the colonial period. Four books on the modern period stand out: Chaitram Singh's *Guyana: Politics in a Plantation Society;* Thomas J. Spinner, Jr.'s *A Political and Social History of Guyana, 1945–1983;* Reynold Burrowes's *The Wild Coast: An Account of Politics in Guyana;* and Henry B. Jeffrey and Colin Baber's *Guyana: Politics, Economics and Society.* (For further information and complete citations, see Bibliography.)

Chapter 2. Guyana: The Society and Its Environment

Georgetown's public market building

THE COMPOSITION OF GUYANESE SOCIETY is a reflection of the country's colonial past. The colony was created by Dutch and British planters who grew sugarcane using the labor of slaves and indentured workers. Ignoring the country's vast interior, the planters constructed dikes and dams that transformed the coast into an arable plain. With the exception of the indigenous Amerindians and a few Europeans, the entire population consists of imported plantation workers or their descendants.

Guyanese culture developed with the adaptation of the forced and voluntary immigrants to the customs of the dominant British. Brought to Guyana as slaves, Africans of diverse backgrounds had been thrown together under conditions that severely constrained their ability to preserve their respective cultural traditions. In adopting Christianity and the values of British colonists, the descendants of the African slaves laid the foundations of today's Afro-Guyanese culture. Arriving later and under somewhat more favorable circumstances, East Indian immigrants were subjected to fewer pressures to assimilate than the Africans had been. As a result, more of their traditional culture was preserved.

Although the culture of independent Guyana has become more truly national, the Guyanese people remain divided by ethnic mistrust. The Guyanese elite that has emerged to replace the colonial administration faces the enormous challenge of satisfying the aspirations of the people concerning economic development and educational opportunity.

Geography

Terrain

With a land area of approximately 197,000 square kilometers, Guyana is about the size of Idaho. The country is situated between 1° and 9° north latitude and between 56° and 62° west longitude. With a 430-kilometer Atlantic coastline on the northeast, Guyana is bounded by Venezuela on the west, Brazil on the west and south, and Suriname on the east. The land comprises three main geographical zones: the coastal plain, the white sand belt, and the interior highlands (see fig. 2).

The coastal plain, which occupies about 5 percent of the country's area, is home to more than 90 percent of its inhabitants. The

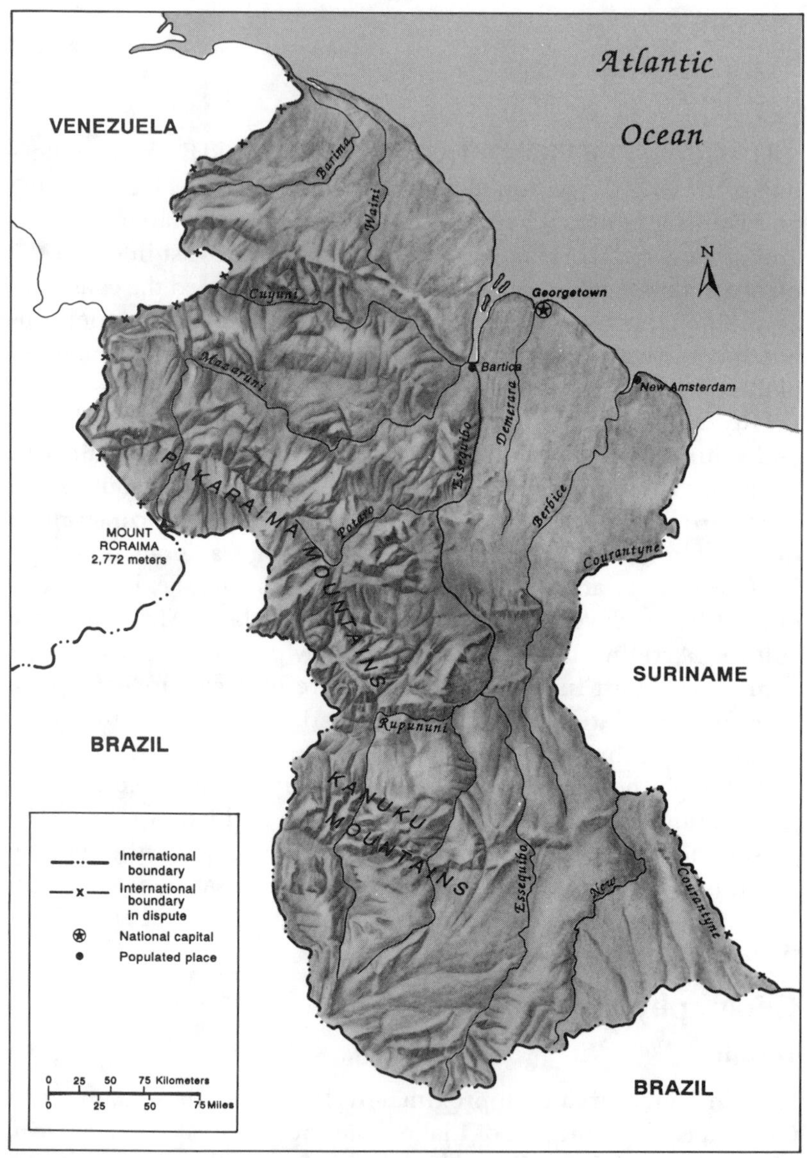

Figure 2. Guyana: Topography and Drainage

plain ranges from five to six kilometers wide and extends from the Courantyne River in the east to the Venezuelan border in the northwest.

The coastal plain is made up largely of alluvial mud swept out to sea by the Amazon River, carried north by ocean currents, and deposited on the Guyanese shores. A rich clay of great fertility, this mud overlays the white sands and clays formed from the erosion of the interior bedrock and carried seaward by the rivers of Guyana. Because much of the coastal plain floods at high tide, efforts to dam and drain this area have gone on since the 1700s (see The Coming of the Europeans, ch. 1).

Guyana has no well-defined shoreline or sandy beaches. Approaching the ocean, the land gradually loses elevation until it includes many areas of marsh and swamp. Seaward from the vegetation line is a region of mud flats, shallow brown water, and sandbars. Off New Amsterdam, these mud flats extend almost twenty-five kilometers. The sandbars and shallow water are a major impediment to shipping, and incoming vessels must partially unload their cargoes offshore in order to reach the docks at Georgetown and New Amsterdam.

A line of swamps forms a barrier between the white sandy hills of the interior and the coastal plain. These swamps, formed when water was prevented from flowing onto coastal croplands by a series of dams, serve as reservoirs during periods of drought.

The white sand belt lies south of the coastal zone. This area is 150 to 250 kilometers wide and consists of low sandy hills interspersed with rocky outcroppings. The white sands support a dense hardwood forest. These sands cannot support crops, and if the trees are removed erosion is rapid and severe. Most of Guyana's reserves of bauxite, gold, and diamonds are found in this region.

The largest of Guyana's three geographical regions is the interior highlands, a series of plateaus, flat-topped mountains, and savannahs that extend from the white sand belt to the country's southern borders. The Pakaraima Mountains dominate the western part of the interior highlands. In this region are found some of the oldest sedimentary rocks in the Western Hemisphere. Mount Roraima, on the Venezuelan border, is part of the Pakaraima range and, at 2,762 meters, is Guyana's tallest peak. Farther south lie the Kaieteur Plateau, a broad, rocky area about 600 meters in elevation; the 1,000-meter high Kanuku Mountains; and the low Acarai Mountains situated on the southern border with Brazil.

Much of the interior highlands consist of grassland. The largest expanse of grassland, the Rupununi Savannah, covers about 15,000 square kilometers in southern Guyana. This savannah also extends far into Venezuela and Brazil. The part in Guyana is split into northern and southern regions by the Kanuku Mountains. The sparse grasses of the savannah in general support only grazing, although Amerindian groups cultivate a few areas along the Rupununi River and in the foothills of the Kanuku Mountains.

Hydrology

Guyana is a water-rich country. The numerous rivers flow into the Atlantic Ocean, generally in a northward direction. A number of rivers in the western part of the country, however, flow eastward into the Essequibo River, draining the Kaieteur Plateau. The Essequibo, the country's major river, runs from the Brazilian border in the south to a wide delta west of Georgetown. The rivers of eastern Guyana cut across the coastal zone, making east-west travel difficult, but they also provide limited water access to the interior. Waterfalls generally limit water transport to the lower reaches of each river. Some of the waterfalls are spectacular; for example, Kaieteur Falls on the Potaro River drops 226 meters, more than four times the height of Niagara Falls.

Drainage throughout most of Guyana is poor and river flow sluggish because the average gradient of the main rivers is only one meter every five kilometers. Swamps and areas of periodic flooding are found in all but the mountainous regions, and all new land projects require extensive drainage networks before they are suitable for agricultural use. The average square kilometer on a sugar plantation, for example, has six kilometers of irrigation canals, eighteen kilometers of large drains, and eighteen kilometers of small drains. These canals occupy nearly one-eighth of the surface area of the average sugarcane field. Some of the larger estates have more than 550 kilometers of canals; Guyana itself has a total of more than 8,000 kilometers. Even Georgetown is below sea level and must depend on dikes for protection from the Demerara River and the Atlantic Ocean.

Climate

Guyana has a tropical climate with almost uniformly high temperatures and humidity, and much rainfall. Seasonal variations in temperature are slight, particularly along the coast. Although the temperature never gets dangerously high, the combination of heat and humidity can at times seem oppressive. The entire area is under the influence of the northeast trade winds, and during the midday and afternoon sea breezes bring relief to the coast. Guyana lies south of the path of Caribbean hurricanes, and none is known to have hit the country.

Temperatures in Georgetown are quite constant, with an average high of 32°C and an average low of 24°C in the hottest month (July), and an average range of 29°C to 23°C in February, the coolest month. The highest temperature ever recorded in the capital was 34°C and the lowest only 20°C. Humidity averages 70 percent year-round. Locations in the interior, away from the moderating influence of the ocean, experience slightly wider variations in daily temperature, and nighttime readings as low as 12°C have been recorded. Humidity in the interior is also slightly lower, averaging around 60 percent.

Rainfall is heaviest in the northwest and lightest in the southeast and interior. Annual averages on the coast near the Venezuelan border are near 2,500 millimeters, farther east at New Amsterdam 2,000 millimeters, and 1,500 millimeters in southern Guyana's Rupununi Savannah. Areas on the northeast sides of mountains that catch the trade winds average as much as 3,500 millimeters of precipitation annually. Although rain falls throughout the year, about 50 percent of the annual total arrives in the summer rainy season that extends from May to the end of July along the coast and from April through September farther inland. Coastal areas have a second rainy season from November through January. Rain generally falls in heavy afternoon showers or thunderstorms. Overcast days are rare; most days include four to eight hours of sunshine from morning through early afternoon.

Population

Demographic Profile

Guyana's population was counted at 758,619 in the census of 1980 and estimated to be 764,000 in 1990. This slow growth was in sharp contrast to the decades following World War II, when the population rose from 375,000 in 1946 to 700,000 in 1970. The natural increase in population in 1990 was 1.9 percent; this growth was almost completely negated, however, by the large numbers of Guyanese who emigrated. The population was relatively young, with 37 percent under fifteen years of age in 1985 (see fig. 3).

Guyana's birthrate, which averaged thirty-two live births per 1,000 residents in the two decades prior to 1940, jumped to an exceptionally high forty live births per 1,000 in the two decades after 1940. The rate began to drop after 1960 and by 1990 had fallen to twenty-five live births per 1,000.

Efforts to control malaria and to improve sanitation in the 1940s resulted in a dramatic decrease in infant mortality and in the overall death rate. In the 1930s, the infant mortality rate was 149 for every 1,000 live births. By 1946 this rate had dropped to eighty-seven per 1,000, and in 1990 it stood at thirty deaths per 1,000 live births. Statistics on the general death rate mirror the decline in the infant

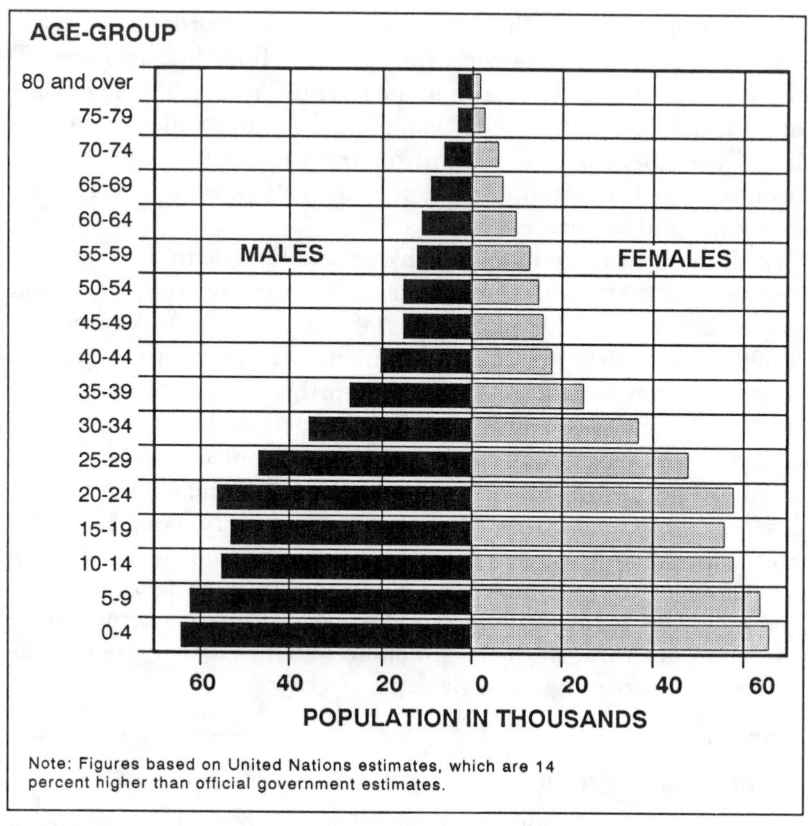

Source: Based on information from Federal Republic of Germany, Statistisches Bundesamt, *Länderbericht Guyana, 1987*, Wiesbaden, 1987, 17.

Figure 3. Guyana: Estimated Population by Age and Sex, 1985

mortality rate. The death rate (including infant mortality) in 1944 was twenty-two per 1,000 residents; in 1963, eight per 1,000; and in 1990, five per 1,000, one of the lowest rates in the Western Hemisphere.

Indo-Guyanese women had a higher birthrate than Afro-Guyanese women in the years after World War II. However, by the early 1960s the fertility rate for Indo-Guyanese women had begun to drop. Statistics for the 1980s showed Indo-Guyanese women marrying at a later age and having fewer children than had been customary in the 1950s. By the 1990s, the difference in birthrates between Indo-Guyanese and Afro-Guyanese women had disappeared.

A general decline in fertility rates among women in all ethnic groups was attributed to the increased availability and use of contraceptives. In 1975 the Guyana Fertility Survey found that 57 percent of women who had been married had used contraceptives at some time and that about 40 percent currently were using them. This high rate of contraceptive use was maintained in the absence of public or private family-planning campaigns.

Ethnic Composition

Ethnic diversity is one of the most significant characteristics of the Guyanese population (see table 2, Appendix A). As of 1980, Guyanese of East Indian descent (Indo-Guyanese) constituted 51 percent of the total population. Guyanese wholly of African descent made up 31 percent of the population. Those listed as of mixed ancestry constituted 12 percent. Since the mixed-ancestry category comprised individuals of partial African ancestry who were usually included in the Afro-Guyanese community, the Afro-Guyanese population in effect constituted 42 percent of the total population. The remainder of the population was composed of Amerindians (4 percent) and individuals of European or Asian descent (3 percent).

A higher growth rate for the Indo-Guyanese population in the post-World War II period resulted in a change in the ethnic composition of Guyanese society. The Indo-Guyanese population grew from 43 percent of the total in 1946 to a majority—51 percent—in 1980. During the same period, the Afro-Guyanese proportion of the population decreased from 49 percent to 42 percent. Although the small European (mostly Portuguese) and Asian (almost entirely Chinese) sectors continued to grow in absolute numbers after World War II, they represented a decreasing proportion of the population.

Population Distribution and Settlement Patterns

Statistics indicate that Guyana is one of the most lightly populated countries in Latin America and the Caribbean. The World Bank (see Glossary) estimated that there were four people per square kilometer in Guyana in 1988, far fewer than the average of twenty people per square kilometer for all of Latin America. However, more than 90 percent of Guyana's population lived along the coast, on a strip constituting only 5 percent of the country's total land area. A more useful figure is the population density per square kilometer of agricultural land, which was estimated at forty-six in 1988. In Latin America as a whole, the average population density on agricultural land was fifty-five per square kilometer.

More than 70 percent of Guyana's coastal population is rural, living on plantations or in villages strung along the coastal road. The villages range in size from several hundred to several thousand inhabitants. The layout of the villages is dictated by the drainage and irrigation systems of the plantations, both active and abandoned. The villages are most heavily concentrated along the estuary of the Demerara River and the eastern environs of Georgetown, near the mouth of the Berbice River close to New Amsterdam, and along the extreme east coast near the Courantyne River (see table 3, Appendix A).

The pattern of population distribution in Guyana is a product of nineteenth-century economic development, which was based on the cultivation of sugarcane (see The Early British Colony and the Labor Problem, ch. 1). Because the swampy coast was fertile and sugar production was geared to export, the large sugar estates confined their operations to a narrow coastal strip. Most of the villages had ethnically diverse populations, but usually one ethnic group predominated. The urban population was predominantly African, but it would be misleading to suggest that all Afro-Guyanese were urban. Indeed, the majority of the Afro-Guyanese population was rural. A far greater majority of Indo-Guyanese, however, lived outside the cities. The interior of the country was left mainly to the Amerindians. Even the later exploitation of timber, bauxite, and manganese in the interior failed to effect any sizeable migration.

Urban Population

Guyana remained a primarily rural country in 1991. The only significant urban area, the capital city of Georgetown, was home to more than 80 percent of the urban population. The smaller towns served primarily as regional distribution centers. Georgetown had an estimated population of 195,000 in 1985 and an annual growth rate of 6.6 percent. Linden, the country's second largest town with a population of 30,000, was a bauxite mining complex on the Demerara River. The port of New Amsterdam in eastern Guyana had a population of about 20,000.

The proportion of the population living in urban areas increased only slightly between 1960, when it was 29 percent, and 1980, when it was 30.5 percent. By 1985, 32.2 percent of the population was living in urban areas.

Emigration

Guyanese statistics indicated an average of 6,080 declared emigrants a year between 1969 and 1976, increasing to an average of 14,400 between 1976 and 1981. Figures for 1976 showed 43 percent of the emigrants going to the United States, 31 percent to Canada, 10 percent to Britain, and 9 percent to the Caribbean. Deteriorating economic conditions caused emigration to increase

Aerial view of the low-lying coast with its Dutch-built seawalls
Aerial view of Georgetown showing the layout designed by the Dutch, mostly on a grid pattern
Courtesy Embassy of Guyana, Washington

sharply in the 1980s. Unofficial estimates put the number leaving the country in the late 1980s at 10,000 to 30,000 annually. Many of these emigrants were reported to be middle-class professionals, largely Indo-Guyanese, who opposed government policies that favored employment of Afro-Guyanese in the public sector. This emigration resulted in a significant loss of skilled personnel.

Ethnic Groups

Guyana's ethnic mix is the direct product of the colonial economy. Except for the Amerindians and a few Europeans, the country's ethnic groups are the descendants of groups brought in to work the early plantations. An economy based on sugar production required a large labor force. Attempts to enslave the Amerindian population failed, and the planters soon turned to African slaves. By 1830 there were 100,000 such slaves in British Guiana.

After the abolition of slavery became totally effective in 1838, the planters found a new source of cheap labor in the form of indentured workers, foreigners recruited to work for a specific number of years, usually five, with the possibility of reenlisting for an additional period and eventually being repatriated. Even before slavery was abolished, the importation of indentured workers began. They were recruited from Portugal, India, China, and the West Indies. Although the terms of indenture were nearly as harsh as slavery, the planters succeeded in bringing about 286,000 persons into the country by the early twentieth century. More than 80 percent of these indentured workers were East Indians; their arrival would profoundly affect Guyana's ethnic composition and the nature of Guyanese society in general.

Afro-Guyanese

Descendants of the Africans, the Afro-Guyanese came to see themselves as the true people of British Guiana, with greater rights to land than the indentured workers who had arrived after them. The fact that planters made land available to East Indians in the late nineteenth century when they had denied land to the Africans several decades earlier reinforced Afro-Guyanese resentment toward other ethnic groups in the colony. The Afro-Guyanese people's perception of themselves as the true Guyanese derived not only from their long history of residence, but also from a sense of superiority based on their literacy, Christianity, and British colonial values.

By the early twentieth century, the majority of the urban population of the country was Afro-Guyanese. Many Afro-Guyanese living in villages had migrated to the towns in search of work. Until the 1930s, Afro-Guyanese, especially those of mixed African and

European descent, comprised the bulk of the nonwhite professional class. During the 1930s, as the Indo-Guyanese began to enter the middle class in large numbers, they began to compete with Afro-Guyanese for professional positions.

Indo-Guyanese

Between 1838 and 1917, almost 240,000 East Indian indentured workers were brought to British Guiana. The indentured workers had the right to be repatriated at the end of their contracts, but as of 1890, most of the East Indian indentured workers had chosen to settle in British Guiana.

Although the great majority of the East Indian immigrants workers were from northern India, there were variations among them in caste and religion. Some 30 percent of the East Indians were from agricultural castes and 31 percent were from low castes or were untouchables. Brahmans, the highest caste, constituted 14 percent of the East Indian immigrants. About 16 percent were Muslims. The only acknowledgment the colonial government and the plantation managers gave to caste differences was their distrust of the Brahmans as potential leaders. East Indian workers were housed together and placed in work gangs without consideration of caste. Unlike the African slaves, the East Indian indentured workers were permitted to retain may of their cultural traditions. But the process of assimilation has made the culture of the modern Indo-Guyanese more homogeneous than that of their caste-conscious immigrant ancestors.

Portuguese and Chinese

The Portuguese were among the first indentured workers brought to Guyana. Portuguese indentured immigration began in 1835 and ended in 1882, with most of the immigrants having arrived by the 1860s. Most of the Portuguese came from the North Atlantic island of Madeira.

Economically successful in Guyana, the Portuguese nonetheless experienced discrimination. Even though of European origin, they were treated as socially inferior by the British plantation owners and officials because of their indentured past and Roman Catholic religion. Despite discrimination, by the end of the nineteenth century the Portuguese were firmly established as an important part of Guyana's middle class and commercial sector.

Indentured Chinese workers first came to British Guiana from the south coast of China in 1853. Relatively few in number, the Chinese became the most acculturated of all the descendants of indentured workers. The Chinese language and most Chinese customs, including religion, disappeared. There were no clans or other extended kinship organizations, and soon most Chinese did not trace their ancestry beyond the first immigrant. Because almost all of the Chinese indentured immigrants were men, they tended to intermarry with both East Indians and Africans, and thus the Chinese of Guyana did not remain as physically distinct as other groups.

Like the Portuguese, the Chinese left the plantations as soon as their indenture contracts were fulfilled. Many entered the retail trade. Other Chinese engaged in farming and pioneered wet-rice production, using techniques they brought from China. The Chinese tended to live in urban settings.

Amerindians

The Amerindians are the descendants of the indigenous people of Guyana; they are broadly grouped into coastal and interior tribes. The term *tribes* is a linguistic and cultural classification rather than a political one. The coastal Amerindians are the Carib, Arawak, and Warao, whose names come from the three language families of the Guyanese Amerindians. The population of coastal Carib in Guyana declined in the nineteenth century, but Arawak and Warao communities can be found near the Pomeroon and Courantyne rivers.

The interior Amerindians are classified into seven tribes: Akawaio, Arekuna, Barama River Carib, Macusi, Patamona, Waiwai, and Wapisiana. The Barama River Carib, Akawaio, Arekuna, and Patamona live in river valleys in western Guyana. Two Amerindian groups live in the Rupununi Savannah region: the Macusi in the northern half and the Wapisiana in the southern half. The Waiwai live in the far south of the country, near the headwaters of the Essequibo River. All of the interior Amerindians originally spoke Carib languages, with the exception of the Wapisiana, whose language is in the Arawak linguistic family.

By the 1990s, all of the Amerindian groups had undergone extensive acculturation. The coastal Amerindians were the most acculturated, sharing many cultural features with lower-class Afro-Guyanese and Indo-Guyanese. There had been considerable intermarriage between coastal Amerindians and Afro-Guyanese. The Waiwai and the Barama River Carib were probably the least acculturated of the Amerindians. Nevertheless, most Amerindians spoke English (or near Brazil, Portuguese) as a first or second language. Almost all Amerindians had been affected by missionary efforts for many decades. Finally, most Amerindians had been integrated in one way or another into the national economic system, though usually at the lowest levels.

Development of Ethnic Identity

One of the dominant characteristics of Guyanese society and politics, ethnicity has received much attention from social scientists and historians. It is an oversimplification to describe Guyanese society as made of up of separate racial groups. Terms such as *Afro-Guyanese* and *Indo-Guyanese* refer to ethnic identities or categories. Significant physical and cultural variations exist within each ethnic category. Thus, two Guyanese with quite different ancestry, political and economic interests, and behavior may share the same ethnic identity.

All of the immigrant groups in British Guiana adapted to the colony's dominant British culture. In many ways, the descendants of the various immigrant groups have come to resemble each other more than their respective ancestors. Moreover, the immigrants' descendants have spread out from their original social niches. Indo-Guyanese are to be found not only on the sugar plantations or in rice-producing communities, but also in the towns, where some are laborers and others are professionals or businessmen. Afro-Guyanese are likewise found at all levels of society.

Among the experiences shared by all of the immigrant groups was labor on the plantations. After the abolition of slavery, the nature of the labor force changed, but not the labor itself. East Indians performed the same work as the slaves before them and lived in the same kind of housing; they were subject to the same management structure on the plantations. All of the immigrant groups were exposed to the same dominant British value system and had to accommodate their own values to it. Africans saw themselves as belonging to different cultural groups; Indian society was differentiated by religion and caste. To the British, however, race was the primary social determinant, and East Indians found themselves categorized as a single race distinct from the Africans.

Perhaps nowhere was assimilation more evident than in language use. English, the official language, has become the primary language of all Guyanese, with the exception of a few elderly Indo-Guyanese and some Amerindians. The universal use of English is a strong unifying cultural force. English also brings the nation closer to other countries of the English-speaking Caribbean, although it has isolated Guyana from Spanish- and Portuguese-speaking Latin America.

As the descendants of the immigrant groups became more Anglicized, cultural differences grew less pronounced, and even physical differences became blurred through intermarriage. The cultural differences that remained took on a symbolic importance as indicators of ethnic identity. Many of these cultural differences had not been passed on by ancestors, but developed in the colony. Guyanese Hinduism, for example, is closer to Islam and Christianity than anything observed by the ancestors of the Indo-Guyanese, yet it serves to rally ethnic solidarity.

Ideologies of Race and Class

Racial stereotypes developed early in the colony. British planters characterized Africans as physically strong but lazy and irresponsible. East Indians were stereotyped as industrious but clannish and greedy. To some extent, these stereotypes were accepted by the immigrant groups themselves, each giving credence to positive stereotypes of itself and negative stereotypes of other groups. The stereotypes provided a quick explanation of behavior and justified competition among groups. Africans were described as improvident when they refused to work for low wages or make long-term contracts with the plantations. East Indians were considered selfish when they minimized their expenses to acquire capital.

In modern Guyana, the association of behavior with ethnicity is less rigid than in colonial days. Where once there was a sharp and uniform distinction between behavior considered "British" and behavior considered "coolie," now there is a continuum of behaviors, which receive different ethnic labels in different contexts. What is considered "British" in a rural village might be considered "coolie" in the capital.

Along with stereotyping, the colonial value system favoring European, specifically British, mores and behavior has persisted. Eurocentrism was promoted by the colonial education system, which idealized British customs. The superiority of British culture was accepted by the ex-slaves, who perceived their Christianity, for example, as an indication that they too were civilized. From the late nineteenth century, the emerging middle class of urban Afro-Guyanese, Indo-Guyanese, and others developed a nationalist ideology based largely on British values. They claimed a place in society because they met standards that had been set by the British.

Family and Kinship Structure

Afro-Guyanese Patterns

The Africans brought to Guyana as slaves came from cultures with highly developed family systems. Slavery had a devastating effect on African social life and especially on family structures. Spouses could be separated, children could be sold away from their mothers, and sexual exploitation by planters was common.

Main Street, Georgetown, with the Cenotaph, a memorial to those who died in the World Wars, in the foreground
Courtesy Leslie B. Johnson, Sr.
Central business district, Main Street, Georgetown
Courtesy Embassy of Guyana, Washington

Although legal marriage was forbidden to the slaves, Africans attempted to sustain relationships between men and women and their children.

The monogamous nuclear family is but one family structure accepted among Afro-Guyanese. Although the Christian church wedding has become a important popular ideal, it is more likely to be achieved by middle-class than by lower-class Afro-Guyanese. For many, a church wedding comes not at the beginning of a union, but as a sort of culmination of a relationship. Many common-law marriages are recognized socially but lack the status of a legal wedding. Afro-Guyanese, especially in the lower socioeconomic groups, may have a series of relationships before entering into a legal or common-law marriage. Some such relationships do not entail the establishment of a separate household. The children of such relationships live with one of the parents, usually the mother.

Because of the variety of conjugal relationships that Afro-Guyanese adults may form over the course of their lives, the composition of households varies. They may be headed by fathers or mothers and may include children from several parents. Afro-Guyanese households tend to be clustered around females rather than males because the men frequently leave their homes in search of paid work. A three-generation household is likely to include daughters with children whose fathers are away or do not live in the household. Children born out of wedlock are not stigmatized.

Indo-Guyanese Patterns

The plantation system had an effect on the family life of East Indians as well as on that of Africans. In rural India, the basic social unit was the large extended family. Caste position was the first criterion in choosing an appropriate mate. In the plantation housing of British Guiana, it was not possible to maintain extended households even if the kin were available. Considerations of caste became less important in choosing a spouse largely because there were so few women among the East Indian indentured workers.

A wedding is not only an ideal to the Indo-Guyanese; it is the usual rite of passage to adulthood. An elaborate wedding is a necessary affirmation of the social prestige of a Hindu family, as well as a major ritual in the life cycle. Muslim weddings are less elaborate, but also confer prestige on the families involved. Parents usually play a role in selecting the first mate. Religion and sect are important in choosing a marriage partner; caste notions may be as well. However, first marriages are not necessarily expected to endure.

An increasing number of East Indian marriages are regarded as legal, especially since Hindu and Muslim clergy have legal authority to perform wedding ceremonies. No social stigma is attached to civil wedding ceremonies, common-law unions, or conjugal unions between couples who remain legally married to others but have ended their past relationships by mutual consent.

The Indo-Guyanese family tends to be organized through male lines. Extended-family members do not necessarily share the same household, but they often live near each other and may engage in economic activities together. Young couples typically live with the husband's family for several years, eventually establishing their own cooking facilities and later their own home. In contrast to Afro-Guyanese practice, three-generation households with males at the head are not uncommon among the Indo-Guyanese. The role of the woman is typically more subordinate in Indo-Guyanese families than in Afro-Guyanese households.

Religion

Christianity, Hinduism, and Islam are the dominant religions in Guyana. The majority of the Indo-Guyanese are Hindus, although a substantial number are Muslims. Some Indo-Guyanese have converted to Christianity, but conversion is often for professional reasons. Some converts continue their Hindu or Muslim rituals in addition to participating in Christian services. Most Afro-Guyanese are Christians, although a few have converted to Hinduism or Islam. Guyana's other ethnic groups are largely Christian. In 1990 some 52 percent of Guyanese were Christian, 34 percent were Hindu, and 9 percent were Muslim. Of the Christians, 65 percent were Protestant and 35 percent Roman Catholic (see table 4, Appendix A).

Christianity's status as Guyana's dominant system of values is a consequence of colonial history. To the European planters, colonial administrators, and missionaries, the profession of Christian beliefs and observance of Christian practices were prerequisites to social acceptance. Even though the planters discouraged the teaching of their religion to the slaves, Christianity eventually became as much the religion of the Africans as of the Europeans. Indeed, after abolition, Christian institutions played an even more important role in the lives of the former slaves than in the lives of the masters. By the time the East Indians and other indentured groups arrived in Guyana, a new syncretic Afro-Guyanese culture in which Christianity played an important part had already been established. Only since the mid-twentieth century, with the growth of the Indo-Guyanese population and the efforts of their ethnic and religious organizations, have Muslim and Hindu values and institutions been recognized as having equal status with those of Guyana's Christians.

Christianity

Among the Christian denominations active in Guyana in the 1990s, the Anglican Church claimed the largest membership: about 125,000 adherents as of 1986. Anglicanism was the state religion of British Guiana until independence. The Roman Catholic Church had a membership of about 94,000 in 1985. The majority of Roman Catholics lived in Georgetown, and the Portuguese were the most active members, although all the ethnic groups were represented. The Presbyterian Church was the third largest denomination, with nearly 39,000 members in 1980. Several other Christian churches had significant memberships in 1980, including the Methodists, Pentecostals, and Seventh-Day Adventists, each of which had about 20,000 members. There were smaller numbers of Baptists, Jehovah's Witnesses, Congregationalists, Nazarenes, Moravians, Ethiopian Orthodox, and other mainstream Christians. Other sects in Guyana included Rastafarianism (see Glossary), which looks to Ethiopia for religious inspiration, and the Hallelujah Church, which combines Christian beliefs with Amerindian traditions. There were also at least 60,000 people describing themselves as Christian who had no formal church affiliation.

Hinduism

The majority of the East Indian immigrants were Hindu, and their dominant sect was Vaishnavite Hinduism. Status differences were attached to castes, and rituals varied with caste status. The higher castes worshipped the classic pantheon of Vishnu and Shiva. Vaishnavite Hinduism remains the predominant religion of the Indo-Guyanese, although it has been considerably modified.

During the indenture period, the East Indian caste system, with its reinforced variations of rites and beliefs within the Vishnu cult, broke down. Hinduism was redefined, and caste-distinguishing practices were eliminated. Christian missionaries attempted to convert East Indians during the indenture period, beginning in 1852, but met with little success. The missionaries blamed the Brahmans for their failure: the Brahmans began administering spiritual rites to all Hindus regardless of caste once the Christian missionaries started proselytizing in the villages, hastening the breakdown of the caste system. After the 1930s, Hindu conversions to Christianity slowed because the status of Hinduism had improved and discrimination against Hindus had diminished.

Orthodox Hinduism stresses the festivities accompanying religious rites. Festivals may last several days and are usually held in times of crisis or prosperity. Because the sponsor of a festival provides a tent and feeds a large number of guests, orthodox Hindu rituals require considerable outlays of money. A Hindu family has difficulty fulfilling ritual obligations unless it has accumulated a surplus of cash.

Since the late 1940s, reform movements have caught the attention of many Guyanese Hindus. The most important, the Arya Samaj movement (Aryan Society), was founded in India in 1875; the first Arya Samaj missionary arrived in Guyana in 1910. Arya Samaj doctrine rejects the idea of caste and the exclusive role of Brahmans as religious leaders. The movement preaches monotheism and opposition to the use of images in worship as well as many traditional Hindu rituals.

Islam

Like the Hindus, Guyana's Muslims are organized into orthodox and reform movements. The Sunnatival Jamaat is the orthodox Sunni (see Glossary) Islamic movement. The largest Islamic organization in the country is the Guyana United Sadr Islamic Anjuman. The reform movement, the Ahmadiyah, was founded in India in the late nineteenth century; its first missionary to Guyana arrived in 1908. The reform movement has had considerable success, even including some Afro-Guyanese among its converts. The rites of orthodox and reform Islam are similar, but the reform movement allows the Quran to be read in English and women to enter a designated section of the mosque. In contrast to the situation found on the Indian subcontinent, Muslims and Hindus experience little friction in Guyana. These two religious communities have a tacit agreement not to proselytize each other's members. In smaller villages, Christians and Muslims come together to participate in each other's ceremonies.

Until the 1970s, Hindu and Muslim holidays were not officially recognized. A number of non-Christian religious days are now public holidays. Hindu holidays include Holi, the spring festival, and Divali, the festival of lights. Muslim holidays include Id al Fitr, the end of Ramadan, the sacred month of fasting; Id al Adha, the feast of sacrifice; and Yaum an Nabi, the birthday of Muhammad. The dates for these holidays vary. An East Indian heritage day is celebrated and on May 5, and an Amerindian festival is held on Republic Day, in February.

Obeah and Amerindian Practices

A number of folk beliefs continue to be practiced in Guyana. Obeah, a folk religion of African origin, incorporates beliefs and practices of all the immigrant groups. Obeah practitioners may be Afro-Guyanese or Indo-Guyanese, and members of all the ethnic groups consult them for help with problems concerning health, work, domestic life, and romance. Some villagers wear charms or use other folk practices to protect themselves from harm.

Traditional Amerindian religious beliefs vary, but shamans play a significant role in all of them. The shaman is believed to communicate with the world of spirits in order to detect sorcery and combat evil. The shaman is also a healer and an adviser, the representative of the village to the spiritual world and sometimes its political leader as well. Missionary activity to the Amerindians has been intense. As a result, the traditional beliefs and practices of all the Amerindian groups have been modified; some have even disappeared.

Cults

The House of Israel was established by a fugitive from the United States, David Hill, also known as Rabbi Edward Washington, who arrived in Guyana in 1972. The cult had no ties to traditional Jewish religion but was a black supremacist movement. In the 1970s, the group claimed a membership of 8,000. The House of Israel had a daily radio program in which it preached that Africans were the original Hebrews and needed to prepare for a racial war. Opponents of the government claimed that the House of Israel constituted a private army for Guyana's ruling party, the People's National Congress (PNC). During an anti-government demonstration, a House of Israel member murdered a Roman Catholic priest because he was on the staff of a religious opposition newspaper, the *Catholic Standard.* The House of Israel also engaged in strikebreaking activities and disruptions of public meetings. Critics of the government alleged that House of Israel members acted with impunity during the government of Linden Forbes Burnham. However, under Hugh Desmond Hoyte, Burnham's successor, Rabbi Washington and key associates were arrested on a long-standing manslaughter charge and imprisoned.

Guyana acquired international notoriety in 1978 following a mass murder-suicide at the commune of the People's Temple of Christ, which had been led by the Reverend Jim Jones, of Oakland, California. In 1974 the People's Temple, a utopian commune, leased a tract of land near Port Kaituma in western Guyana to escape from mounting scrutiny of the group by California authorities. The government welcomed the People's Temple in part because of its interest in populating the interior of the country, especially the area claimed by Venezuela, where Jonestown was situated. Members of the People's Temple also became close to PNC leaders, and the group was allowed to function without interference from the government. Allegations of atrocities by commune leaders and charges that the commune was holding people against their will led a United States congressman, Leo Ryan, to go to Jonestown to investigate the allegations of abuse (see The Cooperative Republic, ch. 1).

Fearing that Congressman Ryan's report on the commune would bring unwanted publicity and restrictions on his operations, Jones had the congressman shot as he was boarding an airplane to return to Georgetown. The United States immediately asked Guyana to send in its army. Before the army could reach Jonestown, however, Jones coerced and cajoled more than 900 members of the commune to commit murder and suicide.

Religion and Politics

Through much of Guyana's history, the Anglican and Roman Catholic churches helped maintain the social and political status quo. The Roman Catholic Church and its newspaper, the *Catholic Standard,* were vocal opponents of the ideology of the People's Progressive Party (PPP) in the 1950s and became closely associated with the conservative United Force. However, in the late 1960s the Roman Catholic Church changed its stance toward social and political issues, and the *Catholic Standard* became more critical of the government. Subsequently, the government forced a number of foreign Roman Catholic priests to leave the country. By the mid-1970s, the Anglicans and other Protestant denominations had joined in the criticisms of government abuse. The Anglican and Roman Catholic churches also worked together, unsuccessfully, to oppose the government's assumption of control of church schools in 1976.

The Guyana Council of Churches was the umbrella organization for sixteen major Christian denominations. Historically, it had been dominated by the Anglican and Roman Catholic churches. The Guyana Council of Churches became an increasingly vocal critic of the government in the 1970s and 1980s, focusing international attention on its shortcomings. The conflict between the government and the Guyana Council of Churches came to a head in 1985, when members of the PNC-influenced House of Israel physically prevented the council from holding its annual meeting. Later that year, police searched the homes of the major Christian church leaders. The PNC maintained the support of a number of smaller Christian denominations, however.

In contrast to the most prominent Christian clergy, who maintained connections with international denominations, Hindu and Muslim leaders depended on strictly local support. For them, resistance to political pressure was more difficult. In the 1970s, the PNC succeeded in splitting many of the important Hindu and Muslim organizations into pro-PNC and pro-PPP factions.

Education

Free education from nursery school through university was a major reason for Guyana's 1990 estimated literacy rate of 96 percent, one of the highest in the Western Hemisphere. As of 1985, the average worker in Guyana had completed 6.8 years of schooling. Families of all ethnic groups and classes took interest in the schooling of their children, and education reform has had a central place in government policy since the 1960s.

The earliest record of schooling in Guyana dates back to Dutch rule and the arrival of a religious instructor in Essequibo in 1685. Because seventeenth- and eighteenth-century planters sent their children to Europe to study, local education developed slowly. Private schools and academies for the children of prospering non-British colonists were established and maintained in the colony during the nineteenth century; the first known reference to the establishment of public schools was made early in the 1800s.

By 1834 there were numerous schools, both elementary and secondary, in British Guiana's urban centers. After the cessation of slavery in 1838, many Africans quickly made use of the educational opportunities open to them. By 1841 there were 101 elementary schools, most of them under the direction of the London Missionary Society. A teacher-training school and a college were opened in the 1850s. Primary education became compulsory in 1876. Truancy, however, was common.

The British planters and bureaucrats discouraged the education of the Indo-Guyanese indentured laborers. The government stated in 1904 that Indo-Guyanese should not be prosecuted if they objected on religious grounds to sending their daughters to school. Planters used this policy to discourage workers from sending their children to school. Not until 1933 was the Indo-Guyanese leadership successful in changing government policy.

For most of the colonial period, secondary education was restricted to the upper and middle classes. With the exception of a very few scholarships, secondary education was paid for by parents,

City Hall, Georgetown. Completed in 1889, it is one of the finest examples of Gothic architecture in South America.
Courtesy Embassy of Guyana, Washington

not the government. Thus, most of the students who completed primary school were excluded from a secondary education.

Guiding the development of the colonial school system was the traditional British view that the purpose of secondary education was to prepare the elite for its role in society. The two best secondary schools, Queen's College and Bishop's High School, both in Georgetown, employed the same curricula and methods used in British "public" schools. During most of the colonial period, there was little interest either in vocational training or in expanding educational opportunities. The requirement of a single, standard certificate based on a highly literary curriculum prevented education reform well into the twentieth century.

In 1961 the government took steps that greatly increased access to education. Many new secondary schools were opened, especially in rural areas, and school fees were abolished. Two years later, the University of Guyana was established. The percentage of children between the ages of twelve and seventeen attending school increased from 63 percent in 1960 to 76 percent in 1985. For those between ages eighteen and twenty-three, school attendance increased almost threefold, from 4.7 percent to 12.9 percent, between 1960 and 1985 (see table 5, Appendix A).

Education Policy and the Teaching Profession

The postindependence government placed particular emphasis on education, both to develop a skilled labor force and to increase opportunity for disadvantaged people. Primary and secondary education was supervised by the Education Department of the Ministry of Education, Social Development, and Culture. District officers inspected schools at the local level. The university and institutions of technical education were administered by the Ministry of Higher Education, established in 1980. In 1988 expenditures on education constituted 6.4 percent of government spending. Many leading members of the government, including presidents Burnham and Hoyte, were former schoolteachers; others were the children of teachers. Yet critics of the government asserted that the education system had undergone decline in the 1970s and 1980s, despite the priority given it by the government. Critics also charged the government with using the school system to disseminate political propaganda.

In 1976 the government abolished private education and became responsible for providing free education from nursery school through the university level. The government took over about 600 schools. The great majority of the private schools taken over by the government had been religious. Most of them had been Christian, and a few had been Hindu or Muslim. The takeover was opposed by the churches and by a large segment of the middle class, which feared a decline in education standards and increased competition from lower-class students.

Guyana had no shortage of teachers through the 1980s. The teaching profession remained an honored one, even though teachers were no longer the most educated members of their community. Teaching had long been a means of advancement for Afro-Guyanese, who made up the majority of teachers until the 1950s; they instructed both Afro-Guyanese and Indo-Guyanese children. Indo-Guyanese began to enter the profession in the 1920s, but there was little room for advancement for non-Christians in the denominational schools. After World War II, Indo-Guyanese took a greater interest in schooling and a large number went into education. Schoolteachers became the largest professional group among the Indo-Guyanese; they tended to teach in government schools, where religious differences were less important. About 7 percent of the primary school instructors in the country were Indo-Guyanese in 1935; by 1965, this segment had increased to 54 percent, surpassing the proportion of Indo-Guyanese in the general population.

Primary Schools

Nursery school was available to Guyanese children for two years, beginning at age four. Children began primary school at age six. Primary schools had six grades: Preparatory A and B and Standards I through IV. Primary schools were attended five hours a day, Monday through Friday. A school year usually had 189 days, beginning in September and ending in July. The school year was divided into three trimesters: Christmas Term, Easter Term, and Summer Term. Primary education for students with disabilities was provided by the Thomas Lands School in Georgetown.

In 1984 there were 368 nursery schools and 418 primary schools in Guyana. In 1981 about 130,000 students attended primary schools, an enrollment rate of 96 percent. With 3,909 teachers in Guyana, the national teacher-pupil ratio was one teacher to thirty-three pupils.

Secondary Schools

Entry into secondary education was based on students' performance in a placement examination, the Secondary School Entrance Examination (SSEE) administered to eleven-year-old students. For those students who scored poorly on the SSEE, a continuation of primary education for three years was also available in the so-called senior department of the primary schools, which were also known as all-age schools. Students who completed primary school or all-age school were eligible to continue in secondary school.

There were three kinds of secondary schools to which students who had taken the SSEE could be admitted: the general secondary school, the multilateral school, and the community high school. General secondary schools had a six-year program, with Forms I through VI. (Form VI was the equivalent of the senior year of high school in the United States.) At the end of the secondary program, students could take the Secondary Schools Proficiency Examination for entry into trade school, or examinations at the General Certificate of Education (GCE) Advanced Level or Caribbean Examination Council examinations for university admission.

The multilateral schools, established in 1974, provided five years of education for students ages ten through eighteen. After a basic three-year course, students concentrated on science, technology, agriculture, home economics, or commerce for their final two years of study. The multilateral schools ended at the Form-V level. The final examinations were for the Ordinary Levels of the GCE.

A third type of secondary school was the community high school, open to students over twelve years of age. During the first half of the four-year program, students were taught basic academic skills as well as prevocational subjects. In the final two years, they concentrated on a vocational area, such as agriculture, arts and crafts, industrial arts, or home economics. The program included on-the-job training.

There were fifty-eight general secondary schools and thirty multilateral and thirty community high schools in Guyana in 1983. In 1981 there were 73,700 secondary students in Guyana, an enrollment rate of 57 percent. The teacher-pupil ratio was one to seventeen.

Institutions of Higher Education

The principal institution of higher education was the University of Guyana; there were also several specialized schools and an elaborate adult education program. Established as an independent institution in 1963, the University of Guyana occupied its campus near Georgetown in 1969. The university had faculties of natural science, social science, arts, technology, and education. In addition to these areas, the university offered bachelor's degrees in public administration, social work, pharmacy, and education. The university also provided an undergraduate degree for law students. The first master's-level graduate program in Guyanese history was started in 1973. Master's degrees have also been awarded in biology, chemistry, economics, education, and political science. There were 2,004 university students in July 1983.

A five-year multilateral school in Georgetown
Graduates at the University of Guyana's graduation exercises
Courtesy Leslie B. Johnson, Sr.

Training of primary and secondary school teachers was provided by three institutions: the Cyril Potter College of Education, the Lilian Dewar College of Education, and the University of Guyana. These institutions provided preservice training, postgraduate diploma courses, and a one-year course for trained teachers, culminating in presentation of a Certificate in Education. Primary teachers underwent a two-year program of study and secondary teachers, a three-year program. The University of Guyana had diploma programs in education that provided certification in vocational training, music, art, physical education, and evaluation. Additional training was provided by the Institute of Education, and in-service training was common.

Among Guyana's vocational institutes were the Government Technical Institute, where mechanics, machine tooling, plumbing, electronic repair, construction, and business were taught; the Industrial Training Centre, run by the Ministry of Labour; the Carnegie School of Home Economics; and the Burrowes School of Art. Agricultural sciences and management were taught at the Guyana School of Agriculture under the direction of the Ministry of Agriculture and by the Burnham Agricultural Institute.

The government created the Kuru Kuru Cooperative College in 1973 and the Cuffy Ideological Institute in 1977 to advance its ideological objective of promoting socialism. The Workers' Education Unit was also formed to provide ideological programs at work.

Adult education was provided by the Extramural Department of the University of Guyana, the Extramural Department of the Kuru Kuru Cooperative College, and the Adult Education Association.

Attitudes Toward Education

Guyana's high literacy and school attendance rates evinced a great interest in education. From the time of slavery, Afro-Guyanese saw education as a means of escape from the drudgery of plantation labor. The schoolteacher became an important figure in village life and a cornerstone of the incipient middle class. Parents made economic sacrifices so their children could attend school. Literacy improved the position of villagers in dealing with the government and commercial institutions. An education created the possibility that one could become a clerk or administrator in the public or private sectors. For the very few who acquired a secondary education, entry into medicine, law, and other professions might become possible.

Until the 1930s, Indo-Guyanese often were opposed to primary schooling for their children. The Indo-Guyanese plantation workers

Mass games, in which school children of all ages perform gymnastics in a large stadium
Courtesy Embassy of Guyana, Washington

feared both discrimination and the influence of Christian education on their children. They were also reluctant to forgo the labor their children provided. In addition, the planters discouraged the workers and their children from pursuing an education. In the 1930s and 1940s, however, a significant number of Indo-Guyanese became successful rice producers and began to regard the education of their children as an opportunity rather than a hindrance. Thereafter, the increasing enrollment of Indo-Guyanese children in elementary and secondary schools reflected the revision in parents' attitudes. New schools were built in the predominantly Indo-Guyanese sugar-estate areas.

Curriculum content was considered secondary to passing examinations and becoming eligible for a white-collar job. For this reason, parents showed little interest in a vocational curriculum that would prepare students for agricultural or mechanical jobs. Parents resisted attempts by the government to channel students into courses that it considered more relevant to Guyana's needs if those courses did not lead to a secondary education.

A high level of demand for expanded educational opportunities persisted in the postindependence period, especially at the secondary level. At the same time, parents continued to exhibit conservatism concerning curricula, not because they favored the traditional course contents, but because they continued to regard an academic curriculum as the best avenue to employment opportunities.

Health and Welfare

Food and Diet

Although the 1990 average daily nutritional intake in Guyana, 2,450 calories, exceeded the Food and Agriculture Organization of the United Nations (FAO) recommended level by about 10 percent, malnutrition remained a problem. Intake of protein calories averaged 62.7 grams, of which 23.1 came from animal sources.

The national food supply generally is adequate, but a high incidence of malnutrition persists, especially in rural areas where deficiencies in vitamin A, iron, folic acid, and protein are common.

Not everyone in Guyana has the means to produce or purchase the food needed for an adequate diet. Also, some foods are not available in sufficient supply to ensure good nutrition. Malnutrition is still estimated to affect more than a third of all children under five years of age.

Peas, rice, and bread are staples in the diet of many Guyanese. Locally grown foods that are high in carbohydrates, such as cassava, plantains, and breadfruit, are widely consumed, but are available only in season. Green and yellow vegetables are plentiful, but are usually of poor quality. Chicken bought in local markets is frequently contaminated with salmonella.

Health

Many of Guyana's health problems are the result of its human geography. Most of the population is crowded in the low-lying coastal plain, where cycles of flooding and drought have historically made sanitation difficult. The coastal plain is a hospitable environment for the malaria-carrying mosquito, and crowded housing on the plantations facilitates the spread of disease. It was not until after World War II that nationwide efforts to improve health conditions were made.

Among the endemic illnesses in Guyana are malaria, typhoid, filariasis, and tuberculosis. Measles remains a common infectious disease. The leading causes of death are circulatory, respiratory, infectious, and parasitic diseases. In the late 1940s, the government began a malaria-control campaign that largely eradicated the disease on the coastal plain. Nevertheless, in 1990 malaria remained a problem in the interior and had returned to some areas of the coast as well. Acquired immune deficiency syndrome (AIDS) also

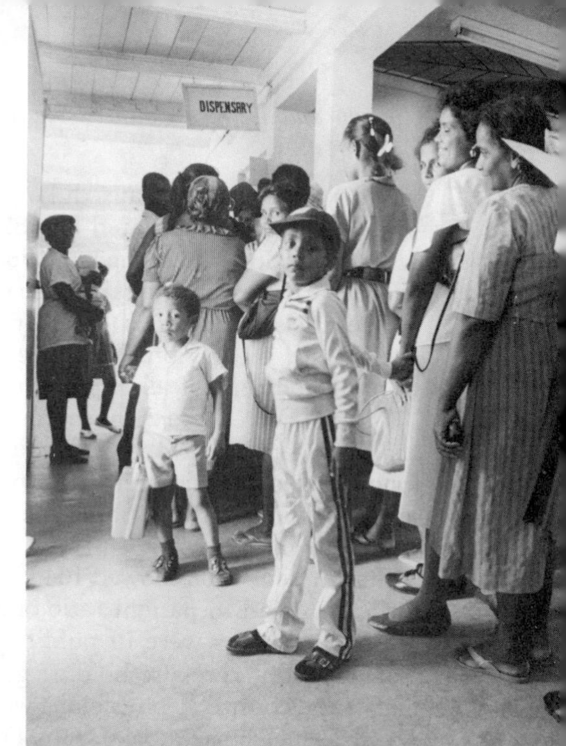

Patients in line to buy medicines subsidized by the government, West Demerara Hospital, west of Georgetown
Courtesy Inter-American Development Bank (David Mangurian)

was a growing problem. A total of 145 cases of AIDS had been reported by the end of 1990.

The infant mortality rate for Guyana in 1988 was 43.9 per 1,000 live births. This figure was considerably below the average rate for Latin America and the Caribbean (52 per 1,000), and was a great improvement over the rate of 141 per 1,000 in the 1930s. However, for low-income families, the rate was 72.6 per 1,000. Life expectancy at birth was estimated at sixty-six years in 1988, about the same as the average for Latin America.

Sewage treatment remains inadequate in many rural households, especially in the villages. More than 90 percent of the urban population, but only 65 percent of the rural population, had access to safe water in 1988. According to World Bank estimates, access to safe water in rural areas had declined 10 percent in the two previous decades because of poor maintenance of purification facilities. In 1960 the government initiated a successful environmental sanitation program in the Essequibo area, where parasitic-infection rates had run between 80 percent and 90 percent. In sugar-estate communities, potable water was supplied by the sugar industry.

Health and Welfare Services

Until World War II, medical facilities in rural areas were inadequate. The extension of workers' compensation to agricultural workers in 1947 and the subsequent establishment of the medical services on the sugar estates did much to improve rural health care. The World Bank estimated that 89 percent of the population had access to health care in the late 1980s. Some children under twelve had been immunized against measles (52 percent), and diphtheria, pertussis, and tetanus (DPT) (67 percent), figures that are about average for the region. Health expenditures by the government were 3.7 percent of all expenditures in 1984.

In 1988 there were 21 hospitals, 47 health clinics, and 115 rural health centers in Guyana. The country counted 2,933 hospital beds for a bed to population ratio of approximately one to 280. Guyana's seven private hospitals and the largest public hospitals are in Georgetown.

Statistics for 1988 showed 164 physicians in Guyana, which made for a physician-to-patient ratio of one to 5,000. About 90 percent of the physicians were in public service. Most physicians in the private sector were also holding government jobs. Approximately half of the country's physicians were expatriates from communist countries, such as Cuba and the Democratic People's Republic of Korea (North Korea), who were assigned to work in Guyana as part of bilateral agreements. These foreign professionals experienced significant language and cultural difficulties in dealing with patients.

Guyana's 789 nurses made for a nurse-to-patient ratio of one to 1,014 in 1988. There were an additional 875 nursing assistants and 409 trained midwives. Because of the shortage of nurses, many health care functions that in developed countries would be performed by nursing personnel were assigned to nursing students. Thirty-eight pharmacists were licensed to operate.

A national insurance program was established in 1969. It covers most workers and self-employed people for disability, sickness, and maternity. The program is administered by the National Insurance Board. Workers with permanent total disabilities are paid their full salary; those with temporary disabilities get at least 60 percent of their salary. Employees with illnesses may receive 60 percent of their salary for up to six months. Women may take maternity leave for up to thirteen weeks with 60 percent of their salary. Guyana also has a pensions system that provides a basis of 30 percent of earnings starting at age sixty-five. Employers and employees alike pay into all of these insurance funds, which are administered by the National Insurance Board. Social security and welfare accounted for 2.7 percent of government expenditures in 1984.

* * *

Current information on Guyanese society is difficult to obtain, especially in book form. Some of the most useful books about Guyana that have appeared since independence include Henry B. Jeffrey and Colin Baber's *Guyana: Politics, Economics and Society,* which focuses on the political system but also contains several interesting analyses and observations on Guyanese social structure and ethnicity, and on the impact of government policies on education and religion; and *A Political and Social History of Guyana, 1945–1983,* by Thomas J. Spinner, Jr., which offers a detailed discussion of the social and economic forces operating in Guyana during the turbulent 1950s and through independence, including most of the Burnham period.

Andrew Sanders's *The Powerless People: An Analysis of the Amerindian People of the Corentyne River* is about the ethnic identity and values of a small population of coastal Amerindians living along the Suriname border. Although the topic sounds somewhat narrow, the analysis offers much on how ethnicity is experienced and handled throughout Guyanese society. The book includes a clear discussion of the various approaches to the study of Guyanese ethnicity taken by social scientists since the 1950s.

Perhaps the most famous book published about Guyana since independence is Walter Rodney's posthumous *A History of the Guyanese Working People, 1881–1905,* published in 1981. Less than a decade after its publication, this book had become a classic in the literature on Caribbean societies. Rodney's careful analysis of the forces shaping Guyanese society at the end of the nineteenth century provides a basis for understanding the conflicts of modern Guyana.

The works of two anthropologists, Raymond T. Smith and Leo A. Despres, are very helpful in understanding Guyanese society between World War II and independence. Smith's *British Guiana* is regarded by many as the best book on Guyanese society in the colonial period. Other works by Smith have focused on kinship structure, especially among Afro-Guyanese. Smith's *The Negro Family in British Guiana: Family Structure and Social Status in the Villages* is a classic of Caribbean anthropology. In the late 1980s, he published a further analysis of his field data in *Kinship and Class in the West Indies: A Genealogical Study of Jamaica and Guyana. Cultural Pluralism and Nationalist Politics in Guyana,* by Leo Despres, is concerned with understanding the nature of ethnicity in Guyana. Despres sees Guyana as an example of a "plural society" composed of separate cultural communities. His analysis is based on fieldwork in Afro-Guyanese and Indo-Guyanese villages.

It is impossible to understand Guyanese society in the second half of the twentieth century without an acquaintance with the economic history of the country. Two works published in the 1970s are very helpful in this regard. Alan H. Adamson's *Sugar Without Slaves: The Political Economy of British Guiana, 1838–1904* looks at the indentured labor system in the nineteenth century. Jay R. Mandle's *The Plantation Economy: Population and Economic Change in Guyana 1838–1960* is concerned with British Guiana from the end of slavery to the closing years of the colonial period.

A number of books on specialized topics were published in the 1980s. *Education for Development or Underdevelopment?*, by M.K. Bacchus, provides an analysis of changes in the Guyanese education system since World War II. Peter Rivière's *Individual and Society in Guiana* is a review of anthropological knowledge about the Amerindian cultures of the Guianas. The book focuses on kinship and political systems at the village level. (For further information and complete citations, see Bibliography.)

Chapter 3. Guyana: The Economy

Worker harvesting rice

GUYANA'S ECONOMY WAS IN DIRE CONDITION in the early 1990s. When the country gained independence in 1966, it was one of the least developed areas in the Western Hemisphere. In the 1970s and 1980s, the economy deteriorated further after the government nationalized foreign-owned companies and took control of almost all economic activity. Output of bauxite, sugar, and rice—the country's three main products—fell sharply. Guyana's gross domestic product (GDP—see Glossary) reflected the decline in output. Real GDP fell during the late 1970s and decreased by an estimated 6 percent per year during the 1980s. The fall in GDP in terms of United States dollars was even more dramatic because of repeated devaluations of the Guyanese dollar (for value of the Guyanese dollar—see Glossary). In 1990 the GDP was only US$275 million. Per capita GDP amounted to less than US$369 per capita, making Guyana one of the poorest countries in the hemisphere (see table 6, Appendix A).

Declining GDP was but one symptom of the malaise that had overcome Guyana's economy in the 1980s. Other indications were the nation's crumbling infrastructure, especially the electrical power supply; the high level of external debt and payments arrears; and the emigration of professionals and skilled workers. Conditions were harsh for the roughly 764,000 people living in the country. In 1990 an estimated 40 percent of workers earned the minimum wage, equivalent to only US$0.50 per day. Three factors—the flourishing illegal economy, the cash remittances that Guyanese citizens received from relatives living abroad, and the country's near self-sufficiency in food production—were all that kept the economic decline from becoming a disaster.

But in the early 1990s, there were signs that twenty years of stagnation and decline could be ending. The government of Guyana was at last coming to grips with the deep economic crisis. The economy's performance had not yet recovered, but the government was dismantling statist policies and opening up the country to foreign investment.

There were two principal reasons for the dramatic policy reversal. The first reason was the death in 1985 of then-President Linden Forbes Burnham, who had been in power since the mid-1960s. Burnham refused to recognize the ill effects of "cooperative" socialism, which he had designed. The second reason for the reversal was Guyana's debt. President Hugh Desmond Hoyte, Burnham's successor, inherited a tremendous external debt burden and large debt payment arrears. By 1988 those arrears exceeded US$885 million (equal to four times the country's annual exports), and Guyana's international creditors had exhausted their patience. Hoyte faced the stark alternatives of having all credit to his country cut off or enacting a package of reforms approved by the International Monetary Fund (IMF—see Glossary). He chose the latter option, launching an ambitious Economic Recovery Program (ERP) in 1988 with the goal of dismantling Guyana's socialist economy and ending the country's self-imposed isolation. "My single ambition," Hoyte told the *Financial Times* in 1989, "is to put this economy right. I want to put it on the path to recovery."

Guyana's economy was still far from recovery in 1991, but the Hoyte government's commitment to reform was clear. The government had cut its budget deficit (in real terms), removed most price controls, legalized foreign currency trading, liberalized trade regulations, encouraged foreign investment, and had begun privatizing state-owned companies. In early 1991, the official and market exchange rates were unified for the first time since independence. Market forces were replacing state intervention; incentives to private individuals were replacing government regulations. Foreign investors appeared ready to tap Guyana's considerable natural resource potential.

Economic reform still faced formidable obstacles, however. Chief among these was the shortage of financial resources to improve the nation's infrastructure and rebuild its productive base. The IMF and other international creditors had refinanced the debt, propping up the financial side of the economy. But Guyana needed additional loans—even though its debt burden was already huge—so that the productive side of the economy could be rebuilt. A second obstacle was the social cost of the government's austerity plan. Guyanese citizens could ill afford to receive lower wages or pay higher taxes to help eliminate the budget deficit. Thus, Guyana needed international assistance for humanitarian as well as economic reasons. For the government then, the economic reform program posed two sizable challenges: to maintain the political initiative at home and to garner the continued support of the international financial community.

Growth and Structure of the Economy

History

Preindependence

Guyana was first colonized by Dutch settlers in the 1600s. Spanish explorers had ignored the area because it lacked obvious mineral wealth. Key features of Guyana's current economic structure, especially the patterns of land use, can be traced to the period of Dutch stewardship. The Dutch West India Company, which administered most of the colony from 1621 to 1792, granted early Dutch and then British settlers ownership over 100-hectare tracts of land (see The Coming of the Europeans, ch. 1). Settlers augmented these narrow coastal tracts by clearing swampland and expanding their holdings inland, for several kilometers in some cases. Many of the large sugar plantations that formed the basis of the colonial economy were established in this manner. Dutch settlers also left their mark on the land. They built a system of dikes and drainage canals on Guyana's low-lying coastal plain, using techniques developed in the Netherlands. Parts of this original sea-defense system continued to operate in the 1990s.

Sugar soon emerged as the most important plantation crop. Sugar was first grown in colonial Guyana in 1658 but was not produced on a large scale until the late 1700s, about 100 years later than in the rest of the Caribbean region. Because Guyana's plantation owners entered the sugar industry late, they were able to import relatively advanced equipment for milling sugarcane. This investment in advanced equipment gave the local sugar industry a firm foundation and made it the leading sector of the local economy. By 1800 there were an estimated 380 sugar estates along the coast. In the 1990s, almost two centuries later, the population was still concentrated on the same coastal strip of land, and sugar was still one of the nation's two most valuable products.

Guyana's distinct ethnic makeup can be traced to conditions that prevailed during the colonial period. To supply the labor required for sugar cultivation, plantation owners at first imported slaves from West Africa. (The indigenous Amerindian population of Guyana was small and lived mostly in the impenetrable interior.) Thousands of slaves were imported each year as plantations expanded; more than 100,000 slaves worked in the colony by 1830 (see Afro-Guyanese, ch. 2).

The British formally took over the colony in 1814. But British Guiana's plantation economy fell into turmoil after 1833, when Britain passed the Act for the Abolition of Slavery Throughout the British Colonies. The law provided a five-year transitional period during which plantation owners were to begin paying soon-to-be-freed slaves for their services. In practice, however, owners alienated the slaves by wringing as much work as possible from them during the last years in bondage. Upon emancipation in 1838, almost all of the former slaves abandoned the plantations. Agricultural production plummeted. Some groups of former slaves were able to buy failed plantations, but they lacked the capital to reconstruct the complex operations after years of neglect. Most former slaves reverted to subsistence farming. By 1848 only 20,000 Africans worked on sugar estates. Even so, few Africans left the country; more than 40 percent of Guyana's postindependence population was descended from African slaves.

Faced with the prospect of a complete extinction of the sugar industry, plantation owners looked abroad for laborers. Free immigrants had little enthusiasm for the harsh working conditions on sugar estates, but indentured servants were less discriminating. Indentured servants typically contracted to work for five years in exchange for a one-way passage to British Guiana as well as food and housing. (In some cases, a return voyage was offered in exchange for extra years of service.) After taking on indentured servants from Portugal, China, and the West Indies (see Glossary), plantation owners turned to what would become the most important source of immigrants: India. About 240,000 indentured East Indians were brought to British Guiana between 1838 and 1917, the date when indentured labor was abolished (see Indo-Guyanese, ch. 2). The British government supported this intraempire transfer of labor. In the short term, the influx of labor saved British Guiana's sugar industry. In the long term, the immigration deeply affected British Guiana's ethnic makeup. Most of the East Indians remained in the colony after completing their terms of indenture; many became independent rice farmers. Their descendants, along with later immigrants from India, account for about half of Guyana's postindependence population.

The racial and ethnic divisions that arose out of the two great waves of immigration into Guyana in the colonial period had a profound effect on the country. The divisions between Afro-Guyanese and Indo-Guyanese persisted into the modern period, in both economic and political terms. In the early 1990s, most Indo-Guyanese were still employed in agriculture, growing sugar and rice, while the majority of Afro-Guyanese lived in Guyana's few urban areas (see Population Distribution and Settlement Patterns, ch. 2).

The most important change in Guyana's economy after the turn of the century was the development of the bauxite (aluminum ore) industry by North American companies. Mining of bauxite began in 1914, and the ore would alternate with sugar as Guyana's most valuable product. Guyana possessed vast reserves of bauxite in the northeast, and by the 1960s, the country had become the world's fourth largest producer (after the Soviet Union, Jamaica, and Suriname). Until the 1980s, Guyana was also the leading producer of calcined bauxite, a high grade of the mineral required for specialized applications.

Postindependence

Guyana achieved political independence in 1966, but economic independence did not immediately follow. Most decisions affecting the economy continued to be made abroad because foreign companies owned most of the agricultural and mining enterprises. Two British companies, Booker McConnell and Jessel Securities, controlled the largest sugar estates and exerted a great deal of influence on the nation. In the early 1970s, the Booker McConnell company alone accounted for almost one-third of Guyana's gross national product (GNP—see Glossary). The company produced 85 percent of Guyana's sugar, employed 13 percent of the work force, and took in 35 percent of the country's foreign exchange earnings.

Two other foreign companies dominated the mining sector: the Demerara Bauxite Company (Demba), a subsidiary of the Aluminum Company of Canada (Alcan); and the Reynolds Bauxite Company, a subsidiary of the Reynolds Metals Company of the United States. Together these firms accounted for 45 percent of the nation's foreign exchange earnings. Foreign companies also controlled the major banks.

The Burnham government, which took office in 1964, saw continued foreign domination of the economy as an obstacle to progress (see Independence and the Burnham Era, ch. 1). As economist DeLisle Worrell pointed out, foreign ownership was considered the root cause of local economic difficulties. Emerging nations of the Caribbean region shared this viewpoint, which was supported by a number of arguments. Foreign-owned companies were said to use inappropriate production technologies in the Caribbean. These technologies were capital intensive, rather than labor intensive, because they had been developed for the industrialized world. Thus, local unemployment remained higher than necessary. Furthermore, local economies were geared to producing only primary products (sugar and bauxite in Guyana) rather than value-added products (processed foods and aluminum parts, for example). Guyana sold its inexpensive primary products abroad at world market prices that made local economies vulnerable to international price swings. At the same time, local economies had to import expensive products, such as machinery, because most small, less-developed countries had no manufacturing base.

According to critics of the country's economic system, foreign companies were satisfied with the existing arrangements and had no incentive to develop the local economies. In short, foreign control was stifling regional aspirations. Many people in Caribbean countries, particularly those with left-leaning political sympathies, called for government control of the economies.

The government moved vigorously to take control of the economy. In 1970 Burnham proclaimed Guyana as the world's first "cooperative republic." He said that the country would continue to welcome foreign investors but that the government would own at least 51 percent of any enterprise operating in Guyana. The Burnham government originally planned not to exceed this 51 percent ownership; it wanted majority control of the companies but wanted to maintain foreign management teams and the flow of foreign investment. In practice, however, major foreign companies balked at the idea of shared ownership, and the Burnham government took complete control of the economy, eliminating both foreign ownership and foreign management.

During the 1970s, Guyana nationalized the major companies operating in the country. Demba became a state-owned corporation in 1971. Three years later, the government took over the Reynolds Bauxite Company. The Burnham government then turned its attention to the sugar industry. Some observers believe the latter move was largely for political reasons; in their view, the Burnham government was seeking to extend its base of support among Indo-Guyanese sugar laborers (see The Cooperative Republic, ch. 1). Guyana nationalized Jessel Securities in 1975 after the company began laying off workers to cut costs. In 1976 the government nationalized the huge Booker McConnell company. By the late 1970s, the government controlled over 80 percent of the economy.

Nationalization of large foreign companies was but one aspect of pervasive government control of economic activity. By the early 1980s, the government had also taken over the bulk of the retailing and distribution systems. It controlled the marketing of all exports, even those few products, such as rice, that were still produced privately. It owned all but two financial institutions and tightly regulated currency exchange. The government controlled prices and even attempted to dictate patterns of consumption by banning a wide range of consumer imports. Local substitutes for even the most basic imports were proposed, such as rice flour for imported wheat flour.

The nationalized economy at first appeared to be performing well. During the early 1970s, world prices of both sugar and bauxite rose, allowing the newly nationalized enterprises to reap sizable profits. Increased government spending helped stimulate the economy, and GDP grew at about 4 percent per year from 1970 to 1975.

In the late 1970s and early 1980s, however, the world commodity prices that had favored Guyana declined, reversing the earlier gains. Economic output dropped as demand for sugar and bauxite fell. Nonetheless, government spending continued at a high rate, and Guyana was forced to begin borrowing abroad. This pattern of declining GDP, continued high levels of government spending, and foreign borrowing was common throughout Latin America in the 1980s.

Guyana's economic decline grew more acute during the 1980s. Unfavorable world prices were only part of the problem. There were two more basic difficulties: the lack of local managers capable of running the large agricultural and mining enterprises, and the lack of investment in those enterprises as government resources were depleted. Bauxite production, which had dropped from 3 million tons per year in the 1960s to 2 million tons in 1971, fell to 1.3 million tons by 1988 (see table 7, Appendix A). Similarly, sugar production declined from 330,000 tons in 1976 to about 245,000 tons in the mid-1980s, and had declined to 168,000 tons by 1988. Rice production never again reached its 1977 peak of 210,000 tons. By 1988, national output of rice was almost 40 percent lower than in 1977.

The decline in productivity was a serious problem, and the Burnham government's reaction to the downturn aggravated the situation. As export revenues fell, foreign exchange became scarce. Rather than attacking the root of the problem, low domestic output, the government attempted to ration foreign exchange. The government regulated all transactions requiring foreign exchange and severely restricted imports. These controls created their own inefficiencies and shortages. More significantly, tight government control encouraged the growth of a large parallel market (see Parallel Economy, this ch.). Smugglers brought in illegal imports, and currency traders circumvented government controls on foreign exchange. Although many citizens began working and trading in the parallel economy, many others were leaving the country. An estimated 72,000 Guyanese, almost one-tenth of the population, emigrated between 1976 and 1981 (see Emigration, ch. 2). Among those who left the country were many of the most skilled managers and entrepreneurs. Finally, the hostile political orientation of the Burnham government foreclosed the possibility of aid from the United States (see Relations with the United States, ch. 4).

The crisis finally came to a head in the late 1980s because of Guyana's unsustainable foreign debt. As export revenues fell, the government began borrowing abroad to finance the purchase of essential imports. External debt ballooned to US$1.7 billion by

1988, almost six times as large as Guyana's official GDP. Because the government funneled the borrowed money into consumption rather than productive investment, Guyana's economy did not grow out of debt. Instead, the government became increasingly unable to meet its debt obligations. Overdue payments, or arrears, reached a staggering US$1 billion in 1988. Rather than risk a curtailment of all foreign credit (even short-term loans for imported machinery and merchandise), the Hoyte government embarked on an IMF-backed austerity and recovery program. The Economic Recovery Program (ERP) introduced in 1988 amounted to a reversal of the statist policies that had dominated Guyana's economy for two decades (see Government Policy, this ch.).

Structure

The structure of Guyana's export-oriented economy in the 1980s was much the same as it had been since colonial times. Sugar, bauxite, and rice were the most important products. In fiscal year (FY—see Glossary) 1989, agriculture accounted for 30 percent of Guyana's official GDP, mining for 10 percent, manufacturing and construction for 15 percent, services for 22 percent, government for 18 percent, and other activities for about 5 percent (see fig. 4). The existence of a large unofficial parallel market in Guyana made it difficult to obtain reliable data on overall economic activity. But according to some estimates, as much as one-half of Guyana's actual economic activity occurred in the parallel market.

The most important agricultural concern was the sugar industry, operated by the state-owned Guyana Sugar Corporation (Guysuco). Sugar production declined significantly during the 1980s. The magnitude of the decline became apparent in 1988, when Guyana imported sugar for the first time in the twentieth century. The second most important agricultural product was rice. In contrast to sugar, rice was produced mostly on privately owned farms, and most rice was consumed domestically. Rice production fluctuated widely during the 1980s. Droughts, floods, and plant disease often interfered with crops, especially in 1988, when Guyana imported rice as well as sugar. Guyana also produced livestock for domestic consumption and exported fishery products (see Livestock, this ch.). Forest resources remained largely unexploited (see Forestry, this ch.).

Bauxite production was the most important part of the mining sector. The major bauxite mines, operated by the Guyana Mining Enterprise Limited (Guymine), were in the Linden area and on the Berbice River at Kwakwani. Bauxite production declined to 1.3 million tons in 1988 compared with the 1966 level of 3 million tons. Guyana also mined gold and diamonds, but the exact value of all of these goods was not known because smugglers commonly absconded with these valuable minerals (see Mining, this ch.).

Processing of sugar, bauxite, rice, and other primary products accounted for three-quarters of Guyana's manufacturing activity. Guyanese industry produced some consumer goods, but the country lacked heavy manufacturers (see Manufacturing, this ch.). The service component of GDP included transport, communications, financial activities, trade, and distribution. Official statistics did not include many services, which the parallel market provided.

Parallel Economy

A growing share of economic activity in Guyana took place outside of the official economy in the 1980s. The rise of the so-called parallel market was alarming for several reasons. In general terms, the parallel economy, or black market, was harmful because it indicated that the official economy was not providing enough goods and services, and that a "norm of illegality" existed in Guyana. More specifically, the illegal economy drained talent and initiative from the official economy, deprived the government of tax revenues, and led to inefficient use of resources. In addition, the parallel market was considered a major source of inflation and currency instability.

The size of Guyana's parallel economy was difficult to estimate because illegal traders and businessmen kept a low profile to avoid both foreign currency regulations and taxation. The *Financial Times* and the *Economist* both estimated in 1989 that the parallel market carried out between US$50 million and US$100 million worth of business annually. By the higher estimate, the parallel economy was about one-third the size of the official economy. Economist Clive Thomas argued in various studies that the parallel economy ranged from one-half to roughly the same size as the official economy.

The key feature of the illegal economy was foreign currency trading, an activity that arose when the government began restricting legal access to foreign exchange. When it introduced foreign exchange controls in the late 1970s, the government was trying to keep Guyana's balance of payments from worsening by controlling the flow of money and goods to and from the country (see Balance of Payments, this ch.). The government also had to restrict access to foreign currency in order to maintain an overvalued exchange rate. If Guyanese citizens had had unlimited access to foreign currency, many of them would have bought United States

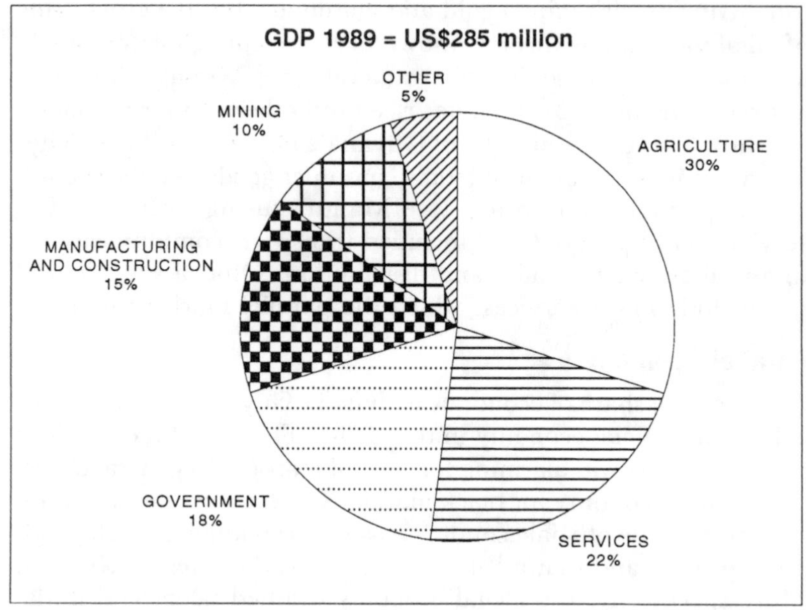

Source: Based on information from Economist Intelligence Unit, *Country Profile: Guyana, Barbados, Windward and Leeward Islands, 1989–90,* London, 1989.

Figure 4. Guyana: Gross Domestic Product (GDP) by Sector of Origin, 1989

dollars, depleting Guyana's foreign exchange reserves, because of their anticipation of devaluations of the Guyanese dollar.

The restriction on foreign exchange helped maintain the fixed exchange rate, but it also created a shortage of foreign currency, making it nearly impossible for individuals and businesses to import essential items (foreign merchants would not accept Guyanese dollars). Street traders filled the gap by supplying much-needed foreign currency; they made a profit by selling foreign currencies at a high price. Thus, the black market exchange rate per United States dollar was about G$60 in early 1989, compared with the official rate of G$33. The *Economist* reported in mid-1990 that brick-sized stacks of G$100 bills were trading for US$1,000 on Georgetown's America Street, dubbed "Wall Street."

The largest currency traders in the country, known as the Big Six, set the parallel exchange rate on a weekly or daily basis by tracking supply and demand, according to Thomas. There were several sources of the foreign currency supply: illegal exports of gold, diamonds, rice, sugar, shrimp, and furniture; cash remittances from abroad; unrecorded expenditures by tourists and visitors;

overinvoicing of imports; and sales of illegal drugs. Demand for foreign currency came primarily from three groups: local producers or retailers needing to import foreign materials or merchandise, investors and savers seeking a safe haven against devaluation of the local currency, and people exchanging local currency because they planned to leave Guyana temporarily or permanently. There was a close relationship between foreign currency trading and other illegal activities such as smuggling, tax evasion, and narcotics sales.

The government responded ambivalently to the parallel market. Official policy restricted illegal economic activity, but in practice, the government often turned a blind eye to the well-developed parallel economy. Government attempts to repress the illegal market, as in the early 1980s, were unsuccessful. Guyana's borders were long and unpatrolled, making smuggling relatively easy. In addition, cash remittances from abroad were common, meaning that many people in Guyana had frequent access to foreign currency and could easily trade on the parallel market. Many observers also noted that the government tolerated the parallel market because it provided goods that were restricted but essential. In fact, even state-owned companies traded on the parallel market.

A fundamental shift in policy toward the parallel economy occurred in the late 1980s, when the Hoyte government began stressing the need for a revitalized private sector. To many people in Guyana, as well as in the international financial community, the existing parallel market was the epitome of private-sector initiative under difficult conditions. The Hoyte government signaled a measure of agreement with this view in 1989 when it legalized and regulated the parallel foreign currency market. The government's aim was to eliminate the illegal economy by absorbing it into the legal economy.

Infrastructure

The country's underdeveloped and decaying infrastructure seriously handicapped Guyana's economy. Many of the basic facilities and services that were taken for granted even in other developing countries were either never present in Guyana or had deteriorated by the late 1980s. This absence of basic infrastructure meant that the country's economic recovery would have to begin at the most fundamental levels. No reform of Guyana's productive sectors was possible without a significant level of investment in electricity, transportation, communications, the water system, and seawalls.

The unreliable supply of electricity in Georgetown and throughout Guyana was "the single most debilitating infrastructural inadequacy," according to Minister of Finance Carl Greenidge. The United

States Embassy reported that the lack of electricity in the Georgetown area was a leading factor in emigration from Guyana. Blackouts of sixteen hours per day were common in 1989–90. Improving the electrical system was a government priority (see Energy Supply, this ch.). Other infrastructural problems also blocked economic development. The poor road system, for example, made it difficult to transport bauxite and blocked efforts to harvest timber (see Transportation, this ch.).

Government Policy

When he took office in 1985, President Desmond Hoyte said he would accelerate "the pursuit of socialist construction." One year later, however, his government began taking the first steps toward dismantling Guyana's statist economy. Faced with a deep economic crisis—declining production levels and an acute balance of payments shortfall—the government began cutting public spending and encouraging foreign investment. At first it was not clear whether this economic reversal was simply a short-term response to the crisis or a long-term change in political philosophy. But after 1986 the Hoyte government continued to move toward a free-market economy under the guidance of the IMF, despite considerable opposition in the country. By 1990 the nation appeared ready to end its disastrous twenty-year experiment with a closed, government-controlled economy.

The Economic Recovery Program

The Hoyte government signaled its commitment to reform in 1988 when it announced a far-reaching Economic Recovery Program (ERP). The plan had four interrelated objectives: to restore economic growth, to incorporate the parallel economy into the official economy, to eliminate external and internal payments imbalances, and to normalize Guyana's financial relations with its foreign creditors.

Restoring Economic Growth

To create a climate favorable for growth, the government removed many of the most onerous limitations on economic activity that had been put in place during the period following independence. First, the government liberalized foreign exchange regulations. For the first time in many years, the government allowed exporters to retain a portion of their foreign currency earnings for future use. Previously, only the government-owned Bank of Guyana had had the legal right to hold foreign currency. Second, the government lifted price controls for many items, although key goods such as petroleum, sugar, and rice remained controlled. Third, the government lifted import prohibitions for almost all items other than food and allowed individuals to import goods directly without government intervention. Fourth, private investment was encouraged by offering streamlined approval of projects and incentives such as tax holidays. To reassure potential foreign investors that Guyana's policy had indeed changed, the government announced in 1988 that "It is no part of Government's policy to nationalize property . . . . The era of nationalizations is therefore to be considered at an end."

Absorbing the Parallel Market

The second major objective of the ERP was to absorb the parallel market into the legal economy. The parallel market was seen as denying tax revenues to the government, adding to inflationary pressures through uncontrolled currency trading, and generally encouraging illegal activity in Guyana. By liberalizing foreign exchange and other regulations, the government began to make inroads into the illegal economy. The 1989 Foreign Currency Act allowed licensed dealers to exchange Guyanese dollars for foreign currency at market-determined rates. By 1990, more than twenty licensed exchange houses operated in Georgetown, taking the place of some illegal currency traders.

A related policy focused on the exchange rates. The government began devaluing the Guyanese dollar so that the official exchange rate would eventually match the market rate. This devaluation process was an essential feature of the recovery program. It not only targeted the parallel economy but also improved the country's export competitiveness. But the devaluations were painful for consumers. In April 1989, the government changed the official exchange rate per United States dollar from G$10 to G$33, instantly tripling the domestic currency price of most imports. The unofficial exchange rate at that time was reportedly G$60 per United States dollar, so the Guyanese dollar was still overvalued at the official rate. As of mid-1990, the disparity between the two rates persisted: the official rate was G$45 but the unofficial rate (at the now legal exchange houses) was G$80 per United States dollar. An important milestone was reached in early 1991 when Guyana adopted a floating exchange, removing the distinction between the official and the market exchange rates. The Guyanese dollar stabilized at US$1 = G$125 in June 1991.

Eliminating Payments Imbalances

The third major goal of the ERP was to eliminate internal and external payments imbalances. In other words, the government was seeking to eliminate the public-sector deficit on the one hand and the current account deficit on the other. The public-sector deficit—the gap between government revenues and overall government spending—had reached 52 percent of GDP by 1986. This level was unsustainable and was an alarming increase over earlier deficits: an average of 12 percent of GDP during 1975–80 and an average of 2 percent of GDP during 1971–75.

The government attacked the public-sector deficit in a straightforward manner: it cut spending and sought to enhance revenues. The government halted all monetary transfers to troubled state-owned enterprises (with the exception of the Guyana Electricity Corporation). As a longer-term measure, the government began studying the public enterprises—the heart of the statist economy—to determine which ones should be privatized (wholly or partially) and which ones should be closed. By 1990 the government had plans to allow significant privatization of the sugar and bauxite industries. In addition, the central government planned to limit expenditures by delaying salary increases and eliminating unnecessary civil service positions. Such fiscal austerity was useful to the economy. Still, the need to service the foreign debt limited the extent to which the government could cut back on spending; the government slated half of 1989 expenditures for interest payments.

The government attempted to raise revenues by absorbing the parallel economy to broaden the tax base, by improving the collection of the consumption tax, and by reducing import duty exemptions. Starting in 1988, the government required companies to pay taxes on earnings from the current year, rather than the previous year. This set of expenditure and revenue policies produced measurable results but failed to eliminate the serious financial difficulties facing the government.

Normalizing International Financial Relations

Even more pressing than the public-sector deficit was Guyana's balance of payments shortfall. The extent of the problem was indicated by the overall balance of payments, which was a record of the flow of goods, services, and capital between Guyana and the rest of the world. The deficit in the current account had increased during the early 1980s, reaching almost 50 percent of GDP in 1986. In effect, this meant that Guyana was receiving more goods and services from the rest of the world than it was providing and was having to pay for the difference. The government paid part of this deficit by using reserves such as stocks of gold. But part of the deficit went unpaid when reserves became depleted. This unpaid portion was critical. Referred to as ''external payment arrears,'' it marked Guyana as a bad credit risk, threatening to completely undermine Guyana's ability to obtain even short-term trade credits from abroad. Accumulated external payment arrears had expanded to almost three times Guyana's official GDP by 1988.

The Hoyte government attempted to decrease the balance of payments deficit by increasing exports and limiting imports; Guyana's trade was close to balanced in 1988, but a sizable trade deficit again appeared in 1990. Low productivity meant that exports did not expand significantly, and the government lacked the resources needed to eliminate the external payments arrears. Therefore, an agreement with the country's foreign creditors was crucial.

The IMF and the World Bank (see Glossary) played a vital role in devising Guyana's economic reform program. The two institutions also helped ensure that the government implemented the planned reforms.

The IMF had curtailed all further lending to Guyana beginning in 1983, because payments on previous loans were overdue. In 1988 the IMF worked with government representatives to draft a reform plan, with the understanding that economic reform within Guyana would lead to renewed international financial support for the country. IMF support was important not only for the resources the institution could provide but also because many other lenders, such as commercial banks and foreign governments, waited for IMF approval before making loans.

In 1989, after Guyana's government had shown a commitment to restructuring the economy, the IMF and the World Bank helped eliminate the external payments arrears. A so-called Donor Support Group led by Canada and the Bank for International Settlements paid US$180 million to enable Guyana to repay arrears. The IMF, the World Bank, and the Caribbean Development Bank then refinanced this amount, essentially replacing Guyana's overdue payments with a new long-term loan. The elimination of the longstanding external payments arrears cleared the way for Guyana to borrow abroad if necessary and allowed it to reschedule other external debts on more favorable terms (see Foreign Debt, this ch.).

Results of the Economic Recovery Program

The reforms introduced by President Hoyte resulted in no immediate progress. A policy framework paper prepared by the government in cooperation with the World Bank and the IMF had predicted that real GDP would grow by 5 percent in 1989. But instead, real GDP fell by 3.3 percent. Economic performance continued to decline in early 1990, according to the United States Embassy. Changes in government policy could not erase the profound difficulties facing the economy: massive foreign debt, emigration of skilled persons, and lack of infrastructure.

But in early 1991, there were signs of improvement: Guyana had rescheduled its debt, making the country eligible for international loans and assistance, and foreign investment surged in the country (see Foreign Investment, this ch.). These changes, preconditions but not guarantees of economic recovery, would not have occurred without the Economic Recovery Program.

Labor

About 240,000 people, or about 55 percent of the adult population (85 percent of adult men and 25 percent of adult women), were economically active in Guyana as of 1990. Official statistics indicated that 16 percent of the economically active persons were unemployed in 1980. In 1985 the government reported that no reliable unemployment estimate was available. Unemployment in 1990 was estimated at between 12 percent and 15 percent. In the mid-1980s, an estimated 30 percent of employed people worked in agriculture, 20 percent in mining and manufacturing, and 50 percent in construction, services, and administration. As with other economic statistics in Guyana, these figures did not include the substantial number of people working in the parallel economy.

The United States Department of State estimated in 1990 that 25 percent of Guyana's work force was unionized. Organized labor in Guyana was closely tied to the major national political parties. In 1990 the largest labor organization, the Trades Union Congress (TUC), comprised eighteen unions, most of which were affiliated with the ruling People's National Congress (PNC) party. President Hoyte was honorary president of the oldest TUC member, the Guyana Labour Union (GLU). British Guiana's best-known labor leader, Hubert Nathaniel Critchlow, started the GLU in 1917 (as the British Guiana Labour Union) when he organized dockworkers. Another important labor organization was the Guyana Agricultural and General Workers' Union (GAWU), which represented 14,000 sugar workers. The predominantly Indo-Guyanese GAWU was associated with the opposition People's Progressive Party (PPP). Intraparty divisions were reflected in labor organizations: in 1988 seven unions left the TUC in protest at PNC electioneering tactics and formed the Federation of Independent Trade Unions of Guyana (FITUG).

Farmer with harvested red chili peppers, Essequibo Islands-West Demerara District
Courtesy Inter-American Development Bank (David Mangurian)

Labor unions played an important role in the anticolonial movement in the 1960s and in the nationalization of foreign companies in the 1970s. But the close ties between the TUC unions and the governing PNC party did not guarantee that workers' interests were always advanced. In 1988 the Guyanese National Assembly adopted a constitutional amendment under which government no longer had to consult with trade unions on labor and social legislation. According to the government, this move was an essential step toward dismantling the statist economy. As part of the reform program, the government effectively cut workers' purchasing power by repeatedly devaluing the Guyanese currency. Wage increases did not keep pace with the devaluations. Prolonged strikes followed, leading to production losses in all major sectors. During wage negotiations in 1990, the unions were again dissatisfied when President Hoyte announced across-the-board pay increases that were significantly lower than what the unions had requested. Economic stabilization was taking precedence over union demands.

Workers in Guyana received overtime pay when they worked in excess of an eight-hour day or a forty-hour week. But in 1990, about 40 percent of the country's workers were in minimum-wage jobs, earning the equivalent of US$0.50 per day (at December 1990 exchange rates). These low wages, often not enough to even cover the costs of commuting to work, helped explain the high rate of emigration. The government barred children under age fourteen from working, but the United States Department of State reported in 1990 that younger children did work, often selling candy, cigarettes, and other items along roads.

Agriculture

Agriculture is the chief economic activity in Guyana. Only the coastal plain, comprising about 5 percent of the country's land area, is suitable for cultivation of crops. Much of this fertile area lies more than one meter below the high-tide level of the sea and has to be protected by a system of dikes and dams, making agricultural expansion expensive and difficult. In the 1980s, there were reports that the 200-year-old system of dikes in Guyana was in a serious state of disrepair. Guyana's remaining land area is divided into a white sand belt, which is forested, and interior highlands consisting of mountains, plateaus, and savanna (see Terrain, ch. 2).

In the 1980s, sugar and rice were the primary agricultural products, as they had been since the nineteenth century. Sugar was produced primarily for export whereas most rice was consumed domestically. Other crops included bananas, coconuts, coffee, cocoa, and citrus fruits. Small amounts of vegetables and tobacco were also produced. During the late 1980s, some farmers succeeded in diversifying into specialty products such as heart-of-palm and asparagus for export to Europe.

Sugar

The extent of Guyana's economic decline in the 1980s was clearly reflected in the performance of the sugar sector. Production levels were halved, from 324,000 tons in 1978 to 168,000 tons in 1988.

A number of factors contributed to the shrinking harvests. The first factor was nationalization. The rapid nationalization of the sugar industry in the mid-1970s led to severe management difficulties and an emigration of talent. The Guyana Sugar Corporation (Guysuco), which took over the sugar plantations, lacked needed experience. Perhaps more important, Guysuco did not have access to the reserves of foreign capital required to maintain sugar plantations and processing mills during economically difficult periods. When production fell, Guysuco became increasingly dependent on state support to pay the salaries of its 20,000 workers. Second, the industry was hard-hit by labor unrest directed at the government of Guyana. A four-week strike in early 1988 and a seven-week strike in 1989 contributed to the low harvests. Third, plant diseases and adverse weather plagued sugar crops. After disease wiped out much of the sugarcane crop in the early 1980s, farmers switched to a disease-resistant but less productive variety.

Extreme weather in the form of both droughts and floods, especially in 1988, also led to smaller harvests.

Guyana exported about 85 percent of its annual sugar output, making sugar the largest source of foreign exchange. But the prospects for sugar exports grew less favorable during the 1980s. Rising production costs after nationalization, along with falling world sugar prices since the late 1970s, placed Guyana in an increasingly uncompetitive position. A 1989 *Financial Times* report estimated production costs in Guyana at almost US$400 per ton, roughly the same as world sugar prices at that time. By early 1991, world sugar prices had declined sharply to under US$200 per ton. Prices were expected to continue decreasing as China, Thailand, and India boosted sugar supplies to record-high levels.

In the face of such keen international competition, Guyana grew increasingly dependent on its access to the subsidized markets of Europe and the United States. The bulk of sugar exports (about 160,000 tons per year in the late 1980s) went to the European Economic Community (EEC) under the Lomé Convention (see Glossary), a special quota arrangement. The benefits of the quota were unmistakable: in 1987, for example, the EEC price of sugar was about US$460 per ton, whereas the world price was only US$154 per ton. (The gap between the two prices was not so dramatic in other years, but it was significant.) Guyana was allowed to sell a much smaller amount of sugar (about 18,000 tons per year in 1989, down from 102,000 tons in 1974) in the United States market at prices comparable to those in the EEC under another quota arrangement, the Caribbean Basin Initiative (see Appendix D). Maintaining preferential access to the European market was a priority in Guyana; in 1988 and 1989, production levels were too low to satisfy the EEC quota, so Guyana imported sugar at low prices and reexported it to the lucrative European market. Even so, Guyana fell 35,000 tons short of filling the quota in 1989 and 13,000 tons short in 1990.

The government of Guyana restructured the sugar industry in the mid-1980s to restore its profitability. The area dedicated to sugar production was reduced from 50,000 hectares to under 40,000 hectares, and two of ten sugarcane-processing mills were closed. Guysuco also diversified into production of dairy products, livestock, citrus, and other items. Profitability improved, but production levels and export earnings remained well below target. In mid-1990, the government took an important step toward long-term reform of the sugar industry—and a symbolically important step toward opening the economy—when Guysuco signed a management contract with the British firms Booker and Tate & Lyle. The Booker company owned most sugar plantations in Guyana until the industry was nationalized in 1976. A study by the two companies reportedly estimated that US$20 million would be needed to rehabilitate Guyana's sugar industry.

Rice

Rice production in Guyana reached a high of over 180,000 tons in 1984 but declined to a low of 130,000 tons in 1988. The fluctuating production levels were the result of disease and inconsistent weather. Droughts and heavy rains had an adverse effect on rice crops because the irrigation and drainage systems in rice-growing areas were poorly maintained. The area under rice cultivation fell from 100,000 hectares in 1964 to 36,000 hectares in 1988, according to the Guyana Rice Producers' Association.

Most rice farms in Guyana were privately owned; the government operated the irrigation systems and rice-processing mills. This division of the industry resulted in several difficulties. According to the United States Embassy, the government neglected irrigation and drainage canals because private farmers refused to pay taxes for their maintenance. Meanwhile, the government-run mills were reportedly slow in paying farmers for their crops. In addition, the government-controlled distribution system for tractors, fuel, spare parts, and fertilizer was highly inefficient, according to some reports. In 1990 the government began privatizing the rice industry by putting several rice mills up for sale.

The bulk of Guyana's rice production was consumed domestically. Even so, exports took on increasing importance during the 1980s as a source of foreign exchange; there were even reports of rice being smuggled out of the country. Guyana shared a quota for rice exports to the EEC with neighboring Suriname but was unable to fill the quota during the late 1980s. In 1988 the government set a 1991 production goal of 240,000 tons and an export goal of 100,000 tons. In the first quarter of 1990, however, exports fell to a record low of 16,000 tons, for an annual rate of less than 70,000 tons. Half of these exports came directly from private farmers, the other half from the Guyana Rice Milling and Marketing Authority.

Forestry

Timber was the least exploited but most abundant natural resource in Guyana in the early 1990s. Forests, many of which reportedly had commercial potential, covered three-quarters of the country's land. Over 1,000 different species of trees were known to grow in the country.

Combine harvesting rice on 162-hectare farm in Mahaica-Berbice Region
Courtesy Inter-American Development Bank (David Mangurian)
Bags of rice awaiting processing, with silos for storage in background
Courtesy Leslie B. Johnson, Sr.

The two main difficulties in timber production were the limited access to the forests and electrical power problems at the major lumber mills. The government and interested groups overseas were addressing both difficulties. The government launched the Upper Demerara Forestry Project in the early 1980s to improve hardwood production on a 220,000-hectare site. In 1985 the International Development Association, part of the World Bank, provided a US$9 million loan for expansion of the forestry industry. In 1990 the government sold the state-owned logging company and announced plans to allow significant Republic of Korea (South Korean) and Malaysian investment in the timber industry. Showing concern for the long-term condition of its forests, the government also planned to set aside 360,000 hectares of rain forest for supervised development and international research into sustainable management.

Fisheries

Fishery products took on increasing importance during the 1980s as potential earners of foreign exchange. By the end of the decade, shrimp had become the third leading earner of foreign exchange after sugar and bauxite. Fisheries production in Guyana totaled about 36,000 tons in 1989, down from 45,000 tons in the mid-1980s. The most valuable portion of the catch was the 3,800 tons of shrimp. Many fishermen reportedly sold their shrimp catch at sea to avoid taxes and earn foreign currency. Thus, shrimp exports may have been much higher than recorded. Shrimp exports were expected to continue increasing as Guyana developed shrimp farms along its coast; Guysuco began operating one such farm in the late 1980s. The bulk of the fisheries catch was sold at the dockside and consumed domestically. A US$5 million fish-processing plant was under construction on the Demerara River in 1990, raising the possibility of frozen fish exports. The government sold Guyana Fisheries Limited, which employed about 5,000 people, to foreign investors in 1990.

Livestock

Livestock production was not a major activity in Guyana because of a shortage of adequate pasture land and the lack of adequate transportation. In 1987 there were an estimated 210,000 cattle, 185,000 pigs, 120,000 sheep, and 15 million chickens in the country. The country imported Cuban Holstein-Zebu cattle in the mid-1980s in an effort to make Guyana self-sufficient in milk production; by 1987 annual production had reached 32 million liters, or only half the target quantity.

Workers cleaning grouper (foreground) and mackerel at the Guyana Limited Fisheries Plant, Georgetown
Courtesy Inter-American Development Bank (David Mangurian)

Mining

Guyana's mining sector offered the best hope of rapid growth in the late 1980s. The government's decision to open the sector to foreign management and investment attracted interest from companies in a number of countries, including the United States, Canada, Brazil, Norway, and Australia. Guyana was known to have sizable reserves of bauxite, gold, and diamonds. Foreign investment was expected to dramatically increase the rate at which those reserves were mined.

Aluminum

Guyana was known to have a 350-million-ton bauxite reserve, one of the world's highest concentrations of the valuable mineral. But production of bauxite dipped sharply after the government nationalized the industry in the 1970s. In the mid-1980s, bauxite production hovered around 1.5 million tons per year, or half the annual level of the 1960s and 1970s. The state-owned Guyana Mining Enterprise Limited (Guymine) suffered repeated losses as a result of inefficient management, declining world prices for bauxite, and prolonged strikes by workers. The losses drained the company's capital reserves and led to deterioration of plants and equipment. Guyana's single alumina plant, located in Linden, used to separate 300,000 tons per year of aluminum oxide from raw bauxite ore until the facility closed in 1982. From then on, Guyana was forced to export only unprocessed bauxite ore, foregoing the added revenues to be gained from refining the mineral.

In the 1970s, Guyana had the advantage of being the world's leading supplier of so-called calcined bauxite, a high grade of the mineral used for lining steel furnaces and other high-temperature applications. After 1981, however, China emerged as a major source of calcined bauxite, and Guyana became known as a less reliable supplier. By the end of the decade, China had displaced Guyana as the leading exporter of calcined bauxite, even though Guyana had the advantage of being closer to the major North American and European markets.

Bauxite mining was concentrated in northeast Guyana. The two largest mines were located at Linden, on the Demerara River directly south of Georgetown, and at Kwakwani on the Berbice River. There was little development of new mining areas during the period of state ownership. But in the late 1980s, the government began offering foreign companies the chance to rebuild and expand the bauxite industry.

The Reynolds Bauxite Company, formerly the owner of the mine at Kwakwani, was one of the first foreign firms allowed back into Guyana. It provided managerial assistance to Guymine beginning in 1985. In the late 1980s, Reynolds began investing an estimated US$25 million to open a bauxite mine at Aroaima on the Berbice River. An elaborate system of tugboats and barges was required to bring the bauxite 126 kilometers down the Berbice River and then 120 kilometers along the coast to Georgetown for transport to the United States. According to the British Economist Intelligence Unit, Reynolds awarded a ten-year transportation contract to Goliath-Knight, an Anglo-Dutch company. The mine was expected to produce 1.5 million tons of bauxite in its first year of operation (July 1990–June 1991) and 2.6 million tons per year by 1995. Guymine was also negotiating to allow Venezuela's Venalum company to begin extracting 600,000 tons per year in the region around Kwakwani.

The government anticipated further development of the bauxite industry in the Linden area. A new mine near Linden, called the East Montgomery North Mine, was expected to open by 1994. It was to take the place of the three largely depleted pits in the area. The government sought significant foreign investment for the project; production was expected to reach 2 million tons per year in the 1990s. Norway's Norsk Hydro was discussing the possibility of reopening the alumina plant near Linden at a cost of about US$100 million. Furthermore, just as the Reynolds company was

Bauxite mining in the interior
Courtesy Leslie B. Johnson, Sr.

returning to the mines it had previously owned, Alcan was negotiating a return to bauxite production facilities in Linden.

Gold and Diamonds

The bauxite sector attracted foreign investment in the late 1980s because companies knew about Guyana's vast reserves and the country's previously formidable production capacity. Gold mining, in contrast, attracted more speculative investment from companies eager to explore the country's neglected potential. Gold production peaked in 1894 at 4,400 kilograms per year but declined to an officially declared level of 160 kilograms per year in 1983. Declared production averaged 500 kilograms per year during the late 1980s, but undeclared production was thought to be five times as high: an estimated 3,000 kilograms of gold were being extracted each year. Individual miners working in southern Guyana smuggled most of the gold they found to Brazil to avoid paying taxes and to avoid receiving Guyana's low official price, which was based on an artificially high exchange rate.

Lured by the prospect of a 1990s gold boom, at least ten foreign companies began operations or preliminary explorations within Guyana in the late 1980s. They brought with them industrial equipment, such as powerful suction dredges, that could extract up to

500 grams of gold from a riverbed in a twelve-hour shift. Three of the largest companies were Canada's Golden Star Resources and Placer Dome, and Brazil's Paranapanema. Others included Australia's Giant Resources, Homestake Mining of the United States, and Britain's Robertson Group. The Guyana Geology and Mines Commission hosted potential investors' visits to the country, and the government promised to pay the market value for gold (US$356 per ounce in May 1991) in United States dollars. The government's promise achieved measurable results in 1990: during the first half of the year, declarations increased by 75 percent over the previous year.

Even if only a few of the proposed foreign investments reached their expected output levels, the government projected that Guyana would still be producing over 6,000 kilograms of gold per year (presumably officially declared by the foreign companies) by the mid-1990s. Paranapanema, drawing on experience in Brazil's tropical terrain, expected to produce 1,500 kilograms per year at its Tassawini joint venture on the northwest Barama River. In the Mahdia region on the Essequibo River, Placer Dome and Golden Star Resources reported that an operation capable of producing 2,000 kilograms per year was probably possible; the companies planned a feasibility study before actually starting operations.

Information on diamond production in Guyana was sketchy because the bulk of the stones were reportedly smuggled out of the country. Declared production fluctuated between 4,000 and 12,000 carats per year in the 1980s. Undeclared production was probably much higher. In 1966 the industry produced about 92,000 carats, 60 percent of which were reported as gem quality.

Industry

Energy Supply

The lack of a reliable supply of electricity in Guyana, especially in Georgetown, was the most severe constraint on economic activity and a major factor in emigration. By 1990 blackouts of sixteen hours per day were common in the capital city, affecting even the presidential mansion. Blackouts occurred without warning and sometimes lasted for several days. Most businesses in Georgetown employed standby generators, raising the demand for imported fuel.

The electricity supply was unreliable because the facilities of the state-owned Guyana Electricity Corporation (GEC) had deteriorated during the 1980s. In 1991 the GEC had a capacity of 253 megawatts of electricity and generated 647 gigawatt-hours of electricity, satisfying about half the estimated demand. The reasons for the shortfall were not only the lack of funds to replace aging generators and to build new power plants, but also periodic fuel shortages because most electrical power was produced thermally. There were other less tangible problems: GEC's finances were inadequate because the cost of electricity was below the cost of production (especially when taking depreciation into account); and the attitude of managers and workers was reportedly very poor. The bauxite and sugar sectors had their own electricity supply system apart from GEC, but they also suffered power shortages.

Two types of efforts were under way in the early 1990s to rectify the electricity shortage. In the short term, GEC was limping along with the help of a small floating generator made in the United States and two ten-megawatt gas-turbine generators borrowed from Brazil. There was also a possibility that electricity would be bought from neighboring Venezuela.

In the longer term, the government was trying to obtain foreign investment and assistance to rebuild the electrical system. GEC planned to hire a consulting firm to help it develop a least-cost expansion program and to improve the pricing of electrical service. International financial organizations were also expected to contribute funds. As early as 1985, the Inter-American Development Bank (IDB) had approved a US$16 million loan for rehabilitation of GEC, and an agreement was reached with an Italian company to build a US$45 million (thirty-megawatt) power station. Both projects were delayed, as were plans to build a hydroelectric plant on the Mazaruni River. The Economist Intelligence Unit reported that GEC rehabilitation still had not started in mid-1990. In 1990 negotiations were under way with the United States firm, Leucadia, to form a joint-venture company for the operation of the electrical system.

Manufacturing

Most manufacturing in Guyana involved the processing of agricultural products (sugar, rice, coconuts, and timber) and minerals (bauxite, gold, and diamonds). The production of alumina from bauxite was suspended in 1982. Guyana produced small quantities of textiles, ceramics, and pharmaceuticals in state-owned factories. Among those industries, the pharmaceutical industry showed the most potential for growth, having attracted investments from Beecham, a British firm, and from Tecno Bago, an Argentine firm. Manufacturers in Guyana also produced wooden furniture, cigarettes, and paints, and other products.

The government was attempting to sell off many of the smaller manufacturing companies as part of the Economic Recovery Program. One of the first state-owned manufacturers to be partially privatized was Demerara Distillers Limited, which produced rum and other alcoholic beverages. The company was relatively successful under state ownership, having become the world's largest producer of rum after Bacardi and the leading supplier of bulk rum (sold under various brand names) to Britain, according to the *Financial Times*. The government owned the majority of the company until 1988, when Demerara Distillers issued 12 million new shares and diluted government ownership to about 47 percent. The government did not appear ready to completely relinquish its hold on the rum producer, however, because it blocked the company's 1990 effort to issue more shares.

Expansion of the manufacturing sector, like expansion in other sectors, depended on increased foreign investment. Many observers noted that with such investment, Guyana could become a supplier of manufactured products to other countries in the Caribbean region. The Commonwealth Advisory Group, affiliated with the Donor Support Group that arranged the refinancing of the debt arrears in 1989, had reported in 1989 that Guyana had the potential for "vibrant and profitable" manufacturing of garments, shoes, leather goods, sawn timber, furniture and other wood products, processed agricultural products, paints, pharmaceuticals, and refrigerators. Preconditions for that sort of development, according to the group, included an easing of the foreign exchange constraint (achieved by 1990); improved infrastructure (telecommunications and transport); a simpler, less burdensome tax system; injections of foreign capital and technical skills; attractive wages for skilled workers; and stable government policy in support of private manufacturing.

Services

Banking

Apart from the Bank of Guyana (the central bank), five commercial banks and two foreign banks operated in Guyana. Three other foreign banks—the Royal Bank of Canada, Chase Manhattan of the United States, and Barclays Bank of Britain—were nationalized in the 1980s. The two remaining foreign-owned banks were Canada's Bank of Nova Scotia and India's Bank of Baroda. The primary activity for commercial banks was lending to the government; private investment opportunities were rare. According to the Economist Intelligence Unit, the public sector accounted for 97 percent of the financial system's claims at the end of 1986.

In 1987 the banks experienced a shock when the government emphasized bond issues rather than borrowing from commercial

Employee sawing hardwood plank for furniture, Ruimveldt, near Georgetown
Courtesy Inter-American Development Bank (David Mangurian)

banks as a way of financing its deficits. This shift in government policy placed the banks in a difficult position because they could make few loans and thus few profits; there were then almost no private entities seeking financing. But commercial banks benefited from the government's legalization of foreign exchange trading in 1989. Until then, the Bank of Guyana had been the only legal source of foreign currency, forcing local banks to hold Guyanese dollars even when a devaluation was expected. Five banks opened *cambios,* or exchange houses, in 1990.

Transportation

Next to the poor supply of electricity, the most serious infrastructure problem was the poor transportation system (see fig. 5). Travel and transport were difficult within Guyana, and there was only one surface link to a neighboring country, a newly paved road to Brazil. The domestic transportation system was minimal: only 500 kilometers of paved roads (mostly along the coast), 5,000 kilometers of gravel roads, 1,500 of earthen roads, and about 28,000 vehicles. Buses were aging and needed to be replaced. Commuting costs for workers were often high enough to dissuade them from leaving home each day. Only the lower portions of the major rivers—Demerara, Essequibo, and Berbice—were navigable, making transport of bauxite and sugar a challenge. Air service within the country was sporadic. The country's two ports, at Georgetown and at New Amsterdam, were also in need of improvement. An *Economist* report about travel to the Marudi Mountain gold mine in the most southern part of Guyana aptly depicted the extremes of inland travel: the trip required a ride on a small plane from Timehri Airport (near Georgetown) to Lethem, followed by a six-hour jeep ride (rain permitting) to Aishalton, and then an eleven-hour walk to the mine.

Guyana's transportation system showed signs of improvement in the early 1990s, when foreign investment and foreign aid began returning to the country. Brazil financed construction of a 300-kilometer road from Kurupukari, in central Guyana, to Lethem, on the western border with Brazil, giving access to much of the interior. The government entered into a joint venture with British Airways to establish a company called Guyana Airports Limited that would operate and develop Timehri Airport and other airports. Air transportation also took a step forward in 1990 when Varig, Brazil's national airline, started weekly air service from Timehri to Boa Vista and Manaus in northern Brazil. Most air travel outside of the country went through Port-of-Spain, Trinidad, or through Caracas, Venezuela.

Communications

Guyana's communications system was on par with its underdeveloped transportation system. There were 27,000 telephones in use in 1983, or 3.3 per 100 people. Two Japanese companies installed a telephone system in 1987, but the telephone network still required an estimated US$150 million in repairs and improvements as of 1988. International direct dialing was available, but calling Guyana from the United States required repeated efforts.

Tele Network, a company from the United States Virgin Islands, agreed to take a majority interest in a telecommunications joint venture starting in late 1990, according to the United States Embassy. The state-owned Guyana Telecommunications Corporation also reached an agreement with a Canadian company, Northern Telecommunications, to rehabilitate the telephone infrastructure, according to *Guyana Business.*

Georgetown had two privately owned television stations that relayed United States programming picked up from satellites and one government-operated station in 1991. The government also operated two amplitude modulation (AM) radio stations in the capital and two frequency modulation (FM) stations, one in Georgetown and one in Lethem.

External Economic Relations

Foreign Trade

Guyana's economy was heavily dependent on foreign trade. Exports and imports both amounted to a large share of GDP. The two largest exports, sugar and bauxite, set the pace for the entire economy. When production of these exports declined in the 1980s, Guyana began to experience severe difficulties. A central element of the IMF-sponsored recovery program introduced in 1988 was to revitalize Guyana's traditional export base.

Exports

Guyana's five leading exports in 1989 were sugar, bauxite, shrimp, rice, and gold. These products together accounted for 90 percent of exports, which amounted to a total of US$204 million in 1990. Other exports included timber, textiles, rum, fruit, and vegetables. Because of the country's limited industrial development, Guyana exported only a few manufactured products, such as refrigerators, freezers, and furniture to other nations in the Caribbean region.

Britain, the United States, and Canada were the destinations for about two-thirds of Guyana's officially recorded exports. Exports

Figure 5. Guyana: Transportation System, 1991

to the United States included bauxite, shrimp, gold, sugar (under a special quota), and clothing. In 1989 Guyana became a beneficiary of the Caribbean Basin Initiative, which eliminated United States customs duties on selected products. Major exports to Britain were bauxite and sugar; the latter was covered by a special quota arrangement with the European Economic Community (see Agriculture, this ch.). Exports to Canada were mainly bauxite and gold. Other markets for Guyana's exports were Germany and Japan.

Imports

Guyana's largest import categories in 1989 were capital goods (mostly machinery) and fuel, followed by other intermediate and consumer goods. The United States supplied about 30 percent of Guyana's merchandise imports, including most machinery and industrial inputs. A surge in imports of capital goods in the late 1980s may have reflected the rebuilding of the bauxite and sugar industries. In 1990 imports amounted to US$250 million.

For most of the 1980s, the largest import category by far was fuel and lubricants; Guyana made special arrangements with its oil-rich neighbors to obtain fuel. Trinidad and Tobago supplied most of Guyana's oil until the mid-1980s, when Guyana fell far behind on its payments. In 1985 the two nations entered into a barter arrangement under which Guyana received oil in exchange for rice. But that agreement broke down within the year, and trade between Trinidad and Tobago and Guyana dropped off. Guyana also had a barter arrangement with Venezuela starting in 1986. Guyana shipped almost one-third of its bauxite (540,000 tons) to Venezuela in 1987 in exchange for fuel. This barter arrangement was essential for Guyana, which had almost no access to credit after the country slipped into arrears on debt to major creditors. But bartering had its drawbacks. In 1989, for example, Guyana suffered recurring fuel shortages when it failed to deliver bauxite shipments to Venezuela.

Foreign Debt

In the early 1990s, Guyana was one of the world's most heavily indebted countries. Its external debt burden was almost US$2 billion in 1990, or about seven times official GDP. The debt burden accumulated in Guyana—as in many other developing countries—beginning in the 1970s. At first, loans were earmarked for development projects. But when rising oil prices adversely affected the balance of payments, Guyana began borrowing to finance imports. Guyana's foreign debt was unlike that of many other Latin American nations because most of it was owed to official creditors (loans from international financial organizations and foreign governments) rather than commercial institutions (loans from foreign banks). Roughly one-third of the debt was owed to the IMF and the World Bank, and one-fourth to neighboring Trinidad and Tobago. Other major creditors were the Caribbean Development Bank and Barbados.

In 1981 Burnham underlined the severity of the debt crisis when he authorized the government to stop making debt-service payments. Arrears on debt repayment and trade credits were simply allowed to accumulate. (Mexico's 1982 announcement of a similar moratorium on its much larger commercial debt sent shock waves through the international financial community.) Guyana's debt moratorium had two serious results. First, unpaid debts and interest payments compounded, leading to rapid growth in total debt. Thus, external debt increased from US$1.2 billion in 1984 to US$1.7 billion in 1987 even though Guyana received few new loans. Second, the buildup of arrears destroyed Guyana's credibility as a debtor. In 1983 the IMF refused to provide further loans; many other international organizations and governments followed suit. The loss of credibility also directly affected Guyana's trade relations: Trinidad and Tobago cut off oil shipments in 1986.

The debt crisis persisted during the 1980s as Guyana remained unable to resume debt service. The country consistently had a deficit in the overall balance of payments, and the government financed the deficit by accumulating even more arrears on debt service payments. By 1989 those arrears exceeded US$1 billion, or five times the value of annual exports. By the late 1980s, the debt crisis threatened to shut down the economy; even short-term trade credits were difficult to obtain. Venezuela began insisting on prepayment in bauxite in exchange for shipments of oil. It was mainly the debt crisis that led the government to agree to an IMF-backed austerity program in 1988.

Temporary debt relief arrived after Guyana agreed to enact the Economic Recovery Program. A Donor Support Group consisting of Guyana's major creditors (Canada, the United States, Britain, Germany, France, Venezuela, and Trinidad and Tobago) provided a bridge loan of US$180 million that enabled the government to pay off arrears to the IMF, the World Bank, and the Caribbean Development Bank. In addition, bilateral creditors agreed to reschedule major portions of Guyana's debt, such as US$460 million owed to Trinidad and Tobago. The complicated refinancing scheme, which was conditioned on rigorous economic reforms within Guyana, removed the massive arrears and allowed Guyana renewed access to international financial support. The IMF and the World Bank extended new loans to Guyana in 1990 for infrastructure projects.

The restoration of Guyana's creditworthiness, however, did not signal an end to its debt problem. Interest payments on the debt were the largest expenditure in the 1990 budget. A priority for the government was to increase foreign currency earnings by expanding

Building a new road through the dense vegetation of the interior
Courtesy Leslie B. Johnson, Sr.

exports, but a large share of export revenues would have to be used to continue debt service. Thus, debt service absorbed scarce resources urgently needed for economic development. There was a possibility that Guyana would receive some measure of debt forgiveness from the United States under the Enterprise for the Americas Initiative (see Glossary), according to 1991 congressional testimony by Undersecretary of the Treasury, David Mulford. But there were few precedents for official debt forgiveness on the scale that Guyana's economy seemed to require.

Balance of Payments

Guyana experienced serious balance of payments difficulties during the late 1980s. The value of imports was roughly in balance with the value of exports in 1988 and 1989 but interest payments on the foreign debt drained the nation's financial resources. The balance of payments situation would have been much worse if Guyana had not withheld payment on much of its debt. Even though it did not include the mounting arrears on debt payments, the deficit in the overall balance of payments averaged US$150 million between 1985 and 1990, or about 50 percent of GDP.

Foreign Investment

Foreign investment was a key element in the Hoyte government's plan to revitalize Guyana's economy. After two decades during which virtually all foreign companies were nationalized, the government was taking great pains in the early 1990s to convince foreign companies that investments in Guyana would be safe and lucrative. According to a government statement, investments were safe because, "The objective circumstances which led to nationalizations during the 1970s no longer exist and the present government has no plans whatsoever to nationalize investment or property." The government allowed investors to enter any sector of the economy, repatriate their profits, and own 100 percent of companies operating in Guyana. To make investment attractive to foreigners, the government introduced a number of incentives (negotiated on a case-by-case basis), including tax holidays of up to ten years, exemption from consumption and capital gains taxes, duty-free import privileges, and support for investment and tax treaties with foreign countries (to avoid double taxation, for example). The government established the Guyana Manufacturing and Industrial Development Agency (Guymida) to streamline the foreign investment process.

The government encouraged foreign investment in a broad range of activities, including agricultural production, agro-industries, fishing and shrimping (including aquaculture), forestry and sawmilling, mining, petroleum, manufacturing, fabrication and assembly industries, tourism and hotel development, construction, electrical power generation (including hydropower), telecommunications, air transport and airport services, shipping and port facilities, and banking and financial services. By 1991 foreign investors were active in a number of these areas. Several companies from the United States, Canada, and other countries were active in bauxite and gold mining as well as infrastructure projects. British companies had invested in the sugar sector, pharmaceutical products, and airport services, among other areas. Brazilian companies were involved in pharmaceuticals, agriculture, and mining.

Some of the most promising investments were in nontraditional areas. A French company, Amazon Caribbean Guyana Limited, was exporting heart-of-palm to Europe. The company employed 100 people. Six European companies were considering investments in engineering or garment manufacturing. A Trinidadian firm, Colonial Life Insurance Company, purchased the assets of the state-owned logging company, Guyana Timbers. The Japanese Nisshan

Ground satellite station at Georgetown
Courtesy Embassy of Guyana, Washington

Suissan company bought another state-owned company, Guyana Fisheries Limited. A United States company, Sahlman Seafoods, operated a shrimp-fishing company.

One activity receiving considerable foreign attention was petroleum exploration. Because fuel was Guyana's costliest import during most of the 1980s, there was great interest in finding domestic sources of oil. An exploration study was completed in 1986, and the results were promising enough to attract a Trinidadian company and a British oil company. Nine petroleum companies were reportedly searching for oil in Guyana's coastal waters by 1990. These companies included Hunt Oil of the United States, the London and Scottish Marine Oil Company of Britain, Broken Hill Proprietary of Australia, and Total from France. The latter company had entered into a joint venture agreement with two small United States companies and was expected to begin drilling test wells in late 1990.

Though foreign investment had begun to flow into Guyana by 1991, many potential investors remained hesitant. One concern was that a change in government could reverse the favorable policies that the Hoyte government had introduced. The Hoyte government maintained that it was planning to change the constitution to remove sections that discouraged potential investors. Other concerns for investors were the lack of infrastructure, the shortage of skilled labor (even though wages were low), and the politicized and strike-prone unions.

Of particular interest to investors from the United States was the possibility that Guyana would become eligible for Internal Revenue Service (IRS) Code, Section 936 funds from United States businesses in Puerto Rico. Under IRS Code, Section 936, United States businesses with branches in Puerto Rico were effectively exempt from income tax on income derived from their Puerto Rican subsidiaries as long as those funds remained in Puerto Rico. In 1986 this tax exemption was expanded to include funds made in Puerto Rico but invested in certain countries of the Caribbean Basin Initiative. The Overseas Private Investment Corporation (OPIC), a United States government organization that provided political risk insurance and loans to United States companies, organized a fact-finding trip to Guyana in 1990.

Foreign Aid

Guyana received little foreign assistance during the early 1980s because aid donors disapproved of the Burnham government's political orientation. According to the government, total aid flows into Guyana were US$71 million in 1981, US$40 million in 1982, US$32 million in 1983, US$23 million in 1985, and US$31 million in 1986.

In the late 1980s, aid donors provided assistance primarily in the form of debt refinancing. Help in clearing Guyana's arrears on its debt was a form of aid because it made the country eligible for various international loans and assistance programs. Guyana was slated to receive assistance from the United States Agency for International Development (AID) in 1991. Beginning in 1988, the year that the Hoyte government announced its Economic Recovery Program, the United States provided about US$7 million (under the Public Law 480 program) in concessional loans for wheat purchases. Guyana also received aid from the EEC, in the form of preferential access to EEC markets and grants for infrastructure development. Canada also provided aid.

Regional Integration

Guyana's strongest regional ties were to the other former British colonies in the Caribbean, rather than to Spanish- or Portuguese-speaking South America. In the hope of becoming the food source and manufacturer for the Caribbean nations, in 1965 Guyana joined Antigua and Barbados in forming the Caribbean Free Trade Association, known as Carifta (see Appendix C). Membership in

Carifta was expanded to thirteen countries in 1968, and in 1973 Carifta was renamed the Caribbean Community and Common Market (Caricom). Caricom appeared to have great potential in the 1970s. The Caricom members, along with Canada, Britain, Mexico, Colombia, and Venezuela, created the Caribbean Development Bank (CDB) as a regional lending body. Another such institution was the Caribbean Investment Corporation.

Caricom's attempts at regional integration have been fraught with economic and political problems. Guyana became the largest debtor to the CDB and hindered the organization's efforts elsewhere in the region when the country had difficulty servicing its debt. When the IMF stopped providing new loans to Guyana in 1983, the CDB did the same, and Guyana was abruptly cut off from major regional assistance. Friction also developed between Guyana and Trinidad and Tobago when Guyana fell behind on its oil payments. In addition, Caricom members were politically divided over the United States invasion of Grenada in 1983.

In the early 1990s, Caricom members were seeking to reinvigorate the organization by creating a customs union. By putting in place a common external tariff, members would take the first step toward removing trade barriers amongst themselves. The proposed tariff structure was to place low rates of duty (as little as 5 percent) on imports that did not compete with goods produced within Caricom, but high rates of duty on competing goods (up to 45 percent). The idea was to protect industries within Caricom countries, which had a combined population of 5.5 million people. In 1991 several members were hesitant about the proposal because it would force Caricom consumers to choose between higher priced imports (since tariffs would be added on to the final price) or a smaller selection of locally produced products. With or without the common tariff, Guyana was far from becoming a major regional supplier of manufactured goods in the early 1990s. Regional integration was less important than the prospect of renewed economic progress at home.

* * *

The best sources of up-to-date information on Guyana's small economy are British publications: the *Financial Times, South,* the *Economist,* and surveys by the Economist Intelligence Unit. The United States Embassy in Georgetown provides annual summaries of economic activity in the *Foreign Economic Trends Report* and the *Investment Climate Statement.* Useful, but difficult to obtain in the United States, are newspapers and periodicals published in Guyana, the *Guyana Chronicle, Guyana Business,* and the *Stabroek News.* Two excellent background readings on Guyana's economy are DeLisle Worrell's "The Impoverishment of Guyana," and Clive Y. Thomas's "Foreign Currency Black Markets: Lessons from Guyana." A historical perspective on labor issues is provided in William L. Cumiford's "Guyana," part of an excellent book on labor in Latin America. (For further information and complete citations, see Bibliography.)

Chapter 4. Guyana: Government and Politics

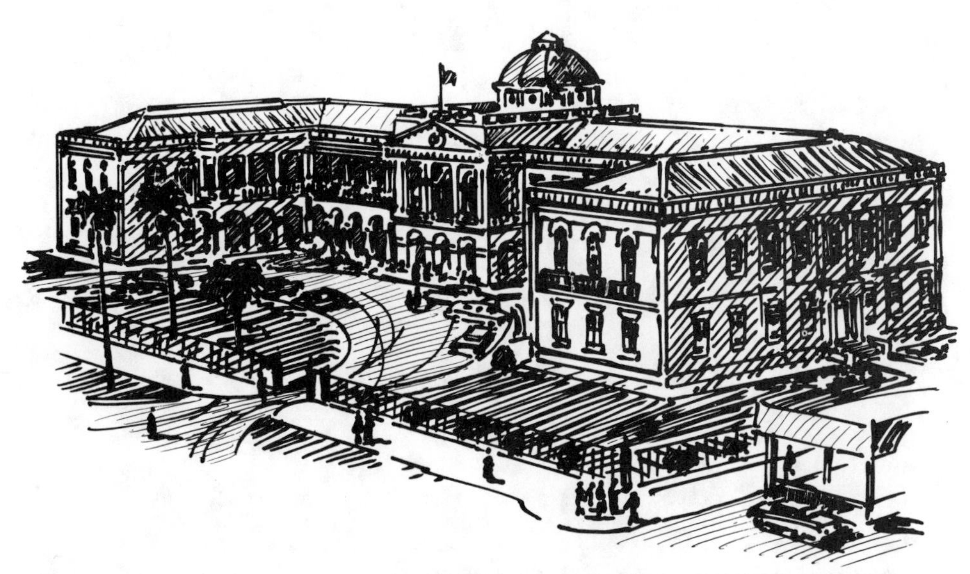

National Assembly building in Georgetown

GUYANA IS OSTENSIBLY a parliamentary-style democracy with a constitution, a National Assembly, a multiparty system, elections, a president chosen by the majority party, a minority leader, and a judicial system based on common law. Despite its democratic institutions, independent Guyana has seen more than two decades of one-party rule and strongman politics, perpetuated by manipulation, racially based voting patterns, and the disenfranchisement of the Guyanese people.

Since 1964 when People's National Congress (PNC) leader Linden Forbes Burnham came to power, Burnham, his successor Hugh Desmond Hoyte, and the PNC have dominated the politics of Guyana. Although Burnham paid lip service to an ambitious political and economic experiment, cooperative socialism, which was to develop Guyana to the benefit of all Guyanese, his paramount concern seemed to be the preservation and enhancement of his own political power. Burnham's true agenda became apparent in 1974, when he announced the subordination of all other institutions in Guyana to the PNC. The late 1970s and early 1980s increasingly saw the government system function primarily to benefit Burnham and his party.

After Burnham's death in 1985, the administration of Desmond Hoyte abandoned many of the authoritarian policies of Hoyte's predecessor. The new president chose to work largely within the framework of the government, tolerated an opposition press, and attempted to downplay the significance of rigid racial political blocs. Whether these moves represented a strengthening of democracy in Guyana or merely a tactical move motivated by economic hardship remained to be determined.

Constitutional Background

Preindependence Constitutions

Guyana's complex constitutional history provides a useful means of understanding the conflict between local interests and those of Britain, the long-time colonial power. The colony's first constitution, the Concept Plan of Redress, was promulgated under Dutch rule in 1792 and remained in effect with modifications under British administration until 1928. Although revised considerably over the years, the Concept Plan of Redress provided for a governor appointed by the colonial power and for a Court of Policy that evolved into the colony's legislature. Reforms throughout the nineteenth century gradually broadened the electoral franchise and lessened the power of the planters in the colonial government (see Transition to British Rule, ch. 1).

As a result of financial difficulties in the 1920s and conflict between the established sugar planters and new rice and bauxite producers, the British government promulgated a new constitution making British Guiana a crown colony (see Glossary). The Court of Policy was replaced by a Legislative Council with thirty members (sixteen appointed and fourteen elected), and executive power was placed in the hands of a governor appointed by officials in London. Modifications throughout the 1930s and 1940s made the majority of members of the Legislative Council subject to popular election and further broadened the franchise (see Political and Social Changes in the 1900s, ch. 1).

The formation of British Guiana's first major political party in 1950 and growing pressure for independence again forced the British to overhaul the political framework. A royal commission proposed a new constitution that would provide for a bicameral legislature consisting of a lower House of Assembly and an upper State Council, a governor appointed by the British, and seven ministers appointed by the House of Assembly. This constitution was put into effect in early 1953. The electoral success of self-proclaimed Marxist-Leninist Cheddi Jagan and his leftist People's Progressive Party (PPP) in the April 1953 elections frightened the colonial authorities. After the new legislature passed a controversial labor bill and pressed for independence, the British suspended the constitution in October 1953 and put in place an interim government whose members were chosen entirely by British authorities (see The PPP's First Government, 1953, ch. 1).

New elections were held in 1957 to choose a majority of members in the new Legislative Council; the rest of the members were chosen by the governor. During its four-year tenure, this government set up a committee to make recommendations on yet another constitution. The committee proposed that a new government be formed with full internal autonomy (see The Second PPP Government, 1957–61, and Racial Politics, ch. 1). Only defense and external affairs would be managed by the British.

In 1961 the new constitution went into effect. The legislature was bicameral: the lower house, a thirty-five-member Legislative Assembly, consisted entirely of elected officials; and the upper house, the thirteen-member Senate, consisted entirely of appointees. The prime minister, who was chosen by the party with a majority of votes in the Legislative Assembly, held the most powerful executive post. Assisting the prime minister were various other ministers. The governor remained the titular head of state. The PPP won the elections of August 1961, and Jagan was named prime minister.

Labor strife and civil disturbances were widespread in 1962 and 1963. In an effort to quell the unrest, the British colonial secretary declared a state of emergency and proposed modifying the constitution to provide for a unicameral fifty-three-member National Assembly and proportional representation. The proposal was adopted, and elections were set for 1964. These elections brought to power a new coalition government headed by the PNC. However, the PPP administration refused to step down. Not until a constitutional amendment was enacted empowering the governor to dismiss the National Assembly was the old government removed from power (see PPP Reelection and Debacle, ch. 1).

Independence Constitution

Independent Guyana's first constitution (a modified version of the 1961 constitution) took effect on the first day of independence, May 26, 1966. It reaffirmed the principle that Guyana was a democratic state founded on the rule of law. The titular head of the country was the British monarch, represented in Guyana by the governor general, who served in a largely ceremonial capacity. Real executive power rested in the prime minister, appointed by the majority party in the unicameral fifty-three-member National Assembly, and his ministers. The first postindependence elections, conducted in 1968, confirmed the dominant role of the PNC and its leader, Forbes Burnham (see Burnham in Power, ch. 1).

On February 23, 1970, the Burnham government proclaimed the Cooperative Republic of Guyana. This move had both economic and political ramifications. The government argued that the country's many resources had been controlled by foreign capitalists and that organizing the population into cooperatives would provide the best path to development.

The 1970 proclamation severed Guyana's last significant constitutional tie to Britain. The governor general, heretofore the ceremonial head of state, was replaced by a president, also a ceremonial figure. Arthur Chung, a Chinese-Guyanese, was the country's first president (see The Cooperative Republic, ch. 1).

Although its ties to the British monarch were broken, Guyana remained within the Commonwealth of Nations (see Appendix B). Membership in the Commonwealth allowed Guyana to reap the benefits of access to markets in Britain and to retain some of the defense arrangements that Britain offered its former colonies. In particular, the British defense umbrella was seen as a deterrent to Venezuelan claims on Guyanese territory (see Relations with Venezuela, this ch.; Guyana-Venezuela Dispute, ch. 5).

Constitution of 1980

As Burnham consolidated his control over Guyanese politics throughout the 1970s, he began to push for changes in the constitution that would muffle opposition. He and his colleagues argued that the changes were necessary to govern in the best interest of the people, free of opposition interference. By the late 1970s, the government and the legislature were PNC-dominated, and the party had declared its hegemony over the civil service, the military, the judiciary, the economic sector, and all other segments of Guyanese society. Burnham called the 1966 constitution inadequate and the product of British conservatism. Nationalization of private enterprise was to be the first step in revamping a system that Burnham felt had been designed to protect private property at the expense of the masses.

Two of the principal architects of the new constitution were the minister of justice and attorney general, Mohammed Shahabbuddeen, and Hugh Desmond Hoyte, the minister of economic planning. Attorney General Shahabbuddeen was given the task of selling the new constitution to the National Assembly and the people. He decried the 1966 constitution as a capitalist document that supported a national economy based on exports and the laws of supply and demand. He argued that the constitution safeguarded the acquisitions of the rich and privileged and did not significantly advance the role of the people in the political process.

The constitution of 1980, promulgated in October of that year, reaffirmed Guyana's status as a cooperative republic within the Commonwealth. It defines a cooperative republic as having the following attributes: political and economic independence, state ownership of the means of production, a citizenry organized into groups such as cooperatives and trade unions, and an economy run on the basis of national economic planning. The constitution states that the country is a democratic and secular state in transition from capitalism to socialism and that the constitution is the highest law in the country, with precedence over all other laws. The constitution guarantees freedom of religion, speech, association, and movement, and prohibits discrimination. It also grants every Guyanese citizen the right to work, to obtain a free education and free medical care, and to own personal property; it also guarantees equal pay for women. However, freedom of expression and other political rights are limited by national interests and the state's duty to ensure fairness in the dissemination of information to the public. Power is distributed among five "Supreme Organs of Democratic Power": the executive president, the cabinet, the National Assembly, the National Congress of Local Democratic Organs, and the Supreme Congress of the People, a special deliberative body consisting of the National Assembly in joint session with the National Congress of Local Democratic Organs. Of these five divisions of government, the executive president in practice has almost unlimited powers (see fig. 6).

The important constitutional changes brought about by the 1980 document were mostly political: the concentration of power in the position of executive president and the creation of local party organizations to ensure Burnham's control over the PNC and, in turn, the party's control over the people. The constitution's economic goals were more posture than substance. The call for nationalization of major industries with just compensation was a moot point, given that 80 percent of the economy was already in the government's hands by 1976. The remaining 20 percent was owned by Guyanese entrepreneurs.

Government Institutions

Executive

The office of executive president is by far the most powerful position in Guyana. The executive president is head of state and commander in chief of the armed forces. He or she has the power to veto any bill passed in the National Assembly and can dissolve the assembly if a veto is overridden.

Elected to a term not to exceed five years concurrent with the term of the incumbent National Assembly, the executive president is the nominee of the party with the largest number of votes in the assembly. There is no limit on the number of times the executive president may be reelected. Grounds for removal from office include inability to function for medical reasons, violations of the constitution as determined by a two-thirds vote of the National Assembly, and findings of gross misconduct by vote of three-quarters of the National Assembly. If a motion to remove the executive president from office passes the National Assembly, he or she has three days to vacate the office or dissolve the legislature. The executive president may postpone national elections in one-year increments for up to five years.

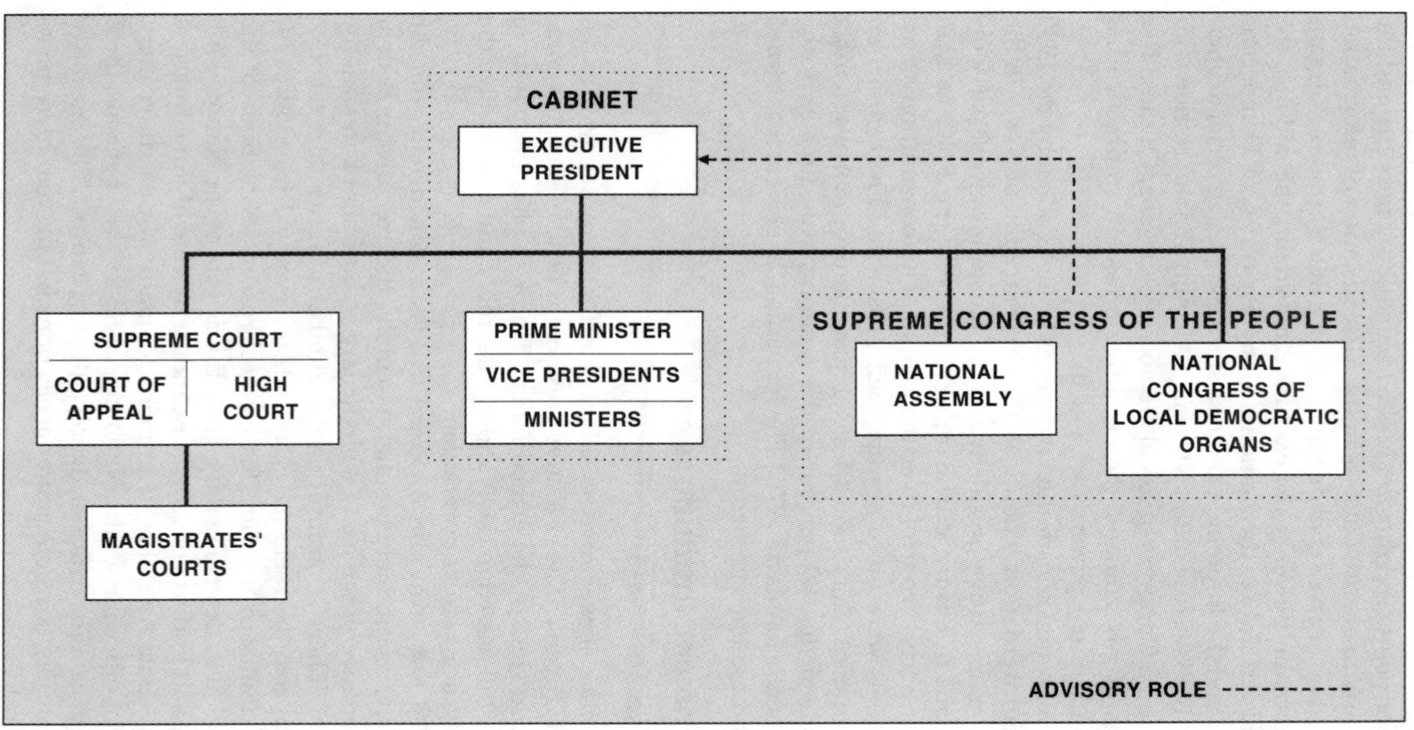

Figure 6. Guyana: Organization of the Government, 1991

The executive president appoints several vice presidents, a prime minister, and various other ministers. This group is known collectively as the cabinet. Although the prime minister and other vice presidents must be selected from the elected members of the National Assembly, other cabinet ministers need not hold an elective post. The number of vice presidents and ministers varies. In 1990 there were two vice presidents and eight ministers. The executive president may dismiss all cabinet members at will.

Legislature

The sixty-five-member unicameral National Assembly constitutes Guyana's legislative branch. Fifty-three members are directly elected though a system of proportional representation, ten members are elected by the regional democratic councils (local legislative bodies for each region), and two members come from the Supreme Congress of the People (a special national-level advisory group). The National Assembly has the power to pass bills and constitutional amendments, which are then sent to the executive president for approval.

The National Assembly has six months to override the presidential veto of a bill. Following an override, the executive president has the authority to dissolve the assembly within twenty-one days and call for new elections. President Burnham used this authority to stifle parliamentary opposition during his administration.

The 1980 constitution provides for the executive president to appoint the minority leader, formerly known as the leader of the opposition. The minority leader must be the elected member of the National Assembly, who, in the president's judgment, is best able to lead the opposition members of the National Assembly. Naming his own chief opponent was yet another tool President Burnham used to control the government apparatus.

Judiciary

Vestiges of a Dutch legal system remain, particularly in the area of land tenure. However, the common law of Britain is the basis for the legal system of Guyana. The judiciary consists of a magistrate's court for each of the ten regions and a Supreme Court consisting of a High Court and a Court of Appeal. The 1980 constitution established the judiciary as an independent branch of the government with the right of judicial review of legislative and executive acts.

The constitution secures the tenure of judicial officers by prescribing their age of retirement (sixty-two or sixty-five), guaranteeing their terms and conditions of service, and preventing their removal from office except for reasons of inability or misconduct established by means of an elaborate judicial procedure. These constitutional arrangements are supplemented by statutory provisions that establish a hierarchy of courts through which the individual under scrutiny may secure enforcement of his civil and political rights.

The lower courts, known as magistrates' courts, have jurisdiction in criminal cases and civil suits involving small claims. The High Court has general jurisdiction in both civil and criminal matters. Criminal cases are always tried by a jury of twelve persons. Appeals of High Court rulings go to the Court of Appeal.

Any person in Guyana has the right to bring charges involving a breach of criminal law. In practice, the police as the official law enforcement body generally institute and undertake criminal prosecutions. Traditionally, the attorney general (a cabinet-level minister) exercises supervisory authority over all criminal prosecutions.

The executive president appoints all judges, with the exception of the chancellor of the High Court (the head of the judiciary), the chief justice of the Court of Appeal, and the chief magistrate. The Judicial Service Commission appoints these top three judges; however, the commission itself is selected by the president. Although selection of the members of the Judicial Service Commission is supposed to be made with opposition input, in fact the opposition has no say in judicial appointments. Observers have noted that trials are generally fair, but if a guilty verdict is reached, the executive president often drops strong hints concerning the magnitude of the sentence he expects for crimes that have received national publicity.

Other National Institutions

The National Congress of Local Democratic Organs is a national body charged with representing the interests of local government. Members of this body are drawn from the regional governments. Each Regional Democratic Council elects two members to sit on the national congress. The constitution also provides for members of other local councils to elect members; however, no other local bodies have been created by the central government. The national congress's role is advisory.

The members of the National Assembly, together with all the members of the National Congress of Local Democratic Organs, form the Supreme Congress of the People. The supreme congress meets at times designated by the executive president to make recommendations to him or her on matters of public interest. It may be dissolved by the executive president by proclamation and is automatically dismissed if the executive president dissolves the National Assembly.

President Hugh Desmond Hoyte with President George Bush, Washington, 1989
Courtesy The White House (Michael Sargent)

Local Government

The 1980 constitution divides Guyana into ten regions, each having a Regional Democratic Council and a regional chairman. Regional councillors serve five-year terms concurrent with the term of the National Assembly, and the councillors of every region elect from among themselves one member to sit in the National Assembly and two members to sit in the National Congress of Local Democratic Organs. The executive president may suspend or dissolve any Regional Democratic Council at will. The system of local governments was designed to decentralize the government and place greater political power in the hands of the people. Resistance by the president to sharing power and the regional governments' fear of dismissal without recourse have, in effect, severely limited the capability of regional government to enact policy.

Six towns in Guyana are incorporated: Georgetown, Corriverton, Linden, New Amsterdam, Bartica, and Anna Regina, northwest of the mouth of the Essequibo River. Each town has a mayor and town council, which are responsible for maintenance of the municipality. However, city officials lack a political mandate or any real power beyond the exercise of municipal duties and are usually political appointees of the PNC.

Civil Service

The civil service is not a neutral body in the traditional British sense. Civil servants are regarded as servants of both the government and the PNC. Opposition to the PNC usually results in the loss of the incumbent's job because the executive president has authority to dismiss anyone whose actions he or she deems contrary to national or party interest. Fear of dismissal and consequently being blacklisted is one of the primary reasons large numbers of Guyanese professionals emigrated in the late 1970s and early 1980s.

Political Dynamics

Electoral Process

The constitution provides for free elections, a secret ballot, and universal suffrage for citizens over the age of eighteen. Voting for the National Assembly is indirect, with voters casting ballots for lists of candidates rather than for individuals. Seats are then apportioned by an Elections Commission on the basis of the percentage each list receives. There is no minimum percentage required for a party to win a seat in the assembly. National elections must be held if the executive president dissolves the National Assembly or no more than five years after a new assembly has been elected. However, the constitution of 1980 allows the executive president to postpone national elections in one-year increments for up to five years.

Despite constitutional guarantees of fair elections, every election since the early 1960s has been tainted by charges of fraud. The most blatant alleged abuse has concerned the votes of expatriate Guyanese. The electoral system allows overseas Guyanese to vote. The number of overseas Guyanese has been said to be inflated, however, and returns have always heavily favored the PNC. Voting districts have been gerrymandered, and the army frequently has been accused of tampering with ballot boxes and breaking up opposition rallies (see Involvement in Political Affairs, ch. 5).

Electoral fraud appeared to diminish during the Hoyte administration. Opposition groups continued to pressure the government to reform the electoral process. In 1991 the executive president agreed to require the use of metal ballot boxes that are less easily tampered with and to permit the Elections Commission to operate more freely. The commission was given the task of producing a new voter list, but by 1991 had failed to do so, prompting the president to declare a state of emergency and postpone national elections.

Billboard promoting progress and the PNC
Courtesy Inter-American Development Bank (David Mangurian)

Political Parties

People's National Congress

The PNC was formed in 1957 when Forbes Burnham broke away from the PPP. The PNC represents the country's Afro-Guyanese community and many of Guyana's intellectuals. The PNC was the main partner in the coalition government formed in 1964 and has been the outright winner of every election held since then. The party held fifty-three seats after the 1980 elections. After the 1985 elections, the PNC held fifty-four seats in the National Assembly—forty-two elected seats and all of the twelve appointed seats (see table 8, Appendix A). The party came under the leadership of Desmond Hoyte following the death of Forbes Burnham in 1985 (see Independence and the Burnham Era, ch. 1).

Ideologically, the PNC has swung from socialism to middle-of-the-road capitalism several times. Although Burnham professed leftist views, the party originally adopted a procapitalist policy as an alternative to the PPP's socialism and to attract members of the Afro-Guyanese middle class. In the mid-1970s, Burnham stated that the PNC was socialist and committed to the nationalization of foreign-owned businesses and to government control of the economy.

In the late 1980s, Executive President Hoyte declared that his predecessor's policies had bankrupted the country and that the PNC would again encourage private investment.

People's Progressive Party

Guyana's oldest political party, the PPP, was founded in 1950 by Cheddi Jagan as a means to push for independence. After the 1961 elections, however, the party came to represent almost exclusively the Indo-Guyanese community. A long-time Marxist-Leninist, Jagan declared in 1969 that the PPP was a communist party and advocated state ownership of all industry. The PPP won elections in 1953, 1957, and 1961, but its leftist policies led to internal unrest and opposition from the British colonial authorities (see Preindependence Government, 1953-66, ch. 1). The PPP had ten National Assembly seats after the 1980 election and in the 1985 elections won eight seats.

Other Political Groups

Concerned that the PPP had been coopted by the more conservative PNC in the early 1970s, a multiethnic group of politicians and intellectuals formed the Working People's Alliance (WPA) in 1973. Originally a loose organization, the WPA became a formal political party in 1979 after three of its leaders were imprisoned by the Burnham government. Its membership is drawn from the Indo-Guyanese and Afro-Guyanese communities, and the party advocates moderately leftist policies. The WPA refused to participate in the 1980 elections, charging that they would be rigged, but won one seat in the 1985 elections.

A small conservative party, the United Force (UF) was founded in 1960 by a wealthy Portuguese businessman to represent Guyana's business community. It also draws support from Guyana's Roman Catholic Church and the small Portuguese, Chinese, and Amerindian populations. The party won two seats in both the 1980 and 1985 elections.

After the 1985 elections, five parties—the PPP, the WPA, the small Democratic Labour Movement, the People's Democratic Movement, and the National Democratic Front—formed the Patriotic Coalition for Democracy (PCD). The PCD promised to push for fair elections and oppose PNC manipulation of the electoral process.

Interest Groups

Trade Unions

Trade unions traditionally have played a major role in Guyana's political life. They began to emerge when Hubert Nathaniel Critchlow mobilized waterfront workers and formed the nation's first labor union, The British Guiana Labour Union (BGLU), in 1917. Since then, union members have become a significant segment of the Guyanese working class. It was from the trade unions that the PPP and PNC evolved and drew their strength.

Most union members work in the public sector, and trade unions historically have had close ties to the ruling government. Many of the twenty-four unions in the Trades Union Congress (TUC), the main umbrella group for trade unions in Guyana, are formally affiliated with the PNC. Unions have the right to choose their own leaders freely, but in practice the ruling party has significant influence over union leadership. Government officials are often also union leaders. For instance, President Hoyte has been named the honorary president of one of the member unions of the TUC.

Government-labor relations have been marred by the PNC's attempts to control and silence the unions. This control initially was secured through the dominance of the Manpower Citizens Association, a pro-PNC union. When the Guyana Agricultural and General Workers' Union (GAWU) entered the TUC in 1976, the size of the GAWU's membership (about 15,000) meant that it would be the largest union in the TUC, a status that would entitle it to the largest number of delegates. The PNC quickly contrived a system whereby the GAWU ended up with far fewer delegates than it had previously been entitled to, and as such the TUC remained under PNC control. From 1982 to 1984, Minister of Labour Kenneth Denny and Minister of Finance Salim Salahuddin held very senior posts in the TUC simultaneously with their ministerial portfolios. In March 1984, the National Assembly passed the Labour Amendment Act, which stipulated that the TUC would henceforth be the only forum through which organized labor could bargain.

The Labour Amendment Act clearly was designed to stifle labor opposition to government policies. The law backfired, however, because reaction to it led to the ouster of the PNC-controlled labor leadership, which was replaced by leaders professing to be more independent. The main resistance to the PNC's control of the TUC came from a seven-union opposition bloc within the TUC, headed by the GAWU. Many unions, including some of the PNC-affiliated ones, began to criticize the government.

In the 1984 TUC elections, the seven-member reform coalition made significant inroads. The coalition candidate for TUC president ran against the PNC candidate and won. The changes in union leadership were a clear indication of the breadth of dissatisfaction with the PNC's efforts to roll back union power, and with Guyana's rapidly deteriorating economy. The seven disaffected unions left the TUC and in 1988 formed the Federation of Independent Trade Unions of Guyana (FITUG).

Media

The 1980 constitution guarantees freedom of the press, but the government owns the nation's largest publication and exercises indirect control over other newspapers by controlling the importation of newsprint. Administrations have also stifled opposition by making frequent charges of libel against the editors of opposition newspapers. The newspaper with the largest circulation is the government-owned *Guyana Chronicle.* The PNC's *New Nation* has the second highest circulation. Smaller newspapers include the PPP's *Mirror,* the independent *Stabroek News,* and the *Catholic Standard,* published by the Roman Catholic Church.

The government's influence over the press has lessened, and increased criticism has been allowed under President Hoyte. The opposition *Stabroek News,* which started out as a weekly, increased publication to six times a week in 1991. It has become widely regarded as the only reliable and nonpartisan source of news in Guyana. At about the same time the *Stabroek News* expanded operations, the PPP's *Mirror* was allowed to import new presses and increase its size from four to sixteen pages per issue.

Religious Organizations

At different times and from different perspectives, the churches of Guyana have been a source of opposition to government policy. In the 1950s, the Christian churches were vocal opponents of Jagan and the PPP's Marxism. These churches also drew international attention with their criticisms of the Burnham government in the 1970s and 1980s.

Much of the criticism of the national government has come from the Guyana Council of Churches (GCC), an umbrella organization of sixteen major Christian denominations. Anglicans and Roman Catholics, confident of foreign support for their positions, often have taken the lead. Some of the smaller churches with ties to the PNC have been instrumental in getting the GCC to soften its criticism. One sect, the House of Israel, has been reported to have close ties to the PNC (see Cults, ch. 2). The sect's members were accused of disrupting a 1985 meeting of the GCC.

Hindu and Muslim religious organizations traditionally have played almost no political role in Guyana. In contrast to many Christian organizations, which receive support from adherents abroad, Hindu and Muslim leaders rely strictly on a local base.

Religious leaders often are dependent on local political bosses, and the PNC has successfully recruited many Hindu and Muslim leaders into party organizations.

Other Groups

The long-standing policy of dividing constituencies into ethnic elements has prevented the establishment of a strong independent business organization. Fear of the Marxist PPP caused many middle-class Afro-Guyanese to support the PNC, beginning in the 1960s. Members of the business community who oppose government policy often do so through participation in the UF.

A movement began in the 1940s to press for improvement in socioeconomic conditions for women. The first formal women's organization was headed by Janet Jagan, wife of Cheddi Jagan, but it soon became merely an arm of Jagan's PPP. There is no national women's organization that spans ethnic groups. Rather, a women's group functions as part of the PPP, and a Women's Affairs Bureau of the ruling government is associated with the PNC.

Foreign Relations

The international relations of the former British colony have been oriented toward the English-speaking world and guided by ideological principles. Except for those countries on Guyana's borders, Latin America is largely ignored. Independent Guyana's foreign policy has had five predominant themes: political nonalignment, support for leftist causes worldwide, promotion of economic unity in the English-speaking Caribbean, opposition to apartheid, and protection of Guyanese territorial integrity in the resolution of the border disputes with Venezuela and Suriname.

Although upholding the principal foreign policy themes, the PNC has adroitly shifted emphasis to reflect changes in domestic policy. To consolidate power against the leftist PPP, PNC foreign policy from 1964 to 1969 was pro-Western. Confident of its domestic power base from 1970 to 1985, the government was nonaligned in international affairs, with strong support for less-developed countries and socialist causes. Guyana established diplomatic ties and symbolic economic ties with the communist governments in Eastern Europe, the Soviet Union, and Cuba. Since Hoyte's accession to the presidency in 1985, foreign policy has again been less supportive of leftist causes, in part to obtain backing for Hoyte's economic programs from Western nations.

Relations with the United States

Guyana's relations with the United States have ranged from

cordial to cool. For the United States, Burnham's policies from 1964 to 1969 were nonthreatening. Burnham assured the United States that he had no intention of pursuing Jagan-style socialism or of nationalizing foreign-owned industries. The United States felt there was little chance of Guyana becoming a second Cuba.

Relations between the two nations cooled significantly after 1969, when Burnham began to support socialism both domestically and internationally. He established the cooperative republic in 1970 and nationalized the sugar and bauxite industries in the mid-1970s. Guyana also became active in the Nonaligned Movement (NAM). Burnham attended the NAM conference in Zambia in 1970 and hosted the conference in Georgetown in 1972. In 1975 the United States accused Guyana of allowing Timehri Airport to be used as a refueling stop for planes transporting Cuban troops to Angola. United States aid to Guyana virtually stopped, and acrimonious rhetoric emanated from both sides.

Under the administration of President Jimmy Carter (1977–81), United States-Guyana relations improved somewhat. The United States ambassador to the United Nations (UN) told the Guyanese government that the region's leaders could expect greater understanding of their alternative development strategies from the Carter administration. When the assistant secretary of state said that the United States did not feel threatened by Guyana's political philosophy, it seemed that the two countries had reached an understanding. This rapprochement led to resumption of United States aid to Guyana.

Relations cooled again with the succession of Ronald Reagan to the United States presidency in 1981. United States aid to Guyana was again halted, and Guyana later was excluded from the Caribbean Basin Initiative (see Appendix D). Relations reached their lowest point after the United States intervened in Grenada in 1983. Burnham had ties to Grenada's New Jewel Movement and was vocal in his opposition to the intervention. He criticized the United States and chastised fellow regional leaders who supported intervention in a speech at the Caribbean Community and Common Market (Caricom—see Appendix C).

After Burnham's death in 1985, United States-Guyanese relations improved under the more market-oriented administration of President Hoyte. The new president welcomed Western aid and investment, and the government stopped its anticapitalist, anti-Western, and socialist rhetoric. The United States responded by resuming wheat shipments in 1986. Frictions remained over the Guyanese electoral process, however.

Relations with Venezuela

Relations between Guyana and Venezuela have been driven by a persistent border dispute (see fig. 7). Venezuela's claim to a mineral-rich five-eighths of Guyana's total land mass dates back to the early nineteenth century (see Origins of the Border Dispute with Venezuela, ch. 1). The dispute was considered settled by arbitration in 1899. Decades later a memo written by a lawyer involved in the arbitration and published posthumously indicated that the tribunal president had coerced several members into assenting to the final decision. In 1962 Venezuela declared that it would no longer abide by the 1899 arbitration on the grounds of this new information.

On February 17, 1966, representatives of Britain, Guyana, and Venezuela signed an agreement in Geneva that established a border commission consisting of two Guyanese and two Venezuelans. The commission failed to reach an agreement, but both countries agreed to resolve their dispute by peaceful means as stipulated in Article 33 of the United Nations Charter. In the meantime, relations remained tense. In February 1967, Venezuela vetoed Guyana's bid to become a member of the Organization of American States (OAS). The Venezuelan government also attempted to sabotage Guyana's development plans for the disputed region by letting it be known to would-be foreign investors that it did not recognize Guyanese jurisdiction.

With Venezuelan backing, several prominent ranching families and Amerindian followers in the southern part of the disputed region began an uprising. The rebels launched a surprise attack on the police outpost at Lethem on January 2, 1969, and several policemen were killed. The government flew police and military forces to the region with orders to raze everything. Only livestock and cattle were spared. The Venezuelan government admitted that some of the Guyanese insurgents had received training in Venezuela and that it would grant refuge to the rebels. Guyana protested this action in the UN.

Venezuela found itself diplomatically isolated, unable even to gain the support of its neighbors in Latin America. Pressure on Venezuela to resolve the dispute led to the Protocol of Port-of-Spain, whereby in 1970 Guyana and Venezuela agreed to a twelve-year moratorium on the dispute. The protocol would be automatically renewed unless either party gave notice of its intention to do otherwise.

In 1981 the Venezuelan president, Luis Hererra Campíns, announced that Venezuela would not renew the protocol. Relations

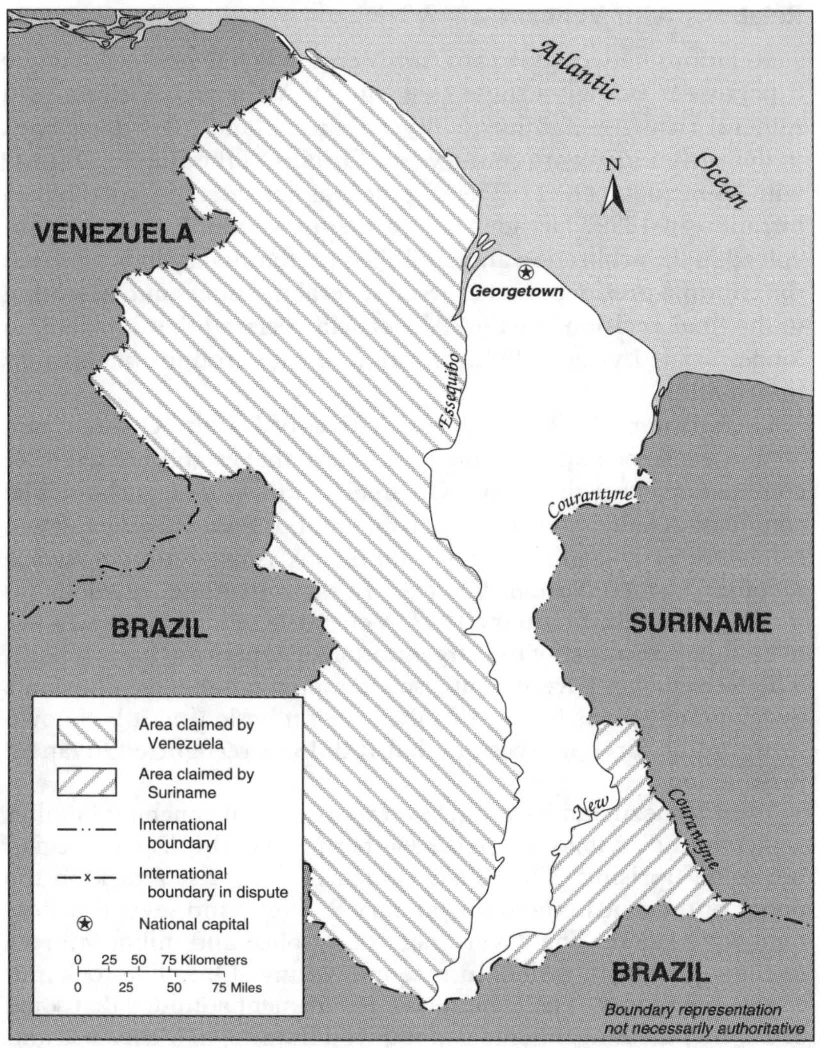

Figure 7. Guyana: Border Disputes

again grew tense. Guyana's government accused Venezuela of massing troops near their common border to invade Guyana. The Venezuelan government denied this accusation, stating that its troops merely were involved in regular maneuvers. The subsequent Argentine invasion of the Falkland Islands (called the Malvinas by Argentina) and the 1983 United States intervention in Grenada were heavily criticized by the Guyanese government, which feared that a precedent had been set for Venezuela to resolve its territorial grievance by force.

In the late 1980s with different administrations in both countries, relations between Venezuela and Guyana improved. Relations became so cordial, in fact, that Venezuela sponsored Guyana's bid for OAS membership in 1990. Although the territorial issue remained unresolved, there seemed little imminent threat of a Venezuelan invasion.

Relations with Brazil

Traditionally, relations between Guyana and Brazil have been good. Brazil has provided small amounts of military assistance to Guyana in the form of jungle warfare training and logistical matériel. Brazil's military assistance to Guyana has been contingent on Guyana's refusal of any military aid from Cuba. In 1975 United States allegations that Guyana was allowing Cuban troops en route to the Angolan civil war to refuel in Guyana made the Brazilian government nervous, and it briefly undertook military maneuvers on its border with Guyana.

In the 1960s, both governments were anxious to complete a highway that would link the Brazilian city of Manaus to Georgetown. Completion of the highway would afford Brazil easy access to an Atlantic port from its northernmost states, and Guyana would gain direct access to Brazilian markets. In 1971 Brazil offered Guyana technical assistance to complete the Guyanese portion from Lethem to Georgetown. The offer was refused, however, and the road was not completed until the early 1990s.

Relations with Suriname

Guyana's relations with Suriname have at times been tense. Suriname has a territorial claim to a triangle of land between the New and Courantyne rivers in southeast Guyana. In 1969 Suriname sent troops into the disputed territory. They were quickly repelled by the Guyanese army. Although Suriname made no further attempts to take the territory by force, two issues continued to trouble relations (see Guyana-Suriname Dispute, ch. 5). The first was the forced repatriation of Guyanese living in Suriname. When Suriname's economic decline began in 1980, Surinamese leader Colonel Desi Bouterse blamed Guyanese immigrants, many of whom were successful rice farmers. The second issue was the matter of fishing rights in the disputed territory. Both countries have periodically detained each other's fishermen and confiscated fishing boats on the Courantyne River.

Relations with Britain

Despite Burnham's anti-Western rhetoric of the 1970s and early 1980s, Guyana has attempted to maintain good relations with Britain, in part to discourage Venezuelan territorial ambitions. Guyana remained in the Commonwealth of Nations after independence and has played an active role in Commonwealth affairs. Guyana strongly criticized the Argentine invasion of the Falkland Islands and was a vocal supporter of Britain in the UN.

Relations with the Commonwealth Caribbean

Guyana under PNC administrations has consistently encouraged greater unity among the English-speaking Caribbean countries. This policy began in 1961 and was in sharp contrast to the policies of the PPP in the 1950s. The Jagan government had refused to join the West Indies Federation because of Indo-Guyanese concerns about becoming an ethnic minority within the federation. In an independent Guyana, the Indo-Guyanese would be in the majority, and Jagan hoped that such an arrangement would secure political power for the Indo-Guyanese and the PPP.

Under the PNC, the Guyanese government joined the Caribbean Free Trade Association (Carifta) with Antigua and Barbados. By 1973 Carifta had become Caricom and had the expanded goal of fostering greater economic, social, and political unity among the member countries. Caricom's headquarters were located in Georgetown, and in 1991 membership included all independent members of the English-speaking Caribbean and Belize.

Despite a trend toward economic union since the 1960s, political relations between Guyana and the English-speaking Caribbean occasionally have been poor. Except for Jamaica and Grenada in the 1970s, all of the English-speaking Caribbean countries were pro-Western and procapitalist. This stance put them in direct conflict with the often anti-Western, anticapitalist rhetoric of the Guyanese government.

The low point in relations came after the United States intervention in Grenada. Burnham heavily criticized other Caribbean leaders for their support of the operation, especially Dominica's prime minister, Eugenia Charles, who played a leading role. The rift between Burnham and the other Commonwealth leaders grew so great that it threatened the future of Caricom.

After Burnham's death in 1985, President Hoyte moved quickly to repair relations. At a well-publicized meeting of Caricom heads of government in 1986, Hoyte posed for a picture with the other leaders. Relations generally were good after that conference.

Relations with Communist Countries

Guyana enjoyed close relations with Cuba in the 1970s and early 1980s. The two countries established diplomatic ties in 1972, and Cuba agreed to provide medical supplies, doctors, and medical training to Guyana. President Burnham flew with Fidel Castro Ruz in Castro's airplane to the NAM conference in Algiers in 1973. Castro made an official state visit to Guyana in August 1973, and Burnham reciprocated in April 1975, when he was decorated with the José Martí National Order, Cuba's highest honor. After the United States intervention in Grenada, Burnham distanced himself somewhat from Cuba, fearing United States intervention in Guyana. Under Hoyte's administration, relations with Cuba have been cordial but not close.

Relations with other communist countries were close under Burnham. Diplomatic relations with China were established in June 1972. In 1975 China agreed to provide interest-free loans to Guyana and to import Guyanese bauxite and sugar. In 1976 the Soviet Union appointed a resident ambassador to Georgetown. Burnham paid official state visits to Bulgaria and China in 1983 to seek increased economic aid.

The rapidly changing world of the 1990s provided numerous challenges for the Guyanese government. Two decades of rule by the Burnham administration had resulted in a profound weakening of the country's democratic process and close ties with socialist countries, punctuated by frequent vocal support for leftist causes around the world. Driven by the need to obtain financial support from the West to rejuvenate a collapsed economy, Burnham's successor, Desmond Hoyte, began loosening ties with socialist regimes and downplaying leftist rhetoric. The fall of communism in the early 1990s only accelerated this trend. Financial help and closer relations with the West, particularly the United States, however, came with a price: free-market reforms and genuine respect for Guyana's democratic institutions. In 1992 it remained to be seen whether Guyana had undergone merely another tactical policy shift as an expedient or was truly set on a path of democracy.

* * *

The literature on Guyanese politics remains relatively limited and perhaps too narrowly focused. The dysfunctional nature of modern Guyanese governance has generated studies of race relations, ideology, and political economy. Lacking are analyses of the post-Burnham period and, most notably, of the absence of progress toward democratization since the late 1980s.

The most current and balanced book-length overview is Chaitram Singh's *Guyana: Politics in a Plantation Society,* a work whose very title is suggestive of the environment the author addresses. In the same vein, but a bit older and less reliable, is *Guyana: Politics, Economics and Society,* by Henry B. Jeffrey and Colin Baber. In addition to the limited journal literature, any reader interested in Guyanese politics should consult, with care, a number of classics, including Leo A. Despres's *Cultural Pluralism and Nationalist Politics in Guyana* and *The West on Trial* by Cheddi Jagan, a fixture on the nation's political scene for almost half a century. Tying many elements together is *Journey to Nowhere: A New World Tragedy,* by well-known author Shiva Naipaul.

The nation's foreign relations are to a degree covered by the above titles. Guyana's nonaligned foreign policy and the border dispute with Venezuela have been the two key subjects. There is little to work with, except for a few journal articles. One exception is *The Venezuela-Guyanese Border Dispute* by Jacqueline Anne Braveboy-Wagner. (For further information and complete citations, see Bibliography.)

Chapter 5. Guyana: National Security

Member of the Guyana Defence Force

THE GUYANA DEFENCE FORCE (GDF) has been Guyana's primary defense service since independence was achieved in 1966. In 1991 the GDF, with a total active strength of only 1,700, was a unified service divided into land, sea, and air elements. The land element was by far the largest of the three, with approximately 1,400 personnel. The Air Command counted 200 personnel; the Maritime Corps, the naval element, had 100 members. The GDF was supplemented by the 2,000 member National Guard Service, a reserve unit. Besides the GDF, Guyana had two paramilitary organizations: the 2,000-member Guyana People's Militia and the 1,500-member Guyana National Service.

Heavily politicized, Guyana's defense organizations were under the control of the leaders of the ruling People's National Congress (PNC). Troops were required to swear public allegiance to the PNC as well as to the nation. Guyana's racial politics affected its armed forces as well; the military was staffed almost entirely by Afro-Guyanese, the ethnic group most associated with the PNC.

The principal role of the armed forces since independence has been to assure internal security, although the GDF has seen some minor action in the course of Guyana's persistent border disputes with two of its neighbors, Venezuela and Suriname. The internal security role overlapped with the duties of the Guyana Police Force, and the two organizations often worked together to intimidate opposition political groups and the Indo-Guyanese, the country's largest ethnic group, or to tamper with electoral counts. The police and the military were unable, however, to control a rising level of violent and petty crime in Georgetown, the nation's capital.

The Armed Forces

The Special Service Unit (SSU) began as a constabulary force in 1964. It became the Guyana Defence Force in 1965. Governor Richard Luyt created the SSU to aid the police in maintaining internal order in British Guiana, as the country was then called. The colonial government's goal was for the SSU to evolve into Guyana's army after independence was granted. A British officer, Colonel Ronald Pope, aided by a British military instructional unit, organized and trained the SSU. The Guyanese component of the SSU's officers and noncommissioned officers was drawn heavily from the Volunteer Force, a reserve unit composed predominantly of Afro-Guyanese civil servants. However, officer candidates were also selected from outside the Volunteer Force and trained in Britain. Once training was completed, the Guyanese officers were rapidly promoted and positioned to assume command from the British upon independence.

The British government strove to ensure an ethnic balance within the SSU. Its reasons were twofold: Guyana was already racially polarized in the 1960s, and the police force consisted mostly of Afro-Guyanese. The British were successful in recruiting a balance of Indo-Guyanese and Afro-Guyanese cadets to fill the junior officer ranks. Indo-Guyanese were also well represented among students at the Mons Officer Cadet Training School in Britain.

The SSU was renamed the Guyana Defence Force in 1965. The transition to complete Guyanese control of the GDF began in 1966, shortly after independence was granted. Prime Minister Linden Forbes Burnham, who also served as minister of defense, oversaw the transition. Major Raymond Sataur, an Indo-Guyanese officer and graduate of the Royal Military Academy at Sandhurst, was heir apparent to the British GDF commander. But perhaps because of ethnic considerations, Burnham selected an Afro-Guyanese officer, Major Clarence Price, as the new commander. After the 1968 election, Burnham began to purge Indo-Guyanese from the GDF's officer corps. By 1970 Afro-Guyanese dominated both the officer and the enlisted ranks of the GDF.

Training of Guyanese officer cadets in Britain ceased in the 1970s. The Guyanese government then established a six-month cadet course at Timehri Airport, south of Georgetown. The ruling PNC began using political and ethnic criteria in selecting officer cadets, instead of relying on educational requirements as had been done in the past (see The Cooperative Republic, ch. 1).

The PNC attempted both to consolidate and expand the loyalty of the GDF by manipulating racial symbols and by materially rewarding loyal soldiers. Politically minded officers portrayed the PNC as the sole protector of Afro-Guyanese interests. These same officers also portrayed the opposition People's Progressive Party (PPP) as an Indo-Guyanese organization whose victory would result in economic and political domination of Afro-Guyanese by Indo-Guyanese. In 1973 an aide to Forbes Burnham openly advocated that the GDF pledge its allegiance to the PNC in addition to its loyalty to the nation. This recommendation was made policy the following year. Although the recommendation was unpopular among career officers, disagreement was not voiced openly for fear of losing high salaries, duty-free cars, housing, and other privileges. Nevertheless, throughout the 1970s and 1980s an undercurrent of

Guyana Defence Force guard of honor in front of the Bank of Guyana building, Georgetown
Courtesy Embassy of Guyana, Washington

tension existed between officers who favored a politically neutral GDF and those who favored political activism.

Mission, Organization, and Capabilities

Responsible for protecting Guyana from external threats, the GDF also concerned itself with internal security, border defense, civic work, and other activities. Some observers viewed the GDF primarily as a partisan internal security force, noting in particular the deployment of its best units to the capital. Yet the military was also a deterrent to the genuine external threat resulting from the border disputes with Venezuela and Suriname (see fig. 7).

In the 1960s, the GDF carried out military operations to counter both external and internal threats. In 1969 the GDF quelled an insurrection in the interior led by ranchers who the government believed had been armed and aided by Venezuela. That same year the GDF expelled Surinamese soldiers from a disputed area in southeastern Guyana.

The GDF maintained a high level of involvement in civic action and national development. Training and logistical support to the agriculture, mining, fishing, and construction sectors received the greatest emphasis. The GDF provided medical support to civilians as needed, and its telecommunications and aviation resources were used during emergencies and in relief operations.

The armed forces were a single unified service comprising ground, naval, and air components. This structure gave the army operational control over the naval and air elements. The president of Guyana was commander in chief of the GDF. The GDF was organized into approximately twenty corps whose activities ranged from training to intelligence to catering and musical performance. Service in the GDF was voluntary, and its membership was overwhelmingly Afro-Guyanese. Women were accepted into the service but constituted only a small percentage of the total force.

The land component of the GDF, by far the dominant service in size and importance, in 1990 had an active strength of approximately 1,400. The principal combat units were two infantry battalions, one guard battalion, one Special Forces battalion, one support weapons battalion, one artillery battery, and one engineer company. The composition of the two infantry battalions was standardized in 1980. Each of these two units consisted of a headquarters company, three rifles companies, and a support company.

Army matériel included armored reconnaissance vehicles, artillery, and surface-to-air missiles. The GDF generally used equipment of British, Soviet, or United States design (see table 9, Appendix A).

The air wing of the GDF was created in 1968. In 1970 it was redesignated the Air Command, GDF. The 200-member Air Command was headquartered at Camp Ayanganna in Georgetown. In the early 1990s, its five aircraft and five helicopters operated from Georgetown's Timehri Airport. The command's primary missions were transportation, communications, and liaison. Secondary missions included counternarcotics and maritime patrolling. All aircraft were civil registered.

A naval section of the GDF was created in 1968 and consisted of four small patrol craft. During the 1970s and 1980s, the naval component gained additional vessels although it remained the smallest element of the GDF; it had four vessels in the early 1990s. Officially known as the Maritime Corps, the naval section numbered 100 personnel in 1991. Based in Georgetown and New Amsterdam, the navy had no marine force or aircraft.

Service in the GDF was voluntary, and the privileged treatment accorded the armed forces was the primary reason for joining the service. Quarters and food were good, and pay was often better than in the civilian sector. A military career offered the advantages of medical care for personnel and their families, a retirement plan, and survivor benefits.

Uniforms were based on a British model. GDF dress for men consisted of tropical khaki shirts and trousers. Short canvas leggings were worn, and the standard headgear was a red beret decorated with the national arms. There was also a ceremonial uniform consisting of a white coat and dark blue trousers. Women had several uniforms, including a khaki blouse and slacks worn with a fatigue hat and a light khaki blouse and skirt worn with a green beret (see fig. 8).

Involvement in Political Affairs

Until 1969 the GDF observed British military ethics, which held that the armed forces should be loyal to the "government of the day" and not otherwise be involved in politics. Beginning in 1973, the PNC regularly used the GDF to help it win every national election. Because of irregularities in previous elections, the opposition parties had argued that the ballots be counted in each electoral district for the 1973 general election. However, the PNC insisted that ballot boxes be taken to three designated counting centers. As occurred in the 1968 elections, opposition members were not allowed to accompany the ballot boxes to the counting centers. On July 16, 1973, election day, GDF personnel shot and killed two PPP members as they protested the removal of ballot boxes from a polling station. Throughout the country, the GDF and police were quick

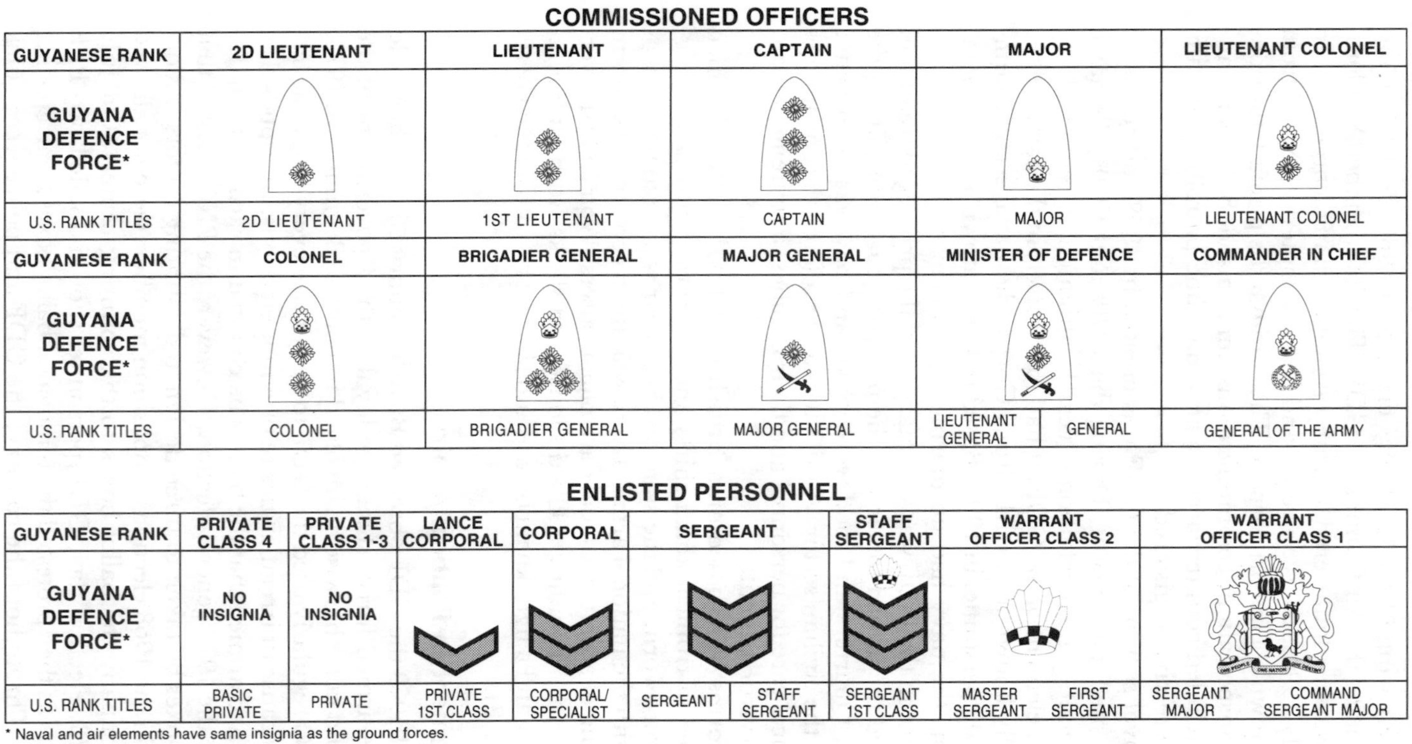

COMMISSIONED OFFICERS

GUYANESE RANK	2D LIEUTENANT	LIEUTENANT	CAPTAIN	MAJOR		LIEUTENANT COLONEL
GUYANA DEFENCE FORCE*						
U.S. RANK TITLES	2D LIEUTENANT	1ST LIEUTENANT	CAPTAIN	MAJOR		LIEUTENANT COLONEL
GUYANESE RANK	COLONEL	BRIGADIER GENERAL	MAJOR GENERAL	MINISTER OF DEFENCE		COMMANDER IN CHIEF
GUYANA DEFENCE FORCE*						
U.S. RANK TITLES	COLONEL	BRIGADIER GENERAL	MAJOR GENERAL	LIEUTENANT GENERAL	GENERAL	GENERAL OF THE ARMY

ENLISTED PERSONNEL

GUYANESE RANK	PRIVATE CLASS 4	PRIVATE CLASS 1-3	LANCE CORPORAL	CORPORAL	SERGEANT		STAFF SERGEANT	WARRANT OFFICER CLASS 2		WARRANT OFFICER CLASS 1	
GUYANA DEFENCE FORCE*	NO INSIGNIA	NO INSIGNIA									
U.S. RANK TITLES	BASIC PRIVATE	PRIVATE	PRIVATE 1ST CLASS	CORPORAL/ SPECIALIST	SERGEANT	STAFF SERGEANT	SERGEANT 1ST CLASS	MASTER SERGEANT	FIRST SERGEANT	SERGEANT MAJOR	COMMAND SERGEANT MAJOR

* Naval and air elements have same insignia as the ground forces.

Figure 8. Guyana: Military Ranks and Insignia, 1991

to resort to force when removing ballot boxes from the electoral districts.

Once they were collected, large numbers of ballot boxes were quarantined at Camp Ayanganna for more than twenty-four hours with no reason given. The PNC apparently had expected to receive a large number of votes in its traditional Georgetown strongholds and initially had allowed a fair count in districts there. When early results showed a low voter turnout, the PNC called on the GDF to intervene.

At the PNC's first biennial congress in 1974, the GDF was required to pledge its allegiance to the PNC. During the 1970s and 1980s, GDF soldiers routinely received political indoctrination. The GDF also scheduled marches to celebrate major PNC political events, such as party congresses.

The PNC's increasing politicization and subordination of the GDF disturbed many members of the officer corps. When some expressed a desire for military neutrality, PNC informants in the armed forces alerted Burnham to the dissension within the GDF. In August 1979, Colonel Ulric Pilgrim, the operational force commander, and Colonel Carl Morgan, a battalion commander, were dismissed. Pilgrim and Morgan had been two of the most popular officers in the GDF. Burnham appointed a PNC loyalist, Colonel David Granger, commander of the GDF. To extend his influence further, Burnham also replaced the army chief of staff, Brigadier General Clarence Price, with a Burnham loyalist who had been a civilian police officer. The appointment of Norman McLean, a former traffic chief, shocked and enraged many GDF officers. The PNC government attempted to rebuild support by issuing a postage stamp in 1981 honoring the GDF.

The general election of December 1980, the first since 1973, was severely criticized by international observers for its irregularities. The security forces were spared blame, except for the police detention on December 9 of Lord Avebury, head of the international observer team.

In preparation for the 1985 elections, the PNC regime reenacted Part II of the National Security Act. This act gave the security forces wide-ranging powers of detention, including the authority to prevent people "from acting in a manner likely to cause subversion of democratic institutions in Guyana." The latitude authorized by the National Security Act intimidated the opposition parties. Reenactment of Part II was quickly followed by army chief of staff McLean's announcement that the army would secure and escort ballot boxes during the election. The PNC's victory was announced on December 12, three days after the election. In response, several civic groups, including the Guyana Bar Association and the Guyana Council of Churches, released a joint communiqué condemning, among other things, "violence and collusion by police and army personnel."

The Security Forces

Mission and Organization

Paramilitary Forces and Special Units

In 1973 a paramilitary organization, the Guyana National Service (GNS), was created. Generally used as a manpower source for public works and services, it also had a limited military potential. The government envisioned the GNS as an organization that would produce "cadres" sufficiently skilled to depart the populated coast and relocate to the underdeveloped interior. According to the GNS's enabling document, the Guyana National Service State Paper, this program would prepare Guyanese to use their time and energies profitably and productively; it would equip them with the knowledge and experience to open up, develop, and live on the rich lands available in the hinterland. It would mobilize and motivate support for the Guyanese people's effort to "feed, clothe, and house" themselves; inculcate the skills and attitudes necessary for nation-building and national development; and transform individuals accustomed to depending upon external aid into self-reliant and productive citizens. The GNS was to encourage the physical and mental discipline necessary for development and to ensure cohesion and unity among the various ethnic, religious, social, and economic groups in Guyana.

The 1,500-person GNS was divided into various corps for young people from ages eight to twenty-five and was integrated into public education. Associated with the Afro-Guyanese-dominated PNC, it was almost exclusively composed of young Afro-Guyanese. The program evolved from an earlier voluntary service group called the Guyana Youth Corps. This organization, whose mission had been to populate the hinterland, failed because of a lack of public support.

The government requirement that University of Guyana students and government scholarship students perform one year of service with the GNS in the republic's interior posed problems for young Indo-Guyanese women. It is customary in Guyana for single women of all ethnic groups to live at home with their parents. When away from home, single women live with relatives or board with families. The Indo-Guyanese were particularly concerned that the GNS program was a scheme to foster interracial relationships.

Many women refused to enter the GNS and, as a result, did not graduate from the university. It became common practice among Indo-Guyanese to attend college overseas to avoid the GNS program.

GNS teaching was highly ideological. Although membership was optional at the elementary and secondary levels, students who did not participate were not provided the results of their high-school placement examinations. Elementary school students who did participate were organized into "Young Brigades" and taught to march and chant party slogans. Later, as high-school juniors, students were encouraged to join the Guyana National Service Cadet Corps. The corps was similar to Cuba's Young Pioneers, with the Guyanese cadets going to field camps for political indoctrination.

The People's Militia was created in 1976 during a period of heightened tension along the Guyana-Venezuela border. Proposed by opposition leader Cheddi Jagan, the militia was envisioned as a more ethnically diverse force than the GDF, which it would replace. Jagan saw the militia as a popular organization that would have branches on every city block and in every village. The government agreed to form the People's Militia, but only as a supplemental security force. Militia members were to engage in their normal occupation until war broke out, at which point they would defend their communities and assist the regular forces.

The government intended the militia units to be autonomous and flexible enough to be self-supporting during emergencies. The militia's force level was set at 2,000. The government's stated goal was to make the militia a broad-based volunteer force. It was initially well received, and both Afro-Guyanese and Indo-Guyanese volunteered. However, preferential treatment of Afro-Guyanese led to an exodus of Indo-Guyanese volunteers. Heavy recruitment in PNC strongholds and sustained political indoctrination ensured that the People's Militia would be loyal to the PNC.

Training in the People's Militia consisted of foot drills for two hours twice a week, plus two Sundays every month. The militia was organized into nine districts, and training was carried out in each of the districts. Uniforms consisted of tan shirts, brown pants, boots, and berets. Members of the militia wore uniforms only during training or during combat. In times of emergency, the militia would be integrated into the GDF.

In 1980 the government created the National Guard Service (NGS) to protect government personnel and state property from theft and subversive activity. The NGS included both security personnel already employed at government facilities and retired police officers and others. The NGS maintained a strength of 2,000 members.

The Young Socialist Movement (YSM) was the youth arm of the PNC, with members throughout Guyana. The YSM maintained a military component with an estimated strength of 2,000. The GDF, GNS, and People's Militia provided its training. Members of the military component usually paraded in military uniforms but without weapons.

Police

In 1891 a paramilitary police force was established in British Guiana. This force became the British Guiana Police Force in June 1939 and after independence, the Guyana Police Force. Headed by a commissioner of police, the force had limited paramilitary capabilities. The 5,000-member force had three major elements: a Mounted Branch trained in riot control, a Rural Constabulary, and a Special Constabulary that served as the police reserve. Additionally, a number of constables were employed by the government and private businesses to guard property.

Informal Paramilitary Groups

House of Israel

During the 1970s and 1980s, a religious group known as the House of Israel became an informal part of the PNC's security apparatus and engaged in actions such as strikebreaking, progovernment demonstrations, political intimidation, and murder (see Cults, ch. 2). The House of Israel was led by an ardent PNC supporter, David Hill, locally known as Rabbi Washington. Hill was an American fugitive wanted for blackmail, larceny, and tax evasion. Despite its name, the House of Israel was neither Israeli nor Jewish-oriented. It was, instead, a black supremacist cult that claimed that Afro-Guyanese were the original Hebrews. Cult adherents further believed that modern-day Jews were, in fact, descendants of other non-Jewish biblical peoples and were in Israel illegally. Serving as a paramilitary force for the PNC, the House of Israel had 8,000 members, including a 300-member guard force known as the "royal cadets."

A 1979 incident illustrates the House of Israel's close relationship with the Burnham administration. A member of the cult, Bilal Ato, murdered a reporter working for an opposition newspaper on July 14, 1979. The reporter had been taking photographs of an antigovernment demonstration when he was stabbed to death. Although the entire incident was filmed by other journalists, the government took three years to bring the case to trial. A former state prosecutor defended Ato. The judge reduced Ato's charge to manslaughter and sentenced him to eight years in prison.

Later in 1979, as well as during the early and mid-1980s, the government used the House of Israel to break strikes and to disrupt public meetings of any group that the government felt might oppose its policies. Observers claimed that House of Israel members were accompanied by police and sometimes wore police uniforms during these incidents. In 1985 House of Israel members allegedly prevented delegates from entering the annual general meeting of the Guyana Council of Churches in Georgetown.

When President Hugh Desmond Hoyte took power in 1985, the House of Israel fell out of government favor. In July 1986, Rabbi Washington and other key House of Israel leaders were arrested and charged with murder. Washington pleaded guilty to manslaughter and received a fifteen-year sentence.

Organized Gangs

From 1980 until mid-1985, organized gangs of Afro-Guyanese terrorized Indo-Guyanese communities. The groups' trademark method of entry led them to be called kick-down-the-door gangs. The gangs were fully armed and used military tactics and techniques. Gang crimes against the Indo-Guyanese included robbery and occasionally rape or murder.

Police response to the gangs caused a civic outcry. The police routinely arrived at victims' homes hours after a crime had occurred, even if notified when the crime was in progress. The half-hearted police response encouraged the growth of the gangs, which became so bold that they began to undertake daylight operations. Fear so paralyzed Indo-Guyanese communities that women in rural areas congregated most of the day by public roads, seeking safety in numbers.

Many analysts believed that the PNC sponsored, or at least tolerated, the kick-down-the-door gangs. Despite stringent gun control laws, gang members carried automatic weapons. One observer called the gangs "policemen by day and bandits by night." The gangs used tactics the PNC had employed against opposition parties, only on a larger scale and with even greater brutality. After Burnham's death in 1985, the gangs disappeared.

Human Rights Violations

Arbitrary detention of civilians, physical abuse of prisoners, and summary executions became standard police behavior during Linden Forbes Burnham's regime (1964–85). During the period, the government routinely refused to conduct public inquiries into killings, even into those in which it was not implicated. In 1973 a University of Guyana lecturer was severely wounded in what many people believed to be an attempted assassination. In 1976 noted PPP member Isahak Basir was severely wounded by police. In 1979 political activist Ohena Koama was shot and killed in Georgetown by police. In October 1979, government minister Vincent Teekah was murdered. In all these cases, no inquest was held. The most infamous murder was the 1980 killing of internationally respected historian and political activist Walter Rodney. The United States Department of State believed the government was implicated in the murder, which occurred when a small radio transmitter in Rodney's possession exploded.

The Guyana Human Rights Association determined that from January 1980 to June 1981 at least twenty-two people were killed by police, and no inquests were ever held. The police stated that all the victims either had attacked police officers or were killed trying to escape.

Another common government practice was to deny opposition groups permission to demonstrate peaceably. On September 17, 1981, the Working People's Alliance organized a demonstration without government permission. The crowd, which numbered fewer than 100, called for higher wages, affirmed Guyana's territorial integrity, and criticized South Africa's apartheid regime. Police intervened in the protest, arrested political leaders Moses Bhagwan and Eusi Kwayana, and beat those demonstrators who would not disperse.

Under the administration of Hugh Desmond Hoyte, who became president in 1985, respect for human rights improved considerably. Although a United States government report stated that in 1991 police abuse of prisoners and electoral manipulation continued, no politically motivated or government-sanctioned extrajudicial killings were reported. No summary executions took place, and there were no reports of politically related disappearances.

The Courts and the Penal System

The Guyanese judicial system consisted of the Supreme Court, which encompassed a Court of Appeal and a High Court, and ten magistrates' courts (see Judiciary, ch. 4). The Court of Appeal, created in June 1966, consisted of a presiding chancellor, the chief justice, and the number of justices of appeal determined by the National Assembly. The High Court consisted of the chief justice as president and several subordinate judges. Its jurisdiction was both original and appellate, and included criminal cases brought before it on indictment. A person convicted by the High Court had the option of resorting to the Court of Appeal. The High Court had unlimited jurisdiction over civil matters and exclusive jurisdiction over probate and divorce. Magistrates had the authority to decide small claims in civil suits and had original jurisdiction in criminal cases.

As a demonstration of PNC dominance over state institutions, the party's flag was flown over the Court of Appeal. This gesture undermined public confidence in the impartiality of the Guyanese judiciary.

Under the constitution of 1980, anyone charged with a criminal offense has the right to a hearing by a court of law, and in the early 1990s this right apparently was being respected. Guyana had a bail system, and defendants were granted public trials. Arrest did not require a warrant issued by a court; the presumption of guilt by a police officer was sufficient. The National Security Act, which had been widely used to detain political dissidents, was repealed in 1991. Although capital punishment was still permitted, no execution had taken place since the 1970s.

A report by the Guyana Human Rights Association indicated that in 1991 the country's three main prisons—at Georgetown, Mazaruni (near New Amsterdam), and New Amsterdam—were overcrowded and in deteriorating condition. Mandatory sentences for narcotics offenses had resulted in a large increase in the inmate population without a corresponding expansion of facilities. The Guyana Human Rights Association claimed that malnutrition and acquired immune deficiency syndrome (AIDS) were widespread in the nation's prisons.

Border Disputes

Guyana-Venezuela Dispute

During the 1800s, Venezuela and British Guiana both laid claim to a large tract (five-eighths of present-day Guyana) between the Essequibo River and the mouth of the Orinoco River (see Origins of the Border Dispute with Venezuela, ch. 1). In 1899 a court of arbitration awarded more than 90 percent of the disputed area to British Guiana, and the matter appeared to be settled. In the early 1960s, however, Venezuela reasserted its claim to the disputed territory (see Relations with Venezuela, ch. 4). In 1966 a commission was established to negotiate a settlement, but border incidents repeatedly interrupted its work. On October 12, 1966, Guyana discovered that Venezuelan military and civilian personnel had occupied the Guyanese half of Ankoko Island in the Cuyuni River.

The Venezuelans had begun developing an airfield and mining facilities on the island. Prime Minister Burnham protested the occupation and demanded Venezuela's complete withdrawal and the removal of the facilities. Dismissing the protest, Venezuela countercharged that Ankoko Island had always been Venezuelan territory. Because Guyana was unable to force a Venezuelan withdrawal, Ankoko Island remained occupied, and Guyanese and Venezuelan military outposts exchanged sporadic gunfire.

The Ankoko Island incident was followed in July 1968 by Venezuela's extension of its territorial waters to twelve nautical miles off its coast, including the disputed region. Because Guyana claimed only a three-nautical-mile limit, Venezuela's decree in effect established a claim over coastal waters from three to twelve nautical miles off Guyana's western coast. Guyana immediately condemned the Venezuelan decree, and Britain voiced its concern to the Venezuelan ambassador in London. Political sparring continued for six months until the incident was overshadowed by new events.

On January 4, 1969, Prime Minister Burnham reported that disturbances had occurred in the Rupununi region of southern Guyana. The historically independent-minded ranchers of the Rupununi Savannah had unsuccessfully attempted a secessionist revolt. The police station in Lethem, the major government post in the region, had been attacked on January 2. Four policemen and one civilian employee of the police had been killed. The insurgents then seized and blocked most area airstrips. The airstrip at Manari, eight kilometers from Lethem, was left open, apparently for the insurgents' own use. Responding quickly, the Guyanese government flew police and GDF forces to Manari. Surprised by the rapid government action, the insurgents fled to Venezuela and order was restored.

The Guyanese government charged that a captured insurgent claimed that the ranchers had developed a plan in December 1968 to create a separate state with Venezuelan aid. Venezuela allegedly transported the insurgents to and from training camps in Venezuela.

After Guyana put down the rebellion, the insurgents took refuge in Venezuelan border towns. Venezuela denied any wrongdoing and declared the insurgents Venezuelan citizens because they had inhabited land claimed by Venezuela. The new citizens were promised land and jobs by the Venezuelan government. Guyana bitterly protested the Venezuelan actions.

The troubled peace along the border was again shattered in February 1970 when Guyanese and Venezuelan forces skirmished for several days. Machine guns and mortars were used during the three days of fighting, which involved Venezuelan troops on Ankoko Island and Guyanese troops at a nearby outpost. On March 3, Venezuela closed the border.

Throughout the troubled period, the border commission had continued to meet. The commission's four-year term expired in early 1970 with the dispute unresolved. Nonetheless, on June 18, 1970, the governments of Venezuela, Britain, and Guyana signed the Protocol of Port-of-Spain. This protocol, which supplemented the 1899 agreement, placed a twelve-year moratorium on the border dispute. The protocol provided for continued discussions, a suspension of territorial claims, and automatic renewal of the protocol if it remained uncontested after the twelve years. In 1981 Venezuela announced that it would not renew the protocol.

Relations between Guyana and Venezuela slowly improved throughout the 1970s and 1980s. In October 1990, the GDF and the Venezuelan Army signed a protocol establishing the framework for improved relations. The protocol covered cooperation in training, sports, and culture, and would remain in force for an indefinite period. The document was a revision of a protocol signed in the 1980s and created a context for future discussions. Protocol signatories were the GDF's acting chief of staff, Brigadier Joe Singh, and Venezuelan army commander Carlos Peñaloza.

Guyana-Suriname Dispute

Suriname reaffirmed a claim to an area in southeastern Guyana, the New River Triangle, after achieving independence from the Netherlands in November 1975. Despite renewed efforts by Guyana and Suriname to reach an agreement, border incidents occurred repeatedly in the late 1970s. In September 1977, Guyana seized a Surinamese trawler and charged it with fishing illegally in Guyana's 200-nautical-mile Exclusive Economic Zone. Suriname retaliated in January 1978 when it withdrew licenses from Guyanese fisherman who worked the Courantyne River, which formed the border between the two nations. Allegations were made that Suriname also used gunboats to harass Guyanese loggers on the river. Renewed talks in 1978 resolved the fishery dispute and led to the Surinamese trawler's return.

In 1979 Guyana's prime minister, Linden Forbes Burnham, and Suriname's prime minister, Henck Arron, signed an agreement establishing fishing rights and reopening the border. However, in 1980 a military coup overthrew Arron's government, and relations deteriorated. Although tensions between Guyana and Suriname improved slightly after Hugh Desmond Hoyte became Guyana's president in 1985, the border dispute remained unresolved in mid-1991.

In 1992 the GDF remained a small politicized force concerned primarily with internal security. As the border dispute with Venezuela edged closer to resolution, Guyana's principal external threat and the defensive role of the GDF diminished. The problems facing the GDF in the 1990s were more internal organizational dilemmas: to define a new mission in a world less ideologically divided and with less belligerent neighbors, and to deal with the legacy of ethnic polarization that two and a half decades of PNC rule had bequeathed to the GDF and to Guyana.

* * *

As of mid-1991, scholarly literature on Guyana's armed forces and other aspects of national security remained limited. Two excellent sources stand out: *Guyana: Politics in a Plantation Society,* by Chaitram Singh, and *Guyana: Politics, Economics, and Society,* by Henry B. Jeffrey and Colin Baber. Current order-of-battle information is available in the International Institute for Strategic Studies' annual, *The Military Balance.* Jacqueline Anne Braveboy-Wagner's *The Venezuela-Guyana Border Dispute* is the definitive reference on Guyana's primary regional problem. (For further information and complete citations, see Bibliography.)

Figure 9. Belize: Administrative Divisions, 1991

Belize: Country Profile

Country

Formal Name: Belize.

Short Form: Belize.

Term for Citizens: Belizean(s).

Capital: Belmopan.

Date of Independence: September 21, 1981, from Britain.

Geography

Size: Approximately 22,960 square kilometers; land area 21,400 square kilometers.

Topography: Country divided into two main physiographic regions. Maya Mountains and associated basins and plateaus dominate southern half of country. Second region comprises northern lowlands and is drained by numerous rivers and streams. Coastline flat and swampy and marked by many lagoons.

Climate: Subtropical climate with pronounced wet and dry seasons; rainy season from approximately June to December, dry season from about January to May. Temperatures vary with elevation and proximity to coast and show little seasonal variation.

Society

Population: Estimated at 191,000 in 1990. Rate of annual growth estimated at 3.0 percent during 1980s.

Education and Literacy: Official literacy rate of 92 percent unreliable, although more realistic figures still favorable by comparison with neighboring countries. Considerable regional inequalities in provision and quality of schooling. Formal education managed by joint partnership of church and state. Compulsory education for youth between ages of five and fourteen years (primary only). Socioeconomic and academic barriers constrain access to secondary and postsecondary education. One university, the University College of Belize, located in Belize City.

NOTE—The Country Profile contains updated information as available.

Health and Welfare: Malaria and enteritis most serious diseases. Significant incidence of moderate to severe malnutrition, particularly among children in rural areas and recent immigrants. Medical care for general population inadequate, especially in rural areas.

Ethnic Groups: By official estimates in late 1980s, roughly 40 percent of population Creole (all or partly African descent), 33 percent Mestizo (Hispanics), 10 percent Maya, 7 percent Garifuna (Afro-Carib), and smaller communities of East Indians, Chinese, Arabs, and Europeans. Extensive migrations during 1980s, however, may have altered ethnic balance.

Languages: English official language; local dialect of English—Belizean Creole—widely spoken by all population groups. Spanish widely spoken outside of Belize City. Additional languages in use include Mayan dialects (Yucatecan, Mopán, and Kekchí), Garifuna, and Low German.

Religion: Majority Roman Catholic, with significant Protestant minorities. Most Anglicans and Methodists reside in Belize City. Evangelical Protestant missionaries active and gaining adherents, especially in rural areas.

Economy

Gross Domestic Product (GDP): US$373 million, or US$1,958 per capita, in 1991.

Agriculture: Although its relative importance to economy declined during the 1980s, agriculture remained one of largest sectors in economy, accounting for 15 percent of GDP in 1990. Three crops—sugar, citrus fruits, and bananas—predominated.

Manufacturing: Small but growing segment of the economy, accounting for 12 percent of the GDP in 1989, consisted primarily of sugar refining and garment industry.

Exports: US$108 million in 1990 (estimated). Major commodities included sugar, clothing, shrimp, molasses, citrus, and bananas.

Imports: US$194 million in 1990 (estimated). Major commodities: machinery, food, manufactured goods, fuel, chemicals, and pharmaceuticals.

Foreign Debt: US$158 million (December 1990).

Currency: Belizean dollar (Bz$) divided into 100 cents. In 1991 US$1 = Bz$2 (fixed rate).

Fiscal year: April 1 to March 31.

Transportation and Communications

Railroads: None.

Roads: Over 2,700 kilometers, of which about 500 kilometers paved, 1,600 gravel, and the rest earthen.

Inland waterways: Over 800 kilometers of river usable by shallow-draught craft.

Ports: Belize City, principal port. Facilities at Big Creek in south of Belize being expanded.

Airports: Belize International (also known as Philip Goldson International) near Belize City is the country's major airport.

Telecommunications: Adequate system. In 1991 over 8,600 telephones, or 4.6 per 100 inhabitants. Broadcast facilities included six amplitude modulation (AM) radio, five frequency modulation (FM) radio, and one television station. One satellite ground station used for international communications.

Government and Politics

Government: Under 1991 constitution, constitutional monarchy with parliamentary government based on British model. Government divided into three independent branches: executive, legislative, and judicial. British monarch titular head of state, but represented by appointed governor general. Real political power held by prime minister, cabinet, and National Assembly composed of twenty-eight-member, elected House of Representatives and appointed Senate, usually of eight members. Prime minister elected by House of Representatives from its own ranks; members of both House of Representatives and Senate may be appointed to cabinet. Country divided into six districts; no corresponding district government. In Belize City and seven other towns, municipal councils elected. The judiciary branch has three levels: Magistrates' courts, Supreme Court, and Court of Appeal.

Politics: Two-party democratic system dominated even before start of internal self-rule in 1964 by People's United Party (PUP). Rival United Democratic Party (UDP) held power from 1984–89 and won again in July 1993. Following September 1989 election and subsequent defection of one UDP representative to PUP, the PUP held sixteen-to-twelve majority in House of Representatives. George Price, long-time leader of PUP, served as prime minister in 1991. PUP and UDP both took centrist-to-conservative political stance, endorsing free-market economy and close relations with United

States. Price described PUP's orientation as Christian Democratic. The UDP considered to have probusiness outlook.

International Organizations: Member of United Nations and its specialized agencies; Organization of American States; Commonwealth of Nations; Caribbean Community and Common Market; and Nonaligned Movement.

National Security

Army: Belize Defence Force (BDF) with total strength of approximately 700. About 1,500 British troops (one infantry battalion) stationed in Ladyville near Belize City.

Navy: Small fifty-member maritime element with main base in Belize City. Ships of British Royal Navy made regular stops in Belize City.

Air Force: Fifteen-member air wing operated out of Belize International Airport. One British Army Air Corps flight and one-half squadron of the Royal Air Force with fighters and ground-attack aircraft stationed in southern Belize.

Military Equipment (1990): British equipment. Ground element of BDF equipped with light infantry weapons, maritime element used two 20-meter patrol boats, air wing operated two small aircraft, one of which armed.

Defense Budget: Almost US$10 million in 1989, 14 percent of total government expenditures. Additionally, Britain spent estimated US$18 million to maintain British forces in Belize.

Internal Security Forces: Belize National Police, about 500 members.

Chapter 6. Belize: Historical Setting

Mayan god of the North Star

TWO THEMES DOMINATE the history of Belize: the outward struggle to establish and maintain an English-speaking nation in an area dominated by Hispanic peoples and culture, and the inward interaction between groups of different races and cultural backgrounds. Understanding contemporary social relations and the politics of Belize depends on understanding these diverse groups and their interpretations of past events.

The first English settlers arrived in the early 1600s in present-day Belize (known as the Settlement of Belize in the Bay of Honduras prior to 1862 and British Honduras from 1862–1973). Their arrival marked the beginning of a conflict with neighboring Spanish settlers that lasted for centuries. For the first 200 years, this conflict was part of the larger rivalry between Britain and Spain. In the early 1800s, after most of the Spanish colonies in the New World became independent, the conflict in Belize evolved into a Guatemalan territorial claim on the area that continued into the 1990s (see fig. 9).

Like many nations that have recently emerged from colonialism, Belize has a population that is fragmented into many racial and cultural groups. The two largest groups are the Creoles (see Glossary), English-speaking or Creole-speaking blacks and people of mixed African and European heritage, and the Mestizos (see Glossary), Spanish-speaking people of mixed Mayan and Spanish background. Two other significant groups are the Garifuna (see Glossary), a group of African and Carib ancestry originally from the Lesser Antilles (see Glossary), and the Maya, descendants of the original inhabitants of Belize.

These groups all have different interpretations of key events in Belize's history. The subjugation of the indigenous people, the rivalry between Spain and Britain, slavery and the process of emancipation, the legacy of colonization, and the position of Belize in the modern world have all been subject to reinterpretation and debate. Despite the gradual emergence of a national identity, the differences among ethnic groups and their divergent outlooks on the present and the past play an important role in Belize today.

Ancient Mayan Civilization

Perhaps as early as 35,000 years ago, nomadic people came from Asia to the Americas across the frozen Bering Strait. In the course of many millennia, their descendants settled in and adapted to different environments, creating many cultures in North America, Central America, and South America. The Mayan culture emerged in the lowland area of the Yucatán Peninsula and the highlands to the south, in what is now southeastern Mexico, Guatemala, western Honduras, and Belize. Many aspects of this culture persist in the area despite nearly half a millennium of European domination. All evidence, whether from archaeology, history, ethnography, or linguistic studies, points to a cultural continuity in this region. The descendants of the first settlers in the area have lived there for at least three millennia.

Prior to about 2500 B.C., some hunting and foraging bands settled in small farming villages. Although hunting and foraging continued to play a part in their subsistence, these farmers domesticated crops such as corn, beans, squash, and chili peppers—which are still the basic foods in Central America. A profusion of languages and subcultures developed within the Mayan core culture. Between about 2500 B.C. and A.D. 250, the basic institutions of Mayan civilization emerged. The peak of this civilization occurred during the classic period, which began about A.D. 250 and ended about 700 years later.

Farmers engaged in various types of agriculture, including labor-intensive irrigated and ridged-field systems and shifting slash-and-burn agriculture. Their products fed the civilization's craft specialists, merchants, warriors, and priest-astronomers, who coordinated agricultural and other seasonal activities with a cycle of rituals in ceremonial centers. These priests, who observed the movements of the sun, moon, planets, and stars, developed a complex mathematical and calendrical system to coordinate various cycles of time and to record specific events on carved stelae.

Belize boasts important sites of the earliest Mayan settlements, majestic ruins of the classic period, and examples of late post-classic ceremonial construction (see fig. 10). About five kilometers west of Orange Walk, is Cuello, a site from perhaps as early as 2,500 B.C. Jars, bowls, and other dishes found there are among the oldest pottery unearthed in present-day Mexico and Central America. The site includes platforms of buildings arranged around a small plaza, indicating a distinctly Mayan community. The presence of shell, hematite, and jade shows that the Maya were trading over long distances as early as 1500 B.C. The Mayan economy, however, was still basically subsistence, combining foraging and cultivation, hunting, and fishing.

Cerros, a site on Chetumal Bay, was a flourishing trade and ceremonial center between about 300 B.C. and A.D. 100. It displays some distinguishing features of early Mayan civilization. The architecture of Mayan civilization included temples and palatial residences organized in groups around plazas. These structures were built of cut stone, covered with stucco, and elaborately decorated and painted. Stylized carvings and paintings of people, animals, and gods, along with sculptured stelae and geometric patterns on buildings, constitute a highly developed style of art. Impressive two-meter-high masks decorate the temple platform at Cerros. These masks, situated on either side of the central stairway, represent a serpent god.

The Maya were skilled at making pottery, carving jade, knapping flint, and making elaborate costumes of feathers. One of the finest carved jade objects of Mayan civilization, the head of the sun god Kinich Ahau, was found in a tomb at the classic period site of Altún Ha, thirty kilometers northwest of present-day Belize City. Settled at least as early as 200 B.C., the Altún Ha area at its peak had an estimated 8,000 to 10,000 inhabitants. At the beginning of the second century A.D., the inhabitants built their first major structure, a temple. The visitor today sees a group of temples, priests' residences, and other buildings around two adjacent plazas. In the vicinity, there are hundreds of other structures, most of which are still unexcavated. The Maya continued to rebuild some of the temples until almost the end of the ninth century. Excavations at Altún Ha have produced evidence suggesting that a revolt, perhaps of peasants against the priestly class, contributed to the downfall of the civilization. People may have continued to live at or to visit the site in the postclassic period, even though the ceremonial centers were left to decay. Some rubbish found at Altún Ha shows that people were at the site in the thirteenth and fourteenth centuries, perhaps to reuse the old structures or undertake pilgrimages to the old religious center.

Other Mayan centers located in Belize include Xunantunich and Baking Pot in Cayo District, Lubaantún and Nimli Punit in Toledo District, and Lamanai on Hill Bank Lagoon in Orange Walk District. Xunantunich, meaning "Lady of the Rock," was occupied perhaps as early as 300 B.C., but most of the architecture there was constructed in the late classic period. As in all the lowland Mayan centers, the inhabitants continually constructed temples and residences over older buildings, enlarging and raising the platforms and structures in the process. The views are breathtaking from Xunantunich's "El Castillo," which, at thirty-nine meters, is the tallest man-made structure in Belize. Lamanai, less accessible to tourists than Altún Ha or Xunantunich, is an important site because it provides archaeological evidence of the Mayan presence over many centuries, beginning around A.D. 150. Substantial

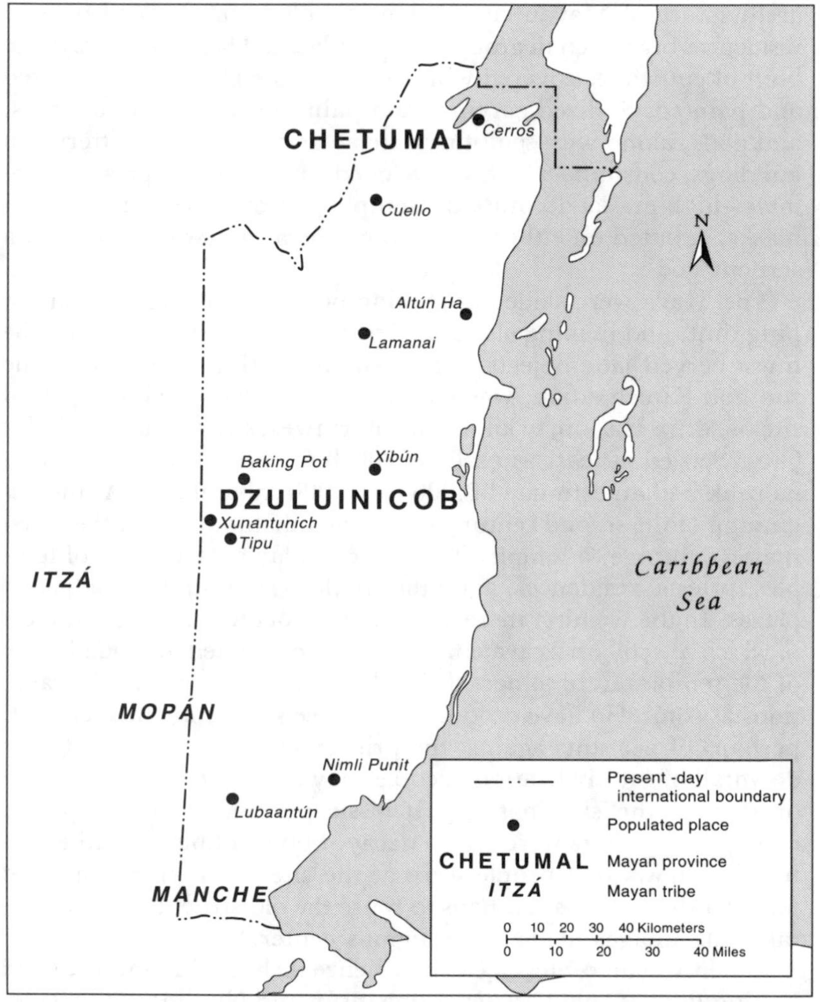

Source: Based on information from Narda Dobson, *A History of Belize*, London, 1973, 35.

Figure 10. Belize: Mayan Settlements, A.D. 700–1700

populations were present throughout the classic and postclassic periods. Indeed, people living in the area were still refacing some of the massive ceremonial buildings after the great centers, such as Tikal in neighboring Guatemala, had been virtually abandoned in the tenth century.

In the late classic period, probably at least 400,000 people inhabited the Belize area. People settled almost every part of the country worth cultivating, as well as the cay (see Glossary) and coastal swamp regions. But in the tenth century, Mayan society suffered a severe breakdown. Construction of public buildings ceased, the administrative centers lost power, and the population declined as social and economic systems lost their coherence. Some people continued to occupy, or perhaps reoccupied, sites such as Altún Ha, Xunantunich, and Lamanai. Still, these sites ceased being splendid ceremonial and civic centers.

The decline of Mayan civilization is still not fully explained. Rather than identifying the collapse as the result of a single factor, many archaeologists now believe that the decline of the Maya was a result of many complex factors and that the decline occurred at different times in different regions.

Increasing information about Mayan culture and society helps explain the development, achievements, and decline of their ancient civilization and suggests more continuities in Mayan history than once had been considered possible. The excavation of sites, such as those at Cuello, Cerros, Altún Ha, Xunantunich, and Lamanai, has shown the extraordinary persistence of Mayan people in Belize over many centuries.

Pre-Columbian Mayan Societies and the Conquest

Colonially oriented historians have asserted that the Maya had left the area long before the arrival of British settlers. But many Maya were still in Belize when the Europeans came in the sixteenth and seventeenth centuries. Archaeological and ethnohistorical research confirms that several groups of Mayan peoples lived in the area now known as Belize in the sixteenth century. The political geography of that period does not coincide with present-day boundaries, so several Mayan provinces lay across the frontiers of modern Belize, Mexico, and Guatemala. The Mayan province of Chetumal, for example, consisted of the northern part of present-day Belize and the southern coast of the Mexican state Quintana Roo. In the south, spreading west over the present-day frontier between Belize and Guatemala, were the Mopán Maya, and still farther south, the Chol-speaking Manche groups. In central Belize lay the province of Dzuluinicob, meaning "land of foreigners" or "foreign people." This province stretched from the New River in the north to the Sittee River in the south, and from close to the present-day Guatemalan border in the west to the sea. The apparent political center of this province was Tipu, located east of modern Benque Viejo del Carmen. Lamanai, several towns on the New River and on the Belize River, and Xibún on the Sibun River, were included in this province.

Christopher Columbus traveled to the Gulf of Honduras during his fourth voyage in 1502. A few years later, two of his navigators, Martín Pinzón and Juan De Solís, sailed northward along the coast of Belize to the Yucatán. In 1519 Hernán Cortés conquered Mexico, and Pedro Arias Dávila founded Panama City. Spain soon sent expeditions to Guatemala and Honduras, and the conquest of the Yucatán began in 1527. When Cortés passed through the southwestern corner of present-day Belize in 1525, there were settlements of Chol-speaking Manche in that area. When the Spanish "pacified" the region in the seventeenth century, they forcibly displaced these settlements to the Guatemalan highlands. The Spanish launched their main incursions into the area from the Yucatán, however, and encountered stiff resistance from the Mayan provinces of Chetumal and Dzuluinicob. The region became a place of refuge from the Spanish invasion, but the escaping Maya brought with them diseases that they had contracted from the Spanish. Subsequent epidemics of smallpox and yellow fever, along with endemic malaria, devastated the indigenous population and weakened its ability to resist conquest.

In the seventeenth century, Spanish missionaries from the Yucatán traveled up the New River and established churches in Mayan settlements with the intention of converting and controlling these people. One such settlement was Tipu, which was excavated in the 1980s. People occupied the site during preclassic, classic, and postclassic times, and through the conquest period until 1707. Although conquered by the Spanish in 1544, Tipu was too far from the colonial centers of power to be effectively controlled for long. Thousands of Maya fled south from the Yucatán in the second half of the sixteenth century, and the people of Tipu rebelled against Spanish authority. Although Tipu was too far south for the Spanish of the Yucatán to control, it was apparently too important to ignore because of its proximity to the Itzá of the Lago Petén Itzá region of present-day Guatemala. In 1618 and 1619, two Franciscans, attempting to convert the people, built a church in Tipu. In 1638 a period of resistance began in Tipu, and by 1642, the entire province of Dzuluinicob was in a state of rebellion. The Maya abandoned eight towns at this time, and some 300 families relocated in Tipu, the center of rebellion. In the 1640s, Tipu's population totaled more than 1,000.

Piracy along the coast increased during this period. In 1642, and again in 1648, pirates sacked Salamanca de Bacalar, the seat of Spanish government in the southern Yucatán. The abandonment of Bacalar ended Spanish control over the Mayan provinces of Chetumal and Dzuluinicob.

Between 1638 and 1695, the Maya living in the area of Tipu enjoyed autonomy from Spanish rule. But in 1696, Spanish soldiers used Tipu as a base from which they pacified the area and supported missionary activities. In 1697 the Spanish conquered the Itzá, and in 1707, the Spanish forcibly resettled the inhabitants of Tipu to the area near Lago Petén Itzá. The political center of the Mayan province of Dzuluinicob ceased to exist at the time that British colonists were becoming increasingly interested in settling the area.

The Emergence of the British Settlement

Colonial Rivalry Between Spain and Britain

In the sixteenth and seventeenth centuries, Spain tried to maintain a monopoly on trade and colonization in its New World colonies, but northern European powers were increasingly attracted to the region by the potential for trade and settlement. These powers resorted to smuggling, piracy, and war in their efforts to challenge and then destroy Spain's monopoly. Early in the seventeenth century, the Dutch, English, and French encroached in areas where Spain was weak: the small islands of the Lesser Antilles, the no-man's-land of the Guianas between the Spanish and Portuguese dominions, and the uncharted coasts of the Yucatán and Central America. Later in the seventeenth century, England effectively challenged Spain in the western Caribbean, capturing Jamaica in 1655 and subsequently using this base to support settlements all along the Caribbean coast from the Yucatán to Nicaragua.

Early in the seventeenth century, on the shores of the Bay of Campeche in southeastern Mexico and on the Yucatán Peninsula, English buccaneers began cutting logwood, which was used in the production of a dye needed by the woolen industry. According to legend, one of these buccaneers, Peter Wallace, called "Ballis" by the Spanish, settled near and gave his name to the Belize River as early as 1638. English buccaneers began using the tortuous coastline of the area as a base from which to attack Spanish ships. Some of the buccaneers may have been refugees expelled by the Spanish in 1641-42 from settlements on islands off the coasts of Nicaragua and Honduras. Buccaneers stopped plundering Spanish logwood ships and started cutting their own wood in the 1650s and 1660s. Logwood extraction then became the main reason for the English settlement for more than a century.

A 1667 treaty, in which the European powers agreed to suppress piracy, encouraged the shift from buccaneering to cutting logwood and led to more permanent settlement. The 1670 Godolphin Treaty between Spain and England confirmed English possession of countries and islands in the Western Hemisphere that England already occupied. Unfortunately, those colonies were not named, and ownership of the coastal area between the Yucatán and Nicaragua remained unclear. Conflict continued between Britain and Spain, over the right of the British to cut logwood and to settle in the region. In 1717 Spain expelled British logwood cutters from the Bay of Campeche west of the Yucatán. This action had the unintended effect of enhancing the significance of the growing British settlement near the Belize River.

The first British settlers lived a rough and disorderly life. According to Captain Nathaniel Uring, who was shipwrecked and forced to live with the logwood cutters for several months in 1720, the British were "generally a rude drunken Crew, some of which have been Pirates." He said he had "but little Comfort living among these Crew of ungovernable Wretches, where was little else to be heard but Blasphemy, Cursing and Swearing."

During the eighteenth century, the Spanish attacked the British settlers repeatedly. In 1717, 1730, 1754, and 1779, the Spanish forced the British to leave the area. The Spanish never settled in the region, however, and the British always returned to expand their trade and settlement. At the end of the Seven Years' War in 1763, the Treaty of Paris conceded to Britain the right to cut and export logwood but asserted Spanish sovereignty over the territory. Still, there was never an agreement on the precise area in which logwood cutters could operate. The Spanish frontier town of Bacalar in the Yucatán, refounded in 1730 after having been deserted for almost a century, became a base for operations against the British. When war broke out again in 1779, the commandant of Bacalar led a successful expedition against the British settlement, which was abandoned until the Treaty of Versailles in 1783 allowed the British to cut logwood in the area between the Hondo and Belize rivers. By that time, however, the logwood trade had declined and mahogany had become the chief export, so the settlers petitioned for a new agreement.

Beginnings of Self-Government and the Plantocracy

The British were reluctant to set up any formal government for the settlement for fear of provoking the Spanish. On their own initiative and without recognition by the British government, the settlers had begun annual elections of magistrates to establish common law for the settlement as early as 1738. In 1765 Rear Admiral Sir William Burnaby, commander in chief of Jamaica, arrived in the settlement and codified and expanded their regulations into a

Lighthouse near Belize City
Courtesy Steven R. Harper

document known as Burnaby's Code (see Constitutional and Political Structures Prior to Independence, ch. 9). When the settlers began returning to the area in 1784, the governor of Jamaica named Colonel Edward Marcus Despard as superintendent to oversee the Settlement of Belize in the Bay of Honduras.

The Convention of London, signed in 1786, allowed the British settlers, known as Baymen, to cut and export logwood and mahogany from the Hondo River in the north southward to the Sibun River. The convention, however, did not allow the Baymen to build fortifications, establish any form of government, military or civil, or develop plantation agriculture. Spain retained sovereignty over the area and asserted the right to inspect the settlement twice a year. Britain also agreed to evacuate its settlement on the Mosquito Coast (Costa de Mosquitos) in eastern Nicaragua. Over 2,000 of these settlers and their slaves arrived in 1787 in the settlement of Belize, reinforcing the British presence.

The last Spanish attack on the British settlement occurred two years after the outbreak of war in 1796. The governor general of the Yucatán commanded a Spanish flotilla of some thirty vessels with some 500 sailors and 2,000 troops and attacked the British colonists in 1798. During several brief engagements culminating in a two-and-a-half-hour battle on September 10, the British drove off the

Spanish. The attack marked Spain's last attempt to control the territory or dislodge the British.

Despite treaties banning local government and plantation agriculture, both activities flourished. In the late eighteenth century, an oligarchy of relatively wealthy settlers controlled the political economy of the British settlement. These settlers claimed about four-fifths of the land available under the Convention of London, through resolutions, called location laws, which they passed in the Public Meeting, the name given to the first legislature. These same men also owned about half of all the slaves in the settlement; controlled imports, exports, and the wholesale and retail trades; and determined taxation. A group of magistrates, whom they elected from among themselves, had executive as well as judicial functions, despite a prohibition on executive action.

The landowners resisted any challenge to their growing political power. Colonel Edward Marcus Despard, the first superintendent appointed by the governor of Jamaica in 1784, was suspended in 1789 when the wealthy cutters challenged his authority. When Superintendent George Arthur attacked what he called the ''monopoly on the part of the monied cutters'' in 1816, he was only partially successful in breaking their monopoly on landholding. He proclaimed that all unclaimed land was henceforth crown land that could be granted only by the crown's representative but continued to allow the existing monopoly of landownership.

Slavery in the Settlement, 1794–1838

Cutting logwood was a simple, small-scale operation, but the settlers imported slaves to help with the work. Slavery in the settlement was associated with the extraction of timber, first logwood and then mahogany, as treaties forbade the production of plantation crops. This difference in economic function gave rise to variations in the organization, conditions, and treatment of slaves. The earliest reference to African slaves in the British settlement appeared in a 1724 Spanish missionary's account, which stated that the British recently had been importing them from Jamaica and Bermuda. A century later, the total slave population numbered about 2,300. Most slaves, even if they were brought through West Indian markets, were born in Africa, probably from around the Bight of Benin, the Congo, and Angola—the principal sources of British slaves in the late eighteenth century. The Eboe, or Ibo, seem to have been particularly numerous; one section of Belize Town was known as Eboe Town in the first half of the nineteenth century. At first, many slaves maintained African ethnic identifications and cultural practices. Gradually, however, the process of assimilation was creating a new, synthetic Creole culture.

The whites, although a minority in the settlement, monopolized power and wealth by dominating the chief economic activities of trade and cutting timber. They also controlled the first legislature and the judicial and administrative institutions. As a result, the British settlers had a disproportionate influence on the development of the Creole culture. Anglican, Baptist, and Methodist missionaries helped devalue and suppress African cultural heritage.

Cutting wood was seasonal work that required workers to spend several months isolated in temporary makeshift camps in the forest, away from families in Belize Town. Settlers needed only one or two slaves to cut logwood, a small tree that grows in clumps near the coast. But as the trade shifted to mahogany in the last quarter of the eighteenth century, the settlers needed more money, land, and slaves for larger-scale operations. After 1770 about 80 percent of all male slaves aged ten years or more cut timber. Huntsmen found the trees, which were then cut, trimmed, and hauled to the riverside. During the rainy season, settlers and slaves floated rafts of untrimmed logs downriver, where the wood was processed for shipment. Huntsmen were highly skilled and valued slaves, as were the axmen who cut the trees while standing on a springy platform four to five meters high. Another group of slaves cared for the oxen that pulled the huge logs to the river. Others trimmed the trees and cleared the tracks. The use of small gangs of slaves for cutting wood reduced the need for close supervision; whip-wielding drivers, who were ubiquitous on large plantations elsewhere, were unknown in the settlement.

The colonial masters used domestic slaves, mostly women and children, to clean their houses; sew, wash, and iron their clothes; prepare and serve their food; and raise their children. Some slaves cultivated provisions that would either be sold or used to save their owners some of the cost of importing food. Other slaves worked as sailors, blacksmiths, nurses, and bakers. Few slaves, however, held jobs requiring a high level of skill. Young people started work by waiting on their masters' tables, where they were taught to obey; then most of the young women continued in domestic work while the young men became woodcutters. This rigid division of labor and the narrow range of work experience of most slaves limited their opportunities after legal emancipation in 1838.

The slaves' experience, although different from that on plantations in other colonies in the region, was nevertheless oppressive. They were frequently the objects of "extreme inhumanity," as a report published in 1820 stated. The settlement's chaplain reported "instances, many instances, of horrible barbarity" against the slaves. The slaves' own actions, including suicide, abortion, murder, escape, and revolt, suggest how they viewed their situation. Slaves who lived in small, scattered, and remote groups could escape with relative ease if they were willing to leave their families. In the eighteenth century, many escaped to the Yucatán, and in the early nineteenth century a steady flow of runaways went to Guatemala and down the coast to Honduras. Some runaways established communities, such as one near the Sibun River, that offered refuge to others. When freedom could be attained by slipping into the bush, revolt was not such a pressing option. Nevertheless, numerous slave revolts took place. The last revolt in 1820, led by two black slaves, Will and Sharper, involved a considerable number of well-armed individuals who "had been treated with very unnecessary harshness by their Owner, and had certainly good grounds for complaint."

One way the settler minority maintained its control was by dividing the slaves from the growing population of free Creole people, who were given limited privileges. Though some Creoles were legally free, they could neither hold commissions in the military nor act as jurors or magistrates, and their economic activities were restricted. They could vote in elections only if they had owned more property and lived in the area longer than whites. Privileges, however, led many free blacks to stress their loyalty and acculturation to British ways. When officials in other colonies of the British West Indies (see Glossary) began giving free blacks expanded legal rights, the British Colonial Office threatened to dissolve the Baymen's Public Meeting unless it followed suit. The "Coloured Subjects of Free Condition" were granted civil rights on July 5, 1831, a few years before the abolition of slavery was completed.

The essence of society, a rigidly hierarchical system in which people were ranked according to race and class, was well established by the time of full emancipation in 1838. The act to abolish slavery throughout the British colonies, passed in 1833, was intended to avoid drastic social changes by effecting emancipation over a five-year transition period. The act included two generous measures for slave owners: a system of "apprenticeship" calculated to extend their control over the former slaves, who were to continue to work for their masters without pay, and compensation for the former slave owners for their loss of property. These measures helped ensure that the majority of the population, even when it was legally freed after apprenticeship ended in 1838, depended on their former owners for work. These owners still monopolized the land. Before 1838, a handful of the inhabitants controlled the settlement and owned most of the people. After 1838 the masters of the settlement, a tiny elite, continued to control the country for over a century by denying access to land and by promoting economic dependency of the freed slaves through a combination of wage advances and company stores.

Emigration of the Garifuna

At the same time that the settlement was grappling with the ramifications of the end of slavery, a new ethnic group, the Garifuna, appeared. In the early 1800s, the Garifuna, descendants of Carib peoples of the Lesser Antilles and of Africans who had escaped from slavery, arrived in the settlement (see Ethnicity, ch. 7). The Garifuna had resisted British and French colonialism in the Lesser Antilles until they were defeated by the British in 1796. After putting down a violent Garifuna rebellion on Saint Vincent, the British moved between 1,700 and 5,000 of the Garifuna across the Caribbean to the Bay Islands (present-day Islas de la Bahía) off the north coast of Honduras. From there they migrated to the Caribbean coasts of Nicaragua, Honduras, Guatemala, and the southern part of present-day Belize. By 1802 about 150 Garifuna had settled in the Stann Creek (present-day Dangriga) area and were engaged in fishing and farming.

Other Garifuna later came to the British settlement of Belize after finding themselves on the wrong side in a civil war in Honduras in 1832. Many Garifuna men soon found wage work alongside slaves as mahogany cutters. In 1841 Dangriga, the Garifuna's largest settlement, was a flourishing village. The American traveler John Stephens described the Garifuna village of Punta Gorda as having 500 inhabitants and producing a wide variety of fruits and vegetables.

The British treated the Garifuna as squatters. In 1857 the British told the Garifuna that they must obtain leases from the crown or risk losing their lands, dwellings, and other buildings. The 1872 Crown Lands Ordinance established reservations for the Garifuna as well as the Maya. The British prevented both groups from owning land and treated them as a source of valuable labor.

The Early Colony

Constitutional Developments, 1850–62

In the 1850s, the power struggle between the superintendent and the planters coincided with events in international diplomacy to produce major constitutional changes. In the Clayton-Bulwer Treaty of 1850, Britain and the United States agreed to promote the construction of a canal across Central America and to refrain from colonizing any part of Central America. The British government interpreted the colonization clause as applying only to any future occupation. But the United States government claimed that Britain was obliged to evacuate the area, particularly after 1853, when President Franklin Pierce's expansionist administration stressed the Monroe Doctrine. Britain yielded on the Bay Islands and the Mosquito Coast in eastern Nicaragua. But in 1854, Britain produced a formal constitution establishing a legislature for its possession of the settlement in present-day Belize.

The Legislative Assembly of 1854 was to have eighteen elected members, each of whom was to have at least £2,400 sterling worth of property. The assembly was also to have three official members appointed by the superintendent. The fact that voters had to have property yielding an income of £27 a year or a salary of a £2,100 a year reinforced the restrictive nature of this legislature. The superintendent could defer or dissolve the assembly at any time, originate legislation, and give or withhold consent to bills. This situation suggested that the legislature was more a chamber of debate than a place where decisions were made. The Colonial Office in London became, therefore, the real political-administrative power in the settlement. This shift in power was reinforced in 1862 when the Settlement of Belize in the Bay of Honduras was declared a British colony called British Honduras, and the crown's representative was elevated to a lieutenant governor, subordinate to the governor of Jamaica.

Mayan Emigration and Conflict

As the British consolidated their settlement and pushed deeper into the interior in search of mahogany in the late eighteenth century, they encountered resistance from the Maya. In the second half of the nineteenth century, however, a combination of events outside and inside the colony redefined the position of the Maya.

During the Caste War in the Yucatán, a devastating struggle that halved the population of the area between 1847 and 1855, thousands of refugees fled to the British settlement. The Legislative Assembly had given large landowners in the colony firm titles to their vast estates in 1855 but did not allow the Maya to own land. The Maya could only rent land or live on reservations. Nevertheless, most of the refugees were small farmers who, by 1857, were growing considerable quantities of sugar, rice, corn, and vegetables in the Northern District (now Corozal and Orange Walk districts). In 1857 the town of Corozal, then six years old, had 4,500 inhabitants, second in population only to Belize Town, which had 7,000 inhabitants. Some Maya, who had fled the strife in the north but had no wish to become subjects of the British, settled in the remote area of the Yalbac Hills, just beyond the woodcutting frontier in the northwest. By 1862 about 1,000 Maya established themselves in ten villages in this area, with the center in San Pedro. One group of Maya, led by Marcos Canul, attacked a mahogany camp on the Bravo River in 1866, demanding ransom for their prisoners and rent for their land. A detachment of British troops sent to San Pedro was defeated by the Maya later that year. Early in 1867, more than 300 British troops marched into the Yalbac Hills and destroyed the Mayan villages, provision stores, and granaries in an attempt to drive them out of the district. The Maya returned, however, and in April 1870, Canul and his men marched into Corozal and occupied the town.

Two years later, Canul and 150 men attacked the barracks at Orange Walk. After several hours of fighting, Canul's group retired. Canul, mortally wounded, died on September 1, 1872. That battle was the last serious attack on the colony.

In the 1880s and 1890s, Mopán and Kekchí Maya fled from forced labor in Guatemala and came to British Honduras. They settled in several villages in southern British Honduras, mainly around San Antonio in Toledo District. The Maya could use crown lands set aside as reservations, but they lacked communal rights. Under the policy of indirect rule, a system of elected *alcaldes* (mayors), adopted from Spanish local government, linked these Maya to the colonial administration. However, the remote area of British Honduras in which they settled, combined with their largely subsistence way of life, resulted in the Mopán and Kekchí Maya maintaining more of their traditional way of life and becoming less assimilated into the colony than the Maya of the north. The Mopán and Kekchí Maya maintained their languages and a strong sense of identity. But in the north, the distinction between Maya and Spanish was increasingly blurred, as a Mestizo culture emerged. In different ways and to different degrees, then, the Maya who returned to British Honduras in the nineteenth century became incorporated into the colony as poor and dispossessed ethnic minorities. By the end of the nineteenth century, the ethnic pattern that remained largely intact throughout the twentieth century was in place: Protestants largely of African descent, who spoke either English or Creole and lived in Belize Town; the Roman Catholic Maya and Mestizos, who spoke Spanish and lived chiefly in the north and west; and the Roman Catholic

Garifuna who spoke English, Spanish, or Garifuna and settled on the southern coast.

Formal Establishment of the Colony, 1862–71

Largely as a result of the costly military expeditions against the Maya, the expenses of administering the new colony of British Honduras increased at a time when the economy was severely depressed. Great landowners and merchants dominated the Legislative Assembly, which controlled the colony's revenues and expenditures. Some of the landowners were also involved in commerce, but their interest differed from the other merchants of Belize Town. The former group resisted the taxation of land and favored an increase in import duties; the latter preferred the opposite. Moreover, the merchants in the town felt relatively secure from Mayan attacks and were unwilling to contribute toward the protection of mahogany camps, whereas the landowners felt that they should not be required to pay taxes on lands given inadequate protection. These conflicting interests produced a stalemate in the Legislative Assembly, which failed to authorize the raising of sufficient revenue. Unable to agree among themselves, the members of the Legislative Assembly surrendered their political privileges and asked for establishment of direct British rule in return for the greater security of crown colony (see Glossary) status. The new constitution was inaugurated in April 1871, and the new legislature became the Legislative Council.

Under the new constitution of 1871, the lieutenant governor and the Legislative Council, consisting of five ex officio or "official" and four appointed or "unofficial" members, governed British Honduras. This constitutional change confirmed and completed a change in the locus and form of power in the colony's political economy that had been evolving during the preceding half century. The change moved power from the old settler oligarchy to the boardrooms of British companies and to the Colonial Office in London.

Colonial Stagnation and Crisis

The Colonial Order, 1871–1931

The forestry industry's control of land and its influence in colonial decision making retarded the development of agriculture and the diversification of the economy. In many parts of the Caribbean, large numbers of former slaves, some of whom had engaged in the cultivation and marketing of food crops, became landowners. British Honduras had vast areas of sparsely populated, unused land.

Nevertheless, landownership was controlled by a small European monopoly, thwarting the evolution of a Creole landowning class from the former slaves. Rather than the former slaves, it was the Garifuna, Maya, and Mestizos who pioneered agriculture in nineteenth-century British Honduras. These groups either rented land or lived as squatters. However, the domination of the land by forestry interests continued to stifle agriculture and kept much of the population dependent on imported foods.

Landownership became even more consolidated during the economic depression of the mid-nineteenth century. Exports of mahogany peaked at over 4 million linear meters in 1846 but fell to about 1.6 million linear meters in 1859 and 8,000 linear meters in 1870, the lowest level since the beginning of the century. Mahogany and logwood continued to account for over 80 percent of the total value of exports, but the price of these goods was so low that the economy was in a state of prolonged depression after the 1850s. Major results of this depression included the decline of the old settler class, the increasing consolidation of capital and the intensification of British landownership. The British Honduras Company emerged as the predominant landowner of the crown colony. The firm originated in a partnership between one of the old settler families and a London merchant and was registered in 1859 as a limited company. The firm expanded, often at the expense of others who were forced to sell their land. In 1875 the firm became the Belize Estate and Produce Company, a London-based business that owned about half of all the privately held land in the colony. The new company was the chief force in British Honduras's political economy for over a century.

This concentration and centralization of capital meant that the direction of the colony's economy was henceforth determined largely in London. It also signaled the eclipse of the old settler elite. By about 1890, most commerce in British Honduras was in the hands of a clique of Scottish and German merchants, most of them newcomers. This clique encouraged consumption of imported goods and thus furthered British Honduras's dependence on Britain. The European minority exercised great influence in the colony's politics, partly because it was guaranteed representation on the wholly appointed Legislative Council. The manager of the Belize Estate and Produce Company, for example, was automatically a member of the council, while members of the emerging Creole elite were excluded from holding seats on the council. The Creoles requested in 1890 that some seats on the council be opened to election (as had occurred in Canada and New Zealand) in the hope of winning seats, but the Legislative Council refused. In 1892 the governor appointed several Creole members, but whites remained the majority. In the 1920s, the Colonial Office supported agitation for an elective council as long as the governor had reserve powers to allow him to push through any measures he considered essential without the council's assent. But the council rejected these provisos, and the issue of restoring elections was postponed.

Despite the prevailing stagnation of the colony's economy and society during most of the century prior to the 1930s, seeds of change were being sown. The mahogany trade remained depressed, and efforts to develop plantation agriculture in several crops, including sugarcane, coffee, cocoa, cotton, bananas, and coconuts, failed. A brief revival in the forestry industry took place early in the twentieth century as new demands for forest products came from the United States. Exports of chicle, a gum taken from the sapodilla tree and used to make chewing gum, propped up the economy from the 1880s. Much of the gum was tapped in Mexican and Guatemalan forests by Mayan *chicleros* who had been recruited by labor contractors in British Honduras. A short-lived boom in the mahogany trade occurred around 1900 in response to growing demand for the wood in the United States, but the ruthless exploitation of the forests without any conservation or reforestation depleted resources. The introduction of tractors and bulldozers opened up new areas in the west and south in the 1920s, but this development led again to only a temporary revival. At that time, mahogany, cedar, and chicle together accounted for 97 percent of forest production and 82 percent of the total value of exports. The economy, which was increasingly oriented toward trade with the United States, remained dependent and underdeveloped.

Creoles, who were well-connected with businesses in the United States, challenged the traditional political-economic connection with Britain as trade with the United States intensified. Men such as Robert S. Turton, the Creole chicle buyer for Wrigley's of Chicago, and Henry I. Melhado, whose merchant family dealt in illicit liquor during prohibition, became major political and economic figures. In 1927 Creole merchants and professionals replaced the representatives of British landowners (except for the manager of the Belize Estate and Produce Company) on the Legislative Council. The participation of this Creole elite in the political process was evidence of emerging social changes that were largely concealed by economic stagnation. These changes accelerated with such force in the 1930s that they ushered in a new era of modern politics.

The Genesis of Modern Politics, 1931–54

The Great Depression shattered the colony's economy, and

Baron Bliss Institute, Belize City
Courtesy Steven R. Harper

unemployment increased rapidly. The *Colonial Report for 1931* stated that "contracts for the purchase of mahogany and chicle, which form the mainstay of the Colony, practically ceased altogether, thereby throwing a large number of the woodcutters and chicle-gatherers out of work." On top of this economic disaster, the worst hurricane in the country's recent history demolished Belize Town on September 10, 1931, killing more than 1,000 people and destroying at least three-quarters of the housing. The British relief response was tardy and inadequate. The British government seized the opportunity to impose tighter control on the colony and endowed the governor with reserve powers, or the power to enact laws in emergency situations without the consent of the Legislative Council. The Legislative Council resisted but eventually passed a resolution agreeing to give the governor reserve powers in order to obtain disaster aid. Meanwhile, people in the town were making shelters out of the wreckage of their houses. The economy continued to decline in 1932 and 1933. The total value of imports and exports in the latter year was little more than one-fourth of what it had been in 1929.

The Belize Estate and Produce Company survived the depression years because of its special connections in British Honduras and London. Since 1875 various members of the Hoare family had been principal directors and maintained a controlling interest in the company. Samuel Hoare, a shareholder and former director, was a former British cabinet member and a friend of Leo Amery, the British secretary of state for the colonies. In 1931 when the company was suffering from the aftereffects of the hurricane and the depression, family member Oliver V.G. Hoare contacted the Colonial Office to discuss the possibility of selling the company to buyers in the United States. The British government rescued the company by granting it an area of virgin mahogany forest and a loan of US$200,000 to erect a sawmill in Belize Town. When the government almost doubled the land tax, the large landowners refused to pay. The government accepted some virtually worthless land in lieu of taxes and in 1935 capitulated completely, reducing the tax to its former rate and annulling the landowners' arrears by making them retroactive to 1931. But small landowners paid their taxes, often at a higher rate.

Robert Turton, the Creole millionaire who made his fortune from chicle exports, defeated C.H. Brown, the expatriate manager of the company, in the first elections for some of the Legislative Council seats in 1936. After the elections, the governor promptly appointed Brown to the council, presumably to maintain the influence of what had for so long been the colony's chief business. But Brown's defeat by Turton, one of the company's chief local business rivals, marked the decline of old British enterprises in relation to the rising Creole entrepreneurs with their United States commercial connections.

Meanwhile, the Belize Estate and Produce Company drove Mayan villagers from their homes in San Jose and Yalbac in the northwest and treated workers in mahogany camps almost like slaves. Investigators of labor conditions in the 1930s were appalled to discover that workers received rations of inferior flour and mess pork and tickets to be exchanged at the commissaries, in lieu of cash wages. As a result, workers and their families suffered from malnutrition and were continually in debt to their employers. The law governing labor contracts, the Masters and Servants Act of 1883, made it a criminal offense for a laborer to breach a contract. The offense was punishable by twenty-eight days of imprisonment with hard labor. In 1931 the governor, Sir John Burdon, rejected proposals to legalize trade unions and to introduce a minimum wage and sickness insurance. The conditions, aggravated by rising unemployment and the disastrous hurricane, were responsible for severe hardship among the poor. The poor responded in 1934 with a series of demonstrations, strikes, petitions, and riots that marked the beginning of modern politics and the independence movement.

Riots, strikes, and rebellions had occurred before, during and after the period of slavery, but the events of the 1930s were modern labor disturbances in the sense that they gave rise to organizations with articulate industrial and political goals. In 1894 mahogany workers rioted against a cut in their real wages caused by devaluation. In 1919 demobilized Creole servicemen protested British racism. But British troops soon stopped these spontaneous protests, which were indicative of discontent but had little lasting effect. In contrast, a group calling itself the Unemployed Brigade marched through Belize Town on February 14, 1934, to present demands to the governor and started a broad movement. Poor people, in desperation, turned to the governor, who responded by creating a little relief work—stone-breaking for US$0.10 a day. The governor also offered a daily ration of two kilograms of cooked rice at the prison gates.

The unemployed, demanding a cash dole, turned to Antonio Soberanis Gómez (1897–1975), who denounced the Unemployed Brigade's leaders at a meeting on March 16, 1934, and took over the movement. For the next few weeks, Soberanis and his colleagues of the Labourers and Unemployed Association (LUA) attacked the governor and his officials, the rich merchants, and the Belize Estate and Produce Company at biweekly meetings attended by 600 to 800 people. The workers demanded relief and a minimum wage. They couched their demands in broad moral and political terms that began to define and develop a new nationalistic and democratic political culture.

Soberanis was jailed under a new sedition law in 1935. Still, the labor agitation achieved a great deal. Of most immediate importance was the creation of relief work by a governor who saw it as a way to avoid civil disturbances. Workers built more than 300 kilometers of roads. The governor also pressed for a semirepresentative government. But when the new constitution was passed in April 1935, it included the restrictive franchise demanded by the appointed majority of the Legislative Council, which had no interest in furthering democracy. High voter-eligibility standards for property and income limited the electorate to the wealthiest 2 percent of the population. Poor people, therefore, could not vote; they could only support members of the Creole middle classes that opposed big-business candidates. The Citizens' Political Party and the LUA endorsed Robert Turton and Arthur Balderamos, a Creole lawyer, who formed the chief opposition in the new council of 1936. Working-class agitation continued, and in 1939 all six seats on the Belize Town Board (the voting requirements allowed for a more representative electorate) went to middle-class Creoles who appeared more sympathetic to labor.

The greatest achievements of the agitation of the 1930s were the labor reforms passed between 1941 and 1943. Trade unions were legalized in 1941, but the laws did not require employers to recognize these unions. Furthermore, the penal clauses of the old Masters and Servants Act rendered the new rights ineffectual. Employers among the unofficial members at the Legislative Council defeated a bill to repeal these penal clauses in August 1941, but the Employers and Workers Bill, passed on April 27, 1943, finally removed breach-of-labor-contract from the criminal code and enabled British Honduras's infant trade unions to pursue the struggle for improving labor conditions. The General Workers' Union (GWU), registered in 1943, quickly expanded into a nationwide organization and provided crucial support for the nationalist movement that took off with the formation of the People's United Party (PUP) in 1950 (see Political Parties, ch. 9). The 1930s were therefore the crucible of modern Belizean politics. It was a decade during which the old phenomena of exploitative labor conditions and authoritarian colonial and industrial relations began to give way to new labor and political processes and institutions.

The same period saw an expansion in voter eligibility. Between 1939 and 1954, less than 2 percent of the population elected six members in the Legislative Council of thirteen members. In 1945 only 822 voters were registered in a population of over 63,000. The proportion of voters increased slightly in 1945, partly because the minimum age for women voters was reduced from thirty to twenty-one years. The devaluation of the British Honduras dollar in 1949 effectively reduced the property and income voter-eligibility standards. Finally, in 1954 British Honduras achieved suffrage for all literate adults as a result of the emerging independence movement. This development was a prelude to the process of constitutional decolonization.

The origins of the independence movement also lay in the 1930s and 1940s. Three groups played important roles in the colony's politics during this period. One group consisted of working-class individuals and emphasized labor issues. This group originated with Soberanis's LUA between 1934 and 1937 and continued through the GWU. The second group, a radical nationalist movement, emerged during World War II. Its leaders came from the LUA and the local branch of Marcus Garvey's Universal Negro Improvement Association. The group called itself variously the British Honduras Independent Labour Party, the People's Republican Party, and the People's National Committee. The third group consisted

Prime Minister George Cadle Price Courtesy Belize Government Information Service

of people who engaged in electoral politics within the narrow limits defined by the constitution and whose goals included a "Natives First" campaign and an extension of the franchise to elect a more representative government.

In 1947 a group of graduates of the elite Saint John's College won control of the Belize City Council and started a newspaper, the *Belize Billboard.* One member of this group, George Cadle Price, topped the polls in the 1947 election when he opposed immigration schemes and import controls and rode a wave of feeling against a British proposal for a federation of its colonies in the Caribbean. Price was an eclectic and pragmatic politician whose ideological position was often obscured under a cloak of religious values and quotations. He has remained the predominant politician in the country since the early 1950s.

The event that precipitated Price's political career and the formation of the PUP was the devaluation of the British Honduras dollar on December 31, 1949. In September 1949, the British government devalued the British pound sterling. In spite of repeated denials by the governor that the British Honduras dollar would be devalued to maintain the old exchange rate with the British pound, devaluation was nevertheless effected by the governor, using his reserve powers in defiance of the Legislative Council. The governor's action angered the nationalists because it reflected the limits of the legislature and revealed the extent of the colonial administration's power. The devaluation enraged labor because it protected the interests of the big transnationals, such as the Belize Estate and Produce Company, whose trade in British pounds would have suffered without devaluation. It subjected British Honduras's middle class, already experiencing widespread unemployment and poverty, to higher prices for goods—especially food—imported from the United States. Devaluation thus united labor, nationalists, and the Creole middle classes in opposition to the colonial administration. On the night that the governor declared the devaluation, the People's Committee was formed and the nascent independence movement suddenly matured.

Between 1950 and 1954, the PUP, formed upon the dissolution of the People's Committee on September 29, 1950, consolidated its organization, established its popular base, and articulated its primary demands. *Belize Billboard* editors Philip Goldson and Leigh Richardson were prominent members of the PUP. They gave the party their full support through anticolonial editorials. The PUP received the crucial support of the GWU, whose president, Clifford Betson, was one of the original members of the People's Committee. Before the end of January 1950, the GWU and the People's Committee were holding joint public meetings and discussing issues such as devaluation, labor legislation, the proposed West Indies Federation, and constitutional reform. Because the GWU was the only mass organization of working people, the early success of the PUP would have been impossible without the support of this union. On April 28, however, the middle-class members of the People's Committee (formerly members of the Christian Social Action Group, to which the founders of the *Belize Billboard* belonged) took over the leadership of the union and gave Betson the dubious honorific title of "patriarch of the union." A year later, George Price, the secretary of the PUP, became vice president of the union. The political leaders took control of the union to use its strength, but the union movement declined as it became increasingly dependent upon politicians in the 1950s.

The PUP concentrated on agitating for constitutional reforms, including universal adult suffrage without a literacy test, an all-elected Legislative Council, an Executive Council chosen by the leader of the majority party in the legislature, the introduction of a ministerial system, and the abolition of the governor's reserve powers. In short, the PUP pushed for representative and responsible government. The colonial administration, alarmed by the growing support for the PUP, retaliated by attacking two of the party's chief public platforms. In July 1951, the governor dissolved the Belize City Council on the pretext that it had shown disloyalty by refusing to display a picture of King George VI. Then, in October, the governor charged *Belize Billboard* publishers and owners, including Richardson and Goldson, with sedition. The governor jailed them for twelve months with hard labor. Soon after, PUP leader John Smith resigned because the party would not agree to fly the British flag at public meetings. The removal of three of four chief leaders was a blow to the party, but the events left Price in a powerful position. In 1952 he comfortably topped the polls in Belize City Council elections. Within just two years, despite persecution and division, the PUP had become a powerful political force, and George Price had clearly become the party's leader.

The colonial administration and the National Party, which consisted of loyalist members of the Legislative Council, portrayed the PUP as pro-Guatemalan and even communist. The leaders of the PUP, however, perceived British Honduras as belonging to neither Britain nor Guatemala. The governor and the National Party failed in their attempts to discredit the PUP on the issue of its contacts with Guatemala, which was then ruled by the democratic, reformist government of President Jacobo Arbenz. When voters went to the polls on April 28, 1954, in the first election under universal literate adult suffrage, the main issue was clearly colonialism—a vote for the PUP was a vote in favor of self-government. Almost 70 percent of the electorate voted. The PUP gained 66.3 percent of the vote and won eight of the nine elected seats in the new Legislative Assembly. Further constitutional reform was unequivocally on the agenda.

Decolonization and the Border Dispute with Guatemala

British Honduras faced two obstacles to independence: British reluctance until the early 1960s to allow citizens to govern themselves, and Guatemala's complete intransigence over its long-standing claim to the entire territory (Guatemala had repeatedly threatened to use force to take over British Honduras). By 1961 Britain was willing to let the colony become independent. From 1964 Britain controlled only defense, foreign affairs, internal security, and the terms and conditions of the public service. On June 1, 1973, the colony's name was changed to Belize in anticipation of independence. After 1975 Britain allowed the colonial government to internationalize its case for independence, so Belizeans participated in international diplomacy even before the area became a sovereign nation. The stalemate in the protracted negotiations between Britain and Guatemala over the future status of Belize led Belizeans to seek the international community's assistance in resolving issues associated with independence. Even after Belize became independent in 1981, however, the territorial dispute remained unsettled.

The territorial dispute's origins lay in the eighteenth-century treaties in which Britain acceded to Spain's assertion of sovereignty while British settlers continued to occupy the sparsely settled and ill-defined area (see Colonial Rivalry Between Spain and Britain, this ch.). The 1786 Convention of London, which affirmed Spanish sovereignty, was never renegotiated, but Spain never attempted to reclaim the area after 1798. Subsequent treaties between Britain and Spain failed to mention the British settlement. By the time Spain lost control of Mexico and Central America in 1821, Britain had extended its control over the area, albeit informally and unsystematically. By the 1830s, Britain regarded the entire territory between the Hondo River and Sarstoon River as British.

The independent republics that emerged from the disintegrating Spanish Empire in the 1820s claimed that they had inherited Spain's sovereign rights in the area. Britain, however, never accepted such a doctrine. Based on this doctrine of inheritance, Mexico and Guatemala asserted claims to Belize. Mexico once claimed the portion of British Honduras north of the Sibun River but dropped the claim in a treaty with Britain in 1893. Since then, Mexico has stated that it would revive the claim only if Guatemala were successful in obtaining all or part of the nation. Still, Mexico was the first nation to recognize Belize as an independent country.

At the center of Guatemala's claim was the 1859 treaty between Britain and Guatemala. From Britain's viewpoint, this treaty merely settled the boundaries of an area already under British dominion. But Guatemala later developed the view that this agreement was a treaty of cession through which Guatemala would give up its territorial claims only under certain conditions, including the construction of a road from Guatemala to the Caribbean coast. Guatemala said it would repudiate the treaty in 1884 but never followed up on the threat. The dispute appeared to have been forgotten until the 1930s, when the government of General Jorge Ubico claimed that the treaty was invalid because the road had not been constructed. Britain argued that because neither the short-lived Central American Federation (1821–39) nor Guatemala had ever exercised any authority in the area or even protested the British presence in the nineteenth century, British Honduras was clearly under British sovereignty. In its constitution of 1945, however, Guatemala stated that British Honduras was the twenty-third department of Guatemala. Since 1954 a succession of military and right-wing governments in Guatemala frequently whipped up nationalist sentiment, generally to divert attention from domestic problems. Guatemala periodically massed troops on the border with Belize in a threatening posture.

Negotiations between Britain and Guatemala began again in 1961, but the elected representatives of British Honduras had no voice in these talks. George Price refused an invitation from Guatemalan President Ydígoras Fuentes to make British Honduras an "associated state" of Guatemala. Price reiterated his goal of leading the colony to independence. In 1963 Guatemala broke off talks and ended diplomatic relations with Britain. In 1965 Britain and Guatemala agreed to have a United States lawyer, appointed by President Lyndon Johnson, mediate the dispute. The lawyer's draft treaty proposed giving Guatemala so much control over the newly independent country, including internal security, defense, and external affairs, that Belize would have become more dependent on Guatemala than it was already on Britain. The United States supported the proposals. All parties in British Honduras, however, denounced the proposals, and Price seized the initiative by demanding independence from Britain with appropriate defense guarantees.

A series of meetings, begun in 1969, ended abruptly in 1972 when Britain announced it was sending an aircraft carrier and 8,000 troops to Belize to conduct amphibious exercises. Guatemala then massed troops on the border. Talks resumed between 1973 and 1975 but again broke off as tensions flared. At this point, the Belizean and British governments, frustrated at dealing with the military-dominated regimes in Guatemala, agreed on a new strategy that would take the case for self-determination to various international forums. The Belize government felt that by gaining international support, it could strengthen its position, weaken Guatemala's claims, and make it harder for Britain to make any concessions.

Belize argued that Guatemala frustrated the country's legitimate aspirations to independence and that Guatemala was pushing an irrelevant claim and disguising its own colonial ambitions by trying to present the dispute as an effort to recover territory lost to a colonial power. Between 1975 and 1981, Belizean leaders stated their case for self-determination at a meeting of the heads of Commonwealth of Nations governments in Jamaica, the conference of ministers of the Nonaligned Movement in Peru, and at meetings of the United Nations (UN). The support of the Nonaligned Movement proved crucial and assured success at the UN.

Latin American governments initially supported Guatemala. Cuba was the first Latin country, in December 1975, to support

Belize in a UN vote that affirmed Belize's right to self-determination, independence, and territorial integrity. The outgoing Mexican president, Luis Echeverría Alvarez, indicated that Mexico would appeal to the Security Council to prevent Guatemala's designs on Belize from threatening peace in the area. In 1976 President Omar Torrijos of Panama began campaigning for Belize's cause, and in 1979 the Sandinista government in Nicaragua declared unequivocal support for an independent Belize.

In each of the annual votes on this issue in the UN, the United States abstained, thereby giving the Guatemalan government some hope that it would retain United States backing. Finally, in November 1980, with Guatemala completely isolated, the UN passed a resolution that demanded the independence of Belize, with all its territory intact, before the next session of the UN in 1981. The UN called on Britain to continue defending the new nation of Belize. It also called on all member countries to offer their assistance.

A last attempt was made to reach an agreement with Guatemala prior to the independence of Belize. The Belizean representatives to the talks made no concessions, and a proposal, called the Heads of Agreement, was initialed on March 11, 1981. However, when ultraright political forces in Guatemala labeled the proposals a sellout, the Guatemalan government refused to ratify the agreement and withdrew from the negotiations. Meanwhile, the opposition in Belize engaged in violent demonstrations against the Heads of Agreement. The demonstrations resulted in four deaths, many injuries, and damage to the property of PUP leaders and their families. A state of emergency was declared. However, the opposition could offer no real alternatives. With the prospect of independence celebrations in the offing, the opposition's morale fell. Independence came to Belize on September 21, 1981, without reaching an agreement with Guatemala (see Relations with Guatemala, ch. 9).

* * *

A good general study of Belize that is historical in its perspective is O. Nigel Bolland's *Belize: A New Nation in Central America.* Narda Dobson's *A History of Belize* is fairly comprehensive but rather dated. More specific studies, in terms of the period or topic covered, include Grant D. Jones's *Maya Resistance to Spanish Rule: Time and History on a Colonial Frontier,* R.A. Humphreys's *The Diplomatic History of British Honduras, 1638–1901,* and Wayne M. Clegern's *British Honduras: Colonial Dead End, 1859–1900.* Humphreys examines the relations between Britain and Spain in the settlement's early years and between Britain and British Honduras's neighbors in the nineteenth century; Clegern focuses on economic and political changes in the late nineteenth century and pays special attention to boundary questions.

Three other books by Bolland analyze specific aspects of Belize's history: *Land in Belize, 1765–1871,* written with Assad Shoman, details the origins and development of the patterns of land use, the land laws, and the concentration of land ownership in the colony's formative years and includes a chapter on the legacy of the plantation economy in the 1970s; *The Formation of a Colonial Society: Belize from Conquest to Crown Colony* studies the social and economic conditions of Belize in the eighteenth and nineteenth centuries, including slavery and emancipation, and the rise and decline of the settlers' political economy; and *Colonialism and Resistance in Belize: Essays in Historical Sociology* is a collection of essays on various topics, including the social relations of the early British settlement, slavery, the emergence of Creole culture, the colonization of the Maya, labor conditions in the century after emancipation, the labor movement and the genesis of modern politics, and the problems of creating nationalism in a multiethnic society.

Cedric H. Grant's *The Making of Modern Belize: Politics, Society, and British Colonialism in Central America* examines in detail Belizean politics between 1950 and 1974, and Assad Shoman's *Party Politics in Belize, 1950–1986* analyses the emergence and development of the electoral and party system. J. Ann Zammit's *The Belize Issue* summarizes the dispute with Guatemala prior to Belize's independence. (For further information and complete citations, see Bibliography.)

Chapter 7. Belize: The Society and Its Environment

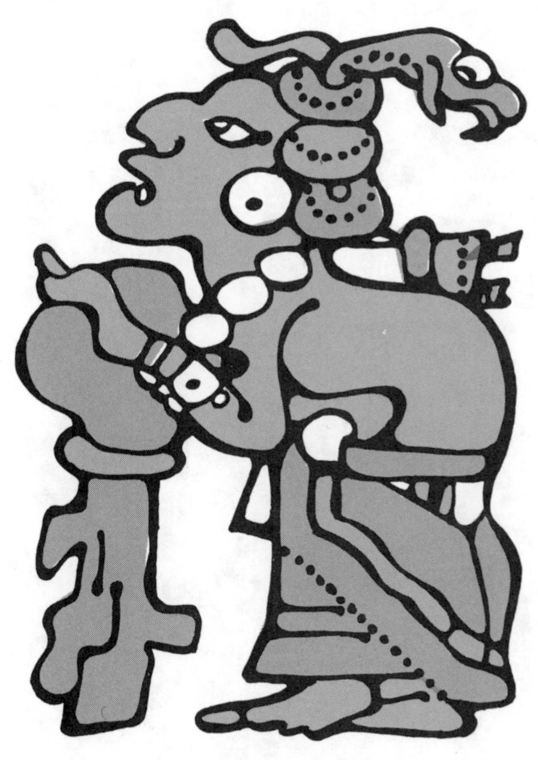

Ixchel, Mayan goddess of medicine and childbirth

BELIZE IS A CULTURAL ANOMALY in Central America, with a society oriented more to Britain, the English-speaking Caribbean countries, and North America than to neighboring Spanish-speaking republics. During the 1980s, efforts to forge a common national identity among a small, multiethnic population challenged the colonial orientations of Belizean society. Regional conflicts, migration, and intensified relationships with the United States also posed challenges.

The deepening of social, economic, and political ties to the United States during the 1980s prompted critics in Belize and abroad to complain that the country merely exchanged one colonial master for another. In addition, emigration of Belizeans to the United States and of Central Americans to Belize further challenged Belizean society, which was already deeply divided by differences of ethnicity, race, and class.

Geography

Boundaries, Area, and Relative Size

Belize is located on the Caribbean coast of northern Central America. It shares a border on the north with the Mexican state of Quintana Roo, on the west with the Guatemalan department of Petén, and on the south with the Guatemalan department of Izabal. To the east in the Caribbean Sea, the second-longest barrier reef in the world flanks much of the 386 kilometers of predominantly marshy coastline. Small cays (see Glossary) totaling about 690 square kilometers dot the reef. The area of the country totals 22,960 square kilometers, an area slightly larger than El Salvador or Massachusetts. The abundance of lagoons along the coasts and in the northern interior reduces the actual land area to 21,400 square kilometers (see fig. 11).

Belize is shaped like a rectangle that extends about 280 kilometers north-south and about 100 kilometers east-west, with a total land boundary length of 516 kilometers. The undulating courses of two rivers, the Hondo and the Sarstoon, define much of the course of the country's northern and southern boundaries. The western border follows no natural features and runs north-south through lowland forest and highland plateau.

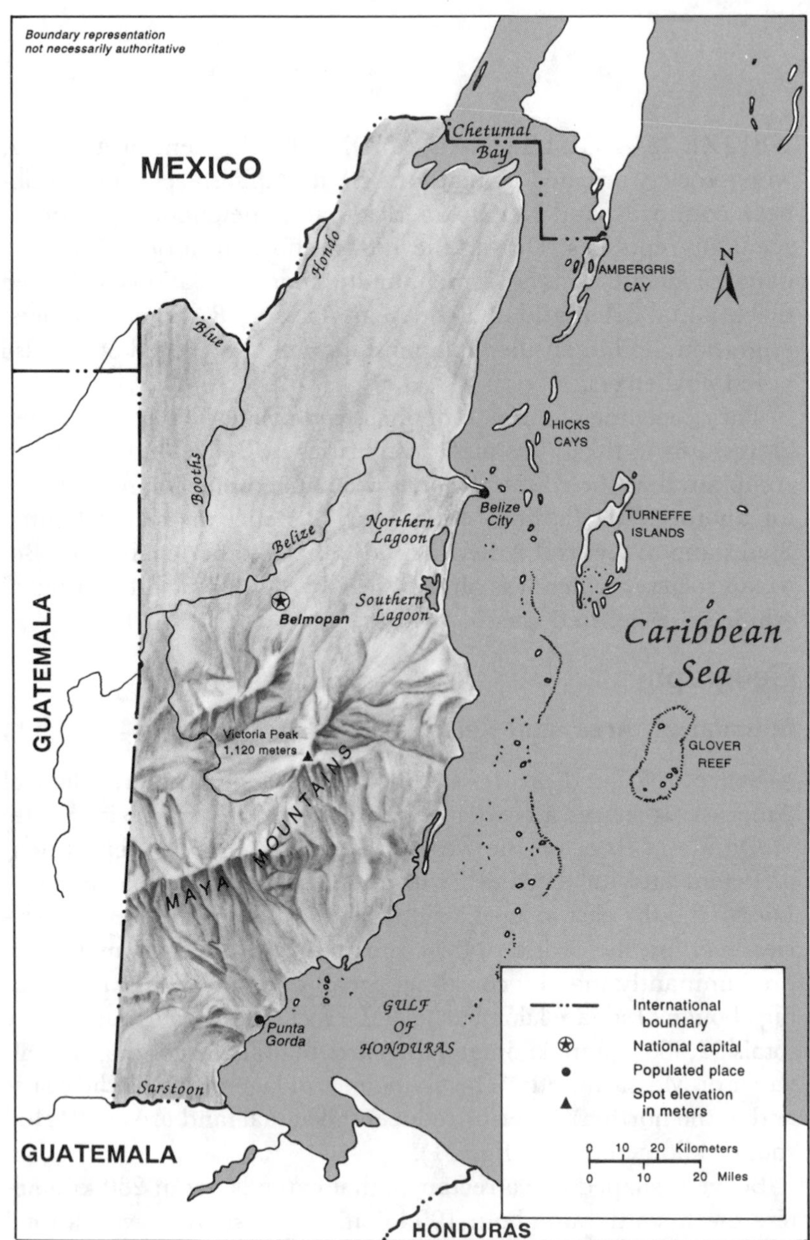

Figure 11. Belize: Topography and Drainage

Geology

Belizean geology consists largely of varieties of limestone, with the notable exception of the Maya Mountains, a large intrusive block of granite and other Paleozoic sediments running northeast to southwest across the south-central part of the country. Several major faults rive these highlands, but much of Belize lies outside the tectonically active zone that underlies most of Central America. During the Cretaceous period, what is now the western part of the Maya Mountains stood above sea level, creating the oldest land surface in Central America, the Mountain Pine Ridge plateau.

The hilly regions surrounding the Maya Mountains are formed from Cretaceous limestone. These areas are characterized by a karst topography that is typified by numerous sinkholes, caverns, and underground streams. In contrast to the Mountain Pine Ridge, some of the soils in these regions are quite fertile and have been cultivated during at least the past 4,000 years.

Much of the northern half of Belize lies on the Yucatán Platform, a tectonically stable region. Although mostly level, this part of the country also has occasional areas of hilly, karst terrain, such as the Yalbac Hills along the western border with Guatemala and the Manatee Hills between Belize City and Dangriga. Alluvial deposits of varying fertility cover the relatively flat landscapes of the coastal plains.

Physical Features

Topographical features divide the Belizean landscape into two main physiographic regions. The most visually striking of these regions is distinguished by the Maya Mountains and the associated basins and plateaus that dominate all but the narrow coastal plain in the southern half of the country. The mountains rise to heights of about 1,100 meters, with the highest point being Victoria Peak (1,120 meters) in the Cockscomb Mountains. Covered with shallow, highly erodible soils of low fertility, these heavily forested highlands are very sparsely inhabited.

The second region comprises the northern lowlands, along with the southern coastal plain. Eighteen major rivers and many perennial streams drain these low-lying areas. The coastline is flat and swampy, with many lagoons, especially in the northern and central parts of the country. Westward from the northern coastal areas, the terrain changes from mangrove swamp to tropical pine savannah and hardwood forest.

The interlocking networks of rivers, creeks, and lagoons have played a key role in the historical geography of Belize. The largest and most historically important river is the Belize, which drains more than one-quarter of the country as it winds along the northern edge of the Maya Mountains across the center of the country to the sea near Belize City. Also known as the Old River, the Belize River is navigable up to the Guatemalan border and served as the main artery of commerce and communication between the interior and the coast until well into the twentieth century. Other historically important rivers include the Sibun, which drains the northeastern edge of the Maya Mountains, and the New River, which flows through the northern sugar-growing areas before emptying into Chetumal Bay. Both of these river valleys possess fertile alluvial soils and have supported considerable cultivation and human settlement.

Natural Resources

Although a number of economically important minerals exist in Belize, none has been found in quantities large enough to warrant their mining (see Mining and Energy, ch. 8). These minerals include dolomite, barite (source of barium), bauxite (source of aluminum), cassite (source of tin), and gold. In 1990 limestone, used in roadbuilding, was the only mineral resource being exploited for either domestic or export use.

The similarity of Belizean geology to that of oil-producing areas of Mexico and Guatemala prompted oil companies, principally from the United States, to explore for petroleum at both offshore and on-land sites in the early 1980s. Initial results were promising, but the pace of exploration slowed later in the decade, and production operations never commenced. As a result, Belize remains almost totally dependent on imported petroleum for its energy needs. However, the country does possess considerable potential for hydroelectric and other renewable energy resources, such as solar and biomass. In the mid-1980s, one Belizean businessman even proposed the construction of a wood-burning power station for the production of electricity, but the idea foundered in the wake of ecological concerns and economic constraints.

Climate

Belize has a tropical climate with pronounced wet and dry seasons, although there are significant variations in weather patterns by region. Temperatures vary according to elevation, proximity to the coast, and the moderating effects of the northeast trade winds off the Caribbean. Average temperatures in the coastal regions range from 24°C in January to 27°C in July. Temperatures are slightly higher inland, except for the southern highland plateaus, such as the Mountain Pine Ridge, where it is noticeably cooler year round. Overall, the seasons are marked more by differences in humidity and rainfall than in temperature.

Average rainfall varies considerably, ranging from 1,350 millimeters in the north and west to over 4,500 millimeters in the extreme south. Seasonal differences in rainfall are greatest in the northern and central regions of the country where, between January and April or May, fewer than 100 millimeters of rain fall per month. The dry season is shorter in the south, normally only lasting from February to April. A shorter, less rainy period, known locally as the "little dry," usually occurs in late July or August, after the initial onset of the rainy season.

Hurricanes have played key—and devastating—roles in Belizean history. In 1931 an unnamed hurricane destroyed over two-thirds of the buildings in Belize City and killed more than 1,000 people. In 1955 Hurricane Janet leveled the northern town of Corozal. Only six years later, Hurricane Hattie struck the central coastal area of the country, with winds in excess of 300 kilometers per hour and four-meter storm tides. The devastation of Belize City for the second time in thirty years prompted the relocation of the capital some eighty kilometers inland to the planned city of Belmopan. The most recent hurricane to devastate Belize was Hurricane Greta, which caused more than US$25 million in damages along the southern coast in 1978.

Population and Settlement Patterns

Size, Growth, and Distribution

Perhaps the most pronounced feature of the Belizean population, aside from its ethnic heterogeneity, is its small size. In 1980 the population was estimated at approximately 145,000. Slightly more than 50 percent of the people resided in eight urban areas, with more than 30 percent in Belize City. By 1990, the pattern of population distribution had changed, with 51.8 percent of the approximately 191,000 Belizeans living in rural areas. The growth in the rural population during the 1980s stemmed primarily from the influx of Central American immigrants who had moved to Belize's countryside. Meanwhile, many urban Belizeans moved to the United States and elsewhere. Even with the increase in its overall population, Belize remained one of the least densely populated countries in the Americas, averaging 8.5 persons per square kilometer in 1991.

Belize is divided administratively into six districts: Corozal, Orange Walk, Belize, Cayo, Stann Creek, and Toledo (see fig. 9). In 1991, more than one in three Belizeans lived in Belize District

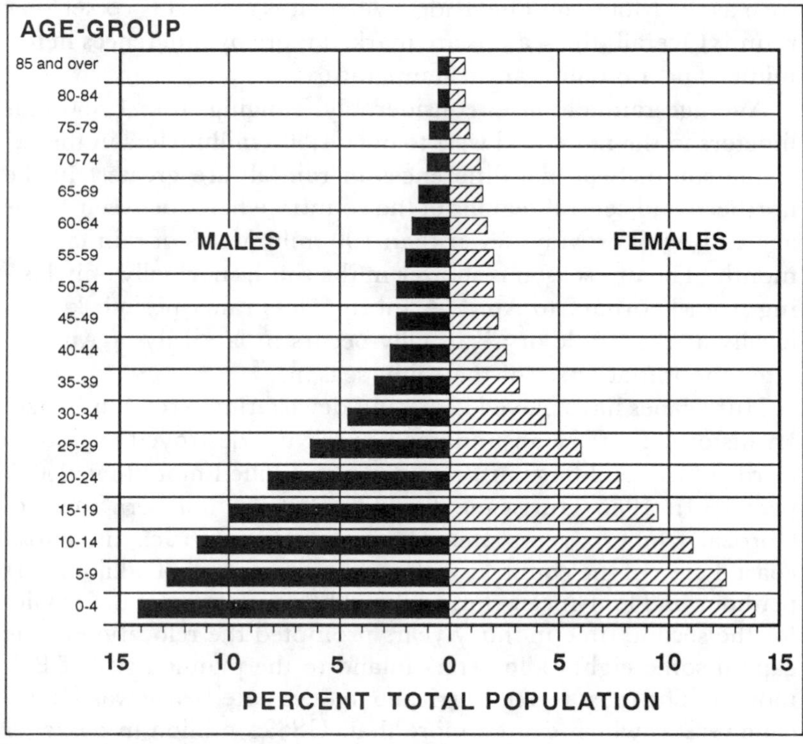

Source: Based on information from Federal Republic of Germany, Statistisches Bundesamt, *Länderbericht Belize, 1987*, Wiesbaden, 1987, 17.

Figure 12. Belize: Estimated Population by Age and Sex, 1986

(including Belize City), which had a population density five times greater than the least populated district, Toledo (see table 10, Appendix A).

As in many other developing societies, the Belizean population was unevenly divided by age and gender (see fig. 12). The ratio of males and females in the population has varied considerably over the last century. In the 1980s, males outnumbered females in most age groups. Shifts in the gender ratio have generally been attributed to changing migration patterns. In the 1940s and 1950s, the emigration stream was predominantly male, but in the 1980s women emigrants outnumbered men.

Consistent with the demographic profile of most developing nations was the general youthfulness of the Belizean population. In 1990 some 46 percent of Belizeans were fourteen years of age or younger and some 58 percent were under the age of twenty.

Regular declines in the death rate have steadily increased the proportion of the population sixty-five years of age and older, to 4.6 percent in 1980.

The average crude birthrate for Belize experienced slow but steady decline, from 44.1 per 1,000 population in 1963 to 35.0 per 1,000 in 1990. The average fertility rate also dropped from nearly 7 children per woman in the late 1960s to 5.4 in 1985. Coupled with declining death and infant mortality rates, the high birthrate between 1970 and 1980 indicated a potential population increase of more than 3.0 percent for the decade. However, the actual increase between 1970 and 1980 was only 1.9 percent, indicating a very high rate of emigration, perhaps involving as many as one in every eight Belizeans. During the 1980s, the rate of natural population increase was about 3.0 percent for the decade. The difference between projected and actual population increase for the period 1980–90 was considerably less than in the 1970s, as the actual rate of increase was some 2.4 percent. The closer correspondence of these two figures reflected not so much a decline in emigration by Belizeans, as the scale and demographic impact of the immigration from the surrounding Central American republics.

Migration

Continuous migration has made it difficult to determine accurately the size and social composition of the Belizean population and to project future growth. Although small numbers of Belizeans have emigrated to Britain, Canada, and the West Indies (see Glossary), the principal destination of most Belizean emigrants has been the United States. Estimates of the Belizean population in the United States have varied between 30,000 and 100,000. The United States Embassy in Belize has estimated that in 1984, about 55,000 Belizeans were residing in the United States, with two of three living there illegally. Settling primarily in New York City, Los Angeles, Chicago, Miami, and New Orleans, most of these emigrants were either Creole (see Glossary) or Garifuna (see Glossary). Their remittances, estimated at US$11 million in 1984, played an important role in the subsistence of many Belizean households, especially in Belize City and Dangriga. Later estimates were that as many as 65,000 Belizeans were living in the United States by mid-1988, with the majority ranging in age from twenty to thirty-four.

Estimates of the immigrant population in Belize also varied widely. According to the 1980 census, more than 10 percent of the population, or roughly 15,000 people, were born in other countries. One of two immigrants came from either Guatemala, Mexico, Honduras, or El Salvador. By the late 1980s, these figures were considerably higher because immigration continued, albeit on a lesser scale, over the course of the decade. The percentages of immigrants who were from Mexico and Central America, the numbers of foreign-born refugees, and the numbers of Belizeans who had been born in other countries all increased. The number of Salvadoran refugees living in Belize was estimated at between 2,000 and 15,000 in the late 1980s, and recent studies claim that between 25,000 and 31,000 citizens of neighboring republics had entered the country since 1977.

The presence of these "aliens," as they were popularly known, was visible in Belize. As of 1991, Salvadoran and Guatemalan vendors lined the sidewalks of Belize City's main commercial street and were prominent in the marketplaces of Orange Walk, Dangriga, and especially the capital, Belmopan. Belizeans derisively dubbed a recently developed satellite shantytown in Belmopan as "Salvapan." Along the remote Hummingbird and Southern highways, the fields of the new migrants cut dramatic swaths in the previously uninhabited forest. This situation raised environmentalists' concerns about soil erosion. Although Central American immigrants have settled throughout the country, they have been most heavily concentrated in the rural areas of Cayo and Toledo districts.

The emigration of English-speaking Creoles and Garifuna to the United States and the immigration of Spanish-speaking Mestizos (see Glossary) from Central America exacerbated ethnic tensions and challenged long-held assumptions regarding the character of Belizean culture, which has traditionally been oriented toward the English-speaking Caribbean. Although they comprised only 40 percent of the total population in 1980, Creoles long considered Belize "their" country—black, English-speaking, and Protestant. Moreover, Guatemala's persistent claim to Belize's territory caused many Belizeans, especially Creoles, to be antagonistic toward Hispanic culture. A key problem in the drive toward building the Belizean nation was the substitution of an ideology of cultural pluralism for undisputed Creole cultural dominance. Neither educational efforts nor political rhetoric has been completely successful in this regard. Indeed, by the early 1990s, many Belizeans were apprehensive of increasing ethnic tension.

The Cultural Diversity of Belizean Society

Ethnicity

The most salient characteristic of Belizean society in the late 1980s was ethnic diversity. Ethnicity in Belize was not reduced to race,

Low-lying land and numerous canals have made Belize City vulnerable to flooding in hurricanes.
Courtesy Steven R. Harper

but instead referred to the collective identities formed through a complex interplay of racial, linguistic, and religious factors, as well as a sense of shared history and custom.

The two largest ethnic groups together constituted almost three-quarters of the population (see table 11, Appendix A). The 1980 census listed 39.7 percent of the population as Creole, a group usually defined as English speakers descended wholly or in part from African slaves imported to work in the colonial mahogany industry. The 1980 census combined the previously separate "black" and "coloured" segments of the population into a single group. Consequently, there was considerable physical diversity among people listed as Creole. A folk system of racial classification further hierarchically divided Creoles on the basis of such physical features as skin shade, facial features, and hair texture. Despite political independence, the colonial social bias toward "clear," or light, skin and European features endured in contemporary Belizean society.

The second largest group, comprising one-third of the population, was identified as Mestizos, or persons of mixed Hispanic-Amerindian origin. In the local Creole vernacular, the Mestizos were known as "Spanish." The physical appearance of the Mestizos varied, but not to the extent that it varied among Creoles. Most Belizean Mestizos were descended from refugees of the mid-nineteenth-century Caste War of Yucatán (see Mayan Emigration and Conflict, ch. 6). The majority of them settled in the northern districts of Corozal and Orange Walk, where they initiated the cultivation of sugarcane in Belize.

Migration during the 1980s had a major impact on the demographic balance between the two largest ethnic groups. As of 1991, the government had not released figures on ethnic identity from the 1990 census, but census officials predicted that Mestizos would equal or outnumber Creoles.

The third largest ethnic population comprised three distinct groups: the Yucatecan, Mopán, and Kekchí Maya. In 1980 one in ten Belizeans belonged to one of the three groups. Belizeans commonly referred to the Yucatecan and Mopán peoples as Maya. Contrary to the statements of colonial historians, some of these Mayan peoples were indeed descendants of the inhabitants of pre-Columbian Belize. Most Kekchí and Mopán, however, emigrated from Guatemala in the late nineteenth century.

The Garifuna, formerly known as the Black Carib, were Belize's fourth largest ethnic grouping, constituting 7 percent of the population in 1980. Descended from African slaves who intermarried with Amerindian inhabitants of the eastern Caribbean islands, the Garifuna were deported to the Gulf of Honduras by the British in the late eighteenth century (see Emigration of the Garifuna, ch. 6). Some Garifuna migrated to the southern Belizean coast, where they established five major settlements. Initially fishermen and subsistence farmers, the Garifuna were gradually incorporated into wage labor in the mahogany industry as early as the 1820s, and later on in the banana and citrus plantations that developed in the Stann Creek Valley and elsewhere in the early twentieth century. Over the course of the twentieth century, an increasing number of Garifuna men became migrant workers, first along the Caribbean coast of Central America, and later in the United States.

Smaller ethnic groups—East Indians (whose forebears came from present-day India), Arabs, Chinese, and Euro-Americans, including a sizeable community of German-speaking Mennonites—made up the remaining 10 present of Belize's population. Of these groups, the East Indian population was the largest. The East Indians were largely descendants of nineteenth-century indentured laborers imported to work the sugar plantations of the Corozal and Toledo districts. By the late 1980s, they had intermarried extensively with other ethnic groups, and, for the most part, they no longer

Queen Street, Belize City, with main post office on right
Courtesy Steven R. Harper

possessed an identifiably East Indian culture. They lived in all of the country's six districts, but were concentrated in Toledo.

There was a second, and much smaller, East Indian community in Belize, composed of Hindi-speaking traders who had immigrated to Belize from Bombay in the 1960s. Living primarily in Belize City and Orange Walk, they formed an aloof, close-knit community that, by the late 1980s, dominated Belize City retail trade and played a major role in currency exchange and speculation.

The smallest ethnic groups—Arabs and Chinese—were also exclusively urban, mercantile populations. Known variously as Turks, Syrians, and Lebanese, many Belizean Arabs were actually Palestinian. Immigrating to Belize in the late nineteenth and early twentieth centuries, they figured prominently as merchants in the Belize and Cayo districts.

A significant number of Chinese were imported as contract laborers in the nineteenth century, but virtually all Chinese people living in Belize in the early 1990s came to the country in the twentieth century. Most resided in Belize City, but at least a few Chinese families lived in every major town. Some were merchants, but most worked in the restaurant and lottery industries. In the late 1980s, the Chinese population increased dramatically because of immigration from Hong Kong and Taiwan.

Belize's small, German-speaking Mennonite population emigrated from Mexico between 1958 and 1962. Numbering more than 5,000, the Mennonites founded numerous settlements in the Orange Walk, Cayo, and Toledo districts. The government granted them complete autonomy over their communities. Nevertheless, they have been slowly integrated into the life of the nation, particularly into the economy. The more progressive Mennonites of Spanish Lookout (Cayo District) and Blue Creek (Orange Walk District) became important suppliers of poultry, eggs, dairy products, and furniture. Still, they remained exempt from military service and were not allowed to vote.

Aside from the Mennonites, the majority of Belize's small white population were British and United States expatriates. Unlike some other Caribbean societies, Belize never supported a large European settler community during the colonial period. Since independence, a large, transient population of United States and British volunteers and international aid personnel has augmented the local European population. In 1986 the United States Peace Corps alone had more than 200 volunteers, the corps's highest volunteer-to-population ratio in the world. By 1991, however, the number of Peace Corps volunteers had dropped to less than 100.

The distribution of officially recognized ethnic groups was highly skewed by region, and each district had its own characteristic cultural orientation. Creoles made up three-quarters of the population of Belize City and the surrounding area but no more than one-third of the population in the other five districts. Mestizos constituted two-thirds of the people in the northern sugar-producing districts of Orange Walk and Corozal, one-half the population of the predominantly agricultural Cayo district, but only about one-tenth of the population in Belize, Stann Creek, and Toledo. Garifuna lived mostly along the coasts of the two southernmost districts of Stann Creek and Toledo; they made up fewer than 3 percent of the population in any of the other four districts. The majority of the country's diverse Mayan population resided mainly in the interior of Toledo (where they constituted some 57 percent of the district's people) and the rural areas of Stann Creek, Orange Walk, and Corozal.

Language

English was the only official language in Belize, but other languages were commonplace. The 1980 census revealed that slightly more than one-half the population spoke English as their first language, and approximately one-third spoke Spanish. In the Corozal and Orange Walk districts, Spanish was the first language of 75 percent of the population, and fewer than 20 percent spoke English by preference. Smaller numbers spoke Mayan dialects, Garifuna, and Low German. The census also estimated that some 62 percent of all Belizeans were bilingual or trilingual. As much as 80 percent of the population was able to speak some English.

The census, however, failed to differentiate between standard English and the local vernacular, Belizean Creole. Some of the people considered to be English speakers could speak only Belizean Creole, or "Broad Creole," whereas others spoke standard English as well. Language competency was largely related to social stratification. English speakers of higher socioeconomic status and education could switch with relative ease between standard English and Belizean Creole. The English-speaking urban and rural poor possessed more limited degrees of competency in standard English.

Linguistic diversity among the English-speaking population reflected and perpetuated social inequality. In Belizean schools, for example, standard English was the sole language of instruction. Studies have shown that students who came to school lacking proficiency in standard English suffered significant problems in comprehension and were often classified by teachers as slow, or problem learners.

Religion

Observers frequently note that Belizeans are a particularly religious people, with almost all the population declaring a specific religious preference in 1980. Indeed, religious institutions were a ubiquitous presence in Belize, especially in the school system, which the Roman Catholic Church and the state managed together. Belize was no longer the intense battleground between competing missionary denominations that it had been in the late nineteenth and early twentieth centuries. Nonetheless, numerous foreign missionaries, mostly evangelical Protestants from the United States, worked in the country in the 1980s.

Of the country's nine major religious groups, the Roman Catholics were the largest, with more than three in five Belizeans claiming to be followers (see table 12, Appendix A). Anglicans and Methodists comprised the two largest Protestant denominations, although they were steadily losing ground to fundamentalist and evangelical sects, such as the Pentecostalists and Seventh-Day Adventists.

Religion was strongly—but not exclusively—associated with ethnicity and region. Catholicism unified most Mestizos, Maya, and Garifuna. Most Creoles were either Anglican or Methodist, but a significant number converted to Roman Catholicism, mainly because of proselytization in Roman Catholic schools. Roman Catholics made up at least 70 percent of the population of all districts, but in Belize City and environs, they made up only 43 percent of the population. In the last two decades, however, evangelical Protestant groups have been particularly successful in making inroads among Creoles, Mestizos, and Maya in Corozal, Orange Walk, and Cayo districts.

A wide range of smaller denominations also flourished in Belize. These groups included Mormons, fundamentalist Protestants, Hindus, and Bahais. Among the Creoles and the Garifuna, there were also small, but socially significant, Black Muslim and Rastafarian (see Glossary) communities.

Official census categories, however, oversimplified religious identity in Belize. Some syncretic beliefs and practices could not be easily categorized. Many Garifuna, for example, although nominally Catholic, continued to uphold their traditional beliefs and practices, such as the *dugu* ritual, through which they honored their ancestors and perpetuated their distinctive cultural identity. The Catholicism of many Maya was similarly inflected with aspects of their own cultural traditions. Among Creoles, the belief in obeah, or witchcraft, endured, particularly among the older generations of the urban and rural poor.

Cultural Pluralism and Ethnic Diversity

Belize might appear to be the archetypical postcolonial "plural society," a mosaic of discrete cultural groups with their own value systems and institutional forms, joined together only by the forces of the marketplace and coercive authority. Indeed, a number of scholars have described Belize as split between two cultural complexes—one English-speaking, and Creole, and the other Spanish-speaking, and Mestizo. Belizean social and cultural diversity was, however, much more complex than this bipolar model suggests. Language and religion cut across ethnic and racial categories. Moreover, race was a complex and elusive concept. For example, both Creoles and Garifuna shared an African heritage, but they were culturally different and had a long-standing enmity toward each other.

Ethnic boundaries in Belize were also notoriously fuzzy. Intermarriage between members of different groups has historically been widespread. Identification of people of mixed ancestry varied considerably; one recent survey of secondary-school students found eight different permutations of Creole identity alone. This variability was not limited to Creoles. Some urban, European-looking Spanish-speakers identified themselves as Maya; many Mestizos

Saint John's Cathedral (Anglican)
Albert Street, Belize City
Courtesy Steven R. Harper

Kingdom Hall of Jehovah's Witnesses,
Regent Street, Belize City
Courtesy Steven R. Harper

no longer spoke Spanish in the home or had become evangelical Protestants.

Not all individuals of multiple ancestries felt comfortable identifying with a particular ethnic group; in the words of one Belizean youth, many Belizeans were "all mix up." A small, but significant number of people eschewed potentially divisive ethnic categories and referred to themselves simply as "Belizeans." Ethnicity competed with other identities, such as those based on status, occupation, and political affiliation, for primacy in social interaction. Belizean society was as divided by class differences as it was by race, language, religion, and ethnicity.

Structure of Belizean Society

Belizean society in the early 1990s was marked by enduring differences in the distribution of wealth, power, and prestige. However, because of the small size of Belize's population and the intimate scale of social relations, the social distance between the rich and the poor, although significant, was nowhere as vast as in other Caribbean and Central American societies, such as Jamaica and El Salvador. Indeed, Belize lacked the violent class and racial conflict that has figured so prominently in the social life of its Central American neighbors.

Still, a decade after independence, political and economic power remained vested in the hands of a relatively small local elite, most of whom were either white, light-skinned Creole, or Mestizo. The sizable middle group, however, was composed of peoples of different ethnic backgrounds. This middle group did not constitute a unified social class, but rather a number of middle- and working-class groups, loosely oriented around shared dispositions toward education, cultural respectability, and possibilities for upward social mobility. These beliefs, and the social practices they engendered, helped distinguish the middle group from the grass roots majority of the Belizean people.

The Upper Sector

In the late 1980s, the elite was a small, socially distinct group whose base of social power lay not in landownership, but in its control of the institutions that mediated relations between Belize and the outside world. The principal economic interests of the elite included commercial and financial enterprises, retail trade, local manufacturing, the state apparatus, and, to a much lesser extent, export agriculture. Foreign firms dominated Belize's agricultural export industry, which was the largest sector of the economy in the 1980s. Foreigners, mostly United States citizens, held 90 percent of Belize's privately owned land, including most of the nation's prime agricultural areas and tourist facilities.

The Belizean elite consisted of people of different status, prestige, and ethnicity. At the top of the power hierarchy were local whites and light-skinned descendants of the nineteenth-century Creole elite. The next group consisted of Creole and Mestizo commercial and professional families whose ancestors first came to political and economic prominence during the late nineteenth and early twentieth centuries. Next in status were some of the Lebanese and Palestinian merchant families who had immigrated to Belize in the early twentieth century.

The more recently arrived Chinese and Indian families comprised another elite group, distinguished from the remaining upper sector by length of residence in the country and by cultural differences. Groups within the elite socialized primarily among themselves.

Shared economic interests and business dealings bonded the different segments of the elite. Other cultural factors also played a role. Intermarriage bound several of the elite families together, although usually without transgressing ethnic or religious boundaries. Religion also served as a partial unifying force; a number of the oldest and most prominent Creole families shared the Catholicism of the Mestizo commercial elite.

Because Belize City was the center of the nation's commercial life, the majority of elite families lived or maintained a residence there, although some prominent families were based in the district towns. In Belize City, elite families lived in the same ocean-front neighborhoods, belonged to the same social clubs, and enjoyed a similar lifestyle centered around the extravagant conspicuous consumption of imported goods.

Education also served to unify the upper sector of society. A generation ago, religious affiliation largely determined which schools children attended. With the decline of the Anglican and Methodist school systems, most elite children, regardless of faith, attended two of Belize's premier Catholic institutions, which provided secondary and postsecondary education. Even after the expansion of secondary and postsecondary schooling in the districts, many of the elite district families continued to send their offspring to Belize City for higher education.

Despite the establishment of a local institution of higher education in 1985, most elite youth attended universities abroad. Their choice of institutions reflected the changing dominant metropolitan cultural orientation of Belizean society. British universities attracted many of the college-bound members of the Belizean elite in the colonial period, but by 1990 the majority pursued their higher education in the United States or, to a lesser extent, in the West Indies.

The Middle Sector

The middle sector of Belizean society was considerably larger, more diverse, and less cohesive than the elite. People in this group lacked the jobs, social status, or economic assets that were typical of the elite, but they were still better off than the rest of society. Some families were "poor relations" of the elite class; others had acquired wealth and prestige over a few generations through higher education or economic success. This large group encompassed the traditional middle class as well as elements of the working classes: not only small businessmen, professionals, teachers, and mid-level civil servants, but also other government workers, smallholders, skilled manual workers, and commercial employees.

The middle sector was stratified according to wealth, level of education, and the status difference between manual and nonmanual occupations. Still, a shared belief system that emphasized cultural respectability, upward social mobility, and the importance of education unified this group. Even more than middle-class families, some working-class families often made great sacrifices to ensure that their children received the best and most extensive education possible.

The middle sector of Belizean society in the 1980s was largely the product of the massive expansion of educational opportunities and the corresponding growth of the "modern" sector of the economy between 1950 and 1980. But as an increasing number of Belizeans earned degrees from education institutions and as the local job market became saturated, families in this group became more concerned in the 1970s and 1980s with maintaining their social position than with upward social mobility. Faced with limited economic prospects in Belize, large numbers migrated to the United States.

The middle sector was culturally diverse and included members of all Belizean ethnic groups, although not in proportion to their numbers in the general population. Relatively few Mayan or Kekchí families, for example, belonged to either the middle or upper working classes. Historical correlations between occupation and ethnic identity endured in the 1980s despite social changes. Middle-sector Creoles were most likely to work in the professions, especially law and accounting, the civil service, and the skilled trades. Considerable numbers of Mestizos were employed by the government, as

Typical house on stilts on low-lying Cay Caulker
Pier and palms on offshore barrier reef island of Cay Caulker
Courtesy Steven R. Harper

well as in small business and farming. Garifuna were particularly well established in the teaching profession.

Ethnic and religious sentiments divided the middle sector to a certain extent. The nationalist movement of the 1950s drew most of its leaders from the Catholic-educated Creole and Mestizo middle class. The Protestant-educated Creole middle class, however, opposed the movement's anti-British, multicultural ethos and the projection of a Central American destiny for Belize. Still, political affiliation defied narrow ethnic or racial lines.

British and North American ideas, particularly those of the United States, largely shaped the beliefs and practices of the middle sector. These influences stemmed not only from the formal education system, but also from the popular culture of North America conveyed through the cinema, magazines, radio, television, and migration. These cultural ideas were as much African-American as Anglo-American. Beginning with the Black Power movement of the late 1960s and early 1970s, middle- and working-class Creole youth increasingly adopted an Afrocentric cultural consciousness that distinguished them both from their elders and other ethnic groups in Belizean society.

The Lower Sector

This sector comprised the bulk of the Belizean population and was popularly known as the grass roots or roots class. It, too, was stratified by occupation and ethnicity. The lower sector consisted of unskilled or semiskilled urban workers, subsistence farmers, agricultural laborers, and the unemployed. These people shared, in addition to poverty and generally poor living conditions, severely limited access to land, higher education, or any other opportunity to change their marginal status. Possibilities for mobility were a main dividing line between the middle and lower sectors of Belizean society.

The ethnic composition of the lower sector varied by region. Most of the country's urban poor lived in predominantly Creole Belize City. With a population four times the size of the next largest urban area, Belize City was home to over half of all unemployed Belizeans in 1980. Many of the employed were engaged in *ketch an kill* jobs, temporary unskilled manual labor. No more than two-thirds of the employed population in 1980 had full-time work.

Educational opportunities beyond the primary level were scarce for most poor urban families. Many children dropped out of school before completing their primary education. Children who finished school often lacked the grades or financial resources to attend secondary school. Because the government generally awarded scholarships according to academic performance rather than financial need, most poor Belizean families continued to lack access to education beyond the primary level.

In further contrast to the upper and middle sectors, many lower-sector households in Belize City were headed by single parents, usually women. Female workers generally received lower incomes than their male counterparts, and women experienced an unemployment rate 250 percent higher than men. In numerous cases, migration of both parents resulted in children being raised by siblings, older relatives, or friends of the family. Some of the more privileged members of Belizean society perceived that increases in juvenile delinquency, crime, and drug use among Belizean urban youth were directly attributable to breakdowns in family structure.

As with the population in general, a large percentage of the urban poor were young. Nationwide, over 40 percent of out-of-school youths aged fifteen to twenty-four lacked work, and youth unemployment rates in Belize City were even higher. Many unemployed youths in Belize City congregated on street corners or met in storefronts known as "bases." These young people were known as baseboys and basegirls. More privileged members of Belizean society tended to categorize baseboys and basegirls as criminals and delinquents, although the only thing many were guilty of was lacking opportunities for education and meaningful work.

Still, the lack of educational and employment prospects for the rural and urban poor in the 1980s did lead to dramatic increases in crime, especially in the drug trade. By the middle of the decade, Belize had become the fourth largest exporter (after Mexico, Colombia, and Jamaica) of marijuana to the United States. By 1987 crack cocaine and gangs had established a foothold among the youthful population of Belize City. By 1991 both gang membership and gang warfare had escalated dramatically, moving off the street corners of the poorer neighborhoods into the schools and major public spaces of Belize City. Gangs, drugs, and violence were the dominant realities with which nearly all Belizean urban youth, especially the poor, had to deal.

Extremely limited access to education and well-paying jobs characterized conditions for the poor in the district towns of Belize. But many people perceived the conditions in these towns as less severe than in Belize City. One exception was Orange Walk, which was known as Rambo Town, owing to the intensity of drug-related violence there in the mid-1980s.

The most limited opportunities for education and economic advancement were found in rural areas. Rural primary schools had much higher rates of absenteeism and attrition than urban schools, and all but three secondary schools were located in Belize City or the major district towns. Furthermore, the demands of agricultural work often prevented many children from attending school.

The rural poor were mostly Mayan and Mestizo subsistence farmers and agricultural laborers, although some Creole and Garifuna families were also included in this category. At the very bottom of both the rural and urban social hierarchies, however, were the Central American aliens who were employed in the lowest paid, least desirable occupations, such as unskilled labor in the sugar, citrus, banana, and marijuana industries.

Social Dynamics

Belize has adopted wholeheartedly, and with much popular support, the rhetoric and practices of the ideologies of development and consumerism, twin hallmarks of a modernizing society. Far-reaching changes have occurred in Belizean society over the last thirty years. The growth of educational opportunities and government employment has facilitated the emergence of a sizable middle class with expanding horizons of consumption. The meaning of education has also changed. Once revered as a scarce privilege guaranteeing social advancement, education is now perceived as a birthright and an essential tool for entering the job market.

Education, migration, and shifts in economic activity have enhanced the power and influence of previously marginal social groups and regions, particularly the Mestizos who inhabited the northern districts. Intermarriage and political mobilization have helped at times to cut across ethnic boundaries and create a nascent sense of national identity. Satellite television, tourism, and emigration have strengthened an already close connection with North America, and immigration has anchored Belize more firmly within Central America and its culture.

But not all of the changes have been positive. Many Belizeans of more than thirty years of age noted the breakdown of traditional notions of authority, respect, and propriety and the obsessive fascination of Belizean youth with North American material culture. Others blamed mass emigration for the dissolution of the Belizean family and a subsequent rise in juvenile delinquency and crime.

Ethnic tensions still regularly intruded into many areas of social interaction and indeed showed signs of intensifying. Possibilities for social mobility existed, but only for some individuals. The school system produced continuously growing numbers of graduates for whom jobs did not exist while it simultaneously excluded growing numbers of the poor from educational opportunity. Emigration to metropolitan countries often siphoned off people with the highest qualifications and the most ambitions, and immigration from neighboring republics promised to reshape the cultural orientation and, quite literally, the complexion of Belizean society.

As Belize entered the 1990s, it faced a number of serious challenges, some of which were common to all postcolonial societies and some of which were the product of the country's unique history and geography. Like other developing societies, Belize faced the challenge of meeting the expanding needs and desires of a rapidly growing population at a time when the country possessed limited natural, financial, and human resources.

Education

Belize's strategy for social development in the 1980s focused on increasing investments in formal education. On the surface, the achievements have been impressive; opportunities for all levels of schooling have greatly increased in the last thirty years. The number of schools grew, enrollment rates rose, and a record number of students graduated in 1990.

These statistics, however, provided only a partial picture. As in many other areas of the Caribbean, enrollments have lagged behind population growth since at least the early 1980s. Large numbers of the urban and rural poor continued to lack access to schooling or dropped out before completing their primary education. But even with high rates of attrition at the primary and secondary levels, the number of graduates exceeded the number of jobs, contributing to "credential inflation," underemployment, and emigration.

Most important, despite three decades of efforts to "decolonize" education, foreign influences in the structure and content of Belizean schooling remained significant during the 1980s. As in the colonial period, a joint partnership of church and state managed the school system, although the terms, nature, and balance of power within this partnership shifted significantly toward the national government, beginning in the 1960s. The Belizean state, however, continued to lack total control over all levels and aspects of schooling. Belize relied heavily on foreign institutions for maintenance and expansion of formal education. These institutions provided financing, staffing, curriculum, planning, and higher education.

The growth and transformation of Belizean education took place in a number of phases, each related to important changes within the political and economic history of the country. During the initial phase, between 1816 and 1892, the church-state partnership became institutionalized. Religious initiative and control, extremely limited state intervention, and vigorous competition of religious denominations for the allegiance of the inhabitants characterized this phase.

The intensification of denominational rivalry, the benign neglect of the colonial state, and the growing influence of United States Jesuit missionaries in education characterized the second phase, which lasted from 1893 to 1934. In 1934 the director of education in Jamaica made a thorough investigation of British Honduras's education system. Various reforms were proposed to increase spending on the school system and improve the standard of education. Implementation of many of these reforms began in the late 1930s.

During the next phase, from the late 1940s and early 1950s, the educational and social activities of the Jesuits influenced the rise of an anti-British, anticolonial nationalist movement. In the late 1950s and early 1960s, Jesuits led efforts to redress the elitist, urban-centered biases of postprimary education that had perpetuated not only social inequality, but also the historical dominance of Belize City over its primarily rural hinterland. By the late 1950s, the Jesuits had emerged as the dominant influence at almost every level of formal education.

With the advent of a large degree of self-rule in 1964, the government began to assert its control over schooling. Formal control over education policy and planning passed from British-born clerics and colonial administrators to British-trained Belizeans. Actual education practice, however, changed very little; the religious denominations continued to determine the direction and pace of educational expansion. United States influence within Belizean schools intensified, not only through the adoption of certain Jesuit practices for systemwide use, but also through the arrival of Peace Corps and other United States volunteer teachers and agencies such as CARE and the Michigan Partners.

As the demand for education outstripped the capacities of the churches—even the Jesuits—to provide it, interdenominational cooperation grew and the state assumed a more central role. By the 1970s, the Belizean government had assumed the leading role in establishing new schools, especially at the secondary and tertiary levels. The government conceived of education as an essential tool in the peaceful struggle for independence. But the expansion of educational opportunities outstripped the state's resources, leading to an intensified reliance on external aid. Since 1981, the United States has provided the bulk of this aid. This situation caused many Belizeans to fear the rise of a new form of imperialist control over the country.

Nowhere were fears of recolonization more realized than in higher education. In 1979 the ruling People's United Party (PUP) government established the Belize College of Arts, Science, and Technology

Students at Belmopan Infant School
Courtesy Steven R. Harper

(Belcast) with the intention of breaking Belize's dependence on the outside world for university education. The PUP envisioned Belcast as a government-run institution, with no participation from the church. Funding was secured from the European Economic Community for the construction of a campus in Belmopan.

The campus was never built because the PUP was swept out of office in a landslide victory for the rival United Democratic Party (UDP) in December 1984. The UDP revoked the Belcast ordinance and invited Ferris State College of Big Rapids, Michigan to establish and manage a new institution, the University College of Belize (UCB). Control over the UCB program rested not with Belizeans, but with the administration of Ferris State College. The birth of UCB embodied Belizean nationalists' worst fears: the country had lost sovereignty over an institution that symbolized Belize's first major effort to break from the country's colonial past in the education sector. The intense controversy arose again in 1991 when it was discovered that Ferris State College had failed to obtain proper accreditation for the UCB program, thus placing into question the value of the degrees UCB had granted since 1987. Following this controversy, the new PUP government revoked its agreement with Ferris State and assumed full control over the institution.

School System

The Belizean school system was a loose aggregate of education subsystems. The system was based on British education and was broken into three levels: primary, secondary, and tertiary. Belizean children began their eight years of primary education with two years of "infant" classes, followed by six "standards." Secondary education was divided into four "forms." Sixth form was a two-year postsecondary course, originally intended to prepare students for the Cambridge Advanced, or "A-Level," examinations. Since the early 1970s, sixth-form institutions have also bestowed Associate of Arts degrees sanctioned by the United States Association of Junior Colleges (see table 13, Appendix A).

In addition to UCB, other postsecondary institutions included Belize Teachers' College, the Belize School of Nursing, and the Belize College of Agriculture. Belize contributes to and participates in the multinational University of the West Indies. The University of the West Indies also maintained a small extramural department in Belize City.

Management of the system varied according to level. In the latter half of the 1980s, religious denominations controlled the majority of primary schools, but the government or private, community-based boards of governors administered more than 50 percent of the secondary institutions. The preponderance of government institutions at the secondary level was a relatively new development; as recently as 1980, the majority of secondary schools were under religious management. Still, denominational representatives retained considerable influence on the managing boards of private, ostensibly nondenominational, institutions.

Secondary schools also differed according to curriculum and cultural orientation. Most private and denominational schools emphasized academic and commercial studies, although some also offered technical-vocational programs. In contrast, the government directly managed nine schools, all of which offered a curriculum oriented to technical-vocational subjects.

In terms of cultural orientation, educational practices, rituals, and valuative criteria spread to Belize's schools from Jesuit institutions in the United States. Jesuit influence even affected such traditional bastions of British pedagogy as the Anglican and Methodist secondary schools and the government-run Belize Technical College. Nearly thirty years of Peace Corps and other United States volunteer teachers have also influenced Belizean educational culture. Technical-vocational education programs by the United States Agency for International Development promise to erode further British pedagogical legacies.

Students at Saint John's College (First Form), Belize City
Courtesy Steven R. Harper

Patterns of Access and Performance

Studies conducted by the Belizean government and outside observers in the late 1980s indicated that between one-quarter and one-third of students enrolled in primary education left school before they reached fourteen, the minimum age at which a student could legally drop out. Dropout rates and absenteeism were higher in rural areas, largely because of the seasonal demand for agricultural labor and the perception that schooling beyond the basic level offered no increased opportunities.

In both rural and urban areas, students who dropped out of primary school (or, indeed, failed to attend) generally belonged to the poorest and least-empowered segments of Belizean society; they were the children of subsistence farmers, agricultural laborers, illegal aliens, and the inhabitants of the urban slums. Without primary school credentials, these individuals faced the continued prospect of lifelong underemployment or unemployment.

Selectivity in the education system intensified at the secondary level. No more than 60 percent of the students who graduated from primary school, or less than 40 percent of all children in that age-group, made the transition to secondary institutions. Again, the percentage of students entering secondary schools was even lower in rural areas, where less than one-third of eligible youth pursued education beyond the primary level as of the early 1980s. Although the construction of new schools in the districts had helped to alleviate this problem, the majority of rural youth still lacked a secondary education.

Primary education was both free and compulsory; secondary schooling was neither. The combined burden of financial and academic requirements excluded not only the poorest, but also the offspring of many working-class parents and even some middle-class families. Government programs and private scholarships failed adequately to address the financial barrier to educational opportunity. Exclusion from secondary schooling had serious consequences for the lives of these youth. A generation ago, a primary education was sufficient for many skilled and semiskilled jobs in the public and private sectors. But by the late 1980s, the value of these credentials had plummeted.

Secondary school credentials, in the form of diplomas and passing grades on exams, have become the minimum criteria for most types of skilled employment. These credentials, too, decreased in value as increasing numbers of students received them. Education in Belize, as elsewhere in the world, was largely synonymous with the earning of credentials.

Attrition, as well as access, was a more serious problem in secondary education than in primary education. Nationwide, only about one-half of the students who entered secondary school completed the course. During the early 1980s, the attrition rate reached higher than 70 percent in a number of city and district schools. The causes of attrition, or wastage, as it was known among administrators, varied but were largely related to socioeconomic factors, such as lack of money, discipline problems, or teenage pregnancy.

Fewer than 15 percent of secondary school graduates made the transition to sixth form. Most graduates of the secondary schools came from only a handful of institutions. Two new secondary institutions opened in the late 1980s, but the number of prospective applicants for the sixth form far exceeded available places. Observers believed that the gap would only grow as secondary schools continued to produce increasing numbers of graduates hungry for more educational credentials.

A university education was a rare opportunity for Belizean youth in the 1980s. Scholarships to foreign universities were extremely limited, although many Belizeans have benefitted from scholarships to Cuban universities. The full costs of university study abroad were beyond the means of all but elite families. Even after the opening of UCB, Belizean students overwhelmingly preferred the prospects of studying at universities in the United States to studying in Belize or at British, West Indian, Canadian, or Latin American institutions. Since 1983, the availability of scholarships to United States universities has increased considerably. Many of these scholarships were the result of United States government programs, such as the Central American Peace Scholarships (CAPS).

Standard of Living

Differences in quality of life reflected and shaped patterns of social inequality in Belize. Access to food, housing, health care, and other necessary or desired goods and services varied most markedly between rural and urban areas, as well as by socioeconomic status. In 1984 the average salary of an employee was Bz$6,000 (for value of the Belizean dollar—see Glossary). Almost two-thirds of the working population earned between Bz$3,000 and Bz$9,000; 20 percent earned less than Bz$3,000.

Despite these differences in wealth, virtually all Belizeans shared a penchant for foreign consumer products. In the 1980s, most Belizeans' aspirations for a high standard of living stemmed not only from the long period of colonial rule, but also from tales of emigrants to the United States and television images of the good life there.

Food and Diet

Despite an abundance of cultivable land, Belize depended on imports of food. Government figures indicated that the average household spent at least 29 percent of its budget on imported food during the 1980s. Urban and upper-income groups averaged higher percentages. Food imports included not only items such as dairy products, canned meats, and vegetables, but also staples such as rice and red kidney beans, which were also produced locally. Diet varied by culture as well as class, with Maya and rural Mestizos preferring large amounts of corn. Garifuna consumed large quantities of fish. The national dish, however, consisted of rice and beans.

Available statistics indicated that at least 40 percent of infants nationwide suffered from at least moderate malnutrition and that 61 percent of children under three years of age suffered some form of malnutrition. Because the government based this conclusion only on surveys of sick persons who visited health clinics, the actual incidence of malnutrition and anemia was probably higher, particularly among the most marginal and impoverished sectors of the population. Poor sanitation in rural areas also contributed to high incidence of intestinal parasites, especially among children.

Nutrition and health were major targets of foreign assistance from sources including the United States Peace Corps, the Cooperative for American Relief Everywhere (CARE), Project Hope, Project Concern, and a variety of international agencies, such as the Pan American Health Organization and the United Nations Children's Fund (UNICEF). At least twelve other organizations, including Canadian and a number of European governments, contributed to health and nutrition programs during the 1980s. Belize's Ministry of Health and other local governmental agencies played a supporting role to these programs.

Health and Welfare

The overall health of Belizeans during the 1980s improved markedly from the colonial period. By 1989 life expectancy at birth had risen to sixty-seven years for males and seventy-two years for females. The death rate dropped from 11.5 per 1,000 in the 1950s to 4.9 per 1,000 in 1980, and the published infant mortality rate declined from 93 per 1,000 in the 1950s to 24.8 per 1,000 in 1986. However, actual infant mortality was probably higher because people living in remote rural areas rarely reported infant deaths. Even so, the infant mortality rate for the largely rural Toledo district was more than double the national rate.

The underreporting of infant deaths in rural areas led the World Health Organization to classify Belize's morbidity and mortality statistics as unreliable. Outside of Belize City, facilities for testing for cases of malaria and dengue fever were inadequate, so the incidence of these illnesses has probably been underestimated. The incidence of other diseases, such as acquired immune deficiency syndrome (AIDS), was also believed to be higher than reported.

Despite a massive *Anopheles* mosquito-eradication campaign in the 1970s, malaria remained Belize's top health problem in the 1980s. After increasing by an annual rate of 30 percent between 1980 and 1983, the number of new cases has since slowed. A more resistant *Plasmodium facilparum* organism (instead of the usual *Plasmodium vivax* variety) caused many of the new cases of the disease. Malaria affected all areas of the country, except for Belize City and the cays, which lacked the *Anopheles* mosquito.

Dengue fever, another disease transmitted by mosquitoes, experienced a resurgence in the 1980s; the disease was thought to have been eradicated in the 1950s. Gastroenteritis and other intestinal diseases also continued to pose major health problems for Belizeans, especially for the rural poor. Although the Latin American cholera outbreak had not troubled Belize by the summer of 1991, health officials expressed fear that it was only a matter of time before the disease reached the country.

As elsewhere in the world, AIDS poses a serious and growing challenge to the Belizean health care system. Until 1990, Belize lacked facilities to test for the AIDS-causing human immunodeficiency virus (HIV). By August of 1990, ninety-four Belizeans had tested positive for HIV (up from an estimated three in 1986), and twenty-four persons had died of AIDS. Although every district of the country was affected, half of the people testing positive for HIV lived in Belize City.

Rivers, streams, and creeks provide 70 percent of Belizean domestic water needs. Although the threat from industrial pollution was still limited in 1990, the lack of effective sewage systems in most communities, along with the use of these same water sources for laundry and bathing, posed significant health risks. Pesticide and fertilizer run-off in agricultural areas also posed potential problems.

Belmopan, a planned capital, was the only Belizean community to be served fully by a municipal sewer system in 1991. After more than ten years of financial and technical support from the Canadian International Development Agency (CIDA), a sewer system for Belize City was completed in the 1980s. However, as recently as 1991, most city households were still not connected to the system.

Government health policy emphasized primary health care, particularly for people most in need, such as children, pregnant women, and the poor. However, health care services were unevenly distributed between rural and urban areas, and many people in need lacked regular access. The government directed most of its health budget in the 1980s toward operating the eight hospitals located in the capital and district towns. Many of these hospitals were old, overcrowded, and in need of equipment and supplies. A new hospital, to be built with European funds, was planned for Belize City. Twenty-nine health centers served the remainder of the population, although less than 50 percent of the facilities were fully staffed. But even the fully staffed centers lacked a complete range of health care services. Only one facility specialized in caring for the disabled and only one in caring for the mentally ill. Both facilities were located in Belize District.

A lack of personnel hindered the development of the Belizean health care system. Fewer than 100 physicians worked in the country in the late 1980s. The country had a school of nursing and a program for medical technicians but lacked a school of medicine. Many Belizeans who went overseas to study medicine never returned home to practice. Indeed, during the 1980s, two of every three government doctors and virtually all of the dentists were foreign citizens.

Legislation protecting the health of Belizean citizens, particularly in the workplace, was weak and poorly enforced. Belize did, however, have a social security system, designed with the help of the United Nations International Labour Organisation. In addition to providing pensions for retired and injured workers, the system also provided short-term benefits for sickness and maternity leave.

* * *

There is a small but growing body of literature on Belizean society. O. Nigel Bolland has been one of the most prolific contributors to this discourse. His *Belize: A New Nation in Central America* is the best general introduction to historical and contemporary social conditions, and his *Colonialism and Resistance in Belize* provides in-depth treatment of more specific issues. Norman Ashcraft's *Colonialism and Underdevelopment: Processes of Political Economic Change in British Honduras,* although dated, still provides a useful overview of rural life.

Most work on Belize, however, appears in the form of articles, conference papers, and unpublished dissertations. The journal *Belizean Studies* serves as a clearinghouse for much of this work. The Society for the Promotion of Education and Research in Belize City publishes collections of recent research, one of which is *Belize: Ethnicity and Development.* (For further information and complete citations, see Bibliography.)

Chapter 8. Belize: The Economy

Mayan god of corn

THE MAIN INFLUENCES on the economy of Belize have been the country's small size and its long history as a colony. As occurred elsewhere in the Caribbean, over the centuries the colony's administrators precariously based its economy on a succession of single raw commodities—logwood in the 1600s and 1700s, mahogany in the 1800s, and then sugar in the mid-1900s. During the 1980s, the dangers of a single-crop economy became brutal realities for the many Caribbean countries that had grown heavily dependent on sugar exports. Sugar prices collapsed, and protectionist trade practices by industrialized countries exacerbated the producers' problem. Belize's experience was no exception. However, the commodity crisis of the 1980s led to economic reform in Belize aimed at diversification and taking the economy definitively beyond the colonial period.

Small economies, such as Belize's, tend to be less diverse and more dependent on exports than larger economies, a situation that makes them volatile and highly vulnerable to outside forces. A small work force and limited capital, dependence on foreign markets and investment funds, and high overhead costs are all factors that have hindered Belize's economic growth. Despite these problems, the economy has steadily improved since independence was achieved in 1981. The British legacy of stable representative government, respect for education, a relatively even distribution of income, and a comparatively high standard of living has attracted increasing amounts of foreign investment. In 1991 the economy was more diverse than ever, the export sector was strong, a growing tourism industry promised increased revenues, and the government had avoided dangerous levels of foreign debt. The outlook for Belize's economy for the remainder of the 1990s seemed bright.

Growth and Structure of the Economy

The Colonial Economy

British Honduras officially became a British colony in 1862, after more than two centuries of vague status (see Colonial Rivalry Between Spain and Britain, ch. 6). Early Spanish settlers based the colonial economy entirely on the export of logwood. British buccaneers first settled in the early 1600s. Giving up their practice of capturing Spanish cargo ships laden with logwood, the erstwhile pirates began to cut the timber themselves. Logwood, a source of black dye, was in great demand in Europe at the time. However, by the end of the eighteenth century, dyes derived from logwood had been largely replaced by synthetic dyes. The decline of the logwood industry during the 1760s and the 1770s was accompanied by fruitless efforts to compensate for lost value by increasing the rate of production and hence the rate of exports. Once they realized the inevitability of failure, the settlers began exploiting other forest products, mainly chicle and mahogany. The latter wood became the mainstay of the economy for most of the next two centuries.

Although the logging of mahogany greatly enriched the colonial economy, particularly during the 1800s, it also seriously disrupted the indigenous Mayan culture. As the British pushed into the interior of the country, there were numerous violent confrontations with the Maya (see Mayan Emigration and Conflict, ch. 6).

In the absence of a forestry policy, the country's mahogany reserves gradually ran low. This depletion, among other factors, led to the decline of the industry in the 1950s. By 1991 forestry accounted for less than 3 percent of gross domestic product (GDP—see Glossary), and mahogany trees were so rare in Belize that one of them, in the center of Belize City, was labeled as if it were a museum piece.

Sugar succeeded logwood and mahogany as the third main staple of the colonial economy. The Maya had cultivated sugar since the mid-1800s, but the modern history of British Honduran sugar production did not begin until 1937, when a small factory was opened at Pembroke Hall (later known as Libertad) in northern Belize.

In 1964 the small mill at Libertad was bought by the large British sugar conglomerate of Tate and Lyle. This event accompanied the beginning of nearly twenty years of great profit. Foreign investment boosted production and productivity, and record prices fueled the growth of the sugar agro-industry. Sugar production increased from 17,000 tons in 1959 to 40,000 tons in 1963, to 70,170 tons in 1973, and to 114,000 tons in 1983. Production decreased rapidly thereafter to 81,700 tons in 1988 and underwent a mild recovery in 1990, when it reached 100,000 tons. The result of drought, smut diseases, froghopper (spittlebug) infestation, occasional labor shortages, and fluctuating demands and prices, the swings in sugar production created severe dislocations in the Belizean economy.

Belize's status as a former British colony has provided benefits that have translated directly or indirectly into economic advantages.

As in many of its former colonies, Britain left behind a well-established two-party political system based on the British model. Belize's democratic tradition made postcolonial stability more likely and appealed to many foreign investors.

The British also left behind a network of education institutions that formed the basis for the country's 93-percent nominal literacy rate and high level of enrollment in secondary schools. As the 1990s began, most of the schools at the primary level were church-administered. Education was compulsory until age fourteen. Health care, too, was better than what was available in most other Central American countries (see Health and Welfare, ch. 7). Belize had a higher daily calorie intake per capita, longer life expectancy, and higher literacy rates than El Salvador, Honduras, or Nicaragua, with quality-of-life statistics comparable to those of Costa Rica, Central America's most prosperous state, or the Bahamas, whose gross national product (GNP—see Glossary) per capita was seven times larger. Another regionally distinctive feature of Belize was its relatively even distribution of income. All these factors have contributed significantly to social stability and economic productivity.

The Small Economy

Belize is roughly the same size as New Hampshire (see Boundaries, Area, and Relative Size, ch. 7). Its population was about 191,000 in 1990. Some 25 percent of the population lived in Belize City and the surrounding area. Almost 25 percent lived in incorporated towns, among them the nation's capital, Belmopan, which had a population of about 4,000. The remaining half of the population was rural. Most rural residents lived in large villages in the north. Except for several towns, the central and southern parts of the country were sparsely inhabited. Among the 185 countries and territories listed in the World Bank (see Glossary) *World Atlas,* only fifteen countries had smaller GNPs than that of Belize.

Small developing economies have certain characteristics that restrict their ability to achieve balanced, sustained economic growth. These constraints include limited supplies of land, labor, and domestic capital; high dependence on foreign capital; limited domestic markets; high unit costs of production for domestic markets; limited bargaining power; relatively high wages driven by preferential trade agreements; and high overhead costs of government services and administration. As a result of these constraints, economic growth in small countries is tied closely to the rate of export growth. Moreover, the open, export-oriented economies of small states tend to be less diverse than those of larger countries. The scarcity of labor and capital demands careful targeting of investments. Finally, limited domestic markets mean less potential for import-substitution industrialization (see Glossary). Hence, the economies of small countries are disproportionately exposed to external shocks that increase import costs or depress export prices for their primary commodities.

The general limitations placed on small economies characterize the situation in Belize, with one exception: Belize is endowed with abundant arable land. Its population density of 8.5 persons per square kilometer in 1991 was one of the lowest in the world. Indeed, Belize depends on immigrant labor to sustain agricultural production, in part because many Belizeans are reluctant to work for the low wages offered in the agricultural sector.

Economic History

Culturally and economically, Belize is more closely linked to the Caribbean than to its Central American neighbors. However, Belize's participation in Caribbean economic integration has not come about easily.

During the 1950s, British Honduras rejected repeated attempts by Britain to incorporate the colony into the proposed West Indies Federation. There were several reasons behind this resistance. One was the fear of being locked into a Caribbean arrangement at the expense of ties with the rest of Central America. Moreover, because wages in British Honduras were higher than in most other British Caribbean territories, the British Hondurans feared that participation in the West Indies Federation might trigger an influx of immigrants from other member states. Indeed, Britain was planning on such an influx.

In 1968 British Honduras began to see the merits of integration with the British Caribbean when the country's ongoing territorial dispute with Guatemala led to rejection of its application to join the Central American Common Market. In 1971 British Honduras joined the Caribbean Free Trade Association (Carifta), which in 1973 became the Caribbean Community and Common Market (Caricom—see Appendix C).

During the Great Depression of the 1930s, British grants were necessary to keep British Honduras economically viable. However, economic ties with Britain gradually were replaced by a growing trade relationship with the United States. This economic link to the United States was seriously weakened by the devaluation of the British pound sterling in September 1949. Respecting the wishes of the middle class, labor, and the colonial legislature, the governor at first refused to devalue the British Honduras dollar and

Central Bank of Belize, Belize City
Courtesy Steven R. Harper

instead kept it at par with the United States dollar. However, three months later, bowing to pressure from Britain and powerful economic interests in British Honduras, the governor overrode the Legislative Council and devalued the colony's currency (see The Genesis of Modern Politics, 1931–54, ch. 6). Imports from the United States then decreased sharply, and imports from Britain rose until they amounted to 35 percent of the total during 1952–54, exceeding the country's imports from the United States. Living costs increased dramatically as a result of the devaluation, and the colony was thrown into turmoil. Anti-British sentiment was widespread and fueled resistance to the British-sponsored West Indies Federation. Imports from the United States did not recover until the late 1950s.

During the 1960s and 1970s, the colony's economy grew rapidly, thanks in large part to the extraordinary success of the sugar sector. During the 1970s, sugar accounted for almost 70 percent of all export revenues. As a result of this high level of dependency, the Belizean economy, although prosperous, entered the 1980s insufficiently diversified and highly susceptible to external shocks.

Growth During 1980–85

In 1980 the average world price of raw sugar had been US$0.13 per kilogram. By 1984 that price had fallen to US$0.02. As sugar prices collapsed, Belize's terms of trade deteriorated, and from 1980 to 1985 GDP grew an average of only 1.2 percent per year. The crisis was compounded in 1982 when, for the first time since 1974, the United States government implemented a sugar quota system. The result was a reduction in total sugar exports from about 5 million tons in 1980–81 to about 1 million tons by 1987.

Also contributing to the worsening of Belize's balance of payments was the sudden collapse of the country's reexport business. As a reexporter, Belize imports goods and then resells them in neighboring countries (primarily Mexico), or merely transports them, collecting fees for port and road facilities. The arrangement is attractive because of Belize's relatively low shipping costs. However, Mexico's economic payment crisis of 1982, which reduced Mexican imports, put a dent in Belize's foreign-exchange earnings as well. Reexports had amounted to 37 percent of export earnings in 1981 but fell to 16 percent in 1983, contributing to a 35-percent drop in total export earnings during that period.

The economic crisis of the early 1980s brought with it escalating trade deficits. In 1981 Belize's net international reserves had stood at US$1.1 million. By the end of 1984, the country had a trade deficit of US$13.6 million.

The economic crisis was a factor in the defeat of the People's United Party government in 1984 (see Political Parties, ch. 9); it also led to implementation of a standby arrangement with the International Monetary Fund (IMF—see Glossary) in December of that year. The IMF agreement marked the beginning of the country's adjustment process. The agreement provided access to 7.1 million units of special drawing rights (SDRs—see Glossary) over a sixteen-month period and called for a reduction of the public-sector deficit and a tightening of the country's credit policy by means of higher reserve requirements and higher interest rates. Credit had expanded at an annual rate of 15 percent from 1981 to 1984 because of escalating government debt.

A small open economy is dependent on developments in external markets and generally experiences few domestically generated inflationary pressures. Belize's currency, the Belizean dollar (see Glossary), had been pegged to the United States dollar at a rate of US$1 = Bz$2 since 1976. Belize's rate of inflation, therefore, was likewise pegged to that of its major trading partner. Between 1980 and 1983, consumer prices increased by 25 percent in Belize. During the same period, they went up 21 percent in the United States. This modest inflation contrasted sharply with the hyperinflation that pushed prices up by more than 1,000 percent per year in many other countries in the region. Yet, the 4-percent difference between

United States and Belizean inflation during those years resulted in a real effective exchange-rate appreciation and, consequently, a worsening of Belize's relative position in the export sector. This trend was later reversed when the Belizean inflation rate fell slightly below that of the United States.

Growth after 1985

After 1986 the Belizean economy improved dramatically, in part because of the adjustment program implemented by the government. These adjustments cut public expenditures and created incentives for diversification of the economy. The country's foreign-exchange receipts from banana and citrus exports multiplied, and tourism became a major contributor to growth. Internal reform coincided with the recovery of the world economy, in particular the revival of the sugar market. Between 1986 and 1990, the Belizean economy grew at an average annual rate of more than 10 percent (see table 14, Appendix A).

Inflation remained low from 1986 to 1990, averaging 2.8 percent and allowing for an effective depreciation of the Belizean dollar relative to the United States dollar. The positive effect of low inflation on Belize's exports was enhanced by the depreciation of the United States dollar during the second half of the 1980s. The more favorable exchange rate enjoyed by the Belizean dollar was central to the vigorous growth the country experienced during the period.

In 1991 estimates showed growth slowing to an annual rate of less than 5 percent. This deceleration was the result of significant shortfalls in banana production following an outbreak of black sigatoka disease and a reduction in citrus production resulting from bad weather. As in most of the Caribbean, tourism was also affected by the recession in the United States and Britain.

Peripheral Factors

Two small but significant factors must be mentioned in any discussion of Belize's economy: the role of British troops and the illegal drug trade. At independence, Belize and Britain agreed that the latter would maintain a garrison of 2,000 soldiers in Belize to deter possible aggression by Guatemala. As of 1991, Guatemala had established diplomatic relations with Belize but continued to claim an undefined part of its territory. The economic impact of the British garrison, then numbering about 1,500 troops, was substantial in the early 1990s. Because of their relatively high incomes and the support services they required, the troops have had a significant impact on the level of employment and the Belizean economy in general. Some analysts have estimated that the British garrison directly or indirectly generated about 15 percent of Belize's GDP.

The drug trade was not factored into the country's GDP statistics, and the impact of this illegal activity on the economy was difficult to measure. Belize played three roles in the drug trade in the early 1990s; the country served as a marijuana producer, as a transshipment route for other drugs, and as a money-laundering center. In the early 1980s, the United States Drug Enforcement Agency placed Belize on its list of leading marijuana producers. Aerial spraying of pesticides was begun in 1984, but was ended that same year because of Belizean concerns about the safety of spraying on legal crops and on the population. The United States government estimated that annual marijuana production in Belize subsequently rose from 35 tons to 850 tons, with an approximate street value of US$120 million. Spraying was resumed in 1985 with different chemicals, and marijuana production declined substantially thereafter.

Belize remained an important transshipment site for drugs other than marijuana in the early 1990s. For instance, in September 1990 Mexican federal judicial police seized approximately 457 kilograms of cocaine, which they suspected had been smuggled into Mexico through the border area between Belize's Hondo River and Santa Teresa, Mexico. The shipment apparently was destined for the United States.

Finally, concerns existed that Belize served as a center for money-laundering. The Central Bank of Belize had the authority to trace large transactions, as well as all foreign-currency transactions. However, the nation's investment law allowed offshore banking in Belize and specifically exempted such activity from the regulatory oversight of the Central Bank.

Government Policy

Economic Diversification

The narrow base of the national economy was recognized as a problem by the Belizean government after the sluggish growth of the early 1980s. In response, the government started a comprehensive program during the second half of the decade focused primarily on eliminating export biases and creating a favorable environment for investment, both foreign and domestic, especially in the nontraditional export sector. The creation of a favorable environment for investment meant eliminating internal and external imbalances and upgrading infrastructures. This process was facilitated by external incentives such as the United States Caribbean Basin Initiative (CBI—see Appendix D). The private sector reacted positively to these changes, and economic growth took off.

The Belizean economy was still insufficiently diversified at the beginning of the 1990s, but major changes in the composition of GDP and exports had provided a basis for sustained growth. The two major changes in the GDP took place in agriculture and tourism. Agriculture declined from a 20 percent share of GDP in 1980 to a 15 percent share in 1990, whereas tourism expenditures increased from a 4 percent share to a 9 percent share (see fig. 13).

The percentage share of each crop within the agricultural sector gave further evidence of how the composition of GDP was changing. Sugar-export receipts had lost half their share of exports by 1990, whereas tourism had tripled its portion, to the point where it nearly equaled receipts from sugar exports. Citrus products also had made remarkable progress, almost doubling their share of exports by 1990. The share of GDP provided by bananas increased, although less steadily.

Balance of Payments

Balance of payments figures also improved in the mid-1980s. From 1980 to 1984, Belize incurred a balance of payments deficit. Effects of the government austerity plan coupled with a rise in exports produced a balance of payments surplus from 1985–90. Between 1988 and 1990, the deficit between exports and imports of goods and services widened again. However, this time the gap was caused by large increases in private-investment expenditures. At the same time, the public sector was accruing surpluses, so the overall balance of payment still showed a surplus.

Investments

The heavy investment in Belize from 1988 to 1990 funded both private-sector and public-sector activity. Public-sector capital investments that were domestically financed, for example, increased from US$3.4 million in 1986–87 to a planned US$38.8 million in 1991–92. Although the domestically funded portion of capital expenditures was budgeted to decrease in 1992, an expected increase in funding from external sources was projected to cause a net gain in new capital expenditures.

Private-sector investment increased from approximately US$17.7 million in 1985 to US$63.7 in 1989, then declined in 1990. Helping make a high level of private-sector investment possible was the increased availability of domestic credit. Analysts estimate that net

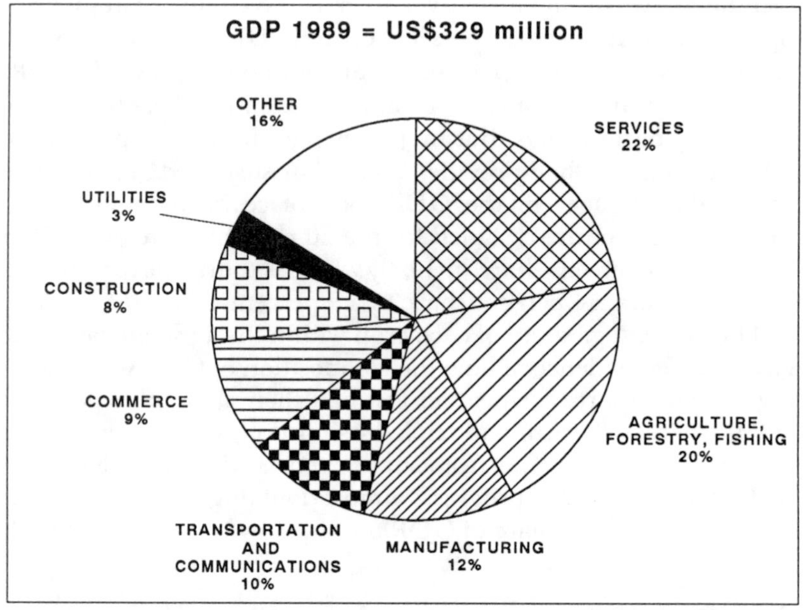

Source: Based on information from Economist Intelligence Unit, *Country Profile: Belize, Bahamas, Bermuda, 1989–90*, London, 1990.

Figure 13. Belize: Gross Domestic Product (GDP) by Sector of Origin, 1989

domestic credit extended to the private sector increased 15.3 percent in 1989 and 17.8 percent in 1990.

The improved health and apparent stability of the Belizean economy also encouraged a surge in foreign direct investment. In 1984 Belize had suffered an outflow of foreign direct investment in equity capital of US$7 million. During the period 1988–90, annual foreign direct investments averaged US$17 million. Contributing to this development was the government's decision to eliminate export biases through various legislative measures. The 1990 Fiscal Incentives Act provided tax holidays and duty exemptions for investments that would benefit the economy. The 1990 Income Tax Act granted tax relief to nontraditional exporters. The legislature in 1990 also approved the Export-Processing Zones Act, which exempted eligible firms from requirements concerning import licenses, quotas, import and export taxes, export licenses, price controls, and other regulatory mechanisms. The first export-processing zones (EPZs) were scheduled to become established in 1993. The concept required designation or development of a physical facility (the zone) similar to an industrial park. As part of the effort to provide a more favorable environment for investment, Prime Minister George Cadle Price also introduced legislation that would lower corporate taxes from 45 percent to 35 percent in fiscal year (FY—see Glossary) 1992.

Fiscal Performance

The consolidation of government finances was a crucial factor in the economic growth of the late 1980s. The first step was the reduction of total expenditures. Between 1981 and 1985, total government expenditures had stood at 34 percent of GDP. Between 1986 and 1990, this proportion was reduced to 31 percent. More significant, however, was the decline of current expenditures as a portion of GDP, from 25 percent to 21 percent. This decline indicated that cuts in government spending were not being made at the expense of development expenditures. Development expenditures as a percentage of GDP actually increased from 7.4 percent between 1981 and 1985 to 8.7 percent between 1986 and 1990.

Statistics for the period 1986–90 also showed an increase in government revenues over 1981–85. These revenues, which had amounted to 24 percent of GDP over the 1981–85 period, increased to 30 percent of GDP in 1986–90. Some of this increase was accounted for by the sale of government assets, which increased capital revenues. The remainder came mainly from higher tax revenues, which rose from 21 percent to 24 percent of GDP.

Lower current expenditures and increased current revenues permitted the Belizean government to experience several years of high surpluses on its current account. In 1990 this surplus on the government's current account was 11 percent. This fiscal consolidation reduced government competition with the private sector in the domestic credit market. Consequently, increased lending to the private sector accelerated growth without increasing the money supply and therefore without threatening currency stability.

External Debt

Improvements in the current and capital accounts facilitated an increase in the country's international reserves from US$5 million in 1984 to US$130 million in 1990. Belize's total external debt more than doubled from US$62.9 million in 1980 to US$158 million in 1990. Despite its relatively low debt burden, Belize formally requested consideration by the United States government for debt reduction and payment of interest into a local environmental fund under the Enterprise for the Americas Initiative (EAI—see Glossary).

Belize has been quite successful in attracting foreign aid. In 1983, two years after the nation became independent, the United States Agency for International Development opened an office in Belize. Between 1983 and 1989, Belize received US$94 million in development assistance. On a per capita basis, in 1991 Belize ranked among the top recipients of United States aid, a position that underscored the close relationship between the two countries. Britain remained Belize's other major benefactor. In 1991 Belize sought membership in the Inter-American Development Bank to assure the continued flow of concessional loans.

Labor

In 1946 the Belizean labor force numbered approximately 20,100 economically active individuals. This pool expanded to 27,000 in 1960, to 33,000 in 1970, and to 46,000 in 1980. By 1990 the active labor force had increased to more than 60,000. Most startling was the increase in female participation. Although women made up only 18 percent of the labor force in 1960, they accounted for one-third in 1991, when 44.5 percent of working-age women were actually economically active, as opposed to only 20.6 percent in 1960. The reason for this relatively high level of female participation was most likely the acute shortage of labor in a country where some 50 percent of the population was aged fifteen and under and also the fact that young women typically are employed in the new low-wage sectors, such as the garment assembly industry.

The labor shortage was eased by the employment of large numbers of migrant workers from Central America. However, relatively high wage rates have been necessary to attract these workers, which, in turn, make Belize a high-cost producer by developing countries' standards. The influx of large numbers of immigrants per year, which has changed the ethnic composition of the population, has also been a source of social tension.

Although Belize has experienced labor shortages, it has also reported relatively high levels of unemployment—around 15 percent in the early 1990s. However, these figures were less a manifestation of job shortages than an indication of labor immobility. Also, many Belizeans chose to be unemployed because they received remittance payments from family abroad. For instance, between 30,000 and 100,000 Belizeans were estimated to reside in the United States.

The members of five major unions accounted for about 15 percent of the labor force. In 1991 more than 1,000 teachers belonged to the Belize National Teachers' Union; the Public Service Union consisted of about the same number of public workers. The largest

Belize Tourist Board, Regent Street, Belize City
Courtesy Steven R. Harper

union outside the public sector was the Christian Workers' Union, which had more than 2,000 members. The General Workers' Union was broad-based and affiliated with the International Confederation of Free Trade Unions. The Democratic Independent Union counted more than 1,200 members in 1991. The National Trades Union Congress of Belize served as an umbrella group for all unions. None of the unions was associated with a political party.

Foreign Economic Relations

Small, open economies depend heavily on preferential trade agreements. Belize's economy benefited from a range of such agreements: the United States sugar quota; the Lomé Convention (see Glossary) of the European Economic Community (EEC—in particular, the Sugar Protocol and the Banana Protocol); the CBI; United States Tariff Schedule 807 program (see Glossary); the Multi-fibre Arrangement; and the EAI.

Preferential trade agreements demonstrate the complexity of international trade relations and their effect on economic progress, especially in developing countries. Preferential trade agreements also provide a reminder that trade liberalization is a double-edged sword for all trade participants, developed and developing alike. For example, there were distinct advantages in the existing quota systems for the Belizean sugar industry in the early 1990s. Quotas guaranteed that Belizean sugar would have access to markets in the EEC and the United States at prices far above world market levels. At the same time, it was also clear that a quota system was a unilateral act, that it limited market access, and that quotas could be changed or eliminated by foreign powers at their will.

Belize was a member of Caricom and benefited from preferential market access to the markets of other member countries. However, Caricom's success at integration was mixed. Between 1984 and 1986, Belize's trade with Caricom members decreased sharply as a result of currency devaluations and a renewal of trade barriers by some member countries. In 1988 Caricom approved a common internal tariff, which was to reinvigorate intraregional trade. However, there were some exceptions to the common internal tariff. Caricom's much-delayed common external tariff was adopted by Belize at the end of 1991. This common tariff changed Belize's duty rates but produced no effect on the budget. High duties on foodstuffs were dropped, and duties on machinery were reduced.

Belizean trade patterns were heavily affected by the country's participation in various bilateral and multilateral trade arrangements. The United States and Britain remained the principal destinations of Belizean exports throughout the 1980s. In the second half of the 1980s, the two accounted for more than 80 percent of total exports in every year. Their respective shares fluctuated from year to year, but their combined total remained practically unchanged. Exports to Caricom countries, which had peaked in 1983 at 14.5 percent of total Belizean exports, plunged to 1.9 percent in 1986, but recovered in 1990 to roughly half their 1983 level.

Agriculture

Sugar

As the 1990s began, sugar was still the Belizean economy's single largest export earner (see table 15, Appendix A). Sugar production involved a unique hybrid of agricultural and industrial activity. Sugarcane cultivation, on the one hand, and the mechanical-chemical transformation of cane into sugar, on the other hand, made for this peculiarity. Both processes needed to be coordinated because of the perishability of the crop.

In Belize small farms in the north produce the bulk of the sugarcane. In the early 1990s, the coordination of the agricultural aspects of sugar production and the organization of cane delivery were the responsibilities of the Cane Farmers' Association. The industrial segment of the sugar-production process was controlled by Belize Sugar Industries Limited (BSIL). Overall coordination of the industry was exercised by the Belize Sugar Board.

Until 1985 Belize had two sugar mills: the Libertad factory in the Corozal District, opened in 1937, and the factory at Tower Hill near Orange Walk Town, opened in 1967. In July 1985, the Libertad factory was closed. By early 1989, Libertad had been reopened and leased to the Jamaican petroleum company Petrojam. Petrojam was to use Libertad for the production of molasses, which was then to be refined in Jamaica into ethanol. Ethanol had duty-free access to the United States market under the CBI arrangement.

The Belizean sugar industry, as elsewhere in the Caribbean, experienced large production and export swings. In 1981 an estimated 30 percent of farmland, formerly used for growing sugarcane, had been abandoned. Yet, at the end of the 1980s, the United States increased its quota for Belize at the expense of Guyana, which was not reaching its allotment, and in early 1990, BSIL reported its largest-ever bulk shipment (17,300 tons of raw sugar) to Canada.

Citrus

Citrus production, mainly oranges and grapefruit, occurs predominantly in Belize's Stann Creek District. The citrus trade began in the 1920s, but became significant only in the 1980s, when Belizean-produced citrus concentrate became exempt from United States tariff duties under the terms of the CBI. Exports of fresh citrus fruit to the United States were restricted, however, because of infestation of the Mediterranean fruit fly. Citrus, much like sugar, underwent sharp price and production fluctuations, although overall export receipts from citrus concentrate markedly increased during the 1980s because of high prices.

In the early 1990s, citrus production was controlled by two processing companies. Founded by a Jamaican family, the Citrus Company of Belize had been controlled since 1984 by the Trinidad Citrus Association. Belize Food Products, the second processor, was owned by Nestlé, the Swiss multinational, until it was sold to a local consortium in 1990. Both processing plants were located near Dangriga on the Caribbean coast.

The future of citrus was uncertain. In 1990 only half of planted citrus hectarage was in production. There were indications that production could double within five years. There were worries, however, about the effect of competition from Mexico or Brazil through preferential access allowed to them via the proposed North American Free Trade Agreement or the EAI.

Bananas

Commercial cultivation of bananas began in the late nineteenth century, when United States and British investors first established plantations. Although the banana trade between British Honduras and New Orleans at first seemed promising, commerce was wiped out in the 1920s by an outbreak of the Panama disease. Another attempt to cultivate bananas was begun by the British during the 1960s, but the plantations were destroyed by hurricanes in 1975 and 1978. The subsequent takeover of banana cultivation by the Banana Control Board, a public enterprise, had the effect of further inhibiting production.

By mid-1985, the Banana Control Board had accumulated debts of US$9 million. The government reacted to the plight of the board by selling the 880 hectares under cultivation to the private sector. Five years later, banana production had almost tripled, and the cultivated area had increased to more than 2,400 hectares. The Banana Control Board was reorganized and retained the responsibility for marketing and research. In 1991 responsibility for the board was passed to the Banana Growers' Association.

Britain was the almost exclusive importer of Belizean bananas. Marketing of exports was handled by Fyffes International, a British subsidiary of the United States company, United Fruit. The special provisions of the Lomé Convention's Banana Protocol allowed Britain to guarantee artificially high prices for bananas to the beneficiaries of the protocol. These prices were above prices in the United States and Germany. The purpose of this special provision was to protect the central export crop of some of the islands of the Lesser Antilles (see Glossary), members of the Commonwealth of Nations, from ruinous competition from low-cost producers in Latin America (see The Commonwealth of Nations, Appendix B).

The preferential access to EEC markets provided by the Lomé Convention was under advisement in 1991 by the EEC in connection with its single-European-market program. It appeared that Belize would be better prepared for a drop in prices than would the islands of the Lesser Antilles, as Belizean producers received far lower prices through the protocol than did their Caribbean neighbors.

New port facilities at Big Creek in southern Stann Creek District were expected to increase banana exports. Until 1990 Belizean bananas had had to go through Puerto Cortés, Honduras, which added to overhead. Fyffes then financed the construction of Big Creek, Belize's only deep-water port. This port was designed to serve as the main shipment point for Belizean bananas.

Belize International Airport near Belize City
Courtesy Steven R. Harper

Between 1989 and 1991, banana production was hampered by cold weather and black sigatoka disease, but production was expected to double in 1992 because of the new port, better disease control, and improved drainage and irrigation systems. The susceptibility of bananas to disease and possible changes in Belize's preferential access to the British market were factors that could limit growth in this sector, however.

Other Crops

Crops other than sugar, citrus, and bananas played a very minor role in the Belizean economy in the early 1990s. Cultivation of nontraditional export crops was encouraged by the CBI as a way of lessening dependence on sugar and banana exports. Trade incentives were offered for nontraditional products, such as tropical fruits or winter fruits and vegetables. This strategy was only moderately successful, however.

Examples of failed attempts at agricultural diversification included AID's sponsorship of the Belize Agri-Business Company, whose purpose was to decrease the dependency of northern farmers on sugarcane by replacing it with cucumbers, okra, and bell peppers for winter export to the United States. The effort failed because of the farmers' reluctance to change and because of poor marketing.

In 1987 the failure of Caribe Farm Industries, the most prominent nontraditional agricultural exporter in the country producing a variety of vegetables, added to the growing frustration with the diversification efforts. Difficulties were also experienced with tropical fruits. The Danish-owned Tropical Produce Company (TPC) had a 570-hectare mango farm in the Monkey River area of the Toledo District. Its produce was grown for the United States market, as well as for European importers, with whom TPC held a ten-year contract. But shipments were erratic because of Mediterranean fruit fly quarantines. For instance, from 1987 to 1990, there were no mango exports from the TPC farm to the United States.

Most production of import-substitution crops resulted from the efforts of two groups, the Maya and the Mennonites. Small farmers, primarily of Mayan descent, grew corn and beans in sparsely populated areas for their own consumption. The immigrant Mennonite community bought 40,000 hectares of forested land along the Hondo River in 1959, constructed a road to Orange Walk, and soon created a thriving business based on dairy products, vegetables, beans, and poultry. Yet, overall production swung widely over the years, closely following price subsidies. The Belize Marketing Board, which supervised production of import-substitution crops, was scheduled to function exclusively as a price stabilization agency by the end of 1992.

Fishing and Forestry

Four fishing cooperatives—Caribeña, the Northern, the National, and Placencia—dominated the fishing industry, which began to flourish in the 1960s. In 1990 fishing accounted for about 2 percent of GDP; 30 percent of the sector's output was for domestic consumption, and the remainder was exported. The primary catches were lobster, shrimp, conch, red snapper, and other fin fish. Overfishing and out-of-season fishing were problems. Shrimp farming, begun with little initial success in the late 1970s, has recently contributed to a boost in shrimp exports (up 43 percent in 1989).

Forestry lost its role as the biggest sector of the Belizean economy decades ago. Its contribution to GDP averaged 2.3 percent during 1980–90. Production rose from 1987 to 1990 because of a high domestic demand for construction materials. Exports consisted primarily of sawn cedar wood. In 1990 volume dropped by 40 percent.

Industry

Mining and Energy

Belize has negligible known mineral deposits, although hopes persisted that large reserves of oil would be found. Extensive drilling, which began in 1981, primarily in the Corozal Basin, has been unsuccessful. Some of the nation's oil has been supplied at concessionary terms because Belize was a signatory in 1988 to the San José Pact with Mexico and Venezuela. This treaty obligated Mexico and Venezuela to offer concessionary credit for at least 20-25 percent of the purchase price of their oil exports to Central American beneficiaries. In August 1991, Venezuela and Mexico increased the oil supplies offered under this agreement.

In the early 1990s, Belize had a limited capacity to generate electricity. Several small diesel generators, mostly powered by oil imported from Mexico, had a total capacity of 34.7 megawatts. In 1990 these plants produced 90 gigawatt-hours of electricity. Mexico agreed in 1990 to supply electricity to the Belize Electricity Board, but electricity remained costly and in short supply.

Manufacturing

The manufacturing sector has been dominated by agro-industries such as sugar-milling, citrus-processing, and processing of domestic foodstuffs. Belize also had a significant garment industry in the early 1990s. Nonagricultural industries that produced import substitutes were highly protected. Their output was limited by the size of the domestic market.

The garment industry was the only export-producing nonagricultural industry of note. As with the country's other major products, its level of exports fluctuated throughout the 1980s. In 1980 the garment industry was Belize's second largest industry. By 1990 the industry had dropped to fourth behind sugar, tourism, and citrus.

Garment manufacturing in Belize was an offshore industry using imported United States cloth. The finished product was then reexported, with the product exempt from United States duties for all but the portion of value added in Belize, per United States Tariff Schedule 807. Belize's garment exports have also benefited from the Multi-fibre Arrangement, which placed a United States import quota on garments from major exporters. Belize was not subject to the United States quota because of its relatively small share of United States imports.

Construction

Beginning in 1985, the construction industry began to grow faster than other sectors of the economy. Growth was especially strong after 1988, when investments in tourism and in the public sector accelerated. The industry continued to benefit from major infrastructural projects, such as the renovation of the Hummingbird Highway (the road linking Belmopan and the coast), the construction of numerous schools and urban housing, and a 24-megawatt hydroelectric project. In 1990 construction accounted for almost 10 percent of GDP.

Tourism

Belize offers some of the most beautiful coral reefs in the Western Hemisphere, as well as more than 175 sandy cay (see Glossary) islands, various archeological sites, about 240 varieties of wild orchids, and about 500 species of birds. Naturally, Belize would appear to be a prime objective for United States tourists. However, a lack of infrastructure has kept the tourism industry relatively underdeveloped.

Apart from making infrastructural improvements such as enlargement of Belize International Airport in 1989 and offering fiscal incentives, the public sector has done little to promote tourism. The unhappy experience of the Colonial Development Corporation (CDC) in the early 1950s may have contributed to the government's hesitancy. In 1953 the CDC opened the Fort George Hotel, realizing that the lack of hotel accommodations in the colony had been an obstacle to investment. The costs of this project were excessive, however, and the architectural difficulties were overwhelming because of the swampy ground on which the hotel was built. The hotel's operations proved to be difficult as well. As a result, CDC's capital in the project had to be written off.

During the 1980s and early 1990s, the tourism sector, despite setbacks, developed into the second most important source of foreign exchange for the Belizean economy. In 1980 tourism receipts had been about a tenth of sugar-export receipts. By 1990 the two sectors were almost equal in size. In 1991 hotel receipts were estimated to have grown by an additional 15 percent. Tourist arrivals almost tripled between 1985 and 1990. In 1990 the Fort George Hotel joined the Radisson chain and doubled its capacity to seventy-six rooms. In 1991 the Ramada Royal Reef Hotel opened with a capacity of 120 rooms. The total number of rooms had increased from 1,176 in 1980 to 2,763 in 1990.

The Belizean Ministry of Tourism has encouraged controlled development of tourism without endangering the country's ecological balance. Although tourism had great potential for growth, the sector was still constrained by poor infrastructure, unsophisticated services, and a shortage of qualified labor.

Other Services

Transportation and Telecommunications

Highways and aircraft were the principal means of transportation in Belize; in 1991 the country had no railroads or significant inland waterways. The Belize River, however, was navigable up to the Guatemalan border, and shallow-draught craft were usable on some 800 kilometers of river. A road renovation program in the 1980s left the country with a much-improved road system. In 1991 Belize had about 500 kilometers of paved highway extending from the Mexican and Guatemalan borders to Belize City, including the new Hummingbird Highway linking Belmopan with Dangriga (see fig. 14). Another 1,600 kilometers of gravel roads linked rural areas and localities in the south. The country's only international airport, Belize International (also called Philip Goldson International), underwent modernization in 1989. Belize City was the main port, but Big Creek in the south was being expanded to accommodate increased banana exports.

The telecommunications network was adequate, with most of the population having access to broadcast facilities. In 1991 the country had 8,650 telephones, or 4.6 per 100 people. A satellite ground station coordinated with the International Telecommunications Satellite Corporation (Intelsat) Atlantic Ocean satellite provided international direct-dial telephone service and television transmission. There were six amplitude modulation (AM) radio stations (four run by Belizean commercial interests and two by the Voice of America), five frequency modulation (FM) stations, and one television transmitter in Belize City.

The highly successful process of privatizing the Belize telecommunications network began in 1988 when the government incorporated Belize Telecommunications Limited (BTL). The government kept 49 percent of the shares of BTL, sold 25 percent to British Telecom, and allowed the rest to be acquired by Belizean investors. Regulatory authority over telecommunications was retained by the government. Receipts from the sale amounted to almost 6 percent of GDP in 1988. The Belizean government also gained a substantial new source of revenue because of taxes, duties, and dividends paid to it by BTL. At the same time, consumers benefited from the increased efficiency of the new company, which more than doubled the number of existing telephone lines. At the beginning of 1992, the government sold all but 3 percent of its remaining shares in BTL for approximately US$15 million.

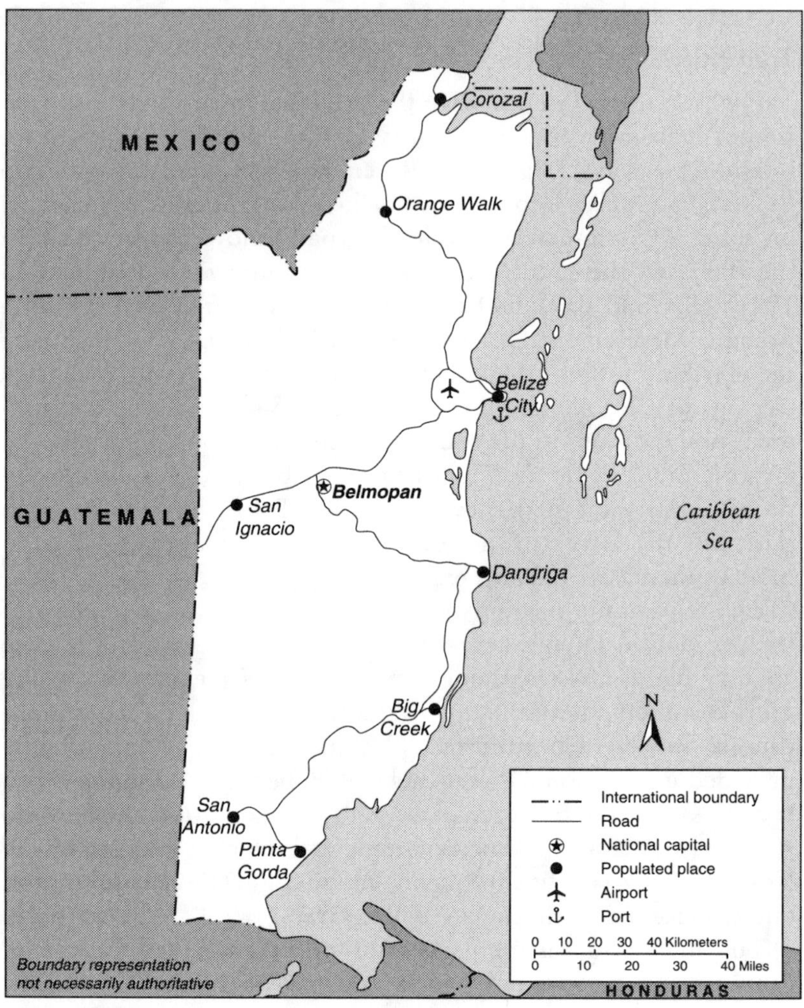

Figure 14. Belize: Transportation System, 1991

Banking and Finance

In the early 1990s, financial institutions in Belize included a central bank, a development bank, commercial banks, and credit unions. The Central Bank of Belize was formed in 1982 as a successor to the Monetary Authority, which had been founded in 1976. The bank held the usual responsibilities of a central bank. The fully government-owned Development Finance Corporation (DFC) was founded in 1963. Its main function was to channel foreign aid into development projects. Personal credit was provided by thirty-eight credit unions. Commercial credit was offered by four commercial banks: Barclays, Bank of Nova Scotia, Atlantic Bank (Honduras), and Banco Serfín (Mexico). These banks have been criticized for preferring short-term trade financing and for charging high interest rates for development loans.

Economic Prospects

The Belizean economy entered the 1990s in much better condition than it had entered the 1980s. The economy was more diverse, export biases had been removed, private-sector incentives and privatization had been well received, private and public investments had reached record levels, the tourism sector had grown and was positioned to become an engine of further growth, and, most important of all, the government had successfully completed a process of fiscal consolidation. All of these gains were financed mainly by direct foreign investment and concessionary funding and accomplished with comparatively low external debt ratios.

Negotiations on trade matters that posed challenges were underway as Belize entered the 1990s. As in most small economies, much of Belize's growth was based on export performance, which depended on preferential trade arrangements. Prices for Belizean sugar exports were 45 percent above world market prices in 1990, and the price of bananas exported to Britain was 30 percent above world market prices. The results of the Uruguay Round of the General Agreement on Tariffs and Trade (GATT—see Glossary) negotiations, the creation of the single European market by 1993, the implementation of action programs under the EAI, and the prospect of a North American Free Trade Agreement would eliminate some of these trade preferences and decrease Belize's exports.

Economic growth could also be affected by a withdrawal of British troops. In 1991 British prime minister John Major gave assurances that the troops would remain despite the diplomatic recognition accorded Belize by Guatemala in September of 1991. But constraints on the British budget might change that position and affect Belize's growth in the future.

The consolidation of government finances was central to the progress made in the second half of the 1980s. Capital expenditures rose sharply in order to cover the cost of providing the physical infrastructure necessary to continued growth. Future increments would have to keep pace with the nation's rate of economic growth. The prospect that Belize would continue on its path to economic development and social progress was good, but the economy nevertheless faced new tests as the century drew to a close.

* * *

Economic literature on Belize is mostly outdated and usually not very comprehensive. The economic chapter in O. Nigel Bolland's book *Belize: A New Nation in Central America* discusses the economic structure of the country in the context of Belize's historical experience. The last chapter in William David Setzekorn's book, *Formerly British Honduras: A Profile of the New Nation of Belize* provides a good understanding of the various sectors of the Belizean economy and their prospects.

The best sources of up-to-date information are the country reports and profiles of the Economist Intelligence Unit and World Bank data. Two relatively recent country guides that also contain economics chapters are Tom Barry's *Belize: A Country Guide* and his *Inside Belize.*

Finally, as a small developing country Belize faces many special constraints. As an aid to understanding these constraints and putting them in the Caribbean context, the most relevant standard piece written on the subject is William G. Demas's *The Economics of Development in Small Countries.* (For further information and complete citations, see Bibliography.)

Chapter 9. Belize: Government and Politics

Mayan sun god

BELIZE'S CONSTITUTIONAL and political institutions have roots in the country's origins as a settlement of British subjects, who carried with them the rights and immunities they had enjoyed in the mother country. British common law included the tradition of recognizing the executive power of the crown in settlements overseas, but the Settlement of Belize in the Bay of Honduras (renamed British Honduras in 1862 and Belize in 1973) enjoyed its own legislative competence. In 1871, however, it surrendered its legacy of self-governance and abolished its elected legislature in order to obtain greater economic and political security as a crown colony (see Glossary).

The colony soon regretted the loss of self-rule and thus began a long campaign to regain an elected legislature that led to internal self-rule in 1964 and culminated in the colony's independence in 1981. From 1950 on, the People's United Party (PUP) spearheaded this campaign under the leadership of George Cadle Price. Price and the PUP have largely defined the nationalist agenda in Belize, and the PUP has won all but one national election in Belize since 1954. Although internal self-rule was achieved in 1964, full independence was delayed because of territorial claims against Belize by Guatemala. These claims were still unresolved in 1991, but British defense guarantees paved the way for Belizean independence on September 21, 1981.

According to its constitution, Belize is a constitutional monarchy, whose titular sovereign, the British monarch, is represented in Belize by a governor general. Actual political power, however, resides in elected representatives in the National Assembly and the cabinet headed by the prime minister. Belize has a political system dominated by two parties, the PUP and the United Democratic Party (UDP). The constitution establishes an independent judiciary and guarantees fundamental human, civil, and political rights.

Constitutional Background

Constitutional and Political Structures prior to Independence

Constitutional and political development in Belize prior to independence in 1981 can be divided into seven stages. The British settlement enjoyed its own legislature, called the Public Meeting, while the crown held executive authority and thus the right to appoint governors. Social, political, and economic factors, however, led British Honduras to surrender its elected legislature, then called the Legislative Assembly, and the legacy of self-governance in order to obtain greater security and economic stability as a crown colony in 1871. The arrangement did not grant the crown, however, the right to revoke or amend the colony's constitution, a right which the monarch held in some colonies. The Parliament of Britain continued to exercise its power to amend British Honduras's constitution in conjunction with relevant legislative bodies in the colony. The rise of trade unions in the 1930s and 1940s and the emergence of a mass political party in the 1950s led to the establishment of institutions that would chart British Honduras's steady course toward internal self-rule and independence.

The Public Meeting and the Superintendent, pre-1854

The ambiguous status of British loggers who settled in Spanish territory hindered the early development of government institutions in the area. Informal meetings to address common security concerns, however, evolved into a rudimentary form of administration, the Public Meeting. Participation in the Public Meetings depended on race, wealth, and length of residency. In 1765 Rear Admiral Sir William Burnaby, commander in chief of Jamaica, compiled the settlement's common law in the Ancient Usages and Customs of the Settlement, or "Burnaby's Code." Burnaby also recommended to the British government that a superintendent be appointed to oversee the settlement. Opposition from the settlers prevented the office of superintendent from being permanently established until 1796. The changing political, economic, and social climate of Central America and the Caribbean, including the emancipation of slaves throughout the British Empire in the 1830s, contributed to a desire to regularize the status of the settlement. As early as 1840, British law displaced Burnaby's Code as the settlement's basic law, and in 1854 a Public Meeting and the British Parliament adopted a new constitution, which created institutions more like those of other British possessions (see Constitutional Developments, 1850–62, ch. 6). The Public Meeting thus ceased to operate.

Elected Legislative Assembly, 1854–70

The new constitution replaced the Public Meeting with a Legislative Assembly with eighteen elected members. In addition, the superintendent appointed three subordinate colonial officials, who served in the assembly as ex officio, or "official," members. The elected members had to be British-born or naturalized subjects and own property worth £2400 sterling. The superintendent, who was appointed by the British government, chaired the assembly and could dissolve it at will. In 1862, when the Settlement of Belize in the Bay of Honduras was officially declared a British colony known as British Honduras, a lieutenant governor subordinate to the governor of Jamaica replaced the superintendent. Later, a governor replaced the lieutenant governor. At the end of the decade, however, the Legislative Assembly petitioned for status as a crown colony, hoping that the crown would thereby shoulder more of the costs of defense. In order to accommodate such status, the Legislative Assembly voted in 1870 to replace itself with an appointed Legislative Council.

Crown Colony, 1871–1935

The governor and his appointed council governed British Honduras after it was declared a crown colony in 1871. The exact composition of the council varied over the years, but its membership until 1936 was always restricted to official members, who held key appointive positions in the colonial administration, and unofficial members, who were appointed by the governor. In drafting a new constitution, the old Legislative Assembly withheld a power from the new governor. Unlike the governors of other crown colonies, the governor of British Honduras lacked reserve powers, the right to enact laws in emergency situations without the consent of the Legislative Council. In 1932, however, the Legislative Council agreed to grant reserve powers to the British Honduran governor in exchange for urgently needed British financial assistance in the wake of a devastating hurricane the previous year.

The Return to Elected Government, 1936–53

Resenting the pressure that had been brought to bear upon them to grant reserve powers, the unofficial members of the Legislative Council successfully lobbied for the inclusion of elected members, as had been offered when the council agreed to grant the governor reserve powers. In 1936 five of the seven unofficial posts of the twelve-member council became elected ones. In 1939 the council expanded to thirteen, the new member being an elected one. The mix of official and appointed members was shuffled several times before the council was replaced in 1954.

The institution of elections for council members, however, did not bring mass political participation. Property requirements for voters and candidates effectively excluded nonwhite people from government. And until 1945, women could not vote before the age of thirty; men could vote when they turned twenty-one. In the 1936 election, only 1,035 voters—1.8 percent of the population—cast ballots. Even as late as 1948, only 2.8 percent of the population voted. After World War II, the cause of self-rule in British Honduras benefited from the growing pressure for self-government and decolonization throughout the British Empire. The labor movement and the PUP, which was founded in 1950, called for greater political participation. In 1947 the Legislative Council appointed a commission of enquiry to make recommendations for constitutional reforms. The commission issued its report in 1952 and recommended moving slowly ahead with reforms, paving the way for an opening of the political system to greater popular participation.

Constitution of 1954 and Extension of Suffrage, 1954–60

The constitution of 1954 extended suffrage to all literate British subjects over the age of twenty-one. The new constitution also replaced the Legislative Council with a Legislative Assembly that had nine elected, three official, and three appointed members and established an Executive Council chaired by the governor. The nine members of the council were drawn from the Legislative Assembly and included the three official members, two of the appointed members, and four of the elected members chosen by the assembly. Although the governor was required to abide by the advice of the Executive Council, he still held reserve powers and controlled the introduction of financial measures into the legislature. In 1955 a quasi-ministerial government was established when three of the elected members of the Executive Council were given responsibility for overseeing three government ministries.

The 1960 Constitution

In 1959 British Honduras undertook another constitutional review, headed by Sir Hillary Blood. Blood's report served as the basis for a constitutional conference in London in 1960 and for reforms that took effect in March 1961. As a result of the review, the composition of the Legislative Assembly and Executive Council changed. In the twenty-five-member assembly, eighteen members were now to be elected from single-member districts, five were to be appointed by the governor (three of these after consultation with the majority and minority party leaders), and two were to be official members. Assembly members served a term of four years.

The eight-member Executive Council included the assembly's majority-party leader, whom the governor appointed as first minister. Two council members were to be official members, and five unofficial members were to be elected by the assembly. Five ministerial posts, including that of first minister, carried portfolios.

Internal Self-Rule, 1964–81

Because the political parties contesting the March 1961 elections had declared their intent to seek full independence, another constitutional conference was held in London in 1963. The conference led to the establishment of full internal self-government under a constitution that took force on January 1, 1964.

The changes introduced by this constitution significantly reduced the powers of the governor, transformed the Executive Council into a cabinet headed by a premier, and established a bicameral National Assembly composed of a House of Representatives and a Senate. The House of Representatives had eighteen members, all of whom were elected. The Senate had eight members, all appointed by the governor after consultation with majority and minority party leaders and other "suitable persons." The Senate's powers were limited to ratifying bills passed by the House or delaying, for up to six months, bills with which it disagreed (but for only one month on financial bills). General elections had to be held at least every five years on a date determined by the prime minister. The governor was still appointed by the crown but in executive matters was now bound by the recommendations of the cabinet. The leader of the majority party in the House of Representatives was to be appointed premier by the governor. Members of both the House and the Senate were eligible for appointment to the cabinet.

The constitution of 1964 established internal self-rule, and Britain had conceded the readiness of the colony for independence as early as 1961. But Guatemalan territorial claims against Belize delayed full independence until 1981 (see Decolonization and the Border Dispute with Guatemela, ch. 6).

Constitution of 1981

Preparation of the Independence Constitution

In the general election of November 1979, the PUP ran on a platform endorsing independence. The PUP's opponent, the UDP, favored delaying independence until the territorial dispute with Guatemala was resolved. Although the PUP won only 52 percent of the vote, it carried thirteen of the eighteen seats in the House of Representatives and thus received a mandate for the preparation of an independence constitution. On January 31, 1981, the government issued the White Paper on the Proposed Terms for the Independence of Belize. The National Assembly appointed a joint select committee to consider the proposed terms and solicit input from all organizations in the country. The committee reported widespread support for a monarchical form of government based on the British parliamentary system but also suggested a number of amendments to the proposal. The House of Representatives adopted the committee's report on March 27, 1981.

The Belize Constitutional Conference was then held at Marlborough House, London, between April 6 and April 14, 1981. Although invited to participate, the leader of the opposition in the House of Representatives and other representatives of the UDP declined to attend. Participating in the meeting at Marlborough House were only the Belizean delegation, headed by C.L.B. Rogers, deputy premier of Belize, and the British delegation headed by Nicholas Ridley, secretary of state for foreign and Commonwealth affairs, along with their respective experts. The report issued by the Belize Constitutional Conference set out the structure and content for the independence constitution.

The British Parliament legislated for the final steps leading to Belizean independence in the Belize Act 1981, which received royal assent on July 28, 1981. The act granted Queen Elizabeth II the power to provide Belize an independence constitution and to set a date for Belizean independence by an Order in Council. The act also recognized Belize's self-governing status with provisions for its right to amend the so-called Constitution Order. The queen issued the order on July 31. In Belize the National Assembly passed the new constitution, the governor gave his assent on September 20, 1981, and Belize became independent the following day.

Structure of the Constitution of 1981

The constitution of 1981 contains twelve chapters and 142 sections. The first five chapters, which cover the sovereignty and territory of Belize, fundamental rights, citizenship, the powers of the governor general, and the executive, were essentially new. Chapters six through ten, which deal with the legislature, the judiciary, the civil service, finances, and miscellaneous details relating primarily to national symbols and government procedures, are based upon the constitution of 1963. Chapters eleven and twelve deal with the transition to independence and the date of the document's commencement.

Procedure for Amending the Constitution

Chapter Six gives the National Assembly the power to amend the constitution, with some sections and articles subject to a more stringent procedure than others. The more stringent procedure applies to changing any of the fundamental rights and freedoms enumerated in Chapter Two; any change in the form of the National Assembly; the establishment of election districts and the conduct of elections; any change relating to the judiciary; and provisions relating to the granting of pardons and commutations, the Belize Advisory Council, the director of public prosecutions, the auditor general, and the public service. Schedule Two and Section Sixty-nine, which detail the amendment process, are also subject to the more stringent procedures. In order for a bill amending any of the above provisions to be presented to the governor general for assent, at least ninety days must pass between the introduction of the bill into the House of Representatives and the start of House proceedings on the second reading (or floor debate) of the bill, and the bill must receive not less than a three-quarters majority vote of all the members of the House of Representatives upon final reading, or passage, of the bill. Bills to amend other sections of the constitution require a vote of not less than a two-thirds majority of all the members of the House for passage upon final reading. Laws amending the constitution were adopted in 1984, 1985, and 1988. These constitutional amendments mainly revised sections defining citizenship and detailing procedures for the appointment and removal of certain government officials and for dividing the country into election districts for the House of Representatives.

Government Institutions

Belize is a constitutional monarchy with a parliamentary form of government based on the British model. The British monarch, Queen Elizabeth II, is the titular head of state and is represented in Belize by a governor general, a position held since independence by Minita Gordon. The governor general has a largely ceremonial role and is expected to be politically neutral. The constitution gives real political power to those who are responsible to the democratically elected House of Representatives, principally the cabinet and the prime minister. The constitution divides the government into three branches—the executive, the legislature, and the judiciary (see fig. 15). Additionally, the civil, or "public," service is overseen by an independent Public Service Commission.

Executive

According to the constitution, executive authority is vested in the British monarch. The governor general and other subordinate officers, however, exercise executive authority on the monarch's behalf. The governor general must be a citizen of Belize, and he or she serves at the pleasure of the queen, not subject to a fixed term of office. The governor general is appointed on the recommendation of the prime minister. The constitution sharply limits the executive authority of the governor general by stating that the

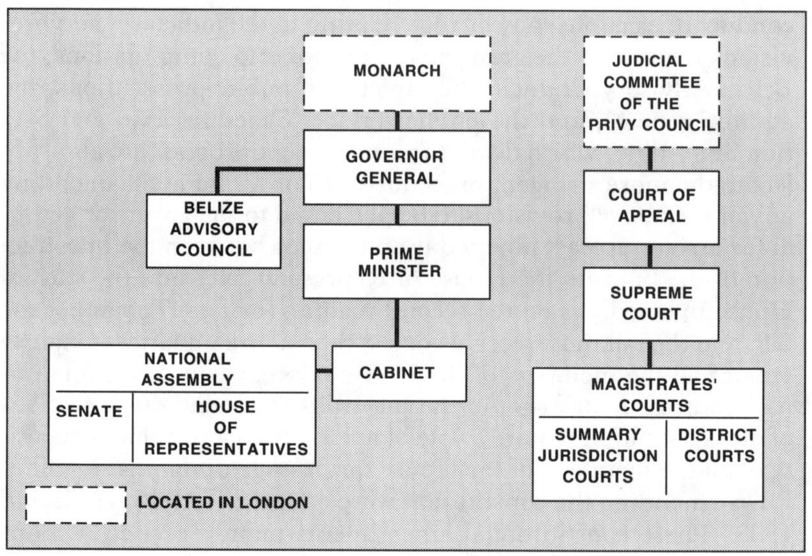

Figure 15. Belize: Organization of the Government, 1991

governor general "shall act in accordance with the advice of the Cabinet or a Minister acting under the general authority of the Cabinet" except in cases in which the constitution or law states otherwise. On some matters, the governor general must consult with other government officials or authorities, but is not bound to act in accordance with their advice.

When appointing a prime minister, the governor general is to appoint "a member of the House of Representatives who is the leader of the political party which commands the support of the majority of the members of that House." If no party has a majority, the governor general is directed to appoint that member "who appears to him likely to command the support of the majority of the members," someone able to assemble a viable coalition government. The constitution empowers the governor general to remove the prime minister from office if a resolution of no confidence is passed by the House of Representatives and the prime minister fails within seven days to resign or advise the governor general to dissolve the National Assembly. If, for example, a party loses its majority in the House through the defection of its members to the opposition party during the life of a National Assembly, the governor general can inform the prime minister that he or she no longer commands a majority in the House, and the governor general is free to appoint a new prime minister.

The cabinet is composed of the prime minister and all other ministers of government. Except for the prime minister and the minister of finance, who must be members of the House of Representatives, cabinet members may come from either the House or the Senate. Neither the speaker of the House nor the president of the Senate, however, may be appointed to the cabinet. The governor general formally appoints the ministers and assigns them their portfolios within the cabinet, but must do so in accordance with the advice of the prime minister. The National Assembly has the power to create ministerial positions not specifically enumerated in the constitution or to delegate this power to the governor general acting on the advice of the prime minister.

The constitution guarantees the executive supremacy of the prime minister and the cabinet. It states:

> The Cabinet shall be the principal executive instrument of policy with general direction and control of the Government and shall be collectively responsible to the National Assembly for any advice given to the Governor General by or under the general authority of the Cabinet and for all things done by or under the authority of any Minister in the execution of his office.

The governor general appoints as leader of the opposition a member of the House who commands the majority support of the opposition members, except in cases where there are no members of the House of Representatives who do not support the government.The leader of the opposition has the right to be consulted by the prime minister or to give binding advice to the governor general in the matter of some appointive government offices.

The Belize Advisory Council is an executive organ that serves as an independent body assisting the governor general. Its primary function is to give binding advice regarding the granting of pardons, commutations, stays of execution, and the removal of justices of appeal who are considered unable to carry out their duties or who have misbehaved in office. The council must have at least seven members including a chairman. The governor general appoints council members in accordance with the advice of the prime minister, who must consult with the leader of the opposition for all appointments and secure his or her concurrence in at least two of the appointments. The chairman must hold, have held, or be qualified to hold the office of judge of a superior court of record.

In addition, at least two members must hold, or have held, high office within the government, and at least one must be a member of a recognized profession in Belize.

Legislature

Belize's National Assembly is a bicameral legislature composed of an elected House of Representatives and an appointed Senate. Chapter Six of the constitution charges the National Assembly with making "laws for the peace, order and good government of Belize." Following national elections, the National Assembly has a life of five years, unless the governor general dissolves it sooner. It must hold at least one session a year. In the event of war, the life of the National Assembly may be extended for one year at a time for up to two years. The governor general almost always exercises his power to dissolve the National Assembly in accordance with the advice of the prime minister, who generally seeks to dissolve the National Assembly at a time when he perceives the ruling party as likely to receive a new mandate from the electorate. Under certain circumstances, however, the governor general may act on his or her own judgment. The governor general may, for example, refuse to dissolve the National Assembly if he or she does not believe dissolution to be in the best interest of the country. A general election must be held within three months after the National Assembly has been dissolved, and senators are to be appointed as soon as practical after the election.

Qualifications for representatives and senators are similar. To be eligible for either chamber, a person must be a citizen of Belize, be at least eighteen years old, and have resided in Belize for at least one year immediately prior to his or her nomination (to the House) or appointment (to the Senate). Members of the armed forces or the police force are barred from serving in either chamber. People holding government office or appointment are barred from membership in the House of Representatives; they are barred from membership in the Senate only if the position is connected with the conduct of elections or compilation of the electoral register. People who are party to any contract with the government or the public service must declare publicly the nature of their contract before the election in order to qualify for election to the House. Potential appointees to the Senate must make such a disclosure to the governor general before their appointment. Sitting members of the National Assembly are also barred from holding government contracts unless the House (or the governor general in the case of senators) waives the ban.

National Assembly building, Belmopan
Courtesy Steven R. Harper

The members of the House of Representatives and the Senate elect their presiding officers, the Speaker of the House and the President of the Senate, respectively. Each chamber may choose one of its own members who is not a government minister, or it may choose some other Belizean citizen who is not a member of either the House or the Senate. A speaker elected from outside the House has no vote within the House of Representatives, but such a president of the Senate does. Both the speaker and the president must be at least thirty years old.

According to the constitution as amended in 1988, the country is to have no fewer than twenty-eight electoral districts, or divisions, each with a nearly equal number of eligible voters and the right to elect one House member. The constitution charges the Elections and Boundaries Commission with making recommendations to the National Assembly when it believes additional electoral divisions are needed. The National Assembly may then enact laws establishing the new divisions. When the constitution took effect in 1981, it mandated that the House would have eighteen elected members; the current number of electoral divisions, and hence elected representatives, was set at twenty-eight in October 1984. Not counting the presiding officer, a quorum of at least seven members is necessary for a sitting of the House of Representatives.

The Senate has eight members (nine, if the Senate elects its presiding officer from outside its membership) who are appointed by the governor general according to the following provisions: five are appointed in accordance with the advice of the prime minister; two with the advice of the leader of the opposition; and one with the advice of the Belize Advisory Council. Not counting the presiding officer, a quorum of three senators is necessary for a sitting of the Senate.

The House of Representatives or the Senate may introduce bills, except ones involving money. Passing a bill requires a simple majority among members who are present and voting. A bill that has been passed by both houses is presented to the governor general, who assents to the bill and publishes the measure in the official *Government Gazette* as law. The governor general's assent is purely pro forma, since he or she acts in accordance with the advice of the cabinet.

The Senate can normally be expected to pass a measure adopted by the House, since a majority of its members are appointed on the advice of the prime minister. Should the Senate, however, reject a measure or amend it in a manner unacceptable to the House, the House still has the power to enact the bill, as long as the Senate received the House's bill at least one month before the end of the session. To enact the bill, the House must pass the measure again at least six months later and in the next session of the National Assembly and send it to the Senate at least one month before the end of the session. Even if the bill is again rejected by the Senate, it still can be presented to the governor general for assent.

Bills involving money are handled under a more restricted procedure and with less opportunity for the Senate to delay them. Only the House of Representatives may introduce these bills. Laws related to taxes may be introduced by the House only with the recommendation or consent of the cabinet. Moreover, if the Senate fails to pass a finance bill without amendments within one month of receiving it from the House, and if the Senate received it at least one month before the end of the session, the bill is presented to the governor general for his or her assent despite the lack of Senate approval.

Laws that are introduced as a result of cabinet decisions are virtually guaranteed passage because the cabinet represents the majority party in the House. Moreover, PUP governments have commonly given all or nearly all PUP House members a cabinet position. The PUP cabinets have consequently constituted a majority of the House membership. Under these circumstances, once the cabinet has agreed on a course of action, debate on the floor of the House is largely irrelevant, since the constitutionally mandated collective responsibility of the cabinet obliges its members to support cabinet decisions on the floor or resign from the cabinet. In contrast, when the UDP won twenty-one seats in the twenty-eight-member House elected in 1984, Prime Minister Manuel Esquivel governed until 1989 with only an eleven-member cabinet, leaving ten other UDP members to be "backbenchers." Political analysts saw this introduction of the backbencher system (an element of the British parliamentary model), as strengthening the House as an institution vis-à-vis the cabinet.

Judiciary

In the Belizean legal system, the judiciary is an independent branch of government. Among the basic legal protections afforded by the constitution to criminal defendants are a presumption of innocence until proven guilty; the rights to be informed of the nature and particulars of the charges, to defend oneself before an independent and impartial court within a reasonable amount of time, and to have the hearings and trial conducted in public; and guarantees against self-incrimination and double jeopardy. In more serious criminal cases, the defendant also has a right to a trial by jury.

Each of the six districts has a Summary Jurisdiction Court, which hears criminal cases, and a District Court, which hears civil cases. Both types of court of first instance are referred to as magistrates' courts because their presiding official is a magistrate. These courts have jurisdiction in less serious civil and criminal cases, but must refer to the Supreme Court more serious criminal cases, as well as any substantive legal questions. Magistrates' courts may impose fines and prison sentences of up to six months. Finding suitable magistrates has proven difficult, even though magistrates need not be trained lawyers. Vacancies have contributed to a backlog of cases and many prolonged acting appointments, a situation that, critics charge, has opened the courts to political manipulation. Law students returning to Belize for summer vacation or retired civil servants often fill the vacancies.

The Supreme Court has unlimited original jurisdiction in both civil and criminal proceedings. In addition to the more serious criminal and civil cases, the Supreme Court hears appeals from the magistrates' courts. The governor general appoints the head of the Supreme Court, the chief justice, "in accordance with the advice of the Prime Minister given after consultation with the Leader of the Opposition." The governor general appoints the other justices, called puisne judges (of which there were two in 1989), "in accordance with the advice of the judicial and legal services section of the Public Service Commission and with the concurrence of the Prime Minister given after consultation with the Leader of the Opposition." Justices may serve until they reach sixty-two, the normal, mandatory retirement age, which may be extended up to the age of seventy. Justices may be removed only for failing to perform their duties or for misbehavior.

The Court of Appeal hears appeals from the Supreme Court. A president heads the Court of Appeal. The governor general appoints the president and the two other justices serving on the court "in accordance with the advice of the Prime Minister given after consultation with the Leader of the Opposition." The constitution sets no fixed term of office for these justices but provides that their terms of office be fixed in their instruments of appointment.

In cases involving the interpretation of the constitution, both criminal and civil cases may be appealed by right beyond the Court of Appeal to the Judicial Committee of the Privy Council in London. The Court of Appeal may also grant permission for such appeals in cases having general or public importance. The crown may grant permission for an appeal of any decision—criminal or civil—of the Court of Appeal.

Public Service

The independent Public Services Commission oversees the public service, which includes the Belize Defence Force (BDF). The Commission consists of a chairman and eighteen other members, including nine ex officio members ranging from the chief justice to the commissioner of police. The governor general appoints the chairman and unofficial members "acting in accordance with the advice of the Prime Minister given after consultation with the Leader of the Opposition." Members of the National Assembly and holders of any public office (except ex officio members) may not be appointed to the commission until being out of office for at least two years. The normal term of office is three years, but the instrument of appointment may specify a shorter period, which must be at least two years. The Public Services Commission has the power to appoint people to public service positions and to discipline employees. The Public Services Commission also has responsibility for setting the code of conduct, fixing salaries, and generally managing the public service.

Under the British model of parliamentary government, public service employees are expected to execute the policies of the cabinet ministers who head the various executive ministries regardless of the ministers' political affiliations. In turn, public service employees are to be insulated from overt political pressure.

Local Government

The country is divided into six political districts, or subdivisions: Belize, Cayo, Corozal, Orange Walk, Stann Creek, and Toledo (see fig. 9). No administrative institutions exist at the district level, however, and there is no regional government between the national government and the municipal and village councils.

Laws enacted by the National Assembly govern the municipal councils, which have limited authority to enact local laws. The primary role of the councils is to oversee sanitation, streets, sewers, parks, and other amenities, and to control markets and slaughterhouses, building codes, and land use. Their revenues come from property and other taxes set by the national government, as well as from grants from the national government. The largest of the eight municipal councils is the one for Belize City, which has a nine-member city council. The other seven municipal governments are the seven-member town boards in Benque Viejo del Carmen, Corozal, Dangriga, Orange Walk, Punta Gorda, San Ignacio, and San Pedro (on Ambergris Cay, off Corozal). Each municipal council elects a mayor from among its members, and elections for the municipal councils are held every three years. The PUP and UDP dominate the municipal elections, and candidates, often recruited on short notice, are highly dependent on their party. The use of at-large elections frequently results in one party winning all of the seats on a council, and this situation tends to make the local elections a popular referendum on the performance of the party in power at the national level. Aliens who have resided for three or more years in a given municipality may register to vote in the municipal elections.

Village councils are a more informal kind of local government. They are not created by law and thus are not vested with any legal powers or functions. Nevertheless, most villages have councils, which operate as community organizations promoting village development and educational, sporting, and civic activities. The village councils have seven members and are chosen every two years in elections overseen by the Ministry of Social Services and Community Development. These elections commonly take place in public meetings, often without voter registration lists or secret ballot. Their informality does not prevent the village councils from becoming politicized, however, and they are often a base of support for or opposition to the local representative in the House of Representatives.

A third form of local government, the *alcalde* (mayor) system, exists in a few Kekchí and Mopán Indian villages. Derived from the Spanish system of local government imposed on the Maya, the *alcalde* system is the only government institution in Belize that is not Anglo-Saxon in origin. Laws enacted in 1854 and 1884 gave the system a legal foundation. Since then, however, the system has declined, largely as the result of a delimitation and regularization of its authority in 1952, the growth of the cash economy, and the diminished importance of subsistence farming and communal labor. Coordination of communal labor had been a key function of the *alcalde.* Annual elections are held to select a first *alcalde,* a second *alcalde,* a secretary, and a village policeman. The *alcalde* has the right to judge disputes over land and crop damage. In minor cases, the *alcalde* has the authority to try and punish offenders. Decision making in the village is generally by consensus after village elders direct open discussion. Women do not participate in these public meetings.

In addition to these forms of local government, Belize grants certain exemptions and rights to three Mennonite communities that immigrated to Belize in the late 1950s and early 1960s. An agreement, or Privilegium (signed in December 1957 between the government and each community), spells out the exemptions, rights, and responsibilities of the Mennonite communities. Under the Privilegium, the Mennonite communities have the right to run their own churches and schools using the Low German language, and their members are exempt from military service, any social security or compulsory insurance system, and the swearing of oaths. In return, the Privilegium commits the Mennonites to invest in the country, be self-supporting, produce food for both the local and export markets, conduct themselves as good citizens, and pay all normal duties and taxes established by law. The Mennonite communities tax themselves in order to make lump-sum property tax payments to the government and to finance schools, and public works, and other internal operations. The communities legally register their land in the name of the community and restrict individual ownership of community land to members in good standing with the Mennonite Church. Other Mennonites also live in Belize with no special arrangements with the government.

Political Dynamics

Electoral Procedures

In contrast to most Central American nations, elections in Belize are notable for their regularity, adherence to democratic principles,

Government House, Belize City
Courtesy Steven R. Harper

and an absence of violence. The Representation of the People Ordinance and the constitution regulate electoral procedures. The constitution established an independent Elections and Boundaries Commission and charged it with the registration of voters, the conduct of elections, establishment of election districts, and all other related matters. The five members of the commission serve five-year terms of office. The governor general appoints all five members in accordance with the advice of the prime minister, who consults with the leader of the opposition before nominating the members. National Assembly members and others who hold public office are barred from appointment.

The constitution guarantees the right to vote to every citizen over the age of eighteen who meets the provisions of the Representation of the People Ordinance. Voting is not compulsory. Employers are required to give their employees time to vote and to pay them for the time they are away at the polls. Polls are open from 7:00 A.M. to 6:00 P.M. on election day, but anyone in line by 6:00 P.M. may vote, no matter how long it may take. The sale of liquor is barred while the polls are open. Certain forms of political campaigning, including television advertisements, political speeches, and the distribution of political buttons, posters, banners, or flags are also prohibited. Canvassing of voters is permitted, except within a 100-meter zone around each polling station. Within this zone, voters may not be disturbed, voter-to-voter conversation is barred, and only election officials may answer questions. The constitution mandates that "votes be cast in a secret ballot."

The Elections and Boundaries Commission maintains a registry of voters and publishes this list for public inspection at its offices and at polling stations. For the September 1989 general election, there were 82,556 registered voters, a 28 percent increase over registration levels for the previous general election in 1984. Of the registered voters in 1989, 72 percent actually voted, a slight decrease from 1984, when 75 percent of the electorate cast ballots. Municipal elections attract a lower turnout. For example, less than 48 percent of the electorate cast ballots in the Belize City municipal elections in 1989.

The right forefinger of voters is marked with indelible ink to help prevent multiple voting. No provision is made for absentee voting, although certain people (for example, members of the BDF, police officers on duty outside their voting district, and persons employed in essential services) may vote by proxy.

Candidates for the House of Representatives are elected from single-member districts. The candidate with the largest number of votes wins the election; in the event of a tie, a new election is held in that district within three months. This type of electoral system usually strengthens the hand of the winning party in relation to its strength at the polls because a party winning narrow victories in a number of districts may obtain a larger majority in the House of Representatives than its share of the popular vote. In 1979, for example, the PUP and the UDP split the vote 52 percent to 47 percent, but the PUP carried thirteen of the eighteen House seats. Similarly, in the 1984 election, the vote was split 53.3 percent to 43.3 percent between the UDP and the PUP, but the UDP won twenty-one of the twenty-eight House seats.

Electoral Process since Independence

Transitional provisions of the 1981 constitution permitted members of the preindependence National Assembly to continue in office until new elections were set. In 1984 Prime Minister George Price called for elections. The PUP under the leadership of George Price held thirteen of the twenty-one seats in the House of Representatives in the years immediately before and after independence. The PUP was beginning to show signs of weakness, however, after having dominated national politics for thirty years. This weakness was evident as early as 1974, when the UDP polled 49 percent of the vote but won only six of eighteen seats. In 1977 the PUP failed to capture a single seat on the Belize City Council. It was not until the general election on December 14, 1984, that the PUP suffered its first defeat at the national level. The UDP under Manuel Esquivel won twenty-one of the twenty-eight seats in the newly enlarged House of Representatives. The PUP won only seven seats; one PUP member defected and later created the Belize Popular Party in 1985. The UDP confirmed its strength when it dominated the municipal elections in March 1985 and won control of five of the eight municipal councils.

A ten-year effort to harness opposition to the PUP culminated in the UDP's victory in the 1984 general election. The UDP campaign focused on economic issues because the PUP had a poor economic record for the 1981-84 period. The UDP stressed its conservative, free-enterprise, and pro-United States approach, but of equal importance in the PUP's defeat was simply the country's readiness for a change. George Price had risen to national prominence in the 1950s, and the PUP had been the ruling party ever since 1964, when internal self-rule was instituted. Price tried to hold the middle ground while the PUP split into left and right camps. Meanwhile, the track record of the UDP at the local level made it a credible alternative to the PUP. Moreover, the leadership of Manuel Esquivel probably enhanced the appeal of the UDP. Esquivel, like George Price, is both Mestizo (see Glossary) and Creole (see Glossary) in origin and thus able to bridge the main ethnic division in the country.

Buoyed by the country's strong economic growth in 1989, Prime Minister Esquivel in July of that year called an election for September 4, several months sooner than necessary. The PUP, however, won the election by a small margin, carrying 50.3 percent of the vote and capturing fifteen seats in the House of Representatives. The UDP won 48.4 percent of vote and thirteen seats. The PUP's fifteen-to-thirteen-seat majority grew to sixteen-to-twelve when a UDP member switched parties in December 1989.

Two issues, the economy and Belizean citizenship, dominated the election. The UDP had overseen an International Monetary Fund (IMF—see Glossary) economic stabilization plan inherited from the previous PUP government and stressed the country's economic progress. The PUP, however, focused on the high unemployment rate, the large trade deficit, and large national debt. It also attacked the government's policy of selling Belizean citizenship to Hong Kong Chinese and accused the UDP of excessive reliance on foreign investment to the detriment of Belizeans. The PUP stated its preference for a mixed economic model under Belizean national control and effectively used the slogan "Belizeans First." The PUP also accused the UDP of political repression and harassment through the control and censorship of the media and the creation of the Security and Intelligence Service (SIS).

Other factors beyond the issues, however, help to explain the UDP's defeat. Having assumed responsibility for governing the country, the UDP neglected its party organization and was plagued by internal divisions before and after the election. The party's newspaper acknowledged that the bitterness of the nominating convention had hurt the UDP. And after the PUP won every seat on the Belize City Council in municipal elections in December 1989, the paper charged that prominent UDP figures had failed to campaign for the party. Meanwhile, the PUP entered the election as a unified, centrist party, which shed its right and left wings.

Personality is an important factor in Belizean politics, and personal vilification is a standard campaign strategy. Many people perceived Esquivel and other UDP ministers as arrogant and snobbish. In contrast, Price was considered a populist, whose personal religiosity and moral austerity always won him—and indirectly the PUP—support from the religious vote.

Despite the diversity of Belizean society, ethnic and religious differences rarely entered overtly into national politics. Parties based on ethnic identity never formed, and no single ethnic group dominated the PUP or the UDP. Nevertheless, ethnic political tension focused on the balance of power between Creoles and others, especially the Mestizos. The Creole middle class of Belize City adopted British culture, language, and religion. This group, the bulwark of British colonialism in Belize, gave Belize City an anti-Central American outlook. Other parts of the country, however, tended to share an ethnic and religious identity with the peoples of Central America. Recent Central American immigration has threatened the balance between Creole and non-Creole, and the UDP attempted to tap resentment toward the refugees in the 1984 election. Although the influx of refugees slowed in the late 1980s, Central American refugees may have accounted for as much as 17 percent of the population in 1989. Most were peasants who were readily absorbed into the agricultural sector, but these Spanish-speaking immigrants may be carrying the seeds of future political tensions by contributing to changes in the ethnic makeup of the country.

George Price and the PUP have long championed Belize's Central American identity. In the late 1950s, Price opposed Belize's inclusion in a proposed West Indies Federation that would have united Belize with the English-speaking Caribbean islands. Joining the federation would have raised the specter of immigration from the islands, which are populated mostly by Creoles and Protestants. This long-standing support for strong ties with Central America undoubtedly contributed to the PUP's strong performance among Spanish-speaking voters in the western and southern parts of the country in the 1989 election. But the PUP by no means had a monopoly on Mestizo voters. Moreover, the PUP's failure to include more Creoles in its top leadership might hurt the party in the future. In fact, the PUP cabinet that was appointed after the 1989 election included only one member that most Belizeans would identify as a Creole. Opponents have charged Price with attempting to "latinize" the country and with selling Belize short in negotiations with Guatemala.

Throughout the 1970s and the 1980s, the number of ethnic associations and councils grew. These associations were dedicated to promoting cultural pride and cohesion, self-reliance, and community participation and action. Although generally seen in a positive light, they were criticized by some observers, who expressed the fear that the revival of ethnic consciousness after several decades of integration was likely to lead Belize into escalating ethnic conflict.

Political Parties

Belize has a functioning two-party political system revolving around the PUP and the UDP. Dissident members of these parties periodically struck out on their own and founded new parties, but they have usually foundered after a few years. In early 1991, no parties besides the PUP and the UDP were active.

People's United Party

Almost since its founding in 1950, the People's United Party (PUP) has been the dominant force in Belizean politics. With the exception of the 1984 election, the PUP has won every national election between 1954 and 1989. The party grew out of a circle of alumni from Saint John's College, a Jesuit-run secondary school. Roman Catholic social-justice theory, derived from such sources as the papal encyclical *Rerum Novarum* and the work of the French neo-Thomistic philosopher Jacques Maritain, had a strong influence on these alumni. The group included many men who later became important political figures, such as George Price, Herbert Fuller, and Philip Goldson. The group won municipal elections in Belize City in the 1940s by addressing national issues and criticizing the colonial regime. Members were then poised to exploit the popular discontent that resulted from the unilateral decision of the governor to devalue the currency in late 1949. The group founded the People's Committee in response to the devaluation, and in September 1950 the People's Committee was reconstituted as the PUP.

The party tapped the organizational strength of the labor movement by piggybacking onto the General Workers' Union (GWU), which had established branches throughout the country during the 1940s. The PUP quickly surpassed the GWU in importance, largely because the overlapping leadership of the GWU and the PUP subordinated the interests of the union to those of the party. The PUP swept the 1954 election, the first one to be held after the introduction of full literate adult suffrage, easily defeating the National Party, a rival sponsored by the colonial government.

The PUP's success, however, set the stage for a split in 1956 over the questions of how far the party should cooperate with the colonial regime and whether to endorse the British initiative for a West Indies Federation. Members favoring cooperation constituted a majority of the PUP's Central Party Council and the party's representatives in the legislature. George Price, however, had the support of the rank and file for his intransigent approach. Following the resignation of the dissident leaders, Price enjoyed undisputed control of the PUP.

Price has been a preeminent politician over the years for several reasons. First, he has been recognized as the ablest and most charismatic politician among the PUP founders, and he has been seen as the spokesman for the anticolonial movement. Second, the party's split in 1956 saw the departure of the PUP's other top leaders, enabling Price to begin building a political machine in which local leaders were personally loyal to him. Third, when the PUP assumed control of the internal government in 1964, the locus of power shifted from the party to the cabinet, which Price was able to choose. Internal party mechanisms and structures began to atrophy, and party conventions served mainly to ratify decisions already made by a small group that Price headed.

The concentration of decision-making power in the hands of a small circle of leaders headed by Price helped the PUP organize across ethnic, class, and rural-urban lines under a common banner of anticolonial nationalism. But by discouraging broad participation in setting party policy, the power arrangement also hindered the rise of younger leaders.

Young members of the PUP's left wing, including Said Musa, V.H. Courtenay, and Assad Shoman, pushed through a new party constitution in 1975 designed to encourage greater participation by the rank and file and to counter declining popular support for the party. The party's older leadership, however, resisted the reformed constitution and effectively blocked its implementation. Observers of Belizean politics have often cited an aging leadership lacking fresh ideas and out of contact with the people, especially with younger voters, as a reason for the PUP's defeat in 1984.

The relatively small leadership circle, however, failed to prevent the rise of factions within the PUP. Although Price has always held a centrist position, the PUP has often been torn by strife between its left and right wings because of conflicting personalities and agendas within the leadership. Observers have also cited party disunity as a factor in the 1984 defeat. In the wake of that defeat, leaders from both the right and left wings abandoned or were expelled from the party. The PUP thus entered the 1989 election more ideologically unified than it had been for many years.

The centrist ideology of the PUP seems to reflect the personal outlook of George Price, who has consistently called the orientation of the party "Christian Democratic," endorsed "wise capitalism," and rejected both "atheistic communism" and "unbridled capitalism."

The primary thrust and ideological appeal of the PUP, however, remained its nationalism and anticolonialism. In the 1989 election, for example, the PUP accused the UDP of having pandered to foreign speculators whose investments did little to help Belizeans. The 1989 PUP platform called for restricting the sale of Belizean property to foreigners, halting the sale of Belizean passports, reducing the role of the United States Agency for International Development (AID) in the country, and nationalizing the University College of Belize, which the UDP government had developed under an agreement with Michigan's Ferris State College. Party documents commit the PUP to "economic democracy," and the party's leaders have endorsed a "mixed economic model with Belizean national control." Still, the PUP has sought investment by foreign firms, including ones from the United States, and the party's differences with the UDP on these matters were often based more on style and rhetoric than on substance.

United Democratic Party

The colonial establishment responded to the political challenge of the PUP by founding the National Party (NP) in 1951. But despite official encouragement, the NP enjoyed little popular support. Ex-PUP members, headed by Philip Goldson, founded the Honduran Independence Party (HIP) after the 1956 split in the PUP. After their defeat by the PUP in elections in 1957, the NP and the HIP parties merged in 1958 to form the National Independence Party (NIP). In 1961 Goldson became party leader but was unable to mount an effective challenge to the PUP. An unsuccessful leadership challenge to Goldson in 1969 led to the formation of the People's Development Movement (PDM), headed by Dean Lindo. Lindo did not try to organize the PDM on a national basis. But in 1969, he formed a coalition with the NIP and ran in a snap election. Suffering a near total defeat, both parties became largely inactive. Probusiness forces within the NIP organized the Liberal Party, probably to strengthen their voice in the anticipated negotiations for a new party. In September 1973, the NIP, the PDM, and the Liberal Party merged to form the United Democratic Party.

With the formation of the UDP in 1973, the outlook for people who opposed the PUP began to brighten. The UDP won 31.8 percent of the vote in 1974 and 46.8 percent in 1979. The PUP, however, still held majorities in the House of Representatives. In the 1979 election, the UDP had expected to receive a boost from the recent enfranchisement of eighteen-year-olds. However, during an election that became a referendum on independence, the party was hurt by its call to delay independence for at least another ten years. Moreover, the party still had to overcome the divisions among its constituencies. Lindo, who had become party leader after the 1974 election, was defeated in his district in 1979. Theodore Aranda, a Garifuna (see Glossary), succeeded Lindo as party leader. After charges and countercharges of racism and incompetence, Aranda resigned from the UDP in 1982 and later formed a Christian Democratic Party (CDP) that merged with the PUP in 1988. Changes in the UDP's constitution enabled Manuel Esquivel, a UDP senator, to be elected the new party leader. Esquivel, who came to the UDP via the Liberal Party, led the party to victory in 1984.

Beyond the weakness of the PUP in 1984, several factors contributed to the UDP's victory. First, Esquivel went beyond simply opposing the PUP and presented a self-assured image for the UDP. Personal initiative and his platform, which emphasized change, played well in the face of the country's poor economic performance in the early 1980s. Second, victories in local elections had made the UDP a more credible party; the UDP had swept Belize City municipal elections in 1983 (Esquivel was a former mayor of Belize City). Finally, Esquivel's mixed Creole and Mestizo heritage probably helped the party make inroads among Mestizo voters. Earlier party leaders, such as Philip Goldson, had long been associated with opposition to what they considered Price's latinization of Belize.

Esquivel was also able to counter PUP criticism of the UDP's economic policy. He noted that the UDP was merely implementing

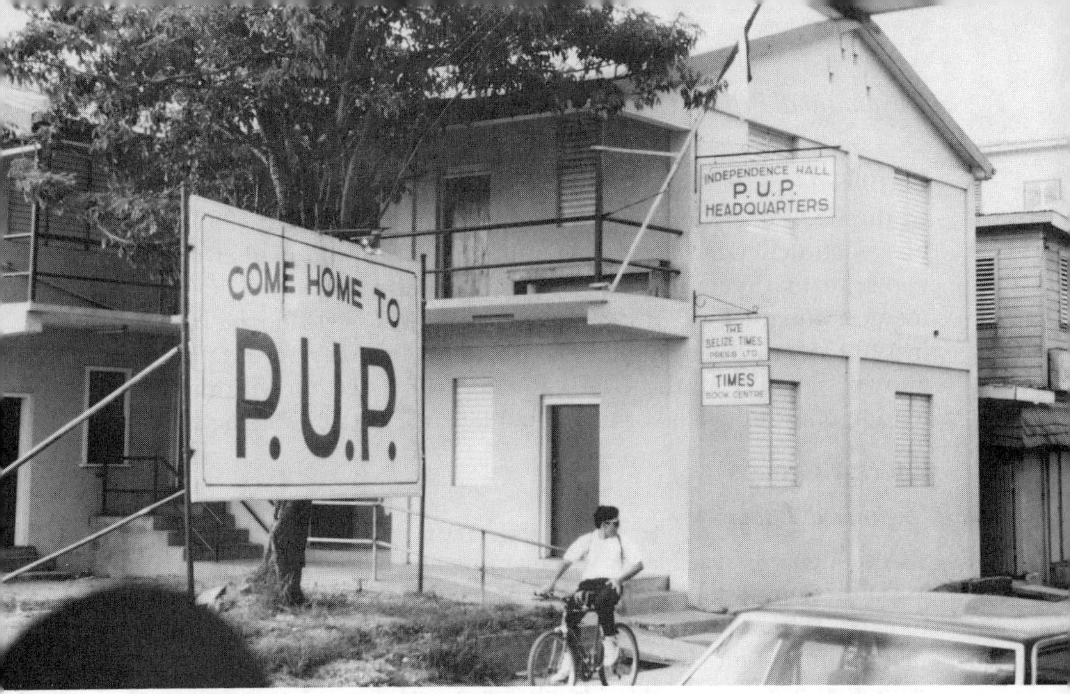

People's United Party headquarters, Belize City
Courtesy Steven R. Harper

an economic policy initiated by the PUP in agreement with the IMF. Esquivel pointed out that many issues criticized by the PUP—the increased presence of AID advisers and Peace Corps volunteers, the construction of radio towers by Voice of America, and the sale of Belizean citizenship—had all begun in the previous PUP government. The UDP distinguished itself from the PUP by highlighting its economic expertise and willingness to implement painful, but necessary, reforms.

Factionalism and disarray emerged in the UDP after its defeat in the September 1989 general election and after postelection recriminations and increased public attention to the private business affairs of many UDP figures. Nevertheless, the party retained its strong political base as the only viable opposition to the PUP. In February 1990, the UDP Executive Council confirmed Esquivel as party leader and Dean Barrow as deputy party leader.

Other Parties

Factionalism within the PUP and the UDP sometimes led to the establishment of new parties. But the track record of these parties was poor. In 1985, for example, expelled right-wing members of the PUP founded the Belizean Popular Party, which received less than 1 percent of the vote in the 1986 Belize City Council elections.

By 1988 the party was apparently defunct. Theodore Aranda founded the CDP following his resignation from the UDP in 1982, but his constituency did not follow him. The CDP won neither of the two seats that it contested in the 1984 general election. The CDP merged with the PUP in 1988, and Aranda was elected to the House in 1989 as a member of the PUP. Cyril Davis, a former UDP senator, resigned from the UDP after the 1989 election with the intention of forming a labor party, but he ended up joining the PUP.

Interest Groups

Organized Labor

Although organized labor was instrumental in the rise of the PUP, its political importance has diminished significantly since the 1950s. In early 1991, organized labor was fragmented, weak, and politically unimportant. In the late 1980s, total union membership was estimated at about 6,000. Membership was divided among some eighteen trade unions. The country's six major trade unions made up the National Trade Union Congress of Belize (NTUCB), which was affiliated with the International Confederation of Free Trade Unions (ICFTU), the Inter-American Regional Organization of Workers (Organización Regional Interamericana de Trabajadores—ORIT), and the Caribbean Congress of Labor. These organizations were philosophically and financially tied to labor organiztions in the United States. The formal ties that once existed with political parties disappeared, and the PUP and the UDP effectively absorbed or neutralized the political voice of the unions once affiliated with them.

The modern labor movement in Belize began in 1934, when Antonio Soberanis Gómez founded the Labourers and Unemployed Association (LUA). Vestiges of the repressive labor laws inherited from the nineteenth-century colonial era were not abolished until 1959, but changes in 1941 and 1943 enabled the British Honduras Workers and Tradesmen's Union (founded by Soberanis in 1939) to register legally as a trade union in 1943. Shortly thereafter, the union changed its name to the General Workers' Union (GWU). Because the GWU's strikes and organizing activities targeted the agricultural and forestry sectors, especially the Belize Estate and Produce Company, its organizational structure in rural areas made it a particularly desirable partner for the PUP in the anticolonial struggle of the 1950s.

Membership in the GWU grew from 350 in 1943 to over 3,000 in the late 1940s and peaked in 1955 at about 12,000. In 1956 membership fell to 700. The union's explosive growth and then rapid decline must be seen in light of its role in the anticolonial movement and the loss of that role to the PUP.

Cooperation in the late 1940s between the GWU and the People's Committee, the forerunner of the PUP, eventually led to the PUP's control of the union through interlocking leadership. Although the PUP drew on the GWU's organizational structure, it abandoned the GWU's socialist ideology in order to attract support from all segments of Belizean society. Having lost its distinct political voice, the GWU ceased playing a key role in the anticolonial movement after the PUP's 1956 internal split, which left the union in the hands of dissident party members. Price's associates founded a rival labor movement, the Christian Workers' Union, hastening the decline of the GWU and lending support to the PUP. The PUP by then had established its own organization throughout the country and no longer needed to rely on outside organizational support.

With its role in the anticolonial movement usurped by the PUP, the labor movement was dormant as a political force during the 1960s and 1970s. The labor movement instead focused its energies on collective bargaining and job-related issues. In the late 1970s, however, a new generation of union activists attempted to reestablish labor's independent political voice through the United General Workers Union (UGWU). This union was formed by the amalgamation of the Belize General Development Workers' Union and the Southern Christian Union in 1979.

Most of the Belizean press, the leadership of both the PUP and UDP, and organized labor (including the Corozal branch of the UGWU, whose leadership had strong ties to the PUP, and the influential Public Services Union, which had close ties to the UDP), were hostile to the UGWU. The hostility stemmed not only from the UGWU's efforts to encroach on what the politicians and their union supporters thought to be their turf, but also from the ideological orientation of the union. Some critics accused the UGWU of being communist because of the union's ties to trade union federations affiliated with the Soviet-controlled World Federation of Trade Unions, its sending of members to study in Cuba and the Soviet Union, its open support for revolutionary movements in Central America, and because of the ideological stance of *Gombay,* a magazine edited by UGWU leaders.

The UGWU (and its rivals) grew rapidly in the late 1970s as it organized banana, citrus, and sugar workers, as well as employees of the Belize Electricity Board and the Development Finance Corporation. Nevertheless, the union's failure to support strikes of other unions severely crippled the UGWU and removed it from the national political scene. These strikes were called to oppose the Heads of Agreement in 1981 and the formation that same year by the Corozal branch of the UGWU of a new union, which overwhelmingly defeated the UGWU in an election to choose a bargaining agent for the sugar workers.

Business Community

The PUP and the UDP depended on the business community for financial support during elections. At one time, the PUP could count on the support of small businessmen, whose interests were negatively affected by the policies of the colonial government. Similarly, big business usually supported the groups that opposed the PUP. By the 1980s, however, this breakdown in support by the business community was no longer generally true. In the election of 1984, for example, the UDP's strong support for free enterprise drew support from small and large business interests. Differences between the economic policies of the two parties were small enough that members of the business community were likely to back whichever party they perceived as the likely winner of any given election. Sometimes, however, they hedged their bets by contributing to both parties.

The Chamber of Commerce and Industry was the leading voice of the business community in Belize and was widely perceived as holding an influential voice in government. It officially endorsed neither political party and sought a good working relationship with the government of the day. It actively lobbied the government and monitored legislation on a variety of issues, such as mercantile policy, economic development, and policies on education and drugs. In its constitution, the chamber states that its objectives include fostering economic growth through the free-enterprise system, strengthening the public-private partnership, and enhancing the investment climate for Belizean and foreign investors. Members of the chamber included supporters of both the PUP and the UDP.

Churches and Religious Institutions

The interaction of churches and religious organizations with the government and political system was informal, but nonetheless powerful. The schools were a key element in this influence. Church-run schools had been the norm in Belize since the early colonial era, and both major political parties continued to endorse the church-state partnership in education. This partnership placed most primary and secondary schools under church control. Thus, the various Christian churches and denominations in Belize did not generally adopt a high political profile, but their schools served as a key adjunct to religious services and their gatherings as a locus for church influence. The most prominent example of such influence was the role that the Jesuit-run secondary school, Saint John's College, played in preparing the leaders of the nationalist movement in the 1940s. Religious influence, especially traditional Roman Catholic social thought, continued to affect Belizean political life in 1991.

Some also attribute the PUP's early anti-British and pro-United States outlook and its predisposition toward the Roman Catholic countries of Central America, rather than toward the predominantly Protestant English-speaking islands of the West Indies (see Glossary), to the influence of the Jesuits and the Roman Catholic Church. Whereas the mainline Protestant churches, such as the Anglican and Methodist churches, were institutionally tied to Britain and the English-speaking West Indies, the Roman Catholic Church in Belize was once a vicariate of the Missouri Province of the Society of Jesus (Jesuits). Jesuits from the United States staffed key positions in the Belizean church. Foreign influence in the Roman Catholic and Protestant churches and schools in Belize had been much criticized. In recent decades, however, Belizeans have increasingly come to occupy leadership positions. By 1990 the top leadership of the country's Roman Catholic Church was Belizean, and a Belizean Jesuit was president of Saint John's College.

No political party or movement in Belize organized itself on the basis of religious affiliation, but Roman Catholics historically were considered to lean more toward the PUP. Protestants, allegedly being more pro-British, leaned more toward the PUP's opposition. Nonetheless, the top leadership of the UDP included many Roman Catholics, including Philip Goldson and Manuel Esquivel. Indeed, the UDP's 1984 victory would not have been possible without strong support from the country's Roman Catholic population.

The existence of a "Roman Catholic vote" in Belize is open to question. Still, politicians avoided taking positions that overtly contradicted Roman Catholic teachings because they feared a reaction from both the hierarchy and the laity. Thus, the presumption of the religious community's opposition to abortion kept the issue of legalizing abortion out of the political debate even through the Roman Catholic Church never sponsored an antiabortion campaign. Furthermore, no politician called for fundamental changes in the church-state partnership in education, which enjoyed strong support across the religious spectrum.

As of the early 1990s, liberal political movements, such as liberation theology, had not taken root in Belize, and the Roman Catholic Church avoided the split between the so-called "traditional" and "popular" churches that divided Roman Catholics in other Central American countries. Moreover, politicians probably overestimated the ability of the Roman Catholic Church to respond as a monolithic institution, and their perception of so-called "Roman Catholic" positions often lacked an awareness of current Roman Catholic thought and practice. The generally conservative outlook of the Belizean Protestant churches, which shared the traditional Roman Catholic position on many moral and social issues, perhaps reinforced politicians' consciousness of religious interests.

Since the 1970s, missionary activities by evangelical and fundamentalist denominations and sects, including the Mormons, Seventh-Day Adventists, and Jehovah's Witnesses, have been changing the religious composition of Belizean society. Although these groups, unlike the mainline Protestant churches, generally had strong ties to mother organizations in the United States and were often considered to be politically conservative, their political impact was negligible at the national level. At the local level, however, the proliferation of denominations and sects, many of which were hostile to one another and to the Roman Catholic Church, could be undermining the sense of common identity within communities. The *alcalde* system of village government, for example, has been disrupted in some Kekchí villages, when the village's Protestant members (who were opposed to the close ties of the traditional leadership with the Roman Catholic Church) have refused to participate in elections or abide by village court decisions.

Consciousness-Raising Organizations

Nongovernmental organizations focusing on charitable and service activities and private enterprise projects have been active for many years in Belize. These groups include Cooperative for American Relief Everywhere (CARE), Project Hope, and Volunteers in Technical Assistance (VITA). But a different type of nongovernmental organization became increasingly common in the 1980s. These organizations had no formal ties to political parties, but they exercised political influence through their efforts to raise the political consciousness or to develop a group identity among their constituencies. These organizations included ethnic-based associations, such as the Toledo Maya Cultural Council, the National Garifuna Council, and the Isaiah Morter Harambe Association; women's groups, such as the Belize Organization for Women and Development (Bowand), Women Against Violence (WAV), and the Belize Rural Women's Association (BRWA); and other groups, such as the Society for the Promotion of Education and Research (SPEAR), whose mission encompassed social and economic analysis, popular education and training, advocacy campaigns to promote social and economic justice, and research, seminars, and publications about Belize. Many of these organizations depended on grants from foreign government development agencies and nongovernment organizations to supplement locally raised funds. The long-term viability of these organizations remained unclear because these grants were often provided only as short-term "seed money."

Mass Communications

The Belizean constitution guarantees freedom of thought and expression. Nevertheless, the constitution permits the enactment of laws to make "reasonable provision" for limiting freedom of expression in the interests of defense, public safety, order, morality, health, and protection of reputations, rights, and freedoms of other persons. Despite the constitution's guarantees, there have been a number of controversies over access to broadcast media for political campaigns and over charges that the former UDP government used the libel laws to intimidate the PUP.

No daily newspapers were published in Belize. Several weeklies were published, but most of these were closely linked to political parties. As of early 1991, *Amandala* was the newspaper with the largest circulation: about 8,500. The paper's editorial line reflected the involvement of its owner and editor, Evan X. Hyde, in the Creole and black consciousness movement in Belize. The *Belize Times,* controlled by George Price, functioned as the official organ of the PUP. Published since 1956, the newspaper had a circulation of about 7,000 as of early 1991. The official UDP newspaper was the *People's Pulse.* Owned outright by the UDP, it began publication in 1988 and had a circulation of 5,000 by early 1991. The pro-business *Reporter,* with a circulation of 5,000 in early 1991, was once an organ of the Chamber of Commerce and Industry but was later bought by a group of businessmen and became an independent publication. The government published a weekly, the *Government Gazette.* Other publications included *Belize Today,* published monthly by the Belize Information Service; the *Chamber Update,* published monthly by the Chamber of Commerce and Industry; monthly newspapers published by the Anglican and the Roman Catholic churches; the quarterly *National Newsmagazine;* and *Spearhead,* a quarterly published by SPEAR.

A second, and older, pro-UPD paper, *Beacon,* suspended publication following the UDP's defeat in September 1989. *Beacon,* which had a circulation of 4,200 in 1989, was not controlled directly by the UDP, but by Dean Lindo, a minister in the Esquivel government. A PUP-affiliated paper, *Disweek,* ceased publication after the

PUP's 1984 electoral defeat. The fate of *Disweek* and *Beacon* points to the dependence of Belizean newspapers on revenue from government-linked advertising. Opposition papers, therefore, could not count on this type of advertising revenue.

Foreign Relations

Relations with the United States

Belize had close and cordial relations with the United States, which was a leading trading partner and principal source of foreign investment and economic assistance. As early as the 1940s, leaders of the anticolonial movement sought close ties with the United States, not only to pressure and embarrass Britain, but also to try to eliminate the colonial government's pro-British trade and economic policies, which were detrimental to many Belizeans.

Since independence, Price and the PUP have charted a foreign policy that proclaimed Belize's nonalignment and affirmed the country's special relationship with the United States. The PUP's favorable attitude toward the United States (when nationalist opinion elsewhere in Latin America and the Caribbean has often been strongly anti-United States and sometimes pro-Cuban) probably reflects the country's colonial experience, which cast Britain, rather than the United States, as the main obstacle to national sovereignty. Additionally, the influential role of Christian Democratic thought on the early nationalist leaders, especially Price, undoubtedly helped steer Belizean political dialogue away from the Marxist influences that have helped shape anti-United States feelings elsewhere in Latin America. Because the PUP and the UDP were in broad agreement on the country's relationship with the United States, the PUP's defeat in 1984 did not upset ties between the United States and Belize. On the contrary, the business-oriented UDP was highly favorable to the ideological outlook of the United States in the 1980s, and the Esquivel government was eager to implement free-market policies to attract United States investment.

United States foreign policy objectives in Belize included the promotion of economic development and political stability under democratic institutions, the promotion of United States commercial interests, the suppression of narcotics trafficking, and the continuation of the marijuana eradication program. Although recognizing Britain as Belize's primary supplier of military aid, the United States sought cooperative military relations with Belize and the development of an apolitical professional military capable of performing defense and counternarcotics functions. AID's plans for the 1991–95 period focused on the agricultural and tourism sectors and were aimed at helping Belize achieve sustainable private-sector-led growth.

In the late 1980s and early 1990s, United States foreign assistance to Belize totaled between US$9.3 million and US$10.7 million a year, a sharp decline from 1985, when it totaled US$25.7 million. Development Assistance and Peace Corps programs accounted for the bulk of the aid. In 1990 Development Assistance totaled US$6.5 million, and Peace Corps programs totaled US$2.5 million. Belize received no food aid from the United States in the 1980s or early 1990s. Although Belize received a total of US$32.0 million in Economic Support Funds (ESF) from 1983 through 1987, it received no funds from this program in the late 1980s and early 1990s. Belize was a beneficiary of the Caribbean Basin Initiative (CBI), under which the United States permits duty-free access to United States markets for imports from most Caribbean Basin countries (see Appendix D).

Military aid made up only a small percentage of United States assistance to Belize. From 1982 through 1990, Belize received over US$3 million in military assistance from the United States. In 1990 military aid totaled about US$615,000.

The PUP and the UDP governments both welcomed assistance from the United States, but this assistance was sometimes the subject of criticism. In the mid-1980s, for example, the presence of Peace Corps volunteers in government offices, the Chamber of Commerce and Industry, and secondary schools raised concerns that jobs were being taken away from Belizeans. People also complained that the volunteers interfered unduly in internal government affairs. In response to this criticism, the Peace Corps reduced the number of volunteers in Belize from more than 200 to fewer than 100 by early 1991. The role of AID consultants in preparing government development plans under the UDP government and the strings attached to aid from the United States have also been subjects of criticism. Belizean officials echoed this criticism because they did not believe that the restrictions (regarding trade and economic liberalizations) on the aid took into account local conditions. Although the Belizean government and business community felt positively about the CBI, they were concerned that the trade-liberalization component of President George Bush's Enterprise for the Americas Initiative (see Glossary) and negotiations for a North American free-trade zone with Mexico might make it impossible for the small countries of the Caribbean to compete with countries such as Mexico and Brazil in the absence of special provisions to preserve existing preferential trade arrangements.

Relations with Guatemala

Guatemala's long-standing territorial claim against Belize delayed normalization of relations between the two countries until September 1991. Guatemala claimed it inherited Spanish sovereignty over the British settlement following Guatemala's independence from Spain, and Spanish sovereignty over the territory had been recognized by Britain in the Convention of London signed in 1786. Britain rejected Guatemala's claim, however, because Guatemala had never effectively occupied present-day Belize's territory. Britain's own occupation of the area and its 1859 treaty with Guatemala, which set boundaries for what soon became British Honduras, paved the way for a British assertion of full sovereignty over the colony in 1862.

The 1859 treaty, however, included a provision for Britain to assist in the construction of a road from Guatemala City to the Caribbean coast. Guatemala has consistently claimed that this provision was a condition for ceding the territory to Britain. Guatemala claims the treaty was never fulfilled because the road was never built, so the country nullified the cession of territory. Britain, which had offered financial contributions toward the road construction at various times, rejected Guatemala's interpretation of the treaty. Britain believed that Guatemala was not in a position to cede the territory because it never possessed sovereignty over British Honduras. Between 1945 and 1985, Guatemalan constitutions claimed British Honduras as part of its national territory. A provision in the charter of the Organization of American States (OAS) reflected Latin American support for Guatemala's claim. The provision effectively barred membership to an independent Belize without a resolution of Guatemala's claim. Latin American support was also reflected in a provision in the treaty that established the Central American Common Market calling for the integration of Belize into Guatemala.

Subsequent negotiations, including United States mediation in 1965, produced recommendations viewed as highly favorable to Guatemala but failed to produce a settlement acceptable to all parties. At various points in the 1960s and 1970s, Guatemala threatened to invade if British Honduras became independent without resolution of its claim. The British military presence in British Honduras forestalled any invasion. To win Guatemalan acceptance of Belizean independence, however, Britain opposed in the 1970s any postindependence security guarantees to Belize and apparently favored ceding a small strip of territory between the Moho and

Sarstoon rivers in southern Belize. Territorial concessions were highly unpopular among Belizeans.

With full independence blocked by the inability to reach agreement with Guatemala and by the unwillingness of Britain to make security guarantees, Belize launched a foreign relations campaign in the mid-1970s to win the support of the world community. Building on support within the Nonaligned Movement, Belize gradually won broad support in the General Assembly of the United Nations (UN). The Latin American community began to shift its support from Guatemala to Belize. Cuba consistently supportly Belize's right to self-determination, Panama and Mexico voiced support for Belize in 1976 and 1977, respectively, and they were joined by Nicaragua in 1979. The United States, however, abstained from voting on Belizean independence resolutions introduced annually in the General Assembly. Then in 1980, with Guatemala refusing to vote and seven countries abstaining, 139 countries, including the United States, voted for a UN resolution calling for Belizean independence with territorial integrity by the end of 1981. The OAS subsequently endorsed this resolution.

Given the international support for this timetable, Belize, Britain, and Guatemala again sought a negotiated settlement. On March 11, 1981, the three parties signed an agreement known as the Heads of Agreements. The agreement laid out sixteen subjects, or heads, that were to be agreed to in a formal treaty at a later date. Popular reaction to the Heads of Agreement was overwhelmingly negative in Belize, and rioting ensued to protest what were perceived to be "unwarranted and dangerous" concessions to Guatemala. Furthermore, Guatemala rejected details of the settlement process and withdrew from the negotiations. The British decision to make security guarantees to Belize, however, enabled Belizean independence to go forward.

Subsequent negotiations with Guatemala in the early 1980s were unsuccessful. In 1985, however, Guatemala promulgated a new constitution that did not include the earlier claims to Belize. Rather, the new constitution treats the Belize question in its transitory provisions, giving the executive the power to take measures to resolve the territorial dispute in accordance with the national interests, but requiring any definitive agreement to be submitted to a popular referendum. The article in the provisions also calls for the government of Guatemala to "promote social, economic, and cultural relations with the population of Belize." After on-and-off negotiations in the late 1980s, including the appointment of a permanent joint commission in 1988, substantial progress was made in 1990, following a meeting between Prime Minister George Price and President

Vinicio Cerezo of Guatemala. In October 1990, Belize's minister of foreign affairs, Said Musa, stated that the preliminary talks on the drafting of a treaty (that would be submitted to popular referenda in both countries) had moved beyond territorial claims to questions of economic cooperation.

On August 14, 1991, Guatemalan president Jorge Serrano Elías acknowledged that Belize was recognized internationally, recognized the right of the Belizean people to self-determination, and stated his willingness to settle the dispute, all without dropping Guatemala's territorial claim. On August 16, 1991, Said Musa introduced a bill to extend Belize's maritime territorial limits to twelve nautical miles, in accord with current international law. The bill stipulated, however, that an exception would be made in the south allowing Guatemala access to international waters from its Caribbean coast in the same way that Mexico has access from its port of Chetumal. Minister Musa has said that the concession to Guatemala was made as a sign of good faith to promote settlement of Guatemala's territorial claim. In a further sign of improving affairs, Guatemala and Belize established full diplomatic relations in September 1991.

Relations with Other Latin American and Caribbean Countries

Maintaining the international support for its independence that Belize won in the 1970s and 1980s remained a main element of the country's foreign policy. Participation in the various regional organizations was seen as both a means toward an end and an objective of this policy. Although George Price and the PUP successfully campaigned against British Honduran participation in the proposed West Indies Federation in the late 1950s, Belize saw itself as a bridge between the English-speaking Caribbean and Central America. The nation had been a member since 1971 of the Caribbean Free Trade Association (Carifta), which later became the Caribbean Community and Common Market (Caricom—see Appendix C). Increasingly active on the political level within that organization, Belize supported an outward-looking strategy for the Caricom countries that would ensure international competitiveness, closer economic cooperation between Caricom and other Caribbean countries, and a common Caricom effort to preserve its limited preferential market access in the face of the growing importance of major trade and economic blocs in Europe and North America.

In November 1989, the OAS—with Guatemalan support—granted Belize permanent observer status and approved full membership for the country in January 1991. This event capped a long effort to overcome obstacles to membership in various regional organizations that had been erected by Guatemala in past years. The OAS charter had effectively barred membership to Belize and Guyana until their territorial disputes with OAS member countries were peacefully resolved. In 1985, however, OAS members modified the charter so that the bar to membership requests from Belize or Guyana expired on December 10, 1990. In February 1991, the Central American heads of government invited Belize to attend their December 1991 summit, the first such invitation received by the country.

During the 1980s, Belize remained on the fringes of the diplomatic initiatives and United States-coordinated military activities in Central America. This situation was due both to Guatemala's presumed opposition to Belize's participation and its fear of being drawn into the regional conflicts of Central America (by 1989 these conflicts had pushed some 30,000 refugees into Belize). Belize has steadfastly supported peaceful resolution of the region's disputes, political pluralism, and noninterference in the internal affairs of other nations. In the late 1980s, Belize stressed its support for the right of both Nicaragua and Panama, which were then under diplomatic, economic, and military pressure from the United States, to choose their own leaders and political systems.

Belize enjoyed warm relations with Mexico, its neighbor to the north. As early as 1958, Mexico stated its desire for a resolution of Belize's territorial problems that would respect the freedom and independence of the Belizean people. Mexico also provided critical support in favor of Belizean independence and territorial integrity in 1977. Although Mexico claimed parts of Belize during the nineteenth century, it signed treaties with both Britain and Guatemala in the course of that century to set the border definitively between Mexico and Belize. As part of its agreement with Britain, Mexico was guaranteed in perpetuity transit rights through Belizean waters connecting the Mexican port of Chetumal with the open seas.

Relations with Britain

Britain maintained approximately 1,500 troops in Belize to guarantee Belizean independence in the face of the Guatemalan territorial claims. The presence of the troops represented an exception to the long-standing British policy of not making military commitments to former colonies. Although the prospects for an agreement with Guatemala looked good in 1991, Minister of Foreign Affairs Said Musa emphasized that the presence of the British troops and an agreement with Guatemala were two separate issues. British officials have stated that the troops would remain even if an agreement were reached. Reasons cited for a continued British military presence in Belize included training the Belize Defence Force, providing British troops with an opportunity to train in a tropical environment, deterring leftist guerrillas from using Belize as a conduit for arms, and balancing the United States military presence in the region with a British presence. Britain spent an estimated US$18 million more per year to maintain its garrison troops in Belize rather than in Britain.

Britain provided Belize with military assistance in the form of training and equipment. Britain also provided interest-free loans totaling US$13.5 million under its multilateral capital aid program for the 1989-94 period. It also provided grants totaling US$1.4 million a year in the early 1990s through the technical cooperation program.

Relations with Other Countries

Depending on international support to guarantee its independence and seeking foreign investment, Belize has sought to expand its diplomatic and economic ties with other nations. It was a member of the UN, the Nonaligned Movement, and the Commonwealth of Nations (see Appendix B). In 1990 Belize appointed a roving ambassador to the European Economic Community. Belize established relations with China in 1987. Then in October 1989, Belize announced a "Two-China" policy and established full diplomatic relations with Taiwan. China swiftly rejected Belize's policy and suspended relations. The switch in relations was apparently motivated by the failure of China to follow through on Belize's expectation of economic assistance, which Taiwan seemed eager to supply.

Following Iraq's invasion of Kuwait in August 1990, Belize supported the UN Security Council resolutions imposing economic and trade sanctions against Iraq and authorizing the use of force to liberate Kuwait. In supporting the UN resolutions, Belize stressed its own interest in seeing the sovereignty and territorial integrity of small, vulnerable states protected. Although it favored peaceful, diplomatic, and political solutions to the crisis, it regarded the use of force by the United States-led coalition to be consistent with those resolutions. Said Musa also called for a comprehensive Middle East peace conference to resolve the long-standing problems of the region, especially of the rights of the Palestinian people, and for the United States and its allies to secure Israeli compliance with relevant UN resolutions. Although Belize did not contribute troops to the coalition forces, an undetermined number of Belizean nationals serving in the United States military saw action in the Persian Gulf War.

* * *

Tom Barry's *Belize: A Country Guide,* Julio A. Fernandez's *Belize: Case Study for Democracy in Central America,* and O. Nigel Bolland's *Belize: A New Nation in Central America* all deal with Belizean politics and government in the postindependence era and are recommended. Assad Shoman's *Party Politics in Belize* is interesting because of the perspective given by a participant in Belizean politics, but it is not as readily available as the above-named works. For an in-depth treatment of the preindependence history, Narda Dobson's *A History of Belize* is an excellent source. (For further information and complete citations, see Bibliography.)

Chapter 10. Belize: National Security

Mayan god of war

SINCE INDEPENDENCE IN 1981, the major threat to Belize's external security has come from Guatemala. Guatemala continued to voice claims on Belize's territory, and various Guatemalan governments have expressed interest in annexing the country's eastern neighbor. As of mid-1991, Belize's dispute with Guatemala had not erupted into hostilities and appeared close to resolution. Nonetheless, the possibility of conflict with Belize's much larger neighbor continued to form the central strategic concern for the country's defense planners. The Belize Defence Force (BDF) helped secure national defense, but the country's sovereignty was essentially guaranteed by Britain, which maintained troops and aircraft in the nation.

The small BDF had a strength of approximately 700. It was principally a lightly armed ground force, but it also had small air and maritime elements. The force assisted the approximately 1,500 British troops and played an aggressive role in counter-narcotics operations. British forces in Belize comprised one infantry battalion, one Army Air Corps flight, and one-half squadron of the Royal Air Force (RAF) equipped with fighter and ground-attack aircraft.

The nation was internally stable; there have been only a few disturbances of public order since independence. These disturbances consisted chiefly of isolated and short-lived public demonstrations or labor activities, and violence rarely erupted in any of the actions. The Belize National Police was responsible for internal security. Civilian authorities controlled the police force, which was generally capable of maintaining public order without resorting to extraordinary means or excessive violence.

Crime associated with international drug trafficking posed the principal challenge to peaceful daily life. The government devoted considerable resources to combating trade in narcotics. Still, Belizeans and foreigners participated in the drug trade because of the opportunity for quick profits and because it was relatively easy to move drugs through this sparsely populated country, where remote areas were difficult to patrol. As a result, the nation continued to be a producer of marijuana and a conduit for cocaine trafficking to the United States.

The central government was responsible for administering criminal justice. The criminal justice system and national penal law were both based on British models. The Supreme Court had jurisdiction over serious criminal offenses. The attorney general and the director of public prosecutions were the top legal officers representing the state in criminal and other issues. The system routinely honored constitutional guarantees regarding fundamental rights and freedoms and the right to a fair trial.

Belize's Military History and Strategic Setting

From the early seventeenth century, the area now known as Belize has had a troubled and disorderly history. The British Settlement of Belize in the Bay of Honduras served as a base for privateers who carried out raids against Spanish vessels transporting gold and silver to Europe. The coral reefs and sand bars of the coast provided hiding places from which to surprise intended targets; these same features offered a place to flee from pursuing warships and other deep-draft vessels unable to navigate the area's shallow passages. By the time piracy had been suppressed, toward the end of the century, settlers—mostly British—had moved into the area's interior to develop lucrative logwood resources (see Colonial Rivalry Between Spain and Britain, ch. 6).

The small British settlement became a target for attacks from neighboring Spanish settlements as the rivalry between the Spanish and British intensified. The first attack took place in 1717 when Spanish and Mayan soldiers entered the area from what is now Guatemala. In the years that followed, Spain made several raids and incursions into various parts of the settlement. British warships were commonly dispatched to the area in response. In times of threat, the settlers at first formed an irregular militia, which was occasionally bolstered by Indians brought in from the Mosquito Coast of what is now Nicaragua and by African slaves from Jamaica. When the threat subsided, the militia disbanded, and residents returned to their usual pursuits, rebuilding what had been destroyed.

After beating back yet another attack in 1754, settlers agreed to build a fort overlooking the harbor near Belize Town and to station a full-time force there. After Spain recognized Britain's right to use the area, the fort was demolished (even though Spain maintained its claim to sovereignty over the area). Hostilities resumed in 1779, however, when local residents fled from Spanish raiders who had kidnapped a number of settlers. This exodus was short-lived; the limits of the British settlement were defined in the Treaty of Versailles in 1783, and British settlers again returned. In 1784 the British governor of Jamaica appointed a superintendent for the settlement (see Beginnings of Self Government and the Plantocracy, ch. 6). Britain also gave the title of commander in chief to the superintendent to enable him, as well as later governors, to organize defense forces. Early the next year, the superintendent established a small garrison.

Spain's last attempt to dislodge the settlers by force took place in 1798 when the Spanish fleet from Yucatán launched an attack on the settlement. Although poorly armed and badly outnumbered, local settlers resisted. Three companies of the British West India Regiment and slaves from Jamaica who had volunteered to serve in exchange for their freedom backed the settlers. The final skirmish involved a sea battle off Saint George's Cay in which local forces, supported by the British sloop H.M.S. *Merlin,* forced a final Spanish retreat.

During the late eighteenth and early nineteenth centuries, the settlement's defense forces were essentially temporary militia. European settlers routinely led the militia, but in times of hostilities, military commissions were opened to all groups, including freed blacks and slaves who sought manumission through enlistment. Although these arrangements appeared to work satisfactorily during times of external threat, the fear of slave rebellions during the mid-1820s prompted concerns regarding the loyalties of black troops, and the local government sent for three or four companies of British troops from Jamaica.

The settlement's chief strategic threat in the nineteenth century came from Spanish colonies that began to receive their independence. The principal and most long-lasting threat came from Guatemala, which did not accept British territorial claims in the area. In 1827 a Guatemalan gunboat threatened local residents, but for the most part, the two sides aired their differences in the diplomatic arena. In 1862, when Britain declared British Honduras a colony, the borders with both Mexico and Guatemala were still undefined. The border with Mexico was finally established in 1893, but uncertainty over the Guatemalan claim continued to affect the strategic outlook of the crown colony (see Glossary) throughout the twentieth century and was responsible for the continued presence of British troops in the territory well after Belize became an independent state.

The most significant threat to public peace in the nineteenth century resulted from clashes with the Maya. At first British forces countered the Mayan raids. Approximately thirty civil police backed the forces, which were stationed in Belize Town. But as clashes grew more serious, it became necessary to impose a land tax to finance armed troops and to call in British regulars from Jamaica. The last battle with Mayan raiding parties took place in 1872, after which many Maya were forced to retire to reservations in the Yucatán (see Mayan Emigration and Conflict, ch. 6).

Another threat to peace throughout the late nineteenth and the early twentieth centuries came from isolated internal disturbances that generally resulted from economic or social tension. In 1894, for instance, mahogany workers rioted after their wages fell as a result of a currency devaluation. Local police and British troops on a warship in the harbor easily subdued the rioters. In 1919 demobilized Creole (see Glossary) soldiers rioted, after returning from service with the British West India Regiment during World War I, in protest against unemployment, homelessness, and high prices. Order was restored only after martial law was proclaimed. Such disturbances did not seriously threaten public peace, but limited outbreaks of public disorder erupted during the 1930s and 1940s, chiefly as a result of harsh economic circumstances, which had contributed to increasing labor militancy (see Interest Groups, ch. 9). By and large, however, British Honduras escaped much of the civil disorder suffered in most of the West Indies (see Glossary) during the period.

During the 1950s, the issue of independence for the colony became a topic of local concern, and by the early 1960s, Britain was willing to support independence. Britain granted the colony internal self-government in 1964 but retained responsibility for defense, internal security, and external relations. Fears arising from Guatemala's continued territorial claims, however, slowed progress toward independence. Between 1962 and 1972, talks between Britain and Guatemala occurred regularly, but even these were abandoned in 1972, after Britain announced it was sending 8,000 servicemen to conduct amphibious exercises in Belize and other parts of the Caribbean. Guatemala responded by massing troops on the border. Although no violence resulted, Britain thereafter increased the size of its regular garrison to act as a deterrent to Guatemalan adventurism. Talks resumed in 1973 but broke off two years later when Guatemala threatened invasion, first in November 1975 and again in July 1977. Britain responded each time by sending in troops and aircraft. Britain kept a battalion of troops, a flight of fighter aircraft, and one-half of a squadron of RAF fighters and ground-attack aircraft in Belize after 1975. In all, the British contingent grew from some 750 personnel in 1970 to about 1,500 in the mid-1970s. By this time, people living in the colony generally agreed that a continued British military presence would be necessary to guarantee security for an independent Belize.

In March 1981, Britain and Guatemala appeared to reach agreement that would clear the way for independence, with Guatemala accepting Belize's independence in return for specified concessions (see Relations with Guatemala, ch. 9). Violent demonstrations in

British military vehicle, Royal Electrical Mechanical Engineers
Courtesy Steven R. Harper

Belize followed this agreement in April 1981. The government proclaimed a state of emergency to deal with protesters who argued that the legitimate security interests of Belize had not been protected. The agreement on independence collapsed in July 1981 as a result of Guatemala's renewed territorial claims on Belize and the violent reaction to the proposed agreement in Belize.

Nevertheless, Belize achieved independence as scheduled on September 21, 1981, and Britain agreed to continue to garrison troops in Belize and to train the new nation's defense force. Guatemala closed the borders with Belize in protest for several months. In 1984 Britain renewed its assurances to keep British troops on hand until the territorial dispute with Guatemala was resolved. Talks between Britain and Guatemala resumed in 1985, and all three countries began the work to draft a treaty to deal with outstanding economic, political, and territorial issues. Progress was interrupted in November 1988 when a Guatemalan gunboat fired on an unarmed British naval vessel in the disputed Gulf of Honduras. Britain dispatched two Royal Air Force Harrier jets to Belize in response, but the incident was quickly resolved after Guatemala indicated it had only fired warning shots at the vessel, which it claimed had strayed into Guatemalan waters.

The Belize Defence Force

As part of moves to develop a local defense force and initiate an independent defense capability, the colony formed the Belize Defence Force (BDF) on January 1, 1978. The BDF drew its strength from the Belize Volunteer Guard, which had formerly acted as a police reserve, and from the paramilitary Belize Police Special Defence Force, which the BDF replaced. The Defence Ordinance of 1977, which formed the legal basis for the creation of a regular force, as well as for volunteer and reserve forces, established the BDF.

In 1978 the new force comprised three active-duty elements, consisting of one rifle, one headquarters, and one training company. Three additional rifle companies and a band made up the volunteer element. The BDF was expanded in 1982, when a second rifle company was added. In 1984 very small air and maritime wings were formed. A third rifle company was added in 1987.

The BDF is charged with the defense of the nation, with support of the civil authority in maintaining order, and with "other duties as defined by the Governor." During its short history, the force has manned border defense posts in conjunction with British forces and provided interpreters and trackers for British patrols. The BDF has also conducted search-and-rescue and other operations in support of the police, customs, immigration, and fisheries departments. As part of its mission to assist the police, the BDF has helped in drug eradication and other antidrug operations. The maritime wing and the air wing have manned emergency frequencies and have launched rescue missions nationwide. The BDF has also provided assistance in times of natural disaster. In 1986 the force took responsibility for coordination of antidrug operations, and in the early 1990s performed an active counter-narcotics role.

Personnel and Training

As of 1991, the BDF had approximately 700 active-duty personnel. An additional 500 Belizeans served in the Volunteer Guard. The law allows for the establishment of obligatory national service whenever normal recruitment falls, but applicants have regularly exceeded openings by at least three-to-one, and enlistment has been entirely voluntary throughout the force's existence. The prospect of a steady job in a country having relatively high unemployment attracted the recruits. Service salaries, which were at least equal to those generally available in the private sector, also contributed to the abundance of recruits. The BDF, moreover, offered several training programs that imparted skills useful in civilian life.

Belize Defence Force naval vessels
Courtesy Steven R. Harper

The BDF drew recruits from all races and all areas of the country. The size of the defense force was about 0.3 percent of the total population and therefore did not drain the country's available work force. As of 1991, an estimated 24,000 men and 23,000 women were of eligible age for active duty. As of 1989, there were twenty-five women soldiers, with spaces for ten more.

The 1977 Defence Ordinance set forth terms of service. The minimum age for enlistment was eighteen. Enlistments were for various terms and included both a period of active service and a subsequent reserve obligation. Under law, service was not to exceed twenty-two years of active duty. Enlistment in the Volunteer Guard was for four-year terms; in a state of emergency, volunteers could be called to permanent service, as could reserve forces. The governor general awarded officer commissions.

Up until 1990, a British loan service officer held the position of commander of the BDF. In June 1990, the first Belizean officer, a lieutenant colonel, assumed command. At the same time, the government created the position of BDF chief of staff, which was also filled by a Belizean officer. Both of the nation's top officers had received training in British military schools.

Recruits underwent a fourteen-week training program focusing on basic weapons skills, marching drills, military tactics, and physical education. Since independence, the BDF's training unit has offered an average of four basic training courses per year. Most training was done at Price Barracks in Ladyville, near Belize City, but additional facilities were available at Camp Oakley, Mountain Pine Ridge, and Hill Bank. Officers, senior noncommissioned officers, and specialists were trained in Britain, Canada, or the United States.

Organization and Equipment

Under the constitution, the governor general serves as commander in chief of the armed forces and exercises administrative control over the three services through the Ministry of National Defence. Since independence, the defense portfolio has usually been held by the prime minister, who has exercised his authority through the permanent secretary for defense. In practice, operational control passed through the BDF commander, assisted by the chief of staff.

In the early 1990s, the BDF was primarily a ground force, consisting essentially of a light infantry battalion made up of three rifle companies and a support company that performed administrative, training, and logistical functions. Its main base was located at Price Barracks, where the majority of personnel were stationed. Operationally, one rifle company was rotated every three months through Belizario Camp near San Ignacio, east of the border with Guatemala. One rifle platoon was also rotated on a monthly basis through Punta Gorda, and BDF personnel manned several observation posts jointly with British forces in Toledo and Cayo districts.

The BDF ground element was equipped with light infantry weapons of British origin (see table 16, Appendix A). These weapons included the L1A1 SLR 7.62mm rifle, the Sterling L2A3 9mm submachine gun, the Bren L4A1 7.62mm light machine gun, and six 81mm mortars.

The BDF had a small maritime arm whose main base was located in the harbor of Belize City. A forward operating base, located in Placentia near Big Creek, enhanced policing and patrolling of the nation's southernmost waters. Operations at Placentia centered mainly on patrolling against drug trafficking and illegal fishing. The maritime arm had fifty personnel, eight of whom were officers. A major commanded this arm, which operated two 20-meter patrol craft. These craft had too great a draft to operate in the shallow waters frequented by smugglers but were effective in search-and-rescue operations and in monitoring illegal immigration.

Police constable assigned to Belize Defence Force maritime arm
Courtesy Steven R. Harper

The BDF's maritime arm shared facilities with British forces that also patrolled the nation's waters.

The BDF also had a very small air wing, which consisted of fifteen personnel and was commanded by a captain. The air wing flew two Britten Norman BN-2B Defenders, one of which was armed. These aircraft usually transported passengers and freight but were also capable of use in parachute resupply, coastal patrol, and search-and-rescue operations. The air wing also had one DO27A crop sprayer to combat drug cultivation. The air wing's main base was the Belize International Airport, but it also used a small airstrip at Punta Gorda.

As of 1991, there were approximately 350 personnel in the reserve force. This force was organized into three rifle companies located at Corozal in the north, at Belize City, and at Dangriga in the south. There was also a small Volunteer Guard with detachments at Belize City, San Ignacio, Orange Walk, Corozal, Dangriga, and Punta Gorda.

Defense Spending

According to the government's 1991 figures, the defense budget for 1989 was Bz$19.9 million (for value of Belizean dollar—see Glossary), or almost US$10 million. The budget total for 1989 amounted to approximately 14 percent of total central government expenditures, up from approximately 4 percent at independence.

The growth of the defense budget mirrored the development and growth of the BDF, although the defense budget was so small that the purchase of even a modest amount of equipment during any single year produced a significant jump in spending.

Compared with other Latin American countries, Belize spent a slightly larger portion of the national budget on defense. The military's portion of the gross domestic product (GDP—see Glossary) was about 3.4 percent in 1988.

Britain formed the largest and most significant element of the country's external defense (see Relations with Britain, ch. 9). Although figures on such assistance were not publicly available, the British government spent an estimated US$18 million annually to maintain British forces in Belize, an amount almost double the Belize defense budget. The British also funded various training programs for BDF officers and other personnel. Observers have estimated that the maintenance of the British garrison in Belize contributed about 15 percent to the nation's GDP.

United States military assistance augmented the Belize defense budget. Assistance to Belize from 1982 through 1990 included approximately US$2.5 million in Foreign Military Sales agreements that went to provide equipment, mostly for counter-narcotics operations. During the same period, the United States also spent approximately US$660,000 on the education of a small number of BDF personnel at United States facilities under the International Military Education and Training (IMET) program. IMET assistance in fiscal year (FY—see Glossary) 1991 totaled US$115,000. The FY 1992 request totaled US$125,000.

Foreign Military Relations

Belize's closest military relations were with Britain. The BDF's rank structure, uniforms, equipment, and organization followed British models, and British regular forces in the nation provided much of the BDF's training.

BDF personnel also trained regularly in Canadian and United States facilities. On occasion, members of the BDF have served abroad in Mexico, Jamaica, El Salvador, and Colombia, usually as observers.

British forces in Belize were headquartered at Ladyville Barracks near Belize City. One battalion represented the bulk of the forces. The battalion was rotated through Belize at regular intervals, usually of six months, and was then replaced by another battalion. Other British military units rounded out this contingent; they included one armored reconnaissance troop, one field artillery battery, and one engineer squadron. British air units consisted of one Army Air

Corps flight and one-half of a squadron of the Royal Air Force, which provided airfield defense. Ships of the Royal Navy, sometimes with Royal Marines embarked, made regular stops at Belize, and in times of tension Britain has shown a willingness to reinforce local forces with aircraft and other units as necessary.

In the early 1990s, Belize had bilateral defense treaties with Britain, the United States and Canada. All of these treaties concerned the provision of military training. Belize was not a signatory to any multilateral defense treaties as of 1991.

Public Order and Internal Security

Public order was well established in the nation. There had been no serious threats to internal stability since independence, and as of 1991, the country was free of insurgencies. Elections were held on a regular basis, and political competition was open. All political parties operated freely and without government or other interference. Organizers of public meetings were required to obtain a permit at least thirty-six hours before the gathering, but such permits were almost always granted and were never denied for political reasons. The government respected constitutionally protected rights and freedoms, which were generally enjoyed by all citizens. Among these protections were the right to free speech, assembly, association, and movement. Unions freely exercised the right to organize and to form confederations (see Labor, ch. 8). The constitution allows unions to strike but permits unions representing essential services to strike only after giving twenty-one days notice to the government ministry concerned. There were no strikes in 1990.

In 1987 the government, then led by the United Democratic Party (UDP), passed a law establishing the Security and Intelligence Service (see Electoral Process since Independence, ch. 9). The new service was intended to protect the nation from espionage, sabotage, subversion, and terrorism. The law charged the service with collecting and evaluating intelligence related to Belize's security and with providing security assessments of certain public servants to various departments of government. These assessments were designed to determine the public servants' loyalty and allegiance to the nation. The opposition People's United Party (PUP) came out firmly against the new service, charging that the government was trying to stifle political opposition and intended to use the service to harass the church, press, judiciary, and civil service. The government never actually formed the new security service, but tensions nevertheless flared between the two political parties over the role of such a service. In January 1988, the political dispute between the two parties evolved into short-lived demonstrations and minor violence after a suspicious fire broke out at the home of the deputy prime minister. Elections in September 1989 resulted in a new PUP government, which, within a few weeks, led a successful effort to repeal the 1987 Security and Intelligence Service Act, abolishing the new service.

Crime

As of 1991, official statistics on the incidence of crime during the 1980s were not available. Still, according to some observers, Belize suffered from relatively high rates of crime. Drug trafficking, in particular, spawned violent crimes of all kinds. The principal trafficking threat came from Colombian organizations that transshipped cocaine through Central America. The extensive domestic cultivation of marijuana posed a significant problem. Growers and traffickers of marijuana were also blamed for much of the country's crime. Most of the cocaine and marijuana was destined for markets in the United States. Some, however, was diverted to local markets. Studies in the mid-1980s revealed that drug abuse was on the rise among Belizeans, especially among teenagers.

During the late 1980s, local law enforcement, backed by the BDF, enjoyed only limited success in combating cocaine traffickers. During the early 1990s, the nation had to rely on foreign assistance, principally from the United States and Britain, to maintain antitrafficking operations. The government's efforts to eradicate marijuana were more effective, however, and the local press carried regular reports on confiscation of the drug or eradication of it through crop spraying. Despite the destruction of large quantities of marijuana, observers estimated that enough marijuana survived herbicidal crop spraying to provide a significant income. Most observers agreed that drug trafficking seemed unlikely to decrease as long as the potential for profit remained high and no alternate crops could net comparable profits for local farmers.

Crime associated with illegal immigration posed another serious challenge for law enforcement. Traditionally, illegal aliens posed problems from an economic and regulatory standpoint. But in the 1980s, some illegal immigrants posed problems from a social standpoint. During the mid-1980s, aliens, who had been hardened by the civil strife and the resulting social chaos in their own countries, were implicated in a number of kidnappings for ransom in northern Belize and for various other violent crimes nationwide. Efforts to address these problems culminated in 1987, when the government stiffened laws to penalize employers who hired illegal aliens. The new legislation also provided for the expeditious expulsion of

Belize police headquarters, Belmopan
Courtesy Steven R. Harper

illegal immigrants. Such laws notwithstanding, the government, working with the United Nations High Commissioner for Refugees, planned and implemented a variety of assistance programs aimed at Belizeans and aliens in an attempt to defuse resentment against the latter. During 1990 Belize did not force or pressure any refugees to return to their countries of origin.

As a reflection of the growing incidence of crime, tourists in the late 1980s began to complain about being openly harassed, particularly on the streets of Belize City. Theft and assault were the two offenses most commonly reported. The government was particularly concerned about publicity surrounding such crime because national economic planning focused on expanding tourism. One response to the problem was imprisonment of "veteran muggers" convicted of repeat offenses.

The Belize National Police

The Belize National Police is descended from the British Honduras Constabulary, which was established in 1886. Constabulary personnel initially numbered 141 and were recruited in Barbados because local men showed no interest in enlisting. The government assigned the early police the task of preserving law and order in the colony. The Constabulary was at first a paramilitary force, but in 1902 it was made into a civil police force.

The constabulary was reorganized after World War I, when soldiers returning from service abroad joined the force. The force was reorganized again in 1957, when its first commissioner of police instituted modernizing reforms that resulted in the force's present form. During the colonial period, expatriate officers filled all senior posts in the police. But with self-government and then independence, more Belizeans assumed positions of authority. The official name of the force was changed to the Belize National Police in 1973, and by the early 1990s the commissioner and all senior police officers were Belizeans.

As of 1991, the force, which was part of the Ministry of Home Affairs, was the sole organization responsible for policing the country and for managing regular immigration matters. A commissioner of police headed the force. The governor general appointed the commissioner with the concurrence of the prime minister after consultation with the leader of the opposition. The commissioner exercised operational and disciplinary control over the police force.

The police force had an authorized strength of approximately 500, a ratio of about three police to every 1,000 inhabitants. Police operations were divided into three territorial divisions: Eastern, which included Belmopan and Belize City; Central; and Western. The force had a small maritime element that operated six shallow-draft motorboats capable of patrolling coastal waters frequented by smugglers.

The force was also divided into three operational branches: General Duties, Crime Investigation, and Tactical Service. The Tactical Service, formed in 1978, assumed the nonmilitary responsibilities of its predecessor, the Police Special Force, which was incorporated into the BDF.

The police underwent training at the Police Training School in Belmopan. In sixteen-week programs, recruits studied general police duties and procedures, criminal law, evidence, traffic management, and firearms. Senior police officers attended a ten-week command course run by the British police in Britain. Police performed their regular duties unarmed, although arms were issued for special duties or in cases of extreme necessity. There were a small number of women police in the force; the first appoinment of a woman to the rank of inspector came in 1989. All personnel were subject to transfer anywhere in the country.

Officers' uniforms resembled those of British police forces. Sergeants and lower ranks wore khaki shirts, blue serge trousers with

Local police headquarters, Belize City
Courtesy Steven R. Harper

a green seam on both sides, and dark blue peaked caps. Some police investigators were not required to wear uniforms.

During the 1980s, the large increase in drug trafficking greatly challenged the police. Unfortunately, some personnel proved vulnerable to corruption by traffickers, and public confidence in the police suffered from charges of official collusion in the drug trade. Public perceptions of the police also suffered from charges that police sometimes resorted to unnecessary force in their efforts to deal with escalating violent crime. During the late 1980s, police leadership began to focus on both problems, expressing a willingness to pursue every allegation of malpractice and to rid the police of unworthy personnel. Penalties for official violators of criminal statutes also increased. The success of these efforts was unclear as of mid-1991.

The Criminal Justice System

The constitution assigns judicial power to the Supreme Court, whose chief justice is appointed on the advice of the prime minister after consultation with the leader of the opposition (see Judiciary, ch. 9). Two other justices also served on the Supreme Court; they were also appointed by the governor general on the advice of the judicial and legal services section of the Public Services Commission. Immediately below the Supreme Court was the Summary

Jurisdiction Court, which was responsible for criminal matters, and the District Court, which heard civil cases. The Summary Jurisdiction Court and the District Court were established in each of the nation's six district capitals: Belize, San Ignacio, Corozal, Orange Walk, Dangriga, and Punta Gorda. Magistrates presided over these courts, which had wide jurisdiction in summary offenses and limited jurisdiction in more serious offenses. Juvenile offenders were tried in district family courts established by the Family Courts Act of 1988.

Magistrates referred serious criminal cases to the Supreme Court, where a jury system was in operation. Appeals from Summary Jurisdiction Court were referred to the Supreme Court; appeals from the Supreme Court were referred to a Court of Appeal, which met on an average of four times a year. Final appeals were made to the Judicial Committee of the Privy Council in London in cases involving interpretation of the constitution.

The principal source of the nation's criminal law was the criminal code of 1980. The code had two sections. The first section defined general legal principles and set forth standards of criminal liability, addressing such issues as intent, negligence, conspiracy, and justifiable force. The second section defined crimes and their punishments.

The criminal code provided for the death penalty for persons convicted of criminal homicide. Under the constitution, the death penalty could be adjudged only after the judge of record submitted a report to the Belize Advisory Council, which in turn advised the attorney general as to the appropriateness of the sentence.

The government amended the criminal code in April 1987 to provide stiffer penalties for rape, kidnapping, blackmail, and robbery. At the same time, the government raised the penalties for offenses subject to summary jurisdiction.

Several other statutes also covered criminal offenses. The most important of these was the Misuse of Drugs Act of 1990, which was the nation's principal drug legislation. This act repealed and replaced the Dangerous Drugs Act of 1980, which was deemed inadequate to meet the challenges of the explosive growth in the drug trade during the 1980s. The 1990 legislation provided for the establishment of a National Drug Abuse Control Council, which was to review the current state of Belize's illegal narcotics trade and advise the prime minister on measures to restrict availability, provide for treatment and rehabilitation, educate the public, and advise farmers on alternate crops. The act called for fines of up to Bz$25,000 and imprisonment of five to ten years for less serious cases of drug trafficking. Persons convicted of more serious offenses by the Supreme Court were liable to fines of not less than Bz$100,000—or three times the street value of the illegal commodities seized—or were subject to seven to fourteen years of imprisonment, or both. Penalties for public officials and members of the National Assembly, the judiciary, the police, and the BDF were more severe. The 1990 law also provided for forfeitures of all aircraft, vessels, and vehicles used in illegal trafficking and for forfeiture of all proceeds derived from this activity.

Criminal procedure followed British models. Officials working under the Directorate of Public Prosecutions handled cases. The constitution protects citizens from arbitrary search or seizure, and the justice system regularly observed these protections. Criminal offenders were also accorded numerous protections. These protections included the right to a public trial and protection against double jeopardy and self-incrimination. All persons were presumed innocent and were entitled to equal protection under the law.

The law required informing detainees of the cause of their arrest within forty-eight hours, and detainees were entitled to communicate with a lawyer. The law also required informing the accused of his or her rights, which included the right to judicial review of the validity of the detention. If arrested, the accused had to be brought before a judge or magistrate within seventy-two hours. The defendant was entitled to be present at all trials, to cross-examine witnesses for the prosecution, and to call witnesses for the defense. The defendant had the right to trial by jury in serious criminal cases. The law guaranteed defendants the right to appeal any decision to the next higher court.

At the end of 1991, the small Belizean defense establishment, including the BDF, existed to maintain internal order and to deter Guatemalan aggression. Actual defense of the country was ultimately in Britain's hands. The 700-member BDF was no match for larger Guatemalan forces but would act merely as a tripwire for British intervention

* * *

As of mid-1991, no definitive studies that dealt comprehensively with national security matters in contemporary Belize had been published. For information on the development of the Belize Defence Force, the reader must search through issues of *Belize Today,* published in Belize City; the *Latin America Report* by the Joint Publications Research Service; and the *Daily Report: Latin America* put out by the Foreign Broadcast Information Service. Current order-of-battle information is available in the International Institute for Strategic Studies' excellent annual, *The Military Balance.* The best overview of conditions of public order is contained in the sections on Belize in *Country Reports on Human Rights Practices,* a report submitted annually by the United States Department of State to the United States Congress. (For further information and complete citations, see Bibliography.)

Appendix A

Table

1 Metric Conversion Coefficients and Factors
2 Guyana: Ethnic Groups, 1960, 1970, and 1980
3 Guyana: Population Statistics by District, 1970
4 Guyana: Religious Affiliation, 1960 and 1990
5 Guyana: Student Enrollment, Selected Years, 1969–70 to 1979–80
6 Guyana: Selected Economic Indicators, 1986–90
7 Guyana: Production of Selected Commodities, 1984–88
8 Guyana: Parliamentary Seats in Elections, 1968–85
9 Guyana: Major Military Equipment, 1991
10 Belize: Population Statistics by District, 1985
11 Belize: Ethnic Groups, 1975 and 1980
12 Belize: Religious Affiliation, 1980
13 Belize: Student Enrollment, Selected Years, 1970–71 to 1985–86
14 Belize: Selected Economic Indicators, 1985–90
15 Belize: Production of Selected Agricultural Commodities, 1984–88
16 Belize: Major Military Equipment, 1991

Table 1. Metric Conversion Coefficients and Factors

When you know	Multiply by	To find
Millimeters	0.04	inches
Centimeters	0.39	inches
Meters	3.3	feet
Kilometers	0.62	miles
Hectares (10,000 m²)	2.47	acres
Square kilometers	0.39	square miles
Cubic meters	35.3	cubic feet
Liters	0.26	gallons
Kilograms	2.2	pounds
Metric tons	0.98	long tons
	1.1	short tons
	2,204	pounds
Degrees Celsius (Centigrade)	1.8 and add 32	degrees Fahrenheit

Table 2. Guyana: Ethnic Groups, 1960, 1970, and 1980 (in percentages)

Ethnic Group	1960	1970	1980
Indo-Guyanese	47	52	51
Afro-Guyanese	45	42	42
Amerindian	4	4	4
European	3	2	—[1]
Asian	1	—[2]	—[1]
TOTAL	100	100	100

[1] In the 1980 census, Europeans and Asians were grouped together as "other" and were 3 percent of the population.

[2] Less than 1 percent.

Source: Based on information from Federal Republic of Germany, Statistisches Bundesamt, *Länderbericht Guyana, 1989,* Wiesbaden, 1989, 19.

Table 3. Guyana: Population Statistics by District, 1970

District in 1970 (District in 1991)[1]	Total Population	Percentage of Total Population
East Demerara (Demerara-Mahaica)	338,000	48.3
East Berbice (East Berbice-Corentyne)	132,500	18.9
Essequibo and Essequibo Islands[2] (Pomeroon-Supenaam and Essequibo Islands-West Demerara)	57,200	8.2
Mazaruni-Potaro (Cuyuni-Mazaruni)	12,700	1.8
Northwest District (Barima-Waini)	16,200	2.3
Rupununi (Potaro-Siparuni and Upper Takutu-Upper Essequibo)	14,200	2.0
West Demerara	78,300	11.2
West Berbice (Mahaica-Berbice)	50,800	7.3
TOTAL	699,900	100.0

[1] Boundaries for districts in 1991 only approximate those in 1970. The new district of Upper Demerara-Berbice was created from parts of West Demerara and East Berbice. The old district of West Demerara was divided into Essequibo Islands-West Demerara, Demerara-Mahaica, and Upper Demerara-Berbice.

[2] The 1970 census combined Essequibo and Essequibo Islands.

Source: Based on information from Federal Republic of Germany, Statistisches Bundesamt, *Länderbericht Guyana, 1987,* Wiesbaden, 1987, 18.

Table 4. Guyana: Religious Affiliation, 1960 and 1990 (in percentages)

Religion	1960	1990
Christian	57	52
Hindu	34	34
Other *	9	14
TOTAL	100	100

* Predominantly Muslim.

Source: Based on information from Federal Republic of Germany, Statistisches Bundesamt, *Länderbericht Guyana, 1987,* Wiesbaden, 1987, 19.

Table 5. Guyana: Student Enrollment, Selected Years, 1969–70 to 1979–80

Level/Type	1969–70	1975–76	1977–78	1979–80
Primary	163,100	196,300 *	166,200 *	164,800
Secondary	18,100			46,600
Trade school	2,000	3,000	3,800	3,600
Teachers' college	500	600	1,000	1,100
University of Guyana	1,100	1,752	1,536	1,889

* Combined primary and secondary school enrollment.

Source: Based on information from Federal Republic of Germany, Statistisches Bundesamt, *Länderbericht Guyana, 1987,* Wiesbaden, 1987, 23.

Table 6. Guyana: Selected Economic Indicators, 1986–90 (in millions of United States dollars unless otherwise indicated)

Indicator	1986	1987	1988	1989	1990
Real GDP [1]	300	303	295	285	275
Real GDP growth [2]	-0.9	0.9	-2.6	-3.3	-2.5
Real GDP per capita [3]	400	403	392	380	369
Real GDP per capita growth [2]	-1.0	0.8	-2.7	-3.4	-2.6
Inflation [2]	7.9	28.7	39.9	89.7	63.6
Trade balance	-50	-21	-1	-8	-46
Overall balance of payments	-140	-137	-106	-181	-194
External debt	1,618	1,719	1,722	1,862	1,960

[1] GDP—gross domestic product, in constant 1988 United States dollars.
[2] In percentages.
[3] In United States dollars.

Source: Based on information from United States, Agency for International Development, *Latin America and the Caribbean: Selected Economic Data,* Washington, 1992, 112.

Table 7. Guyana: Production of Selected Commodities, 1984–88

Commodity	1984	1985	1986	1987	1988
Agricultural					
Rice (thousands of tons)	184	156	183	146	130
Sugar (thousands of tons)	242	243	245	221	168
Mining					
Bauxite (thousands of tons)	1,556	1,599	1,504	1,378	1,300
Diamonds (thousands of carats) *	6.0	11.6	9.1	7.3	4.2
Gold (kilograms) *	345	321	437	666	584

* Quantities include only the amounts channeled through the official economy.

Source: Based on information from Economist Intelligence Unit, *Country Profile: Guyana, Barbados, Windward and Leeward Islands, 1989–90,* London, 1989, 15, 17.

Table 8. Guyana: Parliamentary Seats in Elections, 1968–85

Party	1968	1973	1980	1985
People's National Congress (PNC)	30	37	53	54
People's Progressive Party (PPP)	19	14	10	8
United Force (UF)	4	2 [1]	2	2
Working People's Alliance (WPA)	— [2]	— [2]	0	1
TOTAL	53	53	65	65

[1] Seats originally won by the Liberator Party (LP) but assumed by the UF when the LP boycotted the National Assembly.

[2] Party not established until after 1973 elections.

Table 9. Guyana: Major Military Equipment, 1991

Type and Description	Country of Origin	Number in Inventory
Ground forces		
Armored vehicles		
Shoreland	Britain	3
Artillery		
M-46, 130mm	Soviet Union	6
Mortars		
L16, 81mm	Britain	12
M-43, 120mm	Soviet Union	18
Surface-to-air launchers		
SA-7	-do-	n.a.
Maritime Corps		
Patrol craft	North Korea	4
Air Command		
Light transports		
BN-2A Islander	Britain	4
B-200 Super King	United States	1
Helicopters		
Bell 206	-do-	1
Bell 212	-do-	1
Bell 412	-do-	1
Mi-8	Soviet Union	2

n.a.—not available.

Source: Based on information from *The Military Balance, 1992–1993,* London, 1992, 180.

Table 10. Belize: Population Statistics by District, 1985

District	Total Population	Population Density *
Belize	54,500	13.0
Cayo	27,400	5.1
Corozal	28,000	15.1
Orange Walk	26,600	5.6
Stann Creek	16,500	7.6
Toledo	13,400	2.9
TOTAL	166,400	7.8

* Persons per square kilometer.

Source: Based on information from Federal Republic of Germany, Statistisches Bundesamt, *Länderbericht Belize, 1989,* Wiesbaden, 1989, 18.

Table 11. Belize: Ethnic Groups, 1975 and 1980
(in percentages)

Ethnic Group	1975	1980
Creole	52	40
Mestizo	22	33
Maya	13	10
Garifuna	6	7
European	2	4
Other	5	6
TOTAL	100	100

Source: Based on information from Federal Republic of Germany, Statistisches Bundesamt, *Länderbericht Belize, 1989,* Wiesbaden, 1989, 19.

Table 12. Belize: Religious Affiliation, 1980

Denomination	Total Membership	Percentage of Population
Roman Catholic	89,683	61.7
Anglican	16,152	11.8
Methodist	8,721	6.0
Mennonite	5,669	3.9
Seventh-Day Adventist	4,361	3.0
Other	19,767	13.6
TOTAL	144,353	100.0

Source: Based on information from Federal Republic of Germany, Statistisches Bundesamt, *Länderbericht Belize, 1989,* Wiesbaden, 1989, 20.

Table 13. Belize: Student Enrollment, Selected Years, 1970–71 to 1985–86

Level/Type	1970–71	1975–76	1980–81	1985–86
Primary	31,629	33,444	34,615	39,211
Secondary	4,212	5,008	5,435	6,676
Trade school	n.a.	369	672	n.a.
Teachers' college	75	129	144	n.a.

n.a.—not available.

Source: Based on information from Federal Republic of Germany, Statistisches Bundesamt, *Länderbericht Belize, 1989,* Wiesbaden, 1989, 25.

Table 14. Belize: Selected Economic Indicators, 1985–90
(in millions of United States dollars unless otherwise indicated)

Indicator	1985	1986	1987	1988	1989	1990
Real GDP [1]	201	211	243	265	286	336
Real GDP growth [2]	2.2	4.8	14.3	9.7	13.3	12.1
Real GDP per capita [3]	1,210	1,233	1,376	1,494	1,633	1,762
Real GDP per capita growth [2]	-0.6	1.9	11.6	7.5	10.4	7.9
Inflation [2]	-0.6	2.4	2.0	3.3	2.1	4.0
Trade balance	-44.2	-35.9	-41.3	-61.8	-94.6	-85.6
Overall balance of payments	10.0	10.8	9.8	18.8	11.4	10.5
External debt	118	121	137	139	143	158

[1] GDP—gross domestic product; in constant 1984 United States dollars.
[2] In percentages.
[3] In United States dollars.

Source: Based on information from United States, Agency for International Development, *Latin America and the Caribbean: Selected Economic Data,* Washington, 1992, 92.

Table 15. Belize: Production of Selected Agricultural Commodities, 1984–88
(in thousands of tons)

Commodity	1984	1985	1986	1987	1988
Bananas	12	12	15	25	29
Corn	18	22	20	26	26
Grapefruit	13	19	26	36	34
Molasses	32	28	30	24	23
Oranges	51	47	57	81	60
Rice	6	6	5	5	6
Sugar	102	102	93	82	82

Source: Based on information from Economist Intelligence Unit, *Country Profile: Belize, Bahamas, Bermuda, 1989–90,* London, 1989, 16.

Table 16. Belize: Major Military Equipment, 1991

Type and Description	Country of Origin	Number in Inventory
Ground forces		
Mortars		
81mm	Britain	6
Machine guns		
7.62mm L4A1 Bren	-do-	n.a.
Submachine guns		
9mm L2A3 Sterling	-do-	n.a.
Rifles		
7.62mm L1A1 SLR	-do-	n.a.
Maritime wing		
Patrol craft		
20-meter Wasp	-do-	6
Air wing		
Light transports		
BN-2B Defender	-do-	2

n.a.—not available.

Source: Based on information from *The Military Balance, 1991–1992,* London, 1991, 169.

Appendix B

The Commonwealth of Nations

THE COMMONWEALTH OF NATIONS, more commonly known simply as the Commonwealth, is a voluntary association of independent sovereign states, including Britain and former British territories and existing territories of Britain, Australia, and New Zealand. Any former British territory may seek Commonwealth membership, which is granted by unanimous consent of the members (see table A, this Appendix).

Table A. Members of the Commonwealth of Nations, 1991

Independent Members

Antigua and Barbuda
Australia
Bahamas
Bangladesh
Barbados
Belize
Botswana
Britain
Brunei
Canada
Cyprus
Dominica
Gambia
Ghana
Grenada
Guyana
India
Jamaica
Kenya
Kiribati
Lesotho
Malawi
Malaysia
Maldives
Malta
Mauritius
Namibia
Nauru
New Zealand
Nigeria
Pakistan
Papua New Guinea
Saint Christopher and Nevis
Saint Lucia
Saint Vincent and the Grenadines
Seychelles
Sierra Leone
Singapore
Solomon Islands
Sri Lanka
Swaziland
Tanzania
Tonga
Trinidad and Tobago
Tuvalu
Uganda
Vanuatu

Table A.—Continued

Western Somoa
Zambia
Zimbabwe

Dependencies and Associated States of Britain

Anguilla	Gibraltar
Bermuda	Hong Kong
British Antarctic Territory	Isle of Man
British Indian Ocean Territory	Montserrat
British Virgin Islands	Pitcairn Islands
Cayman Islands	Saint Helena
Channel Islands	Turks and Caicos Islands
Falkland Islands	

Dependencies and Associated States of Australia

Australian Antarctic Territory	Heard and McDonald Islands
Christmas Island	Norfolk Island
Cocos (Keeling) Islands	
Coral Sea Islands Territory	

Dependencies and Associated States of New Zealand

Cook Islands	Ross Dependency
Niue	Tokelau

Source: Based on information from *The Europa Year Book 1987,* 1, London, 1987, 114; *South America, Central America, and the Caribbean, 1993,* London, 1992, 668–69; and United States, Central Intelligence Agency, *The World Factbook, 1991,* Washington, 1991.

Commonwealth member countries recognize the British monarch as the symbolic head of the association. In member nations in which the British monarch serves as the head of state, she or he is represented by an appointed governor general, who is independent of the British government. In other Commonwealth nations, the monarch is represented by a high commissioner, who has the status of an ambassador. Member states meet regularly to discuss issues, coordinate mutual economic and technical assistance, and formulate proposals regarding international economic affairs.

History

The Commonwealth of Nations is a twentieth-century creation, but its origins go back to events in 1867. In that year, the British Parliament passed the British North American Act, creating the self-governing Dominion of Canada. Canada was the first British colony to gain self-government, and from that time on Britain began to redefine its relationship with its colonies. Australia became a dominion in 1900, New Zealand in 1907, and the Union of South Africa in 1910.

Canada, Australia, New Zealand, and the Union of South Africa dispatched troops to aid in the British war effort in World War I. They also participated in the postwar peace conference and in the creation of the League of Nations. Such actions led Britain to acknowledge these countries more as equals than as former colonies.

In 1926 an Imperial Conference of Commonwealth members adopted the Balfour Formula on the status of the dominions. The conference defined the dominions and Britain as "autonomous communities with the Empire, equal in status, in no way subordinate to one another in any aspect of their domestic or external affairs, though united by a common allegiance to the Crown, and freely associated as members of the British Commonwealth of Nations." The formula continued, "Every self-governing member of the Empire is now the master of its destiny. In fact, if not always in form, it is subject to no compulsion whatsoever."

The British government codified these basic principles of equal status and free association in 1931 in the Statute of Westminster, which has been characterized as the "Magna Carta of the Commonwealth." The statute also recognized the full legislative autonomy of the dominions and offered all former colonies the right to secede from the Commonwealth.

The Ottawa Imperial Conference of 1932 added an economic dimension to the Commonwealth by creating the Commonwealth Preference, a system of preferential tariffs that applied to trade between Britain and the other Commonwealth members. Under this system, Britain imported goods from other Commonwealth countries without imposing any tariffs. Commonwealth members were encouraged to negotiate similar trade agreements with one another. For the next decade and a half, the Commonwealth in essence functioned as an economic bloc vis-à-vis the rest of the world. However, following World War II, as world and British trade policies were liberalized, the bloc gradually disintegrated. The Commonwealth Preference was finally terminated in 1977 as a condition of Britain's entrance into the European Economic Community (EEC).

Nevertheless, Commonwealth nations have been linked to the EEC through the Lomé Convention (see Glossary), which offers former colonies of EEC members in Africa, the Pacific, and the Caribbean preferential access to EEC markets and economic assistance. The Lomé Convention is updated every five years.

A new Commonwealth gradually emerged after World War II, reflecting the progress of decolonization and the needs of new members. In the process, the Commonwealth became both more decentralized and more concerned with economic and social needs. In 1947 Britain granted complete independence to India and Pakistan, and in 1948 Ceylon (later Sri Lanka) and Burma (now Myanmar) gained independence. Burma did not join the Commonwealth, but the other three became independent Commonwealth members. In deference to India, a self-declared republic, the Commonwealth dropped the requirement of formal allegiance to the crown. In 1949 the Irish Republic seceded. In 1961 South Africa left the Commonwealth because its racial policies differed from the values of all other Commonwealth members.

During the 1960s and 1970s, a large number of British colonies achieved independence and joined the expanded Commonwealth, including most ex-colonies in sub-Saharan Africa, the Caribbean, and the Pacific. Some former British colonies did not join, however; these included Iraq, Transjordan (now Jordan), British Somaliland (now part of Somalia), Southern Cameroons (now part of Cameroon), and the People's Democratic Republic of Yemen (now part of Yemen). Pakistan left in 1972, after Britain and other members recognized the independence of Bangladesh, formerly East Pakistan, but in 1987 Pakistan rejoined the Commonwealth (see table A, this Appendix).

Principles and Politics

Although the Statute of Westminster affirms the principles of free association and equal status, the contemporary Commonwealth has no written charter or formal treaty. Instead, its governing features are found in a few basic procedures, its periodic declarations of principle, and an organization designed for consultations and mutual assistance. This framework is both flexible and adaptable, and a major reason why the Commonwealth has survived major changes in membership and member interests.

Two central procedures govern the Commonwealth—its process of making decisions by consensus and its biennial meeting of heads of government. The latter is held in odd-numbered years and in different cities and regions within the Commonwealth. In alternate years, senior officials hold policy-review meetings. Finance ministers meet annually; other meetings are held as appropriate.

Over time the Commonwealth has become more oriented toward its less-developed members. Major declarations of principle reflect this trend. The Declaration of Commonwealth Principles, adopted at the 1971 Singapore meeting, affirmed the members' belief "in the liberty of the individual, in equal rights for all citizens regardless of race, color, creed, or political belief, and in their inalienable right to participate by means of free and democratic processes in framing the society in which they live." The declaration also opposed all forms of colonial domination and racial oppression.

The 1977 meeting in Gleneagles, Scotland, issued an Agreement on Apartheid in Sport, reaffirming opposition to apartheid, but allowing each member to decide whether to participate in sporting events with South Africa. The 1979 conference in Lusaka, Zambia, issued both an important framework for a peaceful settlement of Southern Rhodesia's transition to an independent Zimbabwe under black majority rule and a strong Commonwealth declaration condemning racism. Members also adopted the 1981 Melbourne Declaration on relations between the developed and developing nations; the 1983 New Delhi Statement on Economic Action; and the 1983 Goa Declaration on International Security.

The October 1985 meeting in Nassau, the Bahamas, passed resolutions calling for cooperation in fighting international terrorism and drug trafficking, bans on nuclear testing, and prohibition of the use of chemical weapons. As part of the Commonwealth's continuing condemnation of South Africa's racial policies, it also appointed a Commonwealth Group of Eminent Persons (Comgep). The Comgep was tasked to encourage dialogue to end apartheid in South Africa.

Despite a broad consensus among members condemning apartheid, issues concerning South Africa have led to the most serious divisions within the Commonwealth. In 1982 the Commonwealth Games Federation held its first extraordinary meeting to discuss a tour of New Zealand by South African rugby teams. In 1986 over half of the member states pulled their teams out of the Commonwealth Games, held that year in Britain, in protest over South African participation. Conspicuously absent were the predominantly black Caribbean and African states.

Organization and Activities

The central organization for consultation and cooperation is the Commonwealth Secretariat, established in 1965. The Secretariat, located in London, is headed by a secretary general, elected by the heads of government for a five-year term. It organizes conferences and meetings, coordinates a broad range of activities, and disseminates information. Since World War II, member heads of state have attended the biennial meetings. Meetings are also held periodically on specific issues of foreign affairs, defense, finance, and international debt. For example, the national finance ministers routinely meet immediately before the annual meetings of the World Bank (see Glossary) and the International Monetary Fund (see Glossary) to discuss international monetary and economic issues. The Secretariat's departments deal with administration, applied studies in government, economic affairs, education, export market development, food production and rural development, information, international affairs, legal matters, medical affairs, youth, finance, and personnel.

Two permanent directorates are within the Secretariat, the Commonwealth Fund for Technical Cooperation (CFTC) and the Industrial Development Unit. The CFTC was established in April 1971 to provide technical assistance for economic and social development in Commonwealth developing countries. The fund is financed by all Commonwealth nations on a voluntary basis; the CFTC's governing body includes representatives of all its contributors. The Industrial Development Unit promotes the establishment and modernization of industries in member countries.

The Commonwealth Secretariat is funded by member payments, determined individually on the basis of per capita income. Britain pays 30 percent of the Secretariat's budget.

In addition to the Secretariat, a number of Commonwealth components are noteworthy. Government and private funds are sent to less-developed members through the Commonwealth Development Corporation. Specialized organizations include the Commonwealth Agricultural Bureau, the Institute of Commonwealth Studies, the Association of Commonwealth Universities, and various Commonwealth groups for communications, health, the law, the professions, and science and technology. The Commonwealth Games Federation, based in London, has held games every four years since 1930. The Commonwealth also maintains close links with other international organizations, including the United Nations (UN). In October 1976, the UN General Assembly granted the Commonwealth official observer status.

Regional Groupings

Aside from its general departments and specialized organizations, the Commonwealth also has four "regional groupings." One is the Colombo Plan for Cooperative, Economic, and Social Development in Asia and the Pacific, founded in 1951 (originally under a slightly different name) and headquartered in Colombo, Sri Lanka; it is designed to promote economic and social development in Asia and the Pacific. Economic assistance is provided to Commonwealth and non-Commonwealth countries in the region by Australia, Britain, Canada, Japan, and the United States. A related program, the Conference of Heads of Government of Asian and Pacific Commonwealth Member States, began in 1978 and exists to encourage cooperation for regional development.

The other two regional groupings deal with the Caribbean: the Caribbean Community and Common Market (Caricom) and the Organisation of Eastern Caribbean States (OECS), an associate institution of Caricom (see Appendix C). Encompassing Antigua and Barbuda, Dominica, Grenada, Montserrat, Saint Christopher and Nevis, Saint Lucia, and Saint Vincent and the Grenadines, the OECS aims at coordinating member states' development, foreign policy, defense, and relations with international institutions. It also has responsibility for the Eastern Caribbean Currency Authority and the Eastern Caribbean States Supreme Court.

Appendix C

The Caribbean Community and Common Market

IN 1992 THIRTEEN NATIONS located in or bordering on the Caribbean Sea were members of the Caribbean Community and Common Market (Caricom—see table B, this appendix). Observers included Anguilla, Bermuda, the British Virgin Islands, the Dominican Republic, Haiti, the Netherlands Antilles, and Suriname. In 1992 the British Virgin Islands, the Dominican Republic, and the Turks and Caicos Islands were being considered for full membership. The members faced problems typical of many developing societies: high birth rates, unemployment and an unskilled labor force, inadequate infrastructure, balance of payments constraints, and insufficient domestic savings to achieve development goals. In addition, Caricom nations lacked diversified economies and were incapable of producing most capital goods and some basic consumer goods necessary for productive expansion. The Caricom nations, therefore, were forced to rely heavily on imports of essential goods. As a result, development goals were subordinated because of the need to raise foreign exchange to pay for the imports.

Table B. Members of the Caribbean Community and Common Market (Caricom), 1992

Antigua and Barbuda	Jamaica
Bahamas	Montserrat
Barbados	Saint Christopher and Nevis
Belize	Saint Lucia
Dominica	Saint Vincent and the Grenadines
Grenada	Trinidad and Tobago
Guyana	

Source: Based on information from *South America, Central America, and the Caribbean, 1993,* London, 1992, 663–65.

Since 1981 the ability of Caricom nations to raise the needed capital via export expansion has been severely limited by the lack of export diversification and reliance on primary products and tourism services, which are extremely vulnerable to changing forces of demand, supply, and price in the international political economy.

In 1992 intraregional cooperation was urgently needed to create an atmosphere conducive to overcoming the handicaps of small market size, economic fragmentation, and external dependence.

Caricom's goal of regional integration was designed to serve as a catalyst for sustained growth in the short or medium term by allowing for market expansion, harmonization of production strategies, and development of economies of scale. Integration was also expected to promote industrial growth by eliminating excess capacity in the manufacturing sector and by stimulating investment in new sectors of the expanded market. The long-term hope was for balanced growth, minimal unemployment, a higher standard of living, and optimal use of available human and natural resources.

Background and Objectives

Following the example of the European Economic Community (EEC), many nations have organized themselves into regional integration schemes, such as Latin America's Central American Common Market, the Latin America Integration Association, and the Andean Pact. The Commonwealth Caribbean archipelago made a serious move toward establishing a unit of integration by forming the West Indies Federation (WIF) in April 1958. The federation, formed under the auspices of the British, was doomed from the start by nationalistic tendencies and the lack of taxation privileges and failed when Jamaica and Trinidad and Tobago attained independence and withdrew in 1962. Nevertheless, a few institutions, such as the University of the West Indies (UWI) and the Regional Shipping Council, were established under the short-lived federation and continue today. After the demise of the WIF, economist Arthur Lewis attempted to organize a smaller body among the Eastern Caribbean islands; however, his efforts yielded little success, and most of the islands reverted to British colonial status.

The next call for a regional Caribbean community was made in a January 1962 speech by Eric Williams, former prime minister and first head of state of the independent Trinidad and Tobago. However, it was not until the late 1960s that advocates of a new federation focused their attention on the issue of regional integration. In July 1965, the contemporary nations of Antigua and Barbuda, Barbados, and Guyana signed the Treaty of Dickenson Bay, which established the Caribbean Free Trade Association (Carifta). Under the terms of the 1968 Treaty of Saint John's, Carifta was widened to include Anguilla, Dominica, Grenada, Jamaica, Saint Christopher and Nevis, Saint Lucia, Montserrat, Saint Vincent and the Grenadines, and Trinidad and Tobago. Although a free-trade area was established, Carifta did not provide for the free movement of labor and capital or the coordination of agricultural, industrial, defense, and foreign policies. Thus, over the next five years, little progress was made toward creating a regionally integrated unit. In 1970 the prospect of Britain's joining the EEC alerted the islands to their vulnerability to any disruption in their preferential trading ties with Britain. In the same year, economists at the UWI issued a report contending that the creation of a free-trade area alone was not sufficient to procure full gains from regional integration. These events led to the development of the present Caricom structure.

In 1973 the Carifta nations signed the Treaty of Chaguaramas, replacing the ineffective Carifta structure with Caricom. Caricom has three essential components: economic integration based on a regional common market; functional cooperation in such areas as culture, education, health, labor relations, tourism, and transportation; and coordination of foreign and defense policies. Although the regional common market is an integral part of the broader-based community arrangements, it has a completely separate identity juridically. Thus, it was possible for the Bahamas to become a member of the community in 1983, without joining the Common Market. In 1981 the seven Eastern Caribbean island nations—Antigua and Barbuda, Dominica, Grenada, Montserrat, Saint Lucia, Saint Christopher and Nevis, and Saint Vincent and the Grenadines—established an associate entity, the Organisation of Eastern Caribbean States (OECS), which replaced the West Indies States Association (WISA) as the islands' major administrative body. The OECS coordinates development strategies among the member nations and provides for cooperation in economic, foreign policy, and defense matters. The OECS was created after studies indicated that most of the benefits derived from integration were flowing to the larger nations of Caricom (especially Jamaica and Trinidad and Tobago) at the expense of the smaller nations.

Institutional Structure

The institutional structure of Caricom consists of the Heads of Government Conference, Common Market Council of Ministers, Caribbean Community Secretariat, and other special bodies (see fig. A, this Appendix). Unlike in the EEC, these bodies are not supranational; each member has a right of veto and thus retains much of its national sovereignty. Decision making in Caricom, although centralized at some levels, is quite decentralized at others.

The Heads of Government Conference is the supreme decision-making body. Each member state has one vote, and a unanimous

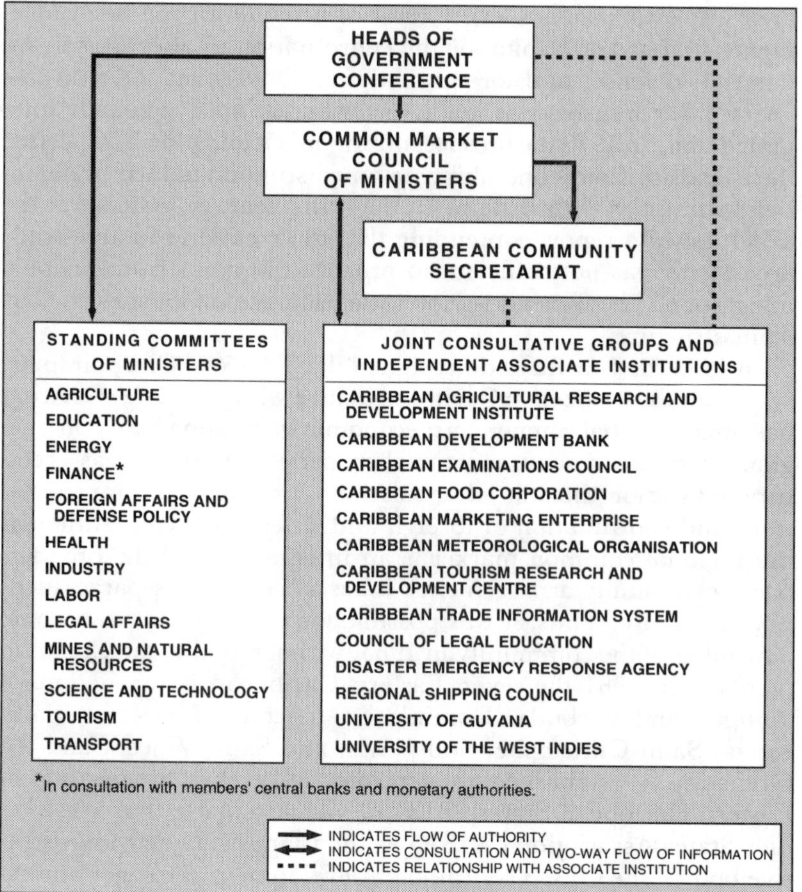

Source: Based on information from Sidney E. Chernick, *The Commonwealth Carribean: The Integration Experience. Baltimore, 1978, 11;* and *South America, Central America, and the Caribbean, 1993,* London, 1992, 668–69.

Figure A. Organization of the Caribbean Community and Common Market (Caricom), 1992

vote is required to legislate decisions or to make policy recommendations. The conference determines the policies to be pursued by Caricom's related institutions. This conference also is responsible for concluding all treaties, making financial disbursements, and maintaining relations with other international organizations.

The Common Market Council of Ministers is the second principal body of Caricom and the principal body of the regional Common Market. The Common Market Council consists of one ministerial representative from each nation. Decisions are also made by unanimous vote, with minor exceptions. This council resolves problems and makes proposals to the Heads of Government Conference to achieve efficient development and operation of the regional common market.

The Caribbean Community Secretariat is Caricom's principal administrative component. The Secretariat operates to serve the interests of the region rather than those of each government. Although the Secretariat has no decision-making power, its discussions, studies, and projects have made it a dynamic element in the integration process.

Other offices responsible for specific sectoral aspects of regional integration are the thirteen Standing Committees of Ministers (health, education, labor, foreign affairs and defense policy, finance, agriculture, mines and natural resources, industry, transport, legal affairs, energy, science and technology, and tourism). In addition, independent associate institutions include the Caribbean Agricultural Research and Development Institute, the Caribbean Development Bank (CDB), the Caribbean Examinations Council, the Caribbean Tourism Research and Development Centre, the Council of Legal Education, the University of Guyana, the UWI, the Disaster Emergency Response Agency, the Caribbean Meteorological Organisation, the Caribbean Food Corporation, the Agricultural Research and Development Institute, the Regional Shipping Council, the Caribbean Trade Information System, and the Caribbean Marketing Enterprise. Finally, the Joint Consultative Group, comprising business, consumer, and trade groups, meets to review the integration process and ensure interest group participation in Caricom activities.

Market Integration Mechanisms

Caricom seeks to achieve economic integration through market forces. The Common Market was established to promote intraregional trade through: trade liberalization by removing duties, licensing arrangements, quotas, and other tariff and nontariff barriers to trade; Rules of Origin; a Common External Tariff (CET) and a Common Protective Policy (CPP); and trade arrangements such as the Agricultural Marketing Protocol and the Oils and Fats Agreement.

The Common Market contains a number of important mechanisms for liberalizing trade. These include eliminating extraregional export duties, removing quantitative restrictions on regional exports, permitting free transit for products of member nations, and eliminating quantitative restrictions on imported goods. Article 28 of the Treaty of Chaguaramas permits the application of quantitative restrictions if the nation has severe balance of payments problems. At the 1987 annual conference, Caricom agreed to abolish all obstacles to trade by October 1988. Seventeen products, however, were allowed an additional three years of protection with all tariffs on them to be removed by 1991.

The Rules of Origin establish the conditions of eligibility of regional products so that they may be considered of Common Market origin and thus qualified for preferential treatment. In 1986 a new set of Rules of Origin was adopted to increase the use of regional products and promote employment, investment, and savings of foreign exchange.

The Treaty of Chaguaramas mandates gradually implementing a CET and CPP. The CET stimulates local production by imposing low tariffs on capital goods and industrial raw materials and higher tariffs on value-added (finished) products. The CPP standardizes quantitative restrictions to protect specific regional industrial sectors. Together, the CET and CPP, coupled with intraregional trade liberalization, were expected to stimulate reciprocal investment and trade among member countries.

The final market integration mechanism aims at providing guaranteed markets and prices for Caricom exports to overcome the volatile trade in primary commodities. The Agricultural Marketing Protocol and the Oils and Fats Agreement regulate intraregional trade via certain buy-and-sell accords at fixed prices resulting from shortages or surpluses within Caricom. Caricom also has a Guaranteed Market Scheme whereby in certain circumstances Jamaica, Barbados, and Trinidad and Tobago will purchase fixed quantities of agroproducts from the other member nations.

Mechanisms of Cooperation in Marketing and Production

Joint regional action in production and marketing activities is viewed by Caricom as a means of coordinating and controlling each member nation's output to avoid injury to other members or to the entire region. Coordinating policies is also intended to encourage specialization and complementary production. One important mechanism in this regard is regional industrial programming aimed at promoting specialization and economic diversification and avoiding duplication of investment. Although industrial programming was first considered in 1973, concrete actions did not begin until 1985. In 1988 members agreed to fully implement the Industrial

Programming Scheme by 1993, but progress toward realizing the plan was slow. The most-cited example of industrial cooperation and integration was a regional alumina refinery that was to use bauxite from Jamaica and Guyana and oil from Trinidad and Tobago. Although the project was thoroughly discussed during the 1970s, it remained doubtful in 1992 that such a project would ever be realized. In addition, there were agricultural programs that represented joint efforts to provide extension, marketing, and research and development services to reduce unit costs, increase quality and yield, and slash imports of basic foodstuffs.

The Regional Food and Nutrition Strategy is the main instrument for Caricom's agricultural development, and it establishes a framework and identifies priorities for a regional approach to agricultural self-sufficiency. The Caribbean Food Corporation, founded in 1976, is the main mechanism for planning and implementing the strategy's objectives. Also, a Food and Nutrition Institute was established at the UWI in Mona, Kingston, Jamaica.

Transportation is indispensable for effective trade, export promotion, and other integration objectives. Cooperation in maritime transportation was envisioned through the West Indies Shipping Corporation (WISCO), which was established in 1961 and restructured in 1975. WISCO theoretically provides services to all Caricom nations. In early 1987, however, Belize, Dominica, and Saint Vincent and the Grenadines withdrew from WISCO, claiming they had received few benefits from the service. WISCO went bankrupt in 1992 and was replaced by the Regional Shipping Council. In 1992 air transportation remained inadequate because of the lack of coordination among the existing airlines. Standardizing air transport by coordinating and planning routes and fares, as well as mergers, was necessary to improve service and reduce costs. A proposal was made in 1991 to restructure and coordinate regional air service.

Tourism is important to the region, providing foreign exchange, increasing employment, encouraging the production of tourist-oriented products and services, and stimulating the construction of basic infrastructure. Some regional cooperation in tourism has been carried out by the Caribbean Tourism Association, the Caribbean Tourism Research and Development Centre (located in Barbados), and at the UWI Hotel Training School in the Bahamas. Nevertheless, in the early 1990s, further cooperation was needed to link the tourism sector to the rest of the economy and to establish regional tourism enterprises.

Mechanisms of Financial Cooperation

Financial cooperation is intended to fulfill the objectives of economic integration by facilitating payments for intraregional trade and by mobilizing investment funds to productive sectors of the economy. The principal vehicle for financial cooperation is Caricom's Multilateral Clearing Facility (CMCF), established in 1977 by the central banks and other financial entities of Caricom's members. The facility's objectives are to reduce the use of foreign exchange and expedite intraregional payments through credit and other financial arrangements. Other related mechanisms include harmonizing exchange rates by pegging the six existing currencies to the United States dollar and by issuing regional traveler's checks through the Central Bank of Trinidad and Tobago. Finally, the CDB contributes to the equitable development of the region by providing low-interest loans for projects and related integration plans.

Functional Cooperation

The Treaty of Chaguaramas also envisioned coordinating efforts in many noneconomic areas. The Caricom structure has formalized and expanded this type of cooperation to include meteorological services and hurricane insurance; health and nutrition services; technical assistance; public utilities; education and job training; broadcasting, printed media, and information; culture and language; social security, labor, and industrial relations; science and technology; and harmonizing the laws and legal systems within Caricom. This cooperation has been successful in improving services to the member nations (especially the smaller ones) and lowering costs of activities through joint ventures. The regional university and health and nutrition systems are examples of successful functional cooperation.

Coordination of Defense and Foreign Policies

The Heads of Government Conference and the Standing Committee of Foreign Ministers of Caricom are responsible for coordinating the defense and foreign policies of member nations to increase their international bargaining power. Caricom has been able to present a regional foreign policy position in defense of the principles of regional security and nonintervention, support of the territorial integrity of Guyana and Belize in their border disputes; and various negotiations for the Lomé Convention (see Glossary), by which many less developed nations have gained preferential access to EEC markets and economic assistance. The Lomé Convention is updated every five years.

Caricom: A Brief Evaluation of the Integration Effort

One method of evaluating Caricom's integration efforts is to look at three of its principal goals: defense and foreign policy coordination, functional cooperation, and economic and trade cooperation. In 1992 some positive results had been achieved in defense and foreign policy coordination. Caribbean expressions of solidarity on issues of regional security and territorial integrity focused international attention on the region and strengthened Caricom's bargaining position in negotiations with regional and extraregional nations and in international forums. Ultimately, however, national concerns have always overshadowed regional interests. The ideological pluralism of the region and the often drastic changes in government orientation have hurt the coordination process through bilateralism and polarization of interests.

Appendix D

Caribbean Basin Initiative

THE CARIBBEAN BASIN INITIATIVE (CBI), enacted by the United States Congress in 1982–83 and modified and expanded in 1990, represented one of the major United States foreign economic policies toward Latin America and the Caribbean in the 1980s and 1990s. Mainly a trade promotion program, the initiative provided duty-free access to the United States market for about 3,000 products; it expanded bilateral economic assistance; and it allowed some limited tax breaks for new United States investors in the region. A number of United States agencies contributed to the formulation and implementation of the policy. Whereas the CBI had improved the region's prosperity only slightly by 1992, it had served nonetheless as a catalyst toward economic diversification in a number of Caribbean Basin countries.

The Reagan Administration's Proposal and Congressional Amendments

On February 24, 1982, in a speech before the Organization of American States, President Ronald Reagan unveiled a new proposal for the economic recovery of Central America and the Caribbean. The Reagan plan expanded duty-free entry of Caribbean Basin exports for up to twelve years and increased economic assistance and tax incentives for new United States investment in the region. The administration's proposal arose in the political context of a successful revolution in Nicaragua, active insurgencies in El Salvador and Guatemala, and leftist coups in Grenada and Suriname. Dramatic political change, coupled with an international economic crisis characterized by high oil prices, unprecedented interest rates, and declining commodity prices, rekindled the interest of United States policy makers in the region.

In September 1982, the 97th Congress passed the foreign aid portion of the president's plan in the form of Public Law 97–257, after scaling back some portions of the proposal, most notably the amount of aid earmarked for El Salvador. Even with congressional amendments, the overwhelming share of the US$350 million in supplemental assistance under the Caribbean Basin Economic Recovery Act, the bill's official name, went toward the most strategically important nations in the region: El Salvador, Costa Rica, Jamaica, the Dominican Republic, and Honduras. Impoverished Haiti, for example, received only US$10 million in supplementary aid. As a result of opposition from domestic labor and industrial interests, the 98th Congress did not pass the trade provisions of the act (as Public Law 98-67) until July 1983. The bill's final version, however, excluded the following items from duty-free coverage: petroleum and petroleum products, sugar, canned tuna, luggage, handbags, certain other leather goods, flat goods, rubber and plastic gloves, footwear, textiles and apparel subject to the Multi-fibre Arrangement, and watches or watch parts manufactured in communist countries. Critics of the initiative argued that with or without these exclusions, it represented more a political policy than a developmental one because new duty-free provisions would provide only limited economic benefits. Congressional sentiment ran against the investment tax exemptions originally included in the bill, and these measures were never approved. Some tax breaks were extended, however, to companies holding business meetings in certain countries.

Section 212 of the act provided the president with the authority to designate beneficiary countries. To qualify, countries had to have a noncommunist government, had to meet specific requirements concerning the expropriation of United States property, had to cooperate in regional antinarcotics efforts, had to recognize arbitral awards to United States citizens, could not provide preferential treatment to the products of developing countries in such a manner as to adversely affect United States trade, had to abstain from the illegal broadcast of United States-copyrighted material, and had to maintain an extradition treaty with the United States. In addition, the act authorized the president to consider eleven discretionary criteria to qualify potential beneficiaries. These included such considerations as the use of subsidies, acceptance of the rules of international trade, and guarantees of workers' rights. President Reagan initially announced twenty-one beneficiary nations or territories from the Caribbean, Central America, and the northern coast of South America. Countries excluded from the list included Cuba, Nicaragua, Guyana, Suriname, Anguilla, the Cayman Islands, and the Turks and Caicos Islands, none of which applied for designation. The Bahamas became a beneficiary nation in March 1985; Aruba became one in January 1986 and Guyana, in November 1988. In March 1988, President Reagan suspended Panama's eligibility because of reported links between that country's government and international narcotics traffickers. Panama's suspension was lifted in 1990 after the United States intervention. The 1991 United States embargo against Haiti after that nation's coup effectively curtailed the CBI's program for Haitian exports (see table C, this Appendix).

Table C. Potential Beneficiaries of the Caribbean Basin Initiative, 1992

Anguilla	Haiti
Antigua and Barbuda	Honduras
Aruba	Jamaica
Bahamas	Montserrat
Barbados	Netherlands Antilles
Belize	Nicaragua
British Virgin Islands	Panama
Cayman Islands	Saint Christopher and Nevis
Costa Rica	Saint Lucia
Dominica	Saint Vincent and the Grenadines
Dominican Republic	Suriname
El Salvador	Trinidad and Tobago
Grenada	Turks and Caicos Islands
Guatemala	United States Virgin Islands
Guyana	

Source: Based on information from United States, International Trade Commission, *Annual Report on the Impact of the Caribbean Basin Economic Recovery Act on U.S. Industries and Consumers: First Report, 1984–85,* Washington, September 1986, 1–8.

The CBI legislation also encompassed other important provisions. Section 213 stipulated the basic product eligibility rule that at least 35 percent of the value-added of the imported product had to originate in a beneficiary country for that country to qualify for duty-free treatment. This section also empowered the president to with-draw duty-free treatment in case of injury to domestic industries resulting from CBI imports. As a result of complaints from Puerto Rico and the United States Virgin Islands that the CBI extended benefits previously reserved for United States overseas territories, section 214 set forth special benefits under the law. These included an increase in beneficiary country content for product eligibility of up to 70 percent, as well as other more technical exemptions. Section 221 also transferred all rum tax proceeds to the treasuries of the two United States possessions. Puerto Rico also benefited from the twin plant plan (see Glossary) which encouraged

United States investors to operate complementary factories in Puerto Rico and in other beneficiary countries. This framework enabled investors to tap funds accumulated under section 936 of the United States Internal Revenue Service Code, known as 936 funds (see Glossary), in order to develop complementary operations if the recipient country had signed a Tax Information Exchange Agreement (TIEA) with the United States. Finally, section 222 permitted tax deductions for business conventions in the region if the country had signed a TIEA.

The CBI Network

The United States Department of State played a central role in designing and implementing the initiative, but many other executive-branch agencies contributed extensively to the policy. The United States Agency for International Development (AID) administered most economic assistance flows, concentrating its efforts on the private sector. The Overseas Private Investment Corporation, the Peace Corps, the Department of Transportation, the Export-Import Bank, and the Customs Service of the Department of the Treasury all enhanced and complemented AID's endeavors. The Department of Commerce, through its Caribbean Basin Information Center and its normal regional offices, provided information packages, investment climate statements, economic trend reports, special product advice, investment missions, a monthly networking newsletter, and other information and services for potential investors. The Department of Agriculture similarly promoted the CBI through frequent agribusiness-marketing workshops and technical assistance missions, and by supplying important regulatory information on United States import standards. The International Trade Commission and the Department of Labor took part by issuing in-depth annual reports on the progress of the CBI and its impact on the United States. The Office of the United States Trade Representative oversaw bilateral investment and textile agreements; and, beginning in 1987, that office hired an ombudsman to direct the CBI Operations Committee, an interagency task force dedicated to the policy's success. Finally, public and private monies helped to create a strong private business and advocacy network to further the aims of the CBI.

The United States government also generated a certain amount of multilateral and bilateral support for the initiative. Mexico, Venezuela, Colombia, and the European Economic Community supported the CBI in a limited way, mainly through the extension of existing programs. Japan increased its aid to the region, as did Canada; on February 17, 1986, the Canadian government offered its own import preference program for the region, a package it dubbed Caribcan. Multilaterals such as the Inter-American Development Bank, the World Bank (see Glossary), and the International Monetary Fund (see Glossary) also cooperated with the initiative through a variety of programs, particularly policy reform efforts coordinated with AID.

Expansion of CBI Benefits and Programs

Visiting the island of Grenada on February 20, 1986, President Reagan announced increased access to the United States market for apparel assembled in the Caribbean Basin in an effort to enlarge the impact of the CBI. Guaranteed access levels for CBI beneficiary countries were provided through import quota negotiations based on previous exports and expected growth under the Tarriff Schedule 807 program (see Glossary). The proposal was the direct result of regional discontent with the limited benefits of the initiative and the expressed fears of regional leaders with regard to mounting protectionist sentiment in the United States. A group of leaders of the English-speaking Caribbean had expressed their dissatisfaction through a detailed letter to President Reagan in late 1985. Regional leaders generally welcomed the small improvement made through the 807 program because of the extraordinary growth in textile production since the inauguration of the CBI.

After a series of regional and Washington-based hearings, in 1987 members of Congress introduced legislation to improve further the benefits of the initiative. By mid-1989, a number of proposals had been combined under the Caribbean Basin Economic Recovery Expansion Act of 1989 (H.R. 1233), which became law on August 20, 1990. Stating that "the existing program has not fully achieved the positive results that were intended," the Expansion Act, dubbed CBI II, proposed an indefinite time extension for duty-free entry of CBI-covered products (previously scheduled to expire September 30, 1995) and the addition of several specific garments and fabrics to be provided reduced or exempted duties. It also guaranteed market access for textiles and footwear via bilateral agreements with all beneficiary nations; potential increases for beneficiary countries in their sugar quotas, through reallocations from other countries that did not reach their allotted share; increased duty-free allowances for United States tourists visiting the region; more flexible criteria for ethanol imports; increased postsecondary scholarships for study in the United States; greater promotion of tourist development; and the trial establishment of preinspection customs facilities to expedite exports. CBI II also sought special measures to enable the Eastern Caribbean and Belize to reap greater benefits from the program, as well as the application of new rules of origin for determining the content of duty-free imports, the employment of internationally recognized workers' rights criteria in evaluating the compliance of beneficiary countries, and a requirement that the president report to Congress every three years on the progress of the initiative.

An Assessment of Progress

One of the major aims of the plan was to increase economic assistance in order to foster sustained economic growth through stimulation of the private sector and the expansion of exports. Beneficiary nations sought increased aid to cushion the impact of the recession of the early 1980s and to provide support during the difficult economic adjustment period of the mid-1980s. The US$350 million in assistance to the region, provided under the auspices of the CBI as a supplement to annual allocations, contributed to a dramatic increase in United States assistance to Central America and the Caribbean, from US$300 million in 1981 to nearly US$1.5 billion in 1985. A large portion of this assistance, however, was motivated by United States strategic concerns rather than developmental ones. For example, El Salvador, engaged in a war against leftist insurgents, received nearly one-third of all assistance throughout this period. Similarly, some strategic countries received allocations in excess of their absorptive capacities while other countries pursued additional United States support. Increased assistance gave the United States significant leverage in encouraging recipient countries to reform their economic policies in such areas as exchange rates, the promotion of increased and diversified exports, the expansion of light manufacturing, reductions in import controls, privatization of state-owned enterprises, the balancing of fiscal accounts, promotion of small business development, and the upgrading of infrastructure. Evidence of the impact of these reforms continued to be inconclusive at the close of the decade, but several countries had begun to open and to diversify their economies, thereby setting the stage, it was hoped, for sustained future growth.

The promotion of increased foreign investment, although not part of the final CBI legislation, continued to be one of the overall goals of the initiative. In 1988 the United States Department of Commerce surveyed Caribbean investment trends in a comprehensive manner, after a previously unsuccessful attempt to quantify CBI-related ventures in 1986. The 1988 survey revealed that significant new investment had taken place in the region during the 1984-88 period, despite the lack of tax credits for United States companies. The 642 United States companies participating in the study accounted for US$1.6 billion in new investment in CBI countries (excluding Panama) and for 116,000 new jobs. Only 150 of these firms (23 percent), however, exported CBI-eligible products; therefore, the CBI was directly related to the creation of only 15 percent of the new jobs. Furthermore, the new investment was highly concentrated; five countries accounted for 67 percent of all new investment. By 1988 the Dominican Republic had surpassed Jamaica as the prime investment location, and it received one-fifth of all the Caribbean Basin's new investment because of the vibrant growth of its industrial free zones. By contrast, Haiti suffered disinvestment because of political unrest, high nonwage costs, and increased regional competition for investment in labor-intensive industry. More than half of all foreign investment was from the United States, followed by the Republic of Korea (South Korea), Canada, and Hong Kong. Although new CBI-related and other foreign investment helped the balance of payments positions of several countries and provided badly needed jobs in manufacturing and tourism, foreign exchange remained scarce in early 1992 and unemployment continued to hover at dangerously high levels in most countries.

The centerpiece of the initiative, however, was neither aid nor investment, but one-way duty-free trade with the United States. An assessment of CBI trade data demonstrated both negative and positive trends. On the negative side, the value of total Caribbean Basin exports generally declined throughout the 1980s because of dwindling prices for the region's traditional exports, such as petroleum, sugar, and bauxite. Except in the case of sugar, this poor performance was attributable almost solely to the vagaries of primary product prices. United States policy clearly damaged sugar exports, however, through the reimposition of sugar quotas in 1981 and through the 75 percent reduction in Caribbean and Central America quotas from 1981 to 1987, a trend that offset export growth among CBI-exempted products. Not only did the region's total exports drop by US$1.8 billion from 1984 to 1990, but its share of the United States market weakened, dropping from 6.5 percent of United States imports in 1980 to 1.6 percent by 1987. As was true of investment, only a small percentage (less than 20 percent) of the growth in nontraditional exports resulted from duty-free entry extended through the CBI. Furthermore, only ten items accounted for the great majority of products that entered the United States market duty-free. Moreover, exports, like investments, were concentrated; only a handful of countries generated the overwhelming share of CBI 806.3 and 807 exports, while some countries suffered substantial declines in exports. Overall, despite import exemptions in the United States market, the United States ran a trade surplus with the region from 1987 to 1989. After years of pursuing the goal of "trade, not aid," United States policy through the CBI continued to provide fewer economic benefits from trade than from aid.

Despite some negative trends, Caribbean Basin countries experienced substantial growth in nontraditional exports during the 1980s. For example, although the area's total exports lagged behind other regions, growth in manufactures and other nontraditional exports far surpassed that of other regions. In fact, some Caribbean Basin countries outperformed even the newly industrialized countries of Asia. The composition of trade shifted markedly away from agricultural commodities and raw materials in favor of nontraditional exports, textiles, and apparel. In 1983 the region's exports broke down as being 78 percent traditional commodities, 17 percent nontraditional ones, and 4 percent textiles and apparel; by 1988, however, traditional exports represented only 37 percent of total exports, compared with 44 percent for nontraditionals, and 19 percent for textiles and apparel. This shift was particularly true of United States imports covered under the 807 provisions; the value of these imports more than doubled from 1983 to 1988. Judging by these statistics, it appeared that although the CBI directly stimulated only limited export growth, its emphasis on nontraditional exports contributed to the restructuring of much of the region's external trade. Such restructuring was especially found among Caribbean countries because of the larger share of depressed primary products in their export baskets relative to those of Central America.

After an initial lag period, CBI trade statistics improved markedly in 1988, and observers expected continued growth in trade and investment. Although many of the structural obstacles to development in the region continued, the broadening of the productive and export base improved long-term prospects for economic growth.

Bibliography

Chapter 1

Adamson, Alan H. *Sugar Without Slaves: The Political Economy of British Guiana, 1838–1904.* New Haven: Yale University Press, 1972.

Akhtar, Shameen. *British Guiana: A Study of Marxism and Racialism in the Caribbean.* Dallas: Southern Methodist University, 1962.

Augies, F.R., S.C. Gordon, D.G. Hall, and M. Reckford. *The Making of the West Indies.* London: Longmans, 1960.

Avebury, and the British Parliamentary Human Rights Group. "Guyana's 1980 Elections: The Politics of Fraud," *Caribbean Review,* 10, Spring 1981, 8–11, 14.

Burnham, Forbes. *A Great Future Together.* Georgetown: Government Printery, 1968.

Burrowes, Reynold A. *The Wild Coast: An Account of Politics in Guyana.* Cambridge, Massachusetts: Schenkman, 1984.

Clementi, Sir Cecil. *A Constitutional History of British Guiana.* London: Macmillan, 1937.

de Caires, David. "Guyana after Burnham: A New Era? Or Is President Hoyte Trapped in the Skin of the PNC?" *Caribbean Affairs,* 1, January–March 1988, 183–93.

Despres, Leo A. *Cultural Pluralism and Nationalist Politics in Guyana.* Chicago: Rand McNally, 1967.

Deveze, Michel. *Antilles, Guyanes, La Mer des Caraïbes de 1492 à 1789.* Paris: Société d'edition d'enseignement supérieur, 1977.

"Dr. Jagan's Address," *Sunday Mirror* [Georgetown], August 7, 1975, 9.

Glascow, R.A. *Guyana: Race and Politics among Africans and East Indians.* The Hague: Nijhoff, 1970.

Hope, Kempe Ronald. "Electoral Politics and Political Development in Post-Independence Guyana," *Electoral Studies,* 4, April 1985, 57–68.

Inter-American Development Bank. *Economic and Social Progress in Latin America: 1982 Report.* Washington: 1982.

Jeffrey, Henry B., and Colin Baber. *Guyana: Politics, Economics, and Society—Beyond the Burnham Era.* Boulder, Colorado: Rienner, 1986.

Latin America and Caribbean Contemporary Record, 7: 1987–88. (Eds., James M. Malloy and Edward A. Gamarra.) New York: Holmes and Meier, 1990.

MacPherson, John. *Caribbean Lands: A Geography of the West Indies.* London: Longmans, Green, 1963.

Mandle, Jay R. *The Plantation Economy: Population and Economic Change in Guyana, 1838–1960.* Philadelphia: Temple University Press, 1973.

Manley, Robert H. *Guyana Emergent: The Post-Independence Struggle for Nondependent Development.* Cambridge, Massachusetts: Schenkman, 1982.

Moore, Brian L. "The Retention of Caste Notions among the Indian Immigrants in British Guiana During the Nineteenth Century," *Comparative Studies in Society and History* [Cambridge, United Kingdom], 19, No. 1, January 1977, 96–107.

Nath, Dwarke. *A History of Indians in British Guiana.* London: Nelson, 1950.

Neuman, Stephanie G. (ed.). *Small States and Segmented Societies.* New York: Praeger, 1976.

Premdas, Ralph R. *Party Politics and Racial Division in Guyana.* (Studies in Race and Nations Series, No. 4.) Denver: University of Colorado Press, 1973.

Ragatz, L.J. *The Fall of the Planter Class in the British Caribbean, 1763–1833.* London: Oxford University Press, 1928.

Rodney, Walter. *A History of the Guyanese Working People, 1881–1905.* Baltimore: Johns Hopkins University Press, 1981.

Singh, Chaitram. *Guyana: Politics in a Plantation Society.* New York: Praeger, 1988.

Spinner, Thomas J., Jr. *A Political and Social History of Guyana, 1945–1983.* Boulder, Colorado: Westview Press, 1984.

Swan, Michael. *British Guiana: The Land of Six Peoples.* London: HMSO, 1957.

Chapter 2

Adamson, Alan H. *Sugar Without Slaves: The Political Economy of British Guiana, 1838–1904.* New Haven: Yale University Press, 1972.

Bacchus, M.K. *Education for Development or Underdevelopment? Guyana's Educational System and Its Implications for the Third World.* (Development Perspectives Series, No. 2.) Waterloo, Canada: Wilfred Laurier University Press, 1980.

Balkaran, Sundat. *Evaluation of the Guyana Fertility Survey, 1975.* (Scientific Reports Series, No. 26.) Voorburg, Netherlands: International Statistical Institute, 1982.

Bartels, Dennis. "Class Conflict and Racist Ideology in the Formation of Modern Guyanese Society," *Canadian Review of Sociology and Anthropology* [Toronto], 14, No. 4, November 1977, 396-405.

Brereton, Bridget, and Winston Dookeran (eds.). *East Indians in the Caribbean: Colonialism and the Struggle for Identity.* (Papers presented to a symposium on East Indians in the Caribbean, The University of the West Indies.) Millwood, New York: Kraus International, 1982.

Burrowes, Reynold A. *The Wild Coast: An Account of Politics in Guyana.* Cambridge, Massachusetts: Schenkman, 1984.

Demographic Yearbook, 1988. New York: United Nations, 1990.

Despres, Leo A. *Cultural Pluralism and Nationalist Politics in Guyana.* Chicago: Rand McNally, 1967.

Drummond, Lee. "The Cultural Continuum: A Theory of Intersystems," *Man* [London], 15, No. 2, 1980, 352–74.

Encyclopedia of the Third World, 1. (Ed., George Thomas Kurian.) New York: Facts on File, 1987.

The Europa World Year Book, 1989, 1. London: Europa, 1989.

Federal Republic of Germany. Statistisches Bundesamt. *Länderbericht Guyana, 1987.* (Statistik des Auslandes Series.) Wiesbaden: 1987.

______. Statistisches Bundesamt. *Länderbericht Guyana, 1989.* (Statistik des Auslandes Series.) Wiesbaden: 1989.

Fredericks, Marcel, John Lennon, Paul Mundy, and Janet Fredericks. *Society and Health in Guyana: The Sociology of Health Care in a Developing Nation.* Durham, North Carolina: Carolina Academic Press, 1986.

"Guyana." Pages 1506–9 in George Thomas Kurian (ed.), *World Education Encyclopedia,* 3. New York: Facts on File, 1988.

Guyana. Ministry of Economic Development. Statistical Bureau. *Guyana: Statistical Digest, January–December 1980.* Georgetown: Bureau, 1980.

Hintzen, Percy C. *The Costs of Regime Survival: Racial Mobilization, Elite Domination, and Control of the State in Guyana and Trinidad.* Cambridge: Cambridge University Press, 1989.

Jayawardena, Chandra. "Culture and Identity in Guyana and Fiji," *Man* [London], 15, No. 3, 1980, 430–50.

______. "Religious Belief and Social Change: Aspects of the Development of Hinduism in British Guiana," *Comparative Studies in Society and History* [Cambridge, United Kingdom], 8, No. 2, January 1966, 211–40.

Jeffrey, Henry B., and Colin Baber. *Guyana: Politics, Economics, and Society—Beyond the Burnham Era.* Boulder, Colorado: Rienner, 1986.

Keyfitz, Nathan, and Wilhelm Fliegler. *World Population Growth and Aging: Demographic Trends in the Late Twentieth Century.* Chicago: University of Chicago Press, 1990.

Landis, Joseph B. "Racial Attitudes of Africans and Indians in Guyana," *Social and Economic Studies* [Kingston, Jamaica], 22, No. 4, December 1968, 426–39.

Mandle, Jay R. *The Plantation Economy: Population and Economic Change in Guyana, 1838–1960.* Philadelphia: Temple University Press, 1973.

Manley, Robert H. *Guyana Emergent: The Post-Independence Struggle for Nondependent Development.* Cambridge, Massachusetts: Schenkman, 1982.

Moore, Brian L. "The Retention of Caste Notions among the Indian Immigrants in British Guiana During the Nineteenth Century," *Comparative Studies in Society and History* [Cambridge, United Kingdom], 19, No. 1, January 1977, 96–107.

Neuman, Stephanie G. (ed.). *Small States and Segmented Societies.* New York: Praeger, 1976.

1990 South American Handbook. (Ed., Ben Box.) Bath, United Kingdom: Trade and Travel, 1989.

Odie-Ali, Stella. "Women in Agriculture: The Case of Guyana," *Social and Economic Studies* [Kingston, Jamaica], 35, No. 2, June 1986, 241–89.

Potter, Lesley M. "The Post-Indenture Experience of East Indians in Guyana, 1873–1921." Pages 71–92 in Bridget Brereton and Winston Dookeran (eds.), *East Indians in the Caribbean: Colonialism and the Struggle for Identity.* (Papers presented to a symposium on East Indians in the Caribbean, the University of the West Indies.) Millwood, New York: Kraus International, 1982.

Premdas, Ralph R. *Party Politics and Racial Division in Guyana.* (Studies in Race and Nations Series, No. 4.) Denver: University of Colorado Press, 1973.

Rivière, Peter. *Individual and Society in Guiana.* Cambridge: Cambridge University Press, 1984.

Roberts, G.W., and J. Byrne. "Summary Statistics on Indenture and Associated Migration Affecting the West Indies, 1834–1918," *Population Studies* [London], 20, No. 1, July 1966, 125–34.

Rodney, Walter. *A History of the Guyanese Working People, 1881–1905.* Baltimore: Johns Hopkins University Press, 1981.

Sanders, Andrew. *The Powerless People: An Analysis of the Amerindians of the Corentyne River.* (Warwick University Caribbean Studies.) London: Macmillian, 1987.

Singh, Chaitram. *Guyana: Politics in a Plantation Society.* New York: Praeger, 1988.

Smith, Raymond T. *British Guiana.* Westport, Connecticut: Greenwood Press, 1980.

______. *Kinship and Class in the West Indies: A Genealogical Study of Jamaica and Guyana.* New York: Cambridge University Press, 1988.

______. *The Negro Family in British Guiana: Family Structure and Social Status in the Villages.* London: Routledge and Kegan Paul, 1956.

______. "Race, Class, and Political Conflict in a Postcolonial Society." Pages 198–226 in Stephanie G. Neuman (ed.), *Small States and Segmented Societies.* New York: Praeger, 1976.

Spinner, Thomas J., Jr. *A Political and Social History of Guyana, 1945–1983.* Boulder, Colorado: Westview Press, 1984.

The Statesman's Year-Book, 1988–1989. (Ed., John Paxton.) New York: St. Martin's Press, 1988.

Strachan, A.J. "Return Migration to Guyana," *Social and Economic Studies* [Kingston, Jamaica], 32, No. 3, September 1983, 121–42.

United States. Department of Health and Human Services. *Social Security Programs Throughout the World, 1985.* Washington: GPO, 1986.

Vasil, Jaj K. *Politics in Bi-Racial Societies: The Third World Experience.* Delhi: Vikas, 1984.

World Bank. *Social Indicators of Development, 1989.* Baltimore: Johns Hopkins University Press, 1989.

______. *World Tables, 1983,* 2. (3d ed.) Baltimore: Johns Hopkins University Press, 1984.

______. *World Tables, 1987.* (4th ed.) Baltimore: Johns Hopkins University Press, 1988.

World Education Encyclopedia, 3. (Ed., George Thomas Kurian.) New York: Facts on File, 1987.

Chapter 3

Bank of Guyana Statistical Bulletin [Georgetown], June 1990, Tables 1–12.

Brock, Philip L., Michael B. Connolly, and Claudio González Vega (eds.). *Latin American Debt and Adjustment.* New York: Praeger, 1989.

Canute, James, and Ivo Dawnay. "Guyana: Financial Times Survey," *Financial Times* [London], May 26, 1989, 17–22.

Commonwealth Advisory Group, *Guyana: Economic Recovery and Beyond,* August 21, 1989, 1–32.

Cumiford, William L. "Guyana." Pages 433–47 in Gerald M.

Greenfield and Sheldon L. Maram (eds.), *Latin American Labor Organizations.* Westport, Connecticut: Greenwood Press, 1987.

Economist Intelligence Unit. *Country Profile: Guyana, Barbados, and Windward and Leeward Islands, 1989–90.* London: 1989.

Economic Panorama of Latin America, 1988. Santiago, Chile: Economic Commission for Latin America and the Caribbean, United Nations, 1988.

The Europa World Year Book, 1989. London: Europa, 1989.

Furtado, Celso. *Economic Development of Latin America.* (2d. ed.; trans., Suzette Macedo.) (Cambridge Latin America Series.) London: Cambridge University Press, 1976.

Greenfield, Gerald M., and Sheldon L. Maram (eds.). *Latin American Labor Organizations.* Westport, Connecticut: Greenwood Press, 1987.

"Guyana Opens Up," *Mining Journal* [London], February 24, 1989, 139.

"Guyana: Poor Man's Gold Rush," *Economist* [London], May 12, 1990, 42, 46.

Inter-American Development Bank. *Economic and Social Progress in Latin America: Regional Integration.* Washington: 1989.

Joffe, George. "Guyana," *South* [London], No. 109, November 1989, 1–22.

Lapper, Richard. "Guyana Wakes Up," *South* [London], No. 95, September 1988, 34–38.

Premdas, Ralph R. "Guyana: Socialist Reconstruction or Political Opportunism?" *Journal of Interamerican Studies and World Affairs,* 20, No. 2, May 1978, 133–63.

Sjaastad, Larry A. "Debt, Depression, and Real Rates of Interest in Latin America." Pages 21–39 in Philip L. Brock, Michael B. Connolly, and Claudio González-Vega (eds.), *Latin American Debt and Adjustment.* New York: Praeger, 1989.

South American Economic Handbook. London: Euromonitor, 1986.

Statistical Abstract of Latin America, 27. (Eds., James Wilkie and Enrique Ochoa.) Los Angeles: Latin American Center, University of California at Los Angeles, 1989.

Thomas, Clive Y. "Foreign Currency Black Markets: Lessons from Guyana," *Social and Economic Studies* [Kingston, Jamaica], 38, No. 2, 137–84.

Thorp, Rosemary (ed.). *Latin America in the 1930s.* London: Macmillan, 1984.

Tomlinson, Alan. "Guyana Seeks Foreign Help to Develop Wealth," *Washington Post,* January 19, 1989.

United States. Agency for International Development. *Latin America and the Caribbean: Selected Economic Data.* Washington: 1992.

______. Department of State. "Foreign Economic Trends Report: Guyana," *Foreign Economic Trends Report,* July 1990, 1-12.

______. Department of State. "Investment Climate Statement: Guyana," *Investment Climate Statement,* June 1990, 1-7.

World Bank. *World Debt Tables.* Washington: 1989.

Worrell, DeLisle. "The Impoverishment of Guyana." Pages 79-109 in Rosemary Thorp (ed.), *Latin America in the 1930s.* London: Macmillan, 1984.

______. *Small Island Economies.* New York: Praeger, 1987.

(Various issues of the following publications were also used in the preparation of this chapter: Economist Intelligence Unit, *Country Report: Guyana, Barbados, and Windward and Leeward Islands* [London]; *Economist* [London]; *Financial Times* [London]; *Guyana Business* [Georgetown]; *Guyana Chronicle* [Georgetown]; the International Monetary Fund's monthly *International Financial Statistics; Latin America Economic Report* [London]; *Latin America Regional Report* [London]; *South* [London]; and *Stabroek News* [Georgetown].)

Chapter 4

Bio Data: His Excellency Cde. H.D. Hoyte S.C., Leader of the People's National Congress, President of the Co-operative Republic of Guyana. Georgetown: Government of Guyana, 1986.

Braveboy-Wagner, Jacqueline Anne. *The Venezuela-Guyana Border Dispute.* Boulder, Colorado: Westview Press, 1984.

Brotherson, Festus Jr. "Burnham-Bashing: Hoyte Fiddles While Guyana Burns," *Caribbean Review,* 3, No. 3, July-September 1990, 16, 17, 79, 81, 82.

______. "Hoyte Takes the Other Road," *Caribbean Contact* [Bridgetown, Barbados], 18, No. 3, November-December 1990, 8, 9.

Burrowes, Reynold A. *The Wild Coast: An Account of Politics in Guyana.* Cambridge, Massachusetts: Schenkman, 1984.

Campbell, Nills Learmond. "Disunity Hoyte's Trump Card," *Caribbean Contact* [Bridgetown, Barbados], 18, No. 3, November-December 1990, 8.

Despres, Les A. *Cultural Pluralism and Nationalist Politics in Guyana.* Chicago: Rand McNally, 1967.

Fauriol, George A. *Foreign Policy Behavior of Caribbean States: Guyana, Haiti, and Jamaica.* Lanham, Maryland: University Press of America, 1984.

French, Howard W. "Guyana Marxist, Mellowed, Makes a Comeback," *New York Times,* July 5, 1991, A10.

"Guyana Teetering," *Economist* [London], June 22, 1991, 46, 48.

Hope, Kempe Ronald. *Guyana: Politics and Development in an Emergent Socialist State.* New York: Mosaic Press, 1985.

Jagan, Cheddi. *The West on Trial.* New York: International, 1972.

Jeffrey, Henry B., and Colin Baber. *Guyana: Politics, Economics, and Society—Beyond the Burnham Era.* Boulder, Colorado: Rienner, 1986.

Lall, Kellawan. "Rise and Fall of the G$," *Mirror* [Georgetown], 1027, August 25, 1991, 1, 4.

Manley, Robert H. *Guyana Emergent: The Post-Independence Struggle for Nondependent Development.* Cambridge, Massachusetts: Schenkman, 1982.

Nagamootoo, Moses. "53,000 Shut Off from Voters' List," *Mirror* [Georgetown], 1027, August 25, 1991, 1, 4.

Naipaul, Shiva. *Journey to Nowhere: A New World Tragedy.* New York: Simon and Schuster, 1986.

Singh, Chattram. *Guyana: Politics in a Plantation Society.* New York: Praeger, 1988.

Spinner, Thomas J., Jr. *A Political and Social History of Guyana, 1945–1983.* Boulder, Colorado: Westview Press, 1984.

Chapter 5

Andrade, John (ed.). *World Police and Paramilitary Forces.* New York: Stockton Press, 1985.

Ashby, Timothy. *The Bear in the Backyard: Moscow's Caribbean Strategy.* Lexington, Massachusetts: Lexington Books, 1987.

Bell, Judith. "Guyana-Suriname." Pages 346–53 in Alan J. Day (ed.), *Border and Territorial Disputes.* Harlow, United Kingdom: Longman Group, 1987.

______. "Guyana-Venezuela." Pages 346–53 in Alan J. Day (ed.), *Border and Territorial Disputes.* Burnt Mill, United Kingdom: Longman, 1987.

Braveboy-Wagner, Jacqueline Anne. *The Venezuela-Guyana Border Dispute.* Boulder, Colorado: Westview Press, 1984.

Damore, Kelley. "Dispute over Essequibo Coast," *Washington Report on the Hemisphere,* 8, No. 21, July 20, 1988, 1–6.

Encyclopedia of the Third World, 2. (Ed., George Thomas Kurian.) New York: Facts on File, 1987.

Encyclopedia of the World's Air Forces. (Ed., Michael J.H. Taylor.) New York: Facts on File, 1988.

English, Adrian J. *Armed Forces of Latin America.* London: Jane's, 1984.

The Europa World Year Book: 1990, 1. London: Europa, 1990.

''GDF Signs Protocol with Venezuelan Army,'' Caribbean News Agency [Bridgetown, Barbados], October 12, 1990. Foreign Broadcast Information Service, *Daily Report: Latin America.* (FBIS-LA-90-199.) October 15, 1990, 57.

''Guyana.'' Pages 264-68 in Arthur S. Banks (ed.), *Political Handbook of The World.* Binghamton, New York: CSA, 1990.

''Guyana.'' Pages 453-56 in Gregory R. Copley (ed.), *Defense and Foreign Affairs Handbook, 1989.* Alexandria, Virginia: International Media, 1989.

Jeffrey, Henry B., and Colin Baber. *Guyana: Politics, Economics, and Society—Beyond the Burnham Era.* Boulder, Colorado: Rienner, 1986.

Keegan, John. *World Armies.* (2d ed.) Detroit: Gale Research, 1983.

McDonald, Scott. ''Guyana.'' Pages 445-58 in James M. Malloy and Eduardo A. Gamarra (eds.), *Latin America and Caribbean Contemporary Record, 7: 1987-88.* New York: Holmes and Meier, 1990.

Manley, Robert H. *Guyana Emergent: The Post-Independence Struggle for Nondependent Development.* Cambridge, Massachusetts: Schenkman, 1979.

Manley, Robert H. ''Cooperative Republic of Guyana.'' Pages 446-50 in George E. Delury (ed.), *World Encyclopedia of Political Systems and Parties,* 1. New York: Facts on File, 1987.

The Military Balance, 1989-1990. London: International Institute for Strategic Studies, 1989.

The Military Balance, 1992-1993. London: International Institute for Strategic Studies, 1992.

Mitrasing, F.E.M. *The Border-Conflict Between Surinam and Guiana.* Paramaribo, Suriname: Kersten, 1975.

Singh, Chaitram. *Guyana: Politics in a Plantation Society.* New York: Praeger, 1988.

Spinner, Thomas J., Jr. ''Guyana Update: Political, Economic, and Moral Bankruptcy,'' *Caribbean Review,* 11, No. 4, Fall 1982, 9-11, 30-32.

SIPRI Yearbook, 1990: World Armaments and Disarmament. New York: Humanities Press, 1990.

Zambrano Velasco, José Alberto. *The Essequibo: Our Historic Claim.* Caracas: Ministry of Foreign Relations, 1982.

Chapter 6

Allsop, S.R.R. ''British Honduras: The Linguistic Dilemma,'' *Caribbean Quarterly* [Kingston, Jamaica], 11, 1965, 54-61.

Ashcraft, Norman. *Colonialism and Underdevelopment: Processes of Political Economic Change in British Honduras.* New York: Teachers College Press, 1973.

Ashcraft, Norman, and Cedric Grant. "The Development and Organization of Education in British Honduras," *Comparative Education Review,* 12, No. 2, 1968, 171–79.

Ashdown, Peter D. "Marcus Garvey, the UNIA, and the Black Cause in British Honduras: 1914–1949," *Journal of Caribbean History* [Kingston, Jamaica], 15, 1981, 41–55.

______. "Race, Class and the Unofficial Majority in British Honduras, 1890–1949." (Ph.D. dissertation.) Brighton, United Kingdom: University of Sussex, 1979.

______. "Sweet-Escott, Swayne, and the Unofficial Majority in the Legislative Council of British Honduras: 1904–1911," *Journal of Imperial and Commonwealth History* [London], 9, No. 1, 1980, 57–75.

Barnett, Carla Natalie. "The Political Economy of Land in Belize: 'Machete Must Fly.'" (Ph.D. dissertation.) Mona, Kingston, Jamaica: University of the West Indies, 1990.

Barry, Tom. *Belize: A Country Guide.* Albuquerque, New Mexico: Inter-Hemispheric Education Resource Center, 1989.

Beckford, George. "B.H. and Regional Economic Integration," *New World Quarterly* [Kingston, Jamaica], 3, No. 4, 1967, 51–53.

Bianchi, W.J. *Belize: The Controversy Between Guatemala and Great Britain over the Territory of British Honduras in Central America.* New York: Las Americas, 1959.

Bloomfield, L.M. *The British Honduras-Guatemala Dispute.* Toronto: Carswell, 1953.

Bolland, O. Nigel. "African Continuities and Creole Culture in Belize Town in the Nineteenth Century." Pages 63–82 in Charles V. Carnegie (ed.), *Afro-Caribbean Villages in Historical Perspective.* Kingston, Jamaica: African-Caribbean Institute of Jamaica, 1987.

______. *Belize: A New Nation in Central America.* Boulder, Colorado: Westview Press, 1986.

______. *Colonialism and Resistance in Belize: Essays in Historical Sociology.* Benque Viejo del Carmen, Belize: Cubola Productions, 1988.

______. *The Formation of a Colonial Society: Belize from Conquest to Crown Colony.* Baltimore: Johns Hopkins University Press, 1977.

______. "Labour Control and Resistance in Belize in the Century after 1838," *Slavery and Abolition* [London], 7, No. 2, 1986, 175–87.

______. "The Labour Movement and the Genesis of Modern Politics in Belize." Pages 258–84 in Malcolm Cross and Gad

Heuman (eds.), *Labour in the Caribbean: From Emancipation to Independence.* London: Macmillan, 1988.

______. "The Maya and the Colonization of Belize in the Nineteenth Century." Pages 69-99 in Grant D. Jones (ed.), *Anthropology and History in Yucatan.* Austin: University of Texas Press, 1977.

______. "The Social Structure and Social Relations of the Settlement in the Bay of Honduras (Belize) in the Eighteenth Century," *Journal of Caribbean History* [Kingston, Jamaica], Nos. 6-7, 1973, 1-42.

______. "Systems of Domination after Slavery: The Control of Land and Labor in the British West Indies after 1838," *Comparative Studies in Society and History* [Cambridge, United Kingston], 23, No. 4, 1981, 591-619.

Bolland, O. Nigel, and Assad Shoman. *Land in Belize, 1765-1871.* Kingston, Jamaica: Institute of Social and Economic Research, 1977.

Broad, David. "Belize: On the Rim of the Cauldron," *Monthly Review,* 1984, 38-42.

Burdon, Sir John Alder (ed.). *Archives of British Honduras.* (3 vols.) London: Sifton Praed, 1931-35.

Cacho, C.P. "British Honduras: A Case of Deviation in Commonwealth Caribbean Decolonization," *New World Quarterly* [Kingston, Jamaica], 3, No. 3, 1967, 33-44.

Carnegie, Charles V. (ed.). *Afro-Caribbean Villages in Historical Perspective.* Kingston, Jamaica: African-Caribbean Institute of Jamaica, 1987.

Chase, Arlen F., and Prudence M. Rice (eds.). *The Lowland Maya Postclassic: Questions and Answers.* Austin: University of Texas Press, 1985.

Clegern, Wayne M. "British Honduras and the Pacification of Yucatan," *The Americas,* 18, 1962, 243-55.

______. *British Honduras: Colonial Dead End, 1859-1900.* Baton Rouge: Louisiana State University Press, 1967.

Craig, Alan K. "Logwood as a Factor in the Settlement of British Honduras," *Caribbean Studies* [Río Piedras, Puerto Rico], 9, 1969, 53-62.

Cross, Malcolm, and Gad Heuman (eds.). *Labour in the Caribbean: From Emancipation to Independence.* London: Macmillan, 1988.

De La Haba, Louis. "Belize: The Awakening Land," *National Geographic,* 141, No. 1, 1972, 124-46.

Dobson, Narda. *A History of Belize.* London: Longman, 1973.

Edgell, Zee. *Beka Lamb.* London: Heinemann, 1982.

Everitt, J.C. "The Recent Migrations of Belize, Central America,"

International Migration Review, 18, No. 2, 1984, 319–25.

Fernandez, Julio A. *Belize: Case Study for Democracy in Central America.* Brookfield, Vermont: Gower, 1989.

Fox, David J. "Recent Work on British Honduras," *Geographical Review,* 52, 1962, 112–17.

Grant, Cedric H. "The Cultural Factor in B.H. Politics," *New World Quarterly* [Kingston, Jamaica], 3, No. 4, 1967, 53–55.

______. *The Making of Modern Belize: Politics, Society, and British Colonialism in Central America.* Cambridge: Cambridge University Press, 1976.

Gregg, Algar Robert. *British Honduras.* London: HMSO, 1968.

Gregory, James. "The Modification of an Interethnic Boundary in Belize," *American Ethnologist,* 3, No. 4, 1976, 683–709.

______. "Pioneers on a Cultural Frontier: The Mopan Maya of British Honduras." (Ph.D. dissertation.) Ann Arbor: University of Michigan, 1972.

Hammond, Norman. "The Prehistory of Belize," *Journal of Field Archaeology* [Belize City], No. 9, 1982, 349–62.

Henderson, Peta M. "The Context of Economic Choice in the Rural Sugar-Growing Area of British Honduras." (M.A. thesis.) Montreal: McGill University, 1969.

Herrmann, Eleanor K. "Health Care in Nineteenth Century British Honduras," *Social Science and Medicine,* 14, No. A, 1980, 353–56.

Highfield, Arnold, and Albert Valdman. *Historicity and Variation in Creole Studies.* Ann Arbor, Michigan: Karoma, 1981.

Howard, Michael C. "Ethnicity and Economic Integration in Southern Belize," *Ethnicity,* 7, 1980, 119–36.

Humphreys, R.A. *The Diplomatic History of British Honduras: 1638–1901.* London: Oxford University Press, 1961.

Jamail, Milton. "Belize: Still Struggling for Independence," *NACLA Report on the Americas,* 18, No. 4, 1984, 8–10.

______. "Belize: Will Independence Mean New Dependence?" *NACLA Report on the Americas,* 18, No. 4, 1984, 13–16.

Jones, Grant D. "Levels of Settlement Alliance Among the San Pedro Maya of Western Belize and Eastern Peten, 1857–1936." Pages 139–89 in Grant D. Jones (ed.), *Anthropology and History in Yucatan.* Austin: University of Texas Press, 1977.

______. "Los Caneros: Sociopolitical Aspects of the History of Agriculture in the Corozal Region of British Honduras." (Ph.D. dissertation.) Waltham, Massachusetts: Brandeis University, 1968.

______. *Maya Resistance to Spanish Rule: Time and History on a Colonial Frontier.* Albuquerque: University of New Mexico Press, 1989.

Jones, Grant D. (ed.). *Anthropology and History in Yucatan.* Austin: University of Texas Press, 1977.

Jones, Grant D., Elizabeth Graham, and Robert R. Kautz. "Archaeology and Ethnohistory on a Spanish Colonial Frontier: An Interim Report on the Macal-Tipu Project in Western Belize." Pages 206–14 in Arlen F. Chase and Prudence M. Rice (eds.), *The Lowland Maya Postclassic: Questions and Answers.* Austin: University of Texas Press, 1985.

Kearns, Kevin C. "Belmopan: Prospects of a New Capital," *Geographical Review,* 43, No. 2, 1973.

Mackie, Euan W. "New Light on the End of Classic Maya Culture at Benque Viejo, British Honduras," *American Antiquity,* 27, 1961, 216–24.

McLeish, J. "British Activities in Yucatan and the Moskito Shore in the Eighteenth Century." (M.A. thesis.) London: University of London, 1926.

Medina, Lauri Kroshus. "Content for Continuity or Change: A Local-Level View of the Organization of Power Relations in the Belizean Citrus Industry," *Caribbean Studies* [Río Piedras, Puerto Rico], 23, Nos. 3 and 4, 1990, 51-67.

Menon, P.K. "The Anglo-Guatemalan Dispute over the Colony of Belize (British Honduras)," *Journal of Latin American Studies,* 2, No. 2, 1979, 343–71.

Minkel, Clarence W., and Ralph H. Alderman. *A Bibliography of British Honduras, 1900–1970.* East Lansing: Michigan State University, 1970.

Moberg, Mark A. "Between Agency and Dependence: Belizean Households in a Changing World System." (Ph.D. dissertation.) Los Angeles: University of California, Los Angeles, 1988.

______. "Class Resistance and Class Hegemony: From Conflict to Co-optation in the Citrus Industry of Belize," *Ethnology,* 29, No. 3, 1990, 189-207.

Muntsh, Albert. "Xaibe: A Mayan Enclave in Northern British Honduras," *Anthropological Quarterly,* 34, 1961, 121–26.

Naylor, R.A. "British Commercial Relations with Central America 1821–51." (Ph.D. dissertation.) New Orleans: Tulane University, 1958.

Parvenu, M. André. "Refugee Migration and Settlement in Belize: The Valley of Peace Project." (M.A. thesis.) Madison: University of Wisconsin, 1986.

Scholes, France V., and Sir Eric Thompson. "The Francisco Perez Probanza of 1654–1656 and the Matricular of Tipu (Belize)." Pages 43–68 in Grant D. Jones (ed.), *Anthropology and History in Yucatan.* Austin: University of Texas Press, 1977.

Setzekorn, William David. *Formerly British Honduras: A Profile of the New Nation of Belize.* Athens: Ohio University Press, 1981.

Shoman, Assad. *Party Politics in Belize, 1950–1986.* Benque Viejo del Carmen, Belize: Cubola Productions, 1987.

Taylor, Douglas M. *The Black Carib of British Honduras.* New York: Wenner-Gren Foundation, 1951.

Thorndike, Anthony E. "Belizean Political Parties: The Independence Crisis and After," *Journal of Commonwealth and Comparative Politics* [London], 21, No. 2, 1983, 195–211.

United Kingdom. British Honduras Land Use Survey. *Land in British Honduras: A Report of the British Honduras Land Use Survey Team.* London: HMSO, 1959.

Waddell, D.A.G. *British Honduras: A Historical and Contemporary Survey.* Westport, Connecticut: Greenwood Press, 1981.

Wilk, Richard R. "Agriculture, Culture, and Domestic Organization among the Kekchi Maya." (Ph.D. dissertation.) Tucson: University of Arizona, 1981.

Woodward, Ralph Lee. *Belize.* Oxford: Clio Press, 1980.

Zammit, J. Ann. *The Belize Issue.* London: Latin America Bureau, 1978.

(Various issues of the following publcations were also used in the preparation of this chapter: *América Indígena* [Mexico City]; *Caribbean Quarterly* [Kingston, Jamaica]; *Caribbean Review;* and *Journal of Belizean Affairs* [Belize City].)

Chapter 7

Ashcraft, Norman. *Colonialism and Underdevelopment: Processes of Political Economic Change in British Honduras.* New York: Teachers College Press, 1973.

Belize. Central Statistical Office. *Abstract of Statistics,* 1986. Belmopan, Belize: 1987.

Bolland, O. Nigel. *Belize: A New Nation in Central America.* Boulder, Colorado: Westview Press, 1986.

______. *Colonialism and Resistance in Belize: Essays in Historical Sociology.* Benque Viejo del Carmen, Belize: Cubola Productions, 1988.

______. "Race, Ethnicity, and National Integration in Belize." (Paper presented at the First Annual Studies on Belize Conference, May 25–26, 1987.) Belize City: University Centre, 1987.

Brockman, C. Thomas. "Ethnic and Racial Relations in Northern Belize," *Ethnicity,* 4, 1977, 246–62.

Esgood, Brule. "The Belize National Survey," *International Third World Studies Journal,* 1, No. 2, Fall 1989, 263–76.

Everitt, J.C. "The Growth and Development in Belize City," *Belizean Studies* [Belize City], 14, No. 1, 1986, 2–45.

______. "The Recent Migrations of Belize, Central America," *International Migration Review,* 18, No. 2. 1984, 319–25.

______. "The Torch Is Passed: Neocolonialism in Belize," *Caribbean Quarterly* [Mona, Kingston, Jamaica], 33, Nos. 3–4, 1987, 42–59.

Federal Republic of Germany. Statistisches Bundesamt. *Länderbericht Belize, 1987.* (Statistik des Auslandes Series.) Wiesbaden: 1987.

______. Statistisches Bundesamt. *Länderbericht Belize, 1989.* (Statistik des Auslandes Series.) Wiesbaden: 1989.

Foster, B. *Heart Drum.* Benque Viejo del Carmen, Belize: Cubola Productions, 1986.

Godfrey, G. *The Sinners Bosonoud.* Benque Viejo del Carmen, Belize: Cubola Productions, 1987.

Grant, Cedric H. *The Making of Modern Belize: Politics, Society, and British Colonialism in Central America.* Cambridge: Cambridge University Press, 1976.

Hartshorn, Gary, et al. *Belize: Country Environmental Profile.* Belize City: R. Nicolait, 1984.

Hyde, Evan. "Celebrations and Contentions," *Amandala* [Belize City], No. 940, 1987, 1.

Jamail, Milton. "Belize: Still Struggling for Independence. *NACLA Report on the Americas,* 18, No. 4, 1984, 8–10.

______. "Belize: Will Independence Mean New Dependence?" *NACLA Report on the Americas.* 18, No. 4, 1984, 13–16.

Jones, Grant D. *The Politics of Agricultural Development in Northern British Honduras.* Winston-Salem, North Carolina: Wake Forest University, 1971.

Krohn, Lita (ed.). *Readings in Belizean History.* Belize City: Belizean Studies, St. John's College, 1987.

Lent, John. "Country of No Return: Belize since Television," *Belizean Studies* [Belize City], 17, No. 1, 1989, 14–36.

Roberts, S.A. "Recent Demographic Trends in Belize." Pages 9–21 in Society for Promotion of Education and Research, *Belize: Ethnicity and Development.* Belize City: 1987.

Rosser, C., L. Snyder, and S. Chaffee. "Belize Release Me, Let Me Go: The Impact of Mass Media on Emigration in Belize," *Belizean Studies* [Belize City], 14, No. 3, 1986, 1–30.

Rutheiser, Charles. *Culture, Schooling, and Neocolonialism in Belize.* (Ph.D. dissertation, Johns Hopkins University, 1991.) Ann Arbor, Michigan: University Microfilms, 1991.

Society for the Promotion of Education and Research. "Belize: Ethnicity and Development." (Paper presented at the First Annual Studies on Belize Conference, May 25-26, 1987.) Belize City: University Centre, 1987.

South America, Central America, and the Caribbean, 1991. London: Europa, 1991.

Topsey, Harriot. "The Ethnic War in Belize." (Paper presented at the First Annual Studies on Belize Conference, May 25-26, 1987.) Belize City: University Centre, 1987.

United States. Agency for International Development. *Belize: Country Development Strategy,* Washington: GPO, 1983.

______. Central Intelligence Agency. *The World Factbook, 1989.* Washington: GPO, 1990.

Wilk, Richard R. "Consumer Goods as Dialogue about Development," *Culture and History* [Copenhagen], 7, 1989, 79-100.

______. "Mayan Ethnicity in Belize," *Cultural Survival Quarterly,* 10, 1986, 73-77.

Chapter 8

Ashcraft, Norman. *Colonialism and Underdevelopment: Processes of Political Economic Change in British Honduras.* New York: Teachers College Press, 1973.

Barry, Tom. *Belize: A Country Guide.* Albuquerque, New Mexico: Inter-Hemispheric Education Resource Center, 1989.

______. *Inside Belize.* Albuquerque, New Mexico: Inter-Hemispheric Education Rsource Center, 1992.

Belize. Government Information Service. *Belize in Figures.* Belmopan: 1991.

Belize. *Off to a Great Start: Mid-Term Report.* Belize City: Government Printery, 1992.

Bolland, O. Nigel. *Belize: A New Nation in Central America.* Boulder, Colorado: Westview Press, 1986.

______. *The Formation of a Colonial Society: Belize from Conquest to Crown Colony.* Baltimore: Johns Hopkins University Press, 1977.

Carey Jones, N.S. *The Pattern of a Dependent Economy: The National Income of British Honduras.* Westport, Connecticut, Greenwood Press, 1972.

Caribbean Development Bank. *Annual Economic Report, 1990: Belize.* Bridgetown, Barbados: 1991.

Demas, William G. *The Economics of Development in Small Countries.* Montreal: McGill University Press, 1965.

Economist Intelligence Unit. *Country Profile: Belize, Bahamas, Bermuda, 1989–90.* London: 1989.

______. *Country Profile: Belize, Bahamas, Bermuda, 1991–92.* London: 1991.

Federal Republic of Germany. Statistisches Bundesamt. *Länderbericht Belize, 1989.* (Statistik des Auslandes Series.) Wiesbaden: 1989.

Furley, Peter A. *Geography of Belize.* London: Collins, 1974.

Grant, Cedric H. "Belize: Multiple External Orientation: The Caribbean Dimension." (Paper presented at the Twelfth International Congress of the Caribbean Studies Association, 1987.) Belize City: 1987.

Hartshorn, Gary. *Belize: Country Environmental Profile, A Field Study.* Belize City: R. Nicolait, 1984.

International Monetary Fund. *Balance of Payment Statistics.* Washington: 1991.

MacDonald, Scott B., Margie Lindsay, and David L. Crumm (eds.). *The Global Debt Crisis.* London: Pinter, 1990.

MacDonald, Scott B., and Georges A. Fauriol (eds.). *The Politics of the Caribbean Basin Sugar Trade.* New York: Praeger, 1991.

Mitchell, Harold. *Europe in the Caribbean.* New York: Cooper Square, 1973.

Setzekorn, William David. *Formerly British Honduras: A Profile of the New Nation of Belize.* Athens, Ohio: Ohio University Press, 1981.

Society for the Promotion of Education and Research. "Belize: Ethnicity, and Development." (Paper presented at the First Annual Studies on Belize Conference, May 25–26, 1987.) Belize City: University Centre, 1987.

United States. Agency for International Development. *Latin America and the Caribbean: Selected Economic Data.* Washington: 1992.

World Bank. *Belize, Economic Report.* Washington: 1984.

______. *The Caribbean: Export Preferences and Performance.* Washington: 1988.

______. *World Bank Atlas.* Washington: 1990.

Zammit, J. Ann. *The Belize Issue.* London: Latin America Bureau, 1978.

(Various issues of the following publication were also used in the preparation of this chapter: Economist Intelligence Unit, *Country Report: Belize, Bahamas, Bermuda* [London].)

Chapter 9

Barry, Tom. *Belize: A Country Guide.* Albuquerque, New Mexico:

Inter-Hemispheric Education Resource Center, 1989.

Belize. Government Information Service. *How We Are Governed.* Belize City: 1990.

______. Independence Secretariat. *Belize: New Nation in Central America.* Belize City: Government Printery, 1972.

______. Ministry of Education. *Belize Today: A Society in Transformation.* Belize City: Sunshine Books, 1984.

Blaustein, Albert P., and Gilbert H. Flanz (eds.). *Constitutions of the Countries of the World.* Dobbs Ferry, New York: Oceana, 1981.

Bolland, O. Nigel. *Belize: A New Nation in Central America.* Boulder, Colorado: Westview Press, 1986.

______. "Race, Ethnicity, and National Integration in Belize." (Paper presented at the First Annual Studies on Belize Conference, May 25-26, 1987.) Belize City: University Centre, 1987.

Byrd, Herman. "Oil in Guatemala: An Economic Factor in the Heads of Agreement." *Belizean Studies* [Belize City], 15, No. 2, 1987, 25-39.

Comisión de Asuntos Internacionales. *México y sus vecinos: Estados Unidos, Guatemala, y Belice.* Mexico City: Partido Revolucionario Institucional, 1982.

Dobson, Narda. *A History of Belize.* London: Longman, 1973.

The Europa World Year Book, 1989. 1. London: Europa, 1989.

Fernandez, Julio A. *Belize: Case Study for Democracy in Central America.* Brookfield, Vermont: Gower, 1989.

Halsbury Laws of England. (3d ed.) London: Butterworth, 1953.

Palacio, Myrtle. "Elections in Belize City—Who Is Participating?" (Paper presented at the First Annual Studies on Belize Conference, May 25-26, 1987.) Belize City: University Centre, 1987.

Sawatzky, Harry Leonard. *They Sought a Country: Mennonite Colonization in Mexico.* Berkeley: University of California Press, 1971.

Shoman, Assad. "The Making and the Breaking of the UGWU." (Paper presented at the First Annual Studies on Belize Conference, May 25-26, 1987.) Belize City: University Centre, 1987.

______. *Party Politics in Belize, 1950-1986.* Benque Viejo del Carmen, Belize: Cubola Productions, 1987.

Waddell, D.A.G. *British Honduras: A Historical and Contemporary Survey.* Westport, Connecticut: Greenwood Press, 1981.

Whatmore, Mark, and Peter Eltringham. *The Real Guide: Guatemala and Belize.* New York: Prentice Hall Press, 1990.

Zammit, J. Ann. *The Belize Issue.* London: Latin America Bureau, 1978.

Chapter 10

Belize. *Constitution*. Belmopan: Government Printery, 1981.

______. *Criminal Code, 1980*. Belmopan: Government Printery, 1980.

______. *Defence Ordinance, 1977*. Belmopan: Government Printery, 1977.

______. *Misuse of Drugs Act, 1990*. Belmopan: Government Printery, 1990.

______. *Security and Intelligence Service Act, 1987*. Belmopan: Government Printery, 1987.

Bolland, O. Nigel. *Belize: A New Nation in Central America*. Boulder, Colorado: Westview Press, 1986.

Caiger, Stephen L. *British Honduras Past and Present*. London: Allen and Unwin, 1951.

Copley, Gregory R. (ed.). *Defense and Foreign Affairs Handbook, 1987–88*. Washington: Perth, 1987.

Dobson, Narda. *A History of Belize*. London: Longman, 1973.

Encyclopedia of the Third World. (Ed., George Thomas Kurian.) New York: Facts on File, 1987.

English, Adrian J. *Regional Defence Profile, No. 1*. Coulsdon, United Kingdom: Jane's Information, 1988.

The Europa World Year Book, 1990. London: Europa, 1990.

Fernandez, Julio A. *Belize: Case Study for Democracy in Central America*. Brookfield, Vermont: Gower, 1989.

Government Finance Statistics Yearbook, 1989. Washington: International Monetary Fund: 1990.

Grant, Cedric H. *The Making of Modern Belize: Politics, Society, and British Colonialism in Central America*. Cambridge: Cambridge University Press, 1976.

Huskey, James L. (ed.). *Lambert's Worldwide Directory of Defense Authorities with International Defense Organizations*. Washington: Lambert, 1983.

Ingleton, Roy D. *Police of the World*. New York: Scribner's, 1979.

Jane's Fighting Ships, 1990–1991. (Ed., Richard Sharpe.) Coulsdon, United Kingdom: Jane's Information, 1990.

Keegan, John (ed.). *World Armies*. New York: Facts on File, 1984.

The Military Balance, 1991–1992. London: International Institute for Strategic Studies, 1991.

Setzekorn, William David. *Formerly British Honduras: A Profile of the New Nation of Belize*. Athens: Ohio University Press, 1981.

United Kingdom. Office of Commonwealth Relations. *The Commonwealth Yearbook, 1990*. London: HMSO, 1990.

United States. Department of Defense. Defense Security Assistance

Agency. *Congressional Presentation for Security Assistance Programs, FY 1992.* Washington: GPO, 1991.

______. Department of Defense. Defense Security Assistance Agency. *Foreign Military Sales, Foreign Military Construction Sales, and Military Assistance as of September 30, 1990.* Washington: GPO, 1990.

______. Department of State. *Country Reports on Human Rights Practices for 1990.* (Report submitted to United States Congress, 102d, 1st Session, Senate, Committee on Foreign Relations, and House of Representatives, Committee on Foreign Affairs.) Washington: GPO, 1991.

World Bank. *World Tables, 1989–90: From the Data Files of the World Bank.* Baltimore: Johns Hopkins University Press, 1990.

World Encyclopedia of Police Forces and Penal Systems. (Ed., George Thomas Kurian.) New York: Facts on File, 1989.

(Various issues of the following publications were also used in the preparation of this chapter: *Belize Today* [Belize City]; Foreign Broadcast Information Service, *Daily Report: Latin America;* Joint Publications Research Service, *Latin American Report;* and *Soldier* [London].)

Appendixes

Abrams, Elliot. "CBI and the U.S. National Interest," *Department of State Bulletin,* April 1986, 84–89.

American Chamber of Commerce of Mexico. *Business Opportunities under the Caribbean Basin Initiative, 1987.* Mexico City: 1986.

Arnold, Guy. *Economic Co-operation in the Commonwealth.* Oxford: Pergamon Press, 1967.

Banks, Arthur S. (ed.). *Political Handbook of the World, 1985–86.* Binghamton, New York: CSA, 1986.

Blake, Byron, and Kenneth Hall. "The Caribbean Community: Administrative and Institutional Aspects," *Journal of Common Market Studies* [Oxford], 16, No. 3, March 1978, 211–28.

Brock, William. "The Caribbean Basin Initiative." Pages xiii–xiv in Kevin P. Power (ed.), *Caribbean Basin Trade and Investment Guide.* Washington: Washington International Press, 1984.

Caribbean and Central American Action. *Caribbean and Central American Databook, 1988.* Washington: 1987.

"Caribbean Community and Common Market—Caricom." Pages 108–9 in *The Europa Year Book 1987: A World Survey,* 1. London: Europa, 1987.

"Caribbean Community and Common Market—Caricom." Pages

663–65 in *South America, Central America, and the Caribbean, 1992.* London: Europa, 1992.

"Caribbean Leaders Back New Moves for Economic Integration," *Caribbean Insight,* 9, No. 7, July 1986, 1–2.

Caribbean Community Secretariat. *Report to the Secretary General of Caricom, 1985.* Georgetown, Guyana: 1986.

______. *Sixth Meeting of the Conference of Caricom Heads of Government. Review of the Caribbean Basin Initiative* (Agenda Item No. 11. Conference held July 1–4, 1985.) Georgetown, Guyana: 1985.

Chernick, Sidney E. *The Commonwealth Caribbean: The Integration Experience.* Baltimore: Johns Hopkins University Press, 1978.

"The Commonwealth." Pages 114–20 in *The Europa Year Book 1987: A World Survey,* 1. London: Europa, 1987.

Day, Alan J. (ed.). *Treaties and Alliances of the World.* Detroit: Gale Research, 1981.

Development Group for Alternative Policies. *Supporting Central American and Caribbean Development: A Critique of the Caribbean Basin Initiative and an Alternative Regional Assistance Plan.* Washington: 1983.

Feinberg, Richard E., Richard Newfarmer, and Bernadette Orr. "Caribbean Basin Initiative: Pros and Cons." Pages 113–28 in Mark Falcoff and Robert Royal (eds.), *The Continuing Crisis: U.S. Policy in Central America and the Caribbean.* Washington: Ethics and Public Policy Center, 1987.

Fox, James W. *Is the Caribbean Basin Initiative Working?* Washington: United States, Agency for International Development, March 7, 1989.

"Glimmer of Hope for Caricom Trade," *Caribbean Insight,* 10, No. 7, March 1987, 1.

Gonzalez, Anthony P. "Future of Caricom: Collective Self-reliance in Decline?," *Caribbean Review,* 13, No. 4, Fall 1984, 8–11, 40.

Gordon, Richard A., and John Venuti. "Exchange of Information under Tax Treaties—An Update," *Tax Management International Journal,* 15, August 8, 1986, 292–98.

Hall, H. Duncan. *Commonwealth: A History of the British Commonwealth of Nations.* London: Van Nostrand Reinhold, 1971.

"In the Caribbean," *Washington Post,* November 3, 1986, A14.

Inter-American Development Bank. *Economic and Social Progress in Latin America: Regional Integration.* Washington: 1984.

______. *Ten Years of Caricom.* Georgetown, Guyana: 1983.

Margain, Eduardo. *Development Challenges and Cooperation in the Commonwealth Caribbean.* Washington: Inter-American Development Bank, 1983.

Martin, Atherton, Steve Hellinger, and Daniel Soloman. *Prospects and Reality: The CBI Revisited.* Washington: Development Group for Alternative Policies, 1985.

Mye, L. Randolph. *Caribbean and Central American Export Performance, 1980 to 1987.* Washington: GPO, 1988.

Overseas Development Council. "The Caribbean Basin Initiative: Update," *Policy Focus,* No. 3, 1985, 1-8.

Palmer, Ransford W. *Problems of Development in Beautiful Countries: Perspectives on the Caribbean.* Lanham, Maryland: North-South Publishing, 1984.

Pastor, Robert. "Sinking in the Caribbean Basin," *Foreign Affairs,* 60, No. 5, Summer 1982, 1038-58.

Payne, Anthony. "Whither Caricom?" The Performance and Prospects of Caribbean Integration in the 1980s," *International Journal,* 40, Spring 1985, 207-28.

Payne, Anthony, and Paul Sutton (eds.). *Dependency under Challenge: The Political Economy of the Commonwealth Caribbean.* London: Butler and Tanner, 1984.

Pregelj, Vladimir N. "CBI II: Expanding the Caribbean Basin Economic Recovery Act." (Library of Congress, Congressional Research Service, Major Issues System, IB89090.) Washington: June 7, 1989.

Ramsaran, Ramesh. "Caricom: The Integration Process in Crisis?" *Journal of World Trade Law,* 12, 1978, 208-17.

Raymond, Nicholas. "Caribbean Basin Revisited," *Editorial Research Reports,* 1, No. 5, February 1985, 83-100.

"The Reagan Caribbean Basin Initiative, Pro and Con," *Congressional Digest,* 62, No. 3, March 1983, 69-96.

Sanford, Jonathan. "Caribbean Basin Initiative." (Library of Congress, Congressional Research Service, Major Issues System, IB82074.) Washington: May 27, 1983.

Sanford, Jonathan, and Lawrence Silverman. *Caribbean Basin Initiative: 1983.* (Library of Congress, Congressional Research Service, Major Issues System, IB83222.) Washington: February 13, 1984.

Schiavone, Giuseppe (ed.). *International Organizations: A Dictionary and Directory.* Chicago: St. James Press, 1983.

Seyler, Daniel J. "The Politics of Development: The Case of Jamaica and the Caribbean Basin Initiative." (Paper presented at the American University, School of International Service, 1986.) Washington: American University, 1986.

South America, Central America, and the Caribbean, 1993. London: Europa, 1992.

Stokes, Bruce. "Reagan's Caribbean Basin Initiative On Track, but Success Still in Doubt," *National Journal,* 17, January 26, 1985, 205-10.

Sullivan, Mark P. ''Caribbean-U.S. Relations: Issues for Congress.'' (Library of Congress, Congressional Research Service, Major Issues System, IB92047.) Washington: January 29, 1993.

Taylor, Jeffrey H. ''Efforts Toward Economic Integration: Caricom as a Case Study.'' (M.A. thesis.) Washington: George Washington University, 1985.

United States. Central Intelligence Agency. *The World Factbook, 1991*. Washington: GPO, 1991.

United States. Congress. 97th, 2d Session. House of Representatives. Committee on Foreign Affairs. *Hearings and Markup Before the Committee on Foreign Affairs and the Subcommittee on International Economic Policy and Trade and the Subcommittee on Inter-American Affairs: The Caribbean Basin Initiative.* Washington: GPO, 1982.

______. Congress. 97th, 2d Session. House of Representatives. Committee on Ways and Means. Subcommittee on Trade. *The Administration's Proposed Trade and Tax Measures Affecting the Caribbean Basin.* (Hearings, March 17–25, 1982.) Washington: GPO, 1982.

______. Congress. 97th, 2d Session. Senate. Committee on Foreign Relations. *Hearings Before the Committee on Foreign Relations: Caribbean Basin Initiative.* Washington: GPO, 1982.

______. Congress. 98th. 1st Session. House of Representatives. Committee on Ways and Means. *Caribbean Basin Economic Recovery.* Washington: GPO, 1983.

______. Congress. 99th, 2d Session. House of Representatives. Committee on Ways and Means. Subcommittee on Oversight. *Review of the Impact and Effectiveness of the Caribbean Basin Initiative.* Washington: GPO, 1986.

______. Congress. 100th, 1st Session. House of Representatives. Committee on Ways and Means. Subcommitte on Oversight. *Report on the Committee Delegation Mission to the Caribbean Basin and the Recommendations to Improve the Effectiveness of the Caribbean Basin Initiative.* Washington: GPO, 1987.

______. Congress. 101th, 1st Session. House of Representatives. Committee on Ways and Means. *Caribbean Basin Economic Recovery Expansion Act of 1989* (Report Nos. 101–36.) Washington: GPO, 1989.

______. Department of Commerce. *Caribbean Basin Initiative: 1986 Guidebook.* Washington: GPO, 1985.

______. Department of Commerce. *Caribbean Basin Initiative: 1987 Guidebook.* Washington: GPO, 1986.

______. Department of Commerce, in cooperation with the United States Agency for International Development. *Caribbean Basin*

Initiative (CBI): 1988 Guidebook for Caribbean Basin Exporters. Washington: GPO, 1988.

———. Department of Commerce. International Trade Administration. *Caribbean Basin Investment Survey.* Washington: GPO, 1990.

———. Department of Commerce. International Trade Administration. *Annual Report on the Impact of the Caribbean Basin Economic Recovery Act on U.S. Industries and Consumers.* (2d Annual Report.) Washington: GPO, 1987.

———. Department of Commerce. International Trade Administration. *Annual Report on the Impact of the Caribbean Basin Economic Recovery Act on U.S. Industries and Consumers.* (3d Annual Report.) Washington: GPO, 1988.

———. Department of Commerce. International Trade Administration. *Annual Report on the Impact of the Caribbean Basin Economic Recovery Act on U.S. Industries and Consumers, First Report 1984–85.* Washington: GPO, September 1986.

———. Department of Labor. *Trade and Employment Effects of the Caribbean Basin Economic Recovery Act.* (3d Annual Report.) Washington: GPO, 1987.

———. Department of Labor. *Trade and Employment Effects of the Caribbean Basin Economic Recovery Act.* (4th Annual Report.) Washington: GPO, 1988.

———. Department of State. *Background on the Caribbean Basin Initiative.* (Special Report No. 97.) Washington: GPO, March 1982.

———. Department of State. Bureau of Inter-American Affairs, Office of Regional Economic Policy. *Report by the United States Department of State on the Caribbean Basin Initiative (CBI).* Washington: GPO, May 1989.

———. Department of State. Bureau of Public Affairs. *GIST Index: Caribbean Basin Initiative.* Washington: GPO, March 1987.

———. General Accounting Office. *Caribbean Basin Initiative: Impact on Selected Countries.* (No. GAO/NSIAD–88–177.) Washington: GPO, 1988.

———. General Accounting Office. *Caribbean Basin Initiative: Legislative and Agency Actions Relating to the CBI. Fact Sheet for the Chairman, Subcommittee on Oversight.* (Report to the Committee on Ways and Means. United States House of Representatives.) Washington: GPO, 1986.

———. General Accounting Office. *Caribbean Basin Initiative: Need for More Reliable Data on Business Activity Resulting from the Initiative.* (No. GAO/NSIAD–86–201BR.) Washington: GPO, 1986.

———. White House. Office of the Press Secretary. *Fact Sheets on the Initiative in President Reagan's Speech at Queens Park, St. George's, Grenada.* Washington: February 20, 1986.

Van Grasstek, Craig. "The Caribbean Basin Initiative: Update," *Policy Focus,* No. 3, 1985.
World Bank. *The Caribbean: Export Preferences and Performance.* Washington: 1988.
Wylie, Scott. "CBI: One Year Later," *Business America,* January 7, 1985, 2–4.
Zegaris, Bruce. "The Caribbean Basin Initiative," *Tax Notes,* 28, August 26, 1985, 1021–25.

Glossary

Belizean dollar (Bz$)—Belizean monetary unit, divided into 100 cents. The official fixed exchange rate of US$1 = Bz$2 was established in 1976 and remained in effect in 1991.

cay—In Belize a low island or reef of sand or coral. The customary spelling in the United States, *key,* is not used in Belize.

Creole—In Belize a term used for an English-speaking person of African or mixed African and European ancestry.

crown colony—A system of British colonial administration under which Britain retained control over defense, foreign affairs, internal security, and various administrative and budget matters. Crown colonies were governed internally by a British-appointed governor and a locally elected assembly. Prior to the Morant Bay Rebellion in Jamaica in 1865, crown colony government was limited to Trinidad and St. Lucia. In 1871 in Belize and in 1928 in Guyana, the representative assemblies were dissolved, and the colonies were governed directly by the Colonial Office in London and by a British-appointed governor who was assisted by a local council, most of whose members were appointed by the governor. In time, however, an increasing number of officials were locally elected rather than appointed. Following the report of the Moyne Commission in 1938, the crown colony system was modified to make local councils even more representative and to give local officials more administrative responsibility. Nevertheless, defense, foreign affairs, and internal security remained the prerogatives of the crown.

Enterprise for the Americas Initiative (EAI)—A plan announced by President George H.W. Bush on June 27, 1990, calling for the United States to negotiate agreements with selected Latin American countries to reduce their official debt to the United States and make funds available through this restructuring for environmental programs; to stimulate private investment; and to take steps to promote extensive trade liberalization with the goal of establishing free trade throughout the Western Hemisphere.

fiscal year (FY)—Guyana's fiscal year is the calendar year. Belize's fiscal year runs from April 1 to March 31.

Garifuna—An ethnic group descended from the Carib of the Eastern Caribbean and from Africans who had escaped from slavery. The Garifuna resisted the British and the French in the Windward Islands until they were defeated by the British in 1796. After putting down a violent Garifuna rebellion on Saint Vincent, the British moved the Garifuna across the Caribbean to the Bay Islands (present-day Islas de la Bahía) in the Gulf of Honduras. From there they migrated to the Caribbean coasts of Nicaragua, Honduras, Guatemala, and southern British Honduras. Garifuna also refers to their language.

General Agreement on Tariffs and Trade (GATT)—An intergovernmental agency related to the United Nations and headquartered in Geneva, GATT was established in 1948 as a multilateral treaty with the aim of liberalizing and stabilizing world trade. GATT's fundamental principles include nondiscriminatory trade among members, protection of domestic trade through the customs tariff, and agreement on tariff levels through negotiations among the contracting parties. The Uruguay Round of major multilateral trade negotiations, the eighth such round of negotiations, began at Punta del Este, Uruguay, in September 1986 and was still underway at the end of 1991.

gross domestic product (GDP)—A measure of the total value of goods and services produced by the domestic economy during a given period, usually one year. GDP is obtained by adding the value contributed by each sector of the economy in the form of profits, compensation to employees, and depreciation (consumption of capital). Only domestic production is included, not income arising from investments and possessions owned abroad, hence the use of the word *domestic* to distinguish GDP from gross national product (*q.v.*).

gross national product (GNP)—The total market value of all final goods and services produced by an economy during a year. GNP is obtained by adding the gross domestic product (*q.v.*) and the income received from abroad by residents less payments remitted abroad to nonresidents.

Guyanese dollar (G$)—Guyanese monetary unit, divided into 100 cents. The Guyanese dollar was repeatedly devalued in the 1980s, the official exchange rate dropping from US$1 = G$4.25 in 1985 to US$1 = G$10 in 1987. In April 1989, the government changed the official exchange rate to US$1 = G$33. The unofficial (market) exchange rate at that time was reportedly US$1 = G$60. In February 1991, the exchange rate was devalued further to align the official rate with the market rate, and the official exchange rate was adjusted weekly to keep this parity. As of June 1991, the official rate was US$1 = G$125.

import-substitution industrialization—An economic development strategy that emphasizes the growth of domestic industries, often by import protection using tariff and nontariff measures. Proponents favor the export of industrial goods over primary products.

International Monetary Fund (IMF)—Established along with the World Bank (*q.v.*) in 1945, the IMF is a specialized agency affiliated with the United Nations that takes responsibility for stabilizing international exchange rates and payments. The main business of the IMF is the provision of loans to its members when they experience balance-of-payments difficulties. These loans often carry conditions that require substantial internal economic adjustments by the recipients.

Lesser Antilles—The easternmost islands of the West Indies (*q.v.*) extending from the Virgin Islands through Trinidad and including the small islands off the north coast of South America. Some of these islands are divided further into two subgroups: the Leeward Islands consisting of the northern part of the Lesser Antilles from the Virgin Islands through Dominica and including Anguilla, Saint Christopher (Saint Kitts), Nevis, Barbuda, Antigua, and Guadeloupe; and the Windward Islands stretching from Martinique through Saint Lucia and Saint Vincent to Grenada. Trinidad, Tobago, Barbados, and the islands off the north coast of South America do not belong to either subgroup. The names *Leeward* and *Windward* refer to their sheltered (leeward) or exposed (windward) position relative to the prevailing northeasterly trade winds.

Lomé Convention—A series of agreements between the European Economic Community (EEC) and a group of African, Caribbean, and Pacific (ACP) states, mainly former European colonies, providing duty-free or preferential access to the EEC market for almost all ACP exports. The Stabilization of Export Earnings Scheme, a mechanism set up by the Lomé Convention, provides compensation for ACP export earnings lost through fluctuations in the world prices of agricultural commodities. The Lomé Convention also provides for limited EEC development aid and investment funds to be disbursed to ACP recipients through the European Development Fund and the European Investment Bank. The Lomé Convention is updated every five years. Lomé I took effect on April 1, 1976; Lomé II, on January 1, 1981; Lomé III, on March 1, 1985; Lomé IV, on March 1, 1990.

Mestizo—In Belize a term used for a Spanish-speaking person of mixed European and Mayan ancestry.

936 funds—Funds deposited by United States-based corporations in the Government Development Bank of Puerto Rico in order

to take advantage of Section 936 of the United States Internal Revenue Service Code, under which income derived from sources in Puerto Rico is exempted from United States income taxes. The funds may be used to help finance twin-plant (*q.v.*) ventures with countries that have signed a bilateral tax information exchange agreement with the United States.

Rastafarian(ism)—An Afro-Christian revivalist cult formed in Jamaica in the early 1920s. The so-called Rastafarian Brethren emphasized rejection of both Jamaican and European culture in favor of eventual repatriation to Africa. Identifying Africa with Ethiopia, Rastafarians viewed then Emperor Haile Selassie of Ethiopia as God incarnate. As hope of returning to Africa dwindled, Rastafarianism became more of a religious than a political movement. Rastafarians developed a system of beliefs compatible with their poverty and aloofness from society and similar to mystical experiences found in other protest religions. Rastas (as they are known in common parlance) have come to symbolize the movement away from white domination and toward a heightened black identity and pride. Rasta thought, reggae music, dance, and literature have been popularized throughout West Indian culture.

special drawing rights (SDRs)—Monetary unit of the International Monetary Fund (IMF) (*q.v.*) based on a basket of international currencies consisting of the United States dollar, the German deutsche mark, the Japanese yen, the British pound sterling, and the French franc.

Sunni (from *sunna,* meaning "custom," in Arabic, giving connotation of orthodoxy in theory and practice)—A member of the larger of the great divisions of Islam.

Tariff Schedule 807 program—Refers to items 806.3 and 807 of the Tariff Schedules of the United States that allow the duty-free entry of goods whose final product contains a certain portion of raw material or labor value added in the Caribbean Basin.

twin plant—Productive arrangements whereby two or more producers in separate countries complementarily share the production of a good or service. Under the Caribbean Basin Initiative (CBI), such arrangements with the government of Puerto Rico potentially benefited from special investment or 936 funds (*q.v.*). The operations of twin plant ventures typically entailed the delegation of assembly or other labor-intensive production stages to plants in a CBI-designated country, from which these semi-finished products would then be shipped duty-free to Puerto Rico for final processing.

[illegible] Ocean—except for islands off the coast of [illegible]—including the small islands off the north coast of South America and the Bermuda Islands. The West Indies are commonly divided into three groups: the Bahamas, which include the Great Inagua [illegible] (more usually, the Bahamas and the Turks and Caicos [illegible]) or the Turks and Caicos; the Greater Antilles, which consist of the four largest islands: Cuba, Hispaniola (the Dominican Republic and Haiti), Jamaica, and Puerto Rico; and the Lesser Antilles (q.v.), which consist of the smaller eastern Caribbean islands stretching from the Virgin Islands southward to Grenada, and the small islands off the coast of South America.

World Bank—The informal name used to designate a group of four affiliated international institutions: the International Bank for Reconstruction and Development (IBRD), the International Development Association (IDA), the International Finance Corporation (IFC), and the Multilateral Investment Guarantee Agency (MIGA). The IBRD, established in 1945, has the primary purpose of providing loans at market-related rates of interest to developing countries at more advanced stages of development. The IDA, a legally separate loan fund but administered by the staff of the IBRD, was set up in 1960 to furnish credits to the poorest developing countries on much easier terms than those of conventional IBRD loans. The IFC, founded in 1956, supplements the activities of the IBRD through loans and assistance designed specifically to encourage the growth of productive private enterprises in less developed countries. The MIGA, founded in 1988, insures private foreign investment in developing countries against various noncommercial risks. The president and certain officers of the IBRD hold the same positions in the IFC. The four institutions are owned by the governments of the countries that subscribe their capital. To participate in the World Bank group, member states must first become members of the International Monetary Fund (q.v.).

West Indies—Term for islands in or bordering the Caribbean Se including the small islands off the north coast of South Amer and the Bahama Islands. The West Indies are commonly di ed into three groups: the Bahamas, which include the C monwealth of the Bahamas and the British crown colony (of the Turks and Caicos; the Greater Antilles, which co of the four largest islands of Cuba, Hispaniola (the Do can Republic and Haiti), Jamaica, and Puerto Rico; an Lesser Antilles (*q.v.*), which consist of the smaller easter islands stretching from the Virgin Islands through Tr and the small islands off the coast of South America.

World Bank—The informal name used to designate a group affiliated international institutions: the International B Reconstruction and Development (IBRD), the Inter Development Association (IDA), the International Fina poration (IFC), and the Multilateral Investment G Agency (MIGA). The IBRD, established in 1945 primary purpose of providing loans at market-relate interest to developing countries at more advanced st velopment. The IDA, a legally separate loan fun ministered by the staff of the IBRD, was set up furnish credits to the poorest developing countries o ier terms than those of conventional IBRD loans founded in 1956, supplements the activities of through loans and assistance designed specifically the growth of productive private enterprises in le countries. The MIGA, founded in 1988, insure eign investment in developing countries against commercial risks. The president and certain IBRD hold the same positions in the IFC. Th tions are owned by the governments of the cou scribe their capital. To participate in the Wor member states must first belong to the Inter tary Fund (*q.v.*).

Index

Acarai Mountains, 33
acquired immune deficiency syndrome (AIDS)
 Belize: 218, 219
 Guyana: 60-61; among prisoners, 145
Act for the Abolition of Slavery Throughout the British Colonies (1833), 69
administration: employment in, 82
Adult Education Association, 58
Africans: as slaves, 40; stereotypes of, 44
African slave descendants, 171, 208
Afro-Guyanese culture, 14, 31; education in, 58; effect of slavery on, 44; family patterns in, 44–46; marriage in, 46; in military, 133, 136; religion in, 47, 50; weddings in, 46; women in, 46
Afro-Guyanese people, 3, 40–41; abandonment of People's Progressive Party by, 20; acculturation of, 43; British values of, 44; conflicts of, with Indo-Guyanese, 3, 70; cooperation of, with other ethnic groups, 12; in elite class, 13; farming by, 70; gangs of, 143; geographic distribution of, 43; in Guyana National Service, 140; in lower class, 42; in middle class, 12, 24; occupations of, xviii, 14; in peasant class, 9; as percentage of population, xx, 37; pressure from, for reform, 12; in professional class, 41; reaction of, to Burnham, 24; religion of, 47; sense of superiority among, 40; social distribution of, 43; social stratification among, 17; suffrage for, 12; as teachers, 55; in urban areas, 38, 40
Agreement on Apartheid in Sport, 323
agricultural: diversification, 85, 239; laborers, 210, 275; production, 102
Agricultural Marketing Protocol, 331, 332
agricultural products (*see also under individual crops*)
 Belize: import of, 173; nontraditional, 239
 Guyana: 84; for export, 84, 97; processing of, 93
Agricultural Research and Development Institute, 331
agriculture
 Belize: 236–240; development of, 172, 173; as percentage of gross domestic product, 231
 Guyana: 84–88; employment in, 82, 226; foreign firms in, 204; importance of, 6; Indo-Guyanese employed in, 70; in Mayan civilization, 158; military support for, 136; as percentage of gross domestic product, 74; ridged-field, 158; slash-and-burn, 158; subsistence, 70
AID. *See* United States Agency for International Development
AIDS. *See* acquired immune deficiency syndrome
air service (Guyana), 96; foreign investment encouraged in, 102
Akawaio tribe, 42
alcalde system, 264, 278; disruption of, 278
Alcan. *See* Aluminum Company of Canada
Altún Ha, 159, 161; excavation of, 161
aluminum (*see also* bauxite), 89–91; prices, 89; production, 89; reserves, 89
Aluminum Company of Canada (Alcan), 71, 91
Amandala, 279
Amazon Caribbean Guyana Limited, 102
Amerindians, 31, 42; acculturation of, 42; attempts to enslave, 40; coastal, 42; festivals of, 49; intermarriage by, 42; language of, 42; in militia, 292; as percentage of population, xx, 37; population of, 6; rebellion by, 23-24, 125; religion of 42, 50; subjugation of, 157
Amery, Leo, 176
Ancient Usages and Customs of the Settlement, 164–65, 250
Andean Pact, 328
Anglican Church, 48; membership in, 48, 201; missionaries of, 167; publications of, 280; role of, 51; schools of, 214
Ankoko Island: seized by Venezuela, 23, 145–46
Anna Regina, 117

anticolonial movement, 83
Antigua and Barbuda, 128, 325, 328
apan jhaat, 22
Arabs, 198, 199; in elite class, 205
Aranda, Theodore, 272, 274
Arawak people, xvii, 3, 42; geographic distribution of, 4; killed by disease, 3; origins of, 4
Arbenz, Jacobo, 181
Arekuna tribe, 42
Argentina: invasion of Falklands by, 126, 128; investment from, 93
Arias Dávila, Pedro, 162
armed forces. *See* Belize Defence Force; Guyana Defence Force
army. *See* Belize Defence Force; Guyana Defence Force
Aroaima, 90
Arron, Henck, 147
Arthur, George, 166
Aryan Society. *See* Arya Samaj movement
Arya Samaj movement, 49
Asians: acculturation of, 43; descendants of, in population, xx, 37
Association of Commonwealth Universities, 324
Atlantic Bank (Honduras), 245
Atlantic Ocean, 34
Ato, Bilal, 142–43
attorney general, 116, 291
Australia: in Commonwealth of Nations, 321, 325; investment of, in mining, 89, 92; petroleum exploration by, 103
Avebury, Lord, 27, 139

Bahais, 202
Baking Pot, 159
balance of payments
  Belize: 228, 231
  Guyana: 101; overall, 80; as percentage of gross domestic product, 101; shortfall in, 80, 101
balance of trade, 81
Balderamos, Arthur, 177
Balfour Formula, 321
Banana Control Board, 238
Banana Growers' Association, 238
Banana Protocol, 235, 238
bananas, xxv, 238–39; attempts to cultivate, 238; exports of, 229, 231, 245; production of, 229, 239
Banco Serfín (Mexico), 245
Bank for International Settlements, 81
banking
  Belize: 244–45
  Guyana: 94–96; foreign investment encouraged in, 102
Bank of Baroda, 94
Bank of Guyana, 94, 96; foreign currency held by, 78
Bank of Nova Scotia, 94, 245
banks, 94
Baptist Church, 48; missionaries of, 167
Barama River Carib tribe, 42
Barbados, 128, 328; debt to, 99
Barclays Bank, 94, 245
barite, 192
Barrow, Dean, 273
Bartica, 117
Basir, Isahak, 144
bauxite (*see also* aluminum)
  Belize: 192
  Guyana: 38, 89–91, 97; calcined, 71, 90; decline in demand for, 73; decline in exports of, 14; decline in production of, 67, 73, 74; demand for, 15; exports of, 74, 97, 98, 99, 100, 129; foreign investment in, 102; in Great Depression, 14; location of, xix, 33; mining of, xviii, 70, 90; prices of, 72; processing, 75, 93; production, 73, 74; reserves, 89
bauxite industry: development of, 70; energy for, 93; foreign investment in, 70; nationalization of, 124; privatization of, 80
Baymen. *See* British settlers
BDF. *See* Belize Defence Force
Beacon, 279–80
Beecham company, 93
Belizario Camp, 298
Belize: etymology of, 163; name change to, 181; national identity of, 210
Belize Advisory Council, 257–58, 306; members of, 257–58; role of, 257
Belize Agri-Business Company, 239
Belizean citizenship, selling of, 267, 272, 273
Belizean Creole, 201
Belizean Popular Party, 273
Belize Billboard, 179, 180
Belize City: Chinese in, 199; city council of, 263; courts in, 306; Creoles in, 200;

East Indians in, 199; elite in, 205; population in, 193, 225; port at, 243
Belize City Council: dissolved, 180; elections, 181
Belize College of Agriculture, 214
Belize College of Arts, Science, and Technology, 212–13; established, 212; funding for, 213
Belize Constitutional Conference, 254; report issued by, 254
Belize Defence Force (BDF), 262, 296–301; active-duty elements, 296; air wing, 299; chain of command in, 298; chief of staff, 297; commander in chief of, 298; commander of, 297; deployment of, 298; enlistment, 296; equipment of, 298–99; foreign service of, 300; formed, 296; maritime arm, 298–99; missions of, 291, 296, 298–99, 302; organization of, 298–99; as percent of population, 297; personnel, 296–97; reserves, 299; salaries, 296; terms of service in, 297; troop strength of, 291, 296; training, 286, 296, 297–98; women in, 297
Belize District, 193, 263; Arabs in, 199; Mestizos in, 200; percentage of population in, 193; population density in, 194
Belize Electricity Board, 241, 275
Belize Estate and Produce Company, 173, 180; in Great Depression, 175; labor conditions in, 176, 274; Maya displaced by, 176
Belize Food Products, 237
Belize General Development Workers' Union, 275
Belize Information Service: publications of, 280
Belize International Airport, 242, 243, 299
Belize Marketing Board, 240
Belize Ministry of Health, 218
Belize Ministry of Home Affairs, 304
Belize Ministry of Social Services and Community Development, 263
Belize Ministry of Tourism, 242
Belize National Police, 303–5; commissioner of, 304; corruption in, 305; established, 303; mission, 303–4; number of, 304; recruitment, 303; role of, in drug eradication, 302; territorial division of, 304; training of, 304; uniforms, 304–5; women in, 304
Belize National Teachers' Union, 234
Belize Organization for Women and Development (Bowand), 278
Belize Police Special Defence Force, 296
Belize Popular Party, 267
Belize River (Old River), 192; named, 163
Belize Rural Women's Association, 278
Belize School of Nursing, 214
Belize Sugar Board, 237
Belize Sugar Industries Limited (BSIL), 237
Belize Teachers' College, 214
Belize Technical College, 214
Belize Telecommunications Limited, 243
Belize Times, 279
Belize Today, 289
Belize Town, 171, 293; population of, 171
Belize Town Board: elections for, 177–78
Belize Volunteer Guard, 296
Belmopan: population in, 225; sewer system in, 219; street vendors in, 196
Benque Viejo del Carmen, 263
Berbice: British takeover of, 8; occupied by Britain, 8; settled, 6
Berbice River, 38, 96
Betson, Clifford, 180
Bhagwan, Moses, 144
Big Creek port, 243
Big Six currency traders, 76
birth control, 36–37; use of, 37
Bishop's High School, 54
Black Friday, 13
Black Muslims, 202
Blood, Hillary, 252
Booker company, 85–86
Booker McConnell company, 71, 72
border disputes
  Belize and Guatemala: 157, 181–84, 226, 249, 334; as obstacle to independence, xxiv, 181, 294–95; origins of, xxiv, 182
  Guyana and Suriname: 123, 147–48, 334; military role in, 133
  Guyana and Venezuela: 10–11, 112, 123, 145–47, 334; arbitration of, 10–11, 125; commission on, 147; decision of, 11; military role in, xx, 133; resurgence of, 23, 125–26, 145, 146–47
Bouterse, Desi, 127
Bowand. *See* Belize Organization for

Women and Development
Brazil: financial aid from, 127; investment from, 102; investment of, in mining, 89, 92, 102; military assistance from, 127; relations with, 127
Britain: aid from, 234, 286, 325; border disputes settled by, 125; control of Belize by, 182; dependence on, 173; in Donor Support Group, 100; economic ties of, with Belize, 226; education in, 205, 217; emigration to, 38; exports to, 94, 97, 98; French war with, 8; imports from, 227; influence of, on Belize, xxv, 208, 286; investment from, 71, 92, 93, 102; matériel from, 286; migration of Belizeans to, 195; military aid from, 280, 302; military training in, 297, 298, 300; negotiations of, with Guatemala, 183, 282, 294–95; occupation of Dutch colonies by, 8; petroleum exploration by, 103; relations of, with Belize, 285–86; relations of, with Guyana, 128; relations of, with Venezuela, 10; rivalry of, with Spain, 157, 163–64, 165, 292; settlers from, 69; trade with, 236; war of, with Netherlands, 8
British Airways, 96
British Colonial Office, 168
British culture, 44; acculturation to, xvii, 43, 168, 269; superiority of, 44
British Guiana: as crown colony, 14
British Guiana Labour Union (BGLU): founded, 13, 82, 121
British Guiana Mining Company, 10
British Guiana Police Force, 142
British Honduras, 157; constitution of, 172; established, 170, 172, 251
British Honduras Company: as landowner, 173
British Honduras Constabulary, 303–4
British Honduras Independent Labour Party, 178
British Honduras Workers and Tradesmen's Union, 274
British immigrants, 7, 200
British North American Act (1867), 321
British rule
  Belize: 249–55; legacy of, 224–25; legal system under, 250; Mayan resistance to, 170
  Guyana: education under, 52; elections under, 17; political parties under, 17–18; social organization under, 9; transition to, 7–9
British settlers, xviii; arrival of, in Belize, xxiii, 157; dissipation of, 164; government of, xxiii, 164, 166; logging by, 165; Spanish attacks on, xxiii, 164, 165–66, 292, 293
British settlements, 163; Mayan attacks on, 171
British Telecom, 243
British troops, 280, 285–86, 295; headquarters of, 300; influence of, on Belizean economy, 229–30, 245, 286, 300; need for, 294; organization of, 291, 300–301; origins of, 293; as protection against invasion by Guatemala, xxiv, 282; withdrawal of, xxvi
British West India Regiment, 293, 294
British West Indies, 168
Broken Hill Proprietary, 103
Brown, C.H., 176
BSIL. *See* Belize Sugar Industries Limited
budget deficit, 80; reduced, 68
Bulgaria: relations with, 129
Burdon, John, 176
Burma: withdrawal from Commonwealth of Nations, 322
Burnaby, William, 164, 250
Burnaby's Code, 164–65, 250
Burnham, Linden Forbes, xviii, xix, 3, 147; background of, 17; conflict of, with Jagan, 15–16, 18–19; consolidation of power by, xx, 25, 112, 113; death of, xxi, 27, 67; as minister of defense, 134; People's National Congress under, 119; as prime minister, 22–27, 111; racial conflict provoked by, 20; support for, 20, 24
Burnham administration (*see also* cooperative republic) (1964–85), 22–27; authoritarian policies of, 109; conflict of, with Guyana Council of Churches, 51–52; criticism of, xx, 51; economic policies of, 22–23; economy under, 100; election fraud under, 24; House of Israel under, 50, 51; human rights abuses under, 143–44; leftist policies of, 24; opposition of, to intervention in Grenada, 124, 128, schools controlled by, 51; view of People's Temple of Christ, 26; violence by, xx
Burnham Agricultural Institute, 58
Burrowes School of Art, 58
Bush, George, 281

business community, 276; political role of, 276

cabinet (Belize): laws introduced by, 260-61; members of, 257
Cambridge Advanced examinations, 214
Camp Oakley, 298
Canada: assistance from, 81, 104, 325, 340-41; in Commonwealth of Nations, 321, 325; in Donor Support Group, 100; education in, 217; emigration to, 38, 195; exports to, 97, 98-99, 237; influence of, on Belize, 208, 210; investment from, 70, 92, 97, 102, 343; investment of, in mining, 89; military training in, 298, 300
Canadian International Development Agency (CIDA), 219
Cane Farmers' Association, 236
Canul, Marcos, 171
capital goods, 99
CARE, 212, 218, 279
Caribbean Agricultural Research and Development Institute, 331
Caribbean Basin Economic Recovery Act. *See* Caribbean Basin Initiative
Caribbean Basin Economic Recovery Expansion Act (1989), 341
Caribbean Basin Initiative, 85, 98, 104, 124, 231, 235, 239, 281, 337-44; amendments to, 337; amount of assistance, 342; beneficiary countries, 338; criticisms of, 338; expansion of benefits and programs, 341; exports in, 343-44; goals of, 342; impact of, 342; imports in, 344; motivations for, 342; multilateral support, 340; network, 340-1; Operations Committee, 340; proposal for, 337; provisions of, 337; requirements for assistance, 338; sources of investment, 342; special benefits under, 339; targets of assistance, 337-38; trade provisions, 338; twin plant plan, 339-40
Caribbean Community and Common Market (Caricom), 105, 124, 128, 325, 327-35; common tariff in, 236; components of, 329; customs union created by, 105; defense policy coordination, 334; effectiveness of, 335; financial cooperation, 334; foreign exchange needs, 327; foreign policy coordination, 334; functional cooperation, 334; goals of, 328; imports by, 327; industrial programming, 332-33; institutional structure of, 329-31; market integration mechanisms, 331-32; mechanisms for liberalizing trade, 331-32; membership in, 284; members of, 327; observers in, 327; problems of, 105; production and marketing cooperation, 332-33; regional integration by, 328, 335; tourism cooperation, 333; trade with, 236; transportation cooperation, 333
Caribbean Community Secretariat, 331
Caribbean Congress of Labor, 274
Caribbean countries (*see also* regional integration): economic assistance to, 342; economic problems of, 327-28; emigration to, 38; exports from, 343-44; foreign exchange needed by, 327, 343; foreign investment in, 343; imports by, 327, 344; relations with, 128; tourism in, 333; unemployment in, 343
Caribbean Development Bank, 81, 331; created, 105; debt to, 99, 100
Caribbean Examinations Council, 56, 331
Caribbean Food Corporation, 331, 333
Caribbean Free Trade Association (Carifta), 226; formed, 104, 328; membership in, 23, 104-5, 128, 226, 284, 328; replaced, 329
Caribbean Marketing Enterprise, 331
Caribbean Meteorological Organisation, 331
Caribbean Tourism Association, 333
Caribbean Tourism Research and Development Centre, 331, 333
Caribbean Trade Information System, 331
Caribcan, 341
Caribe Farm Industries, 240
Carib people, xvii, 3, 42; geographic distribution of, 4; killed by disease, 3; Lesser Antilles settled by, 4; origins of, 4
Caricom. *See* Caribbean Community and Common Market
Caricom's Multilateral Clearing Facility, 334
Carifta. *See* Caribbean Free Trade Association

Carnegie School of Home Economics, 58
Carter, Jimmy, xxii, 124
Carter Center, xxi
cassite, 192
caste, 41, 46; breakdown of, 48
Caste War, 170, 198
Castro Ruz, Fidel, 20, 129
Catholic Standard, 50, 51, 122
cays, 161, 189, 242
Cayo District, 193, 263; Arabs in, 199; Central American immigrants in, 196; Mennonites in, 200; Mestizos in, 200; religion of, 202
CDC. *See* Colonial Development Corporation
cedar, 174
Central America: immigrants to Belize from, xxv, xxvi, 189, 193, 196, 210, 285; influence of, on Belize, 210; migrant laborers from, 234; orientation of Belize toward, 268-69, 277, 285
Central American Common Market, 226, 328; support by, for Guatemala's claim to Belize, 282
Central American Federation, 182
Central Bank of Belize, 230, 244
Cerezo, Vinicio, 284
Cerros, 158-59; excavation of, 161
CFTC. *See* Commonwealth Fund for Technical Cooperation
Chamber of Commerce and Industry: Peace Corps volunteers in, 281; political role of, 276; publications of, 280
Chamber Update, 279
Charles, Eugenia, 128
Chase, Ashton, 17
Chase Manhattan Bank, 94
Chetumal Bay, 192
Chetumal province, 162
chicle: exports of, 174, 175, 224; production, 174
child labor, 83-84
China, 90; indentured servants recruited from, 40; relations with, 129, 286; trade with, 129
Chinese people
- Belize: 198, 199; in elite class, 205
- Guyana: 41-42; acculturation of, 41-42, 43; intermarriage by, 42; as percentage of population, 37; as sugar plantation workers, xviii, 10, 70; in urban areas, 42

Chol language, 162
Christian Democratic Party, 272, 274
Christianity (*see also under individual denominations*), 47-48; Hindu conversions to, 48; percentage of followers in population, xx, 47; politics and, 52; role of, 47; status of, 48; syncretic, 47
Christian missions. *See* missions; missionaries
Christian Social Action Group, 180
Christian Workers' Union, 235, 275
Chung, Arthur, 111
churches
- Belize: involvement of, in education, 276-77; political role of, 276-78
- Guyana: opposition of, to government, 122; opposition of, to political parties, 122

CIDA. *See* Canadian International Development Agency
Citizens' Political Party, 177
citrus, xxv, 237; exports of, 229, 231, 237; production of, 229, 237
Citrus Company of Belize, 237
civil service, 118; loyalty in, 118
Clayton-Bulwer Treaty (1850), 169-70
Cleveland, Grover, 11
climate
- Belize: 192-93; rainfall, 193; seasons, 192, 193; temperatures, 192-93
- Guyana: 34-35; humidity, 34; rainfall, 34, 35; temperature, 34-35

clothing: exports of, 98
coastal plain, xix, 31-33; as percentage of land area, 84; rainfall in, 35
cocaine, 209, 291, 302
Cockscomb Mountains, 191
College of Electors, 11; abolished, 12
Colombia, 340; Belize Defence Force deployed to, 300
Colombo Plan for Cooperative, Economic, and Social Development in Asia and the Pacific, 324-25
Colonial Development Corporation (CDC), 242
Colonial Life Insurance Company, 102
Colonial Report for 1931, 175
Columbus, Christopher, xvii, xxiii, 3, 4, 6, 162
Combined Court, 12, 14; abolished, 14; members of, 11; responsibilities of, 11
Comgep. *See* Commonwealth Group of Eminent Persons

commercial sector
Belize: 166
Guyana: 41, 42
commodity crisis, 223
Common External Tariff, 331, 332
Common Market Council of Ministers, 330-31
Common Protective Policy, 331, 332
Commonwealth Advisory Group, 94
Commonwealth Agricultural Bureau, 324
Commonwealth Development Corporation, 324
Commonwealth Fund for Technical Cooperation (CFTC), 324
Commonwealth Games Federation, 323, 324
Commonwealth Group of Eminent Persons (Comgep), 323
Commonwealth of Nations: activities of, 324; Belize as member of, 286; Belize's case for independence presented to, xxiv 183; benefits of, 111; history of, 321-22; meetings of, 322-23; members of, 320; membership in, 111-12, 128, 319; monarch in, 320; organization of, 324; origins of, 321; politics of, 322-23; principles of, 322-23; procedures of, 322-23; purpose of, 319; regional groupings in, 324-25; status of dominions in, 321; trade with, 238
Commonwealth Preference, 321
Commonwealth Secretariat, 323-24
communications
Belize: 243, 279-80
Guyana: 97; foreign investment in, 97, 102; need for investment in, 77, 97
communism, 120; church opposition to, 122; fall of, 129
communist countries: Guyana's relations with, 129
Concept Plan of Redress, 8, 109
Conference of Foreign Ministers of Nonaligned Countries, 24
Conference of Heads of Government of Asian and Pacific Commonwealth Member States, 325
Congregationalist Church, 48
conjugal relationships: Afro-Guyanese, 46; Indo-Guyanese, 47
constitution
Belize:
constitution of 1854, 250
constitution of 1954, 252
constitution of 1960, 252
constitution of 1981, 253-55; elections under, 265; freedom of expression under, 279; preparation of, 253-54; procedure of amending, 254-55; right under, 301; structure of, 254
Guyana:
constitution of 1792, 109
constitution of 1871, 172
constitution of 1928, 14, 18
constitution of 1953, 110
constitution of 1957, xix
constitution of 1961, 21, 110, 111-12; amendments to, 22, 24, 111; legislature under, 21; prime minister under, 21
constitution of 1980, xx, 112-13; distribution of power under, 113; elections under, 118; executive under, xx, 26; guarantees under, 112-113; judicial system under, 145; promulgated, 26
constitutional conference (Guyana) (1964), 23
constitutional reform
Belize: agitation for, 180; recommendations for, 252
Guyana: 12; agitation for, 12; resistance to, 12
constitutional structure (Belize); preindependence, 249-55
construction
Belize: 241-42; growth of, 241; as percentage of gross domestic product, 242
Guyana: 241; employment in, 82; foreign investment encouraged in, 102; military support for, 136; as percentage of gross domestic product, 74
consumer goods: import of, 99, 217
consumerism, 210
contraception. *See* birth control
Convention of London (1786), 165, 182, 282
Cooperative for American Relief Everywhere. *See* CARE
Cooperative Republic of Guyana, 24-27, 109; attributes of, 112; declared, xx, 24, 72, 111, 124
Corozal: courts in, 306; Maya in, 200;

Mestizos in, 200; municipal government of, 263; population of, 170
Corozal Basin, 241
Corozal District, 193, 263; Mestizos in, 198; religion of, 202; Spanish language in, 200-201
Corriverton, 117
Cortés, Hernán, 162
Council of Legal Education, 331
Courantyne River, 38
Courtenay, V.H., 270
Court of Appeal
Belize: 262
Guyana: 115, 144-45; jurisdiction of, 116; political loyalty in, 145
Court of Policy (Dutch), 110; abolished, 14; altered, 12; functions of, 11; membership of, 8, 11; replaced, 110
courts of justice (Dutch): functions of, 11; membership of, 8, 11
court system
Belize: 261-62
Guyana: 115-16, 144-45; subservience of, to People's National Congress, 145
Costa de Mosquitos. *See* Mosquito Coast
credit, 232
credit unions, 245
Creole language, 171
Creole people, xxiv, xxv, 157, 267; acculturation of, 168, 269; antagonism of, to Hispanic culture, 196; in Belize city, 200; culture of, 167; in elite class, 205; emigration of, 195, 196; identification as, 202; legal rights of, 168; on Legislative Council, 174; occupations of, 206; percentage of, in population, 197; physical features of, 197; protests by, 177; religion of, 201, 202, 208; suppression of culture, 167
crime
Belize: 209, 210, 291, 302-3
Guyana: 133
criminal code of 1980 (Belize), 306
criminal justice system
Belize: 291, 3057; defendants' rights in, 261, 307; procedure, 307; punishment in, 306
Guyana: punishment in, 145
Critchlow, Hubert Nathaniel, 13, 82, 121
crown colony of Belize, 250; petition for status as, 251
Crown Lands Ordinance (1872), 169
Cuba: equipment to Guyana from, 21; loans to Guyana from, 21; physicians to Guyana from, 62; relations of, with Guyana, 22, 123, 129; support by, for Belize's independence, 183-84, 283; university scholarships in, 216
Cuello, 158; excavation of, 161
Cuffy, 7
Cuffy Ideological Institute, 58
currency
Belize: devaluations of, 178, 179-80, 227, 229, 270, 294; pegged to U.S. dollar, 228
Guyana: devaluations of, 67, 79; exchange rates, 75-76; instability of, 75; trading, 75
current accounts
Belize: 233
Guyana: 80-81
Cyril Potter College of Education, 58

dairy products, 85
dams, 31, 84
Dangerous Drugs Act (1980), 306
Dangriga, 169; courts in, 306; municipal government of, 263; street vendors in, 196
Davis, Cyril, 274
Davson, Henry K., 12
death: causes of, 60-61
debt, external
Belize: 233-34; amount of, 233; ratio, 245
Guyana: xx, 67, 99-101; amount of, 68, 73-74, 99, 100; forgiveness, 101; as percentage of gross domestic product, 74, 99; refinancing, 104
debt payments arrears, 67, 68, 74, 100; elimination of, 81; as percentage of gross domestic product, 81
debt service, 101; refusal to pay, 100
Declaration of Commonwealth Principles, 323
Defence Ordinance of 1977, 296, 297
defense spending, 299-300; external aid for, 300; as percentage of federal spending, 299; as percentage of gross domestic product, 300
Demba. *See* Demerara Bauxite Company
Demerara: courts in, 8; economic growth

in, 7; occupied by Britain, 8; settled, 6, 7
Demerara Bauxite Company (Demba), 71, 72
Demerara Distillers Limited, 94
Demerara River, 7, 34, 38, 96
Democratic Independent Union, 235
Democratic Labour Movement, 120
demonstrations, xix, 302; forbidden, 144; labor, 176
Denny, Kenneth, 121
dentists, 219
De Solís, Juan, 162
Despard, Edward Marcus, 165; suspended, 166
development expenditures, 233
Development Finance Corporation, 244–45, 275
diamonds, 92; location of, xix, 33; mining of, 75; processing, 93; production of, 92; reserves of, 89; smuggling of, 75, 76, 92
diet
Belize: 225
Guyana: 60
dikes, xviii, 3, 7, 31, 34, 69, 84
Directorate of Public Prosecutions, 292, 307
Disaster Emergency Response Agency, 331
disease, 60–61, 218; intestinal, 218; native Americans killed by, 3, 162
District Court, 261, 306
Disweek, 279–80
Divali, 49
Donor Support Group, 81, 94, 100
drainage, 38; canals, xviii, 3, 34, 69, 86
drought, 85, 86
drug abuse, 302
drug trafficking, 77, 209, 230, 291, 302; and Belize's economy, 229, 230; foreign assistance in fighting, 302; role of Belize Defence Force in fighting, 291, 296, 298; role of Belize National Police in fighting, 302, 304–5
Dutch rule (*see also* Netherlands), 3, 6; attraction of immigrants under, 7; judiciary under, 8; recognized, 6
Dutch settlements, xvii, 6, 163
Dutch West India Company, 6, 69; poor administration of, 8; problems of, 7–8
Dzuluinicob province, 161, 162; rebellion in, 162
EAI. *See* Enterprise for the Americas Initiative
Eastern Caribbean Currency Authority, 325
Eastern Caribbean States Supreme Court, 325
East Indians (*see also* Indians)
Belize: 198–99; in elite class, 205
Guyana: culture of, 31; as indentured servants, 10, 13, 43, 70; as rice farmers, 70; stereotypes of, 44; as sugar plantation workers, 10
East Montgomery North Mine, 90
Eboe. *See* Ibo
Echeverría Alvarez, Luis, 184
economic: activity, constraints on, 92; crisis, 27, 38; diversification, xxv, 230–31; problems, 327–28; structure, 74–75
economic growth
Belize: 225, 227–29, 229–30; factors hindering, 223
Guyana: in Demerara, 7; in Essequibo, 7; restoration of, 78–79
economic policies: under Burnham, 22–23; under Hoyte, 28
Economic Recovery Program (ERP) (Guyana), 68, 74, 78–82, 97, 100; effect of, on workers, 83; manufacturing under, 93; results of, 81–82
economic reform
Belize: 223
Guyana: under Hoyte, xxi, 67–68; objectives of, 78; obstacles to, 68
economic stabilization plan (Belize), 268
economy
Belize: British influence on, 173, 229; colonial, 223–25; constraints on, 225–26; growth of, 227; history of, 226–27; peripheral factors in, 229–30
Guyana: closed, dismantling of, 67; Dutch influence on, 69; free-market, 27; government control of, 72, 75; under Hoyte, xxi, 78
economy, parallel, (Guyana), 27, 74, 75–77, 79; absorption of, 79; foreign exchange in, 73; government response to, 77; illegal imports in, 73; problems caused by, 75; services provided by, 75; size of, 75; state enterprises in, 77
education (*see also* schools)
Belize: 211–17; access to, 209, 210,

211, 212, 215-17; aid for, 212; attrition rates, 211, 215, 216; British influence on, 225; church control of, 211-12, 214, 276-78; demand for, 212, 216, 223; of elite, 205; foreign influences on, 211; government control of, 214; investment in, 211; of lower class, 208; of middle class, 206; overseas, 205, 216-17; primary, 214, 216; secondary, 214, 216; technical, 214; university, 216; value of, 216

Guyana: 52-60; accessibility to, 54; adult, 58; attitudes toward, 58-60; under British rule, 52-54, 59; decline in, 54; demand for, 59-60; development of, 52; of elite, 52-54; government emphasis on, 54; government spending on, 54; importance of, 52, 58; of Indo-Guyanese, 58-59, 141; of middle class, 52-54; overseas, 141; post-secondary, 56-58, 141; primary, 54; reform, 52; restrictions on, 52-54; right to, 112; secondary, 52-54

EEC. *See* European Economic Community

election fraud, xx, 24, 27, 118, 137, 139-40; ballot box tampering, 118, 137-40; gerrymandering, 118; voting by expatriates, 118

elections

Belize: of Belize City Council, 181; among British settlers, 164; campaign strategies in, 268; under constitution of 1964, 253; under constitution of 1984, 265; local, 263; of National Assembly, 258; of 1936, 176, 252; of 1939, 177-78; of 1948, 252; of 1954, 181, 270; of 1979, 253; of 1984, 213, 267; of 1989, 267-68, 302; of 1993, xxvi-xxvii

Guyana: under constitution of 1980, 118; institution of, 110; of 1950, 17; of 1953, xviii, 18, 110; of 1957, xix, 19-20, 110; of 1961, xix, 21, 111; of 1964, xix, 22; of 1968, xx, 24; of 1973, xx, 24; of 1978, 25; of 1980, 27, 139-40; of 1985, xxi, 27; of 1986, 27; of 1992, xxi-xxii; postponement of, xxi, 113, 118; reform of, xxi, 118

Elections Assistance Board, xxi

Elections and Boundaries Commission, 259, 265; voter register of, 266

electoral districts, 259, 263

electoral process

Belize: 264-66

Guyana: 118

electric power

Belize: 192; generation, 241; shortages, 241

Guyana: blackouts, 92; demand for, 92; facilities, 92; foreign investment encouraged in, 102; generation problems, 88; need for investment in, 77, 92; private production of, 93; shortages, xxi, 27, 67, 77-78, 92

elite class

Belize: 204-6; base of social power, 204; in Belize City, 205; under British rule, 173; control by, 169; economic interests of, 204; education of, 205-6; ethnic groups in, 205; lifestyle of, 205; marriage in, 205

Guyana: 31; Afro-Guyanese in, 13, 17; education of, 52-54

Elizabeth II (queen), 255

El Salvador: Belize Defence Force deployed to, 300; immigrants to Belize from, 195

emigration

Belize: 194; causes of, 210; of Garifuna, 169; of parents, 209; rate of, 195; to United States, 189, 193, 206

Guyana: 38-40; annual, 38, 40; causes of, 38, 78, 92; destinations of, 38; of managers, 73, 84; of professionals, 67; of skilled workers, 67

Employers and Workers Bill (1943), 178

energy resources

Belize: 192, 241

Guyana: 92-93

English language

Belize: xvii, 171, 172, 200, 201

Guyana: xvii, 42, 43

Enmore shootings, 17

Enterprise for the Americas Initiative, 101, 233, 235, 237, 281

EPZ. *See* export-processing zones
ERP. *See* Economic Recovery Program
Esquivel, Manuel, 261, 277; ethnicity of, 267, 272; as leader of UDP, xxvi, 267, 272, 273; as prime minister, xxvii
Essequibo: courts in, 8; economic growth in, 7; occupied by Britain, 8; settled, 6
Essequibo River, 6, 34, 94
Ethiopian Orthodox Church, 48
ethnic: associations, 269, 278; cleavage, 19, 31; diversity, xx, xxv, 196, 202–4
ethnic groups (*see also under individual groups*)
  Belize: cultural patterns in, 171–72; distribution of, 198, 200; impact of immigration on, 198; marriage among, 202; in middle class, 206; tensions among, 210, 268
  Guyana: 40–44; importance of differences among, 43–44; introduction of, 9–10; political parties of, 16; political polarization of, 16; animosity between, 70; stereotypes of, 44
ethnic identity
  Belize: 196–200, 202–3; factors in, 197; and religion, 201
  Guyana: 43–44
European Economic Community (EEC), 328; assistance from, 104, 213, 340; Belize's ambassador to, 286; Britain in, 321; exports to, 85, 86, 98, 235, 245; relations with, 123
Europeans
  Belize: 198
  Guyana: xx, 37, 43
Exclusive Economic Zone, 147
executive branch (*see also* executive president; president): of Belize, 244–50, 255–58; of Guyana, 113–15
Executive Council (Belize), 252, 253; members, 252
executive president, xx, 26, 113–15; appointments by, 115, 116; as commander in chief, 136; grounds for removal of, 113; loyalty to, 118; powers of, 113–15, 117, 118; term of, 113
Export-Import Bank, 340
export-processing zones (EPZs), 232–33
Export-Processing Zones Act (1990), 232
exports (*see also under individual products*)
  Belize: of cedar, 174; of chicle, 174; under colonial rule, 166; growth of, 225; of logwood, 173, 223; of mahogany, 173, 174; of sugar, 227
  Guyana: 97–99; of crops, 84; decline in, 14; of diamonds, 76; of gold, 76; in Great Depression, 14; illegal, 76; of rice, 76, 86; of shrimp, 76, 88; as source of foreign exchange, 86; of sugar, 76, 85; value of, 97

Falkland Islands (Malvinas): invasion by Argentina, 126, 128
families: Afro-Guyanese, 44–46; Indo-Guyanese, 47
Federation of Independent Trade Unions of Guyana (FITUG), 82, 122
Ferris State College, 213, 271
financial institutions, 72; foreign investment encouraged in, 102
financial relations, international: normalization of, 80–81
Financial Times, 68, 75, 85, 94
Fiscal Incentives Act (1990), 232
fiscal performance, 233
fishing, 240, 298; as percentage of gross domestic product, 240
FITUG. *See* Federation of Independent Trade Unions of Guyana
floods, 85, 86
food
  Belize: access to, 217; import of, 173, 217
  Guyana: 60; production, self-sufficiency in, 67
Food and Nutrition Institute, 333
foreign assistance
  Belize: 234; from Canada, 218; from European Economic Community, 218; from relief agencies, 218; strings attached to, 281; from United States, 217
  Guyana: 104; aid flows, 104; from Brazil, 96; from Canada, 104; for energy production, 93; from European Economic Community, 104; for transportation, 96; from United States, 104, 124
foreign: borrowing, 73; debt. *See* debt, external; economic relations, 235–36
foreign currency: demand for, 77; illegal trading of, 75; legalized trading of, 68,

78; shortage of, 76; sources of, 76–77; traders, 76
Foreign Currency Act (1979), 79
foreign exchange
  Belize: earnings, 228; rate, 229
  Guyana: attempt to ration, 73, 75–76; decline in, 73; earnings, 71; illegal, 73; legalization of, 96; liberalization of, 78, 79; regulation of, 72, 78, 79; restrictions on, 76, 94; rice as source of, 86; sugar as source of, 85
foreign exchange rates: black market, 76; floating, 79; official, 76, 79; overvalued, 75; unified, 68; unofficial, 79
foreign holdings
  Belize: 204–5; in agriculture, 204; of property, 271
  Guyana: nationalization of, 20–21
foreign investment
  Belize: 232, 245; creation of climate for, 230–31, 271; in sugar industry, 224, 224
  Guyana: 72, 102–4; in agricultural production, 102; in bauxite industry, 70, 90; concerns regarding, 103–4; encouragement of, 68, 78, 102; in energy production ,93; in fishing industry, 88, 102; in manufacturing, 93–94; in mining industry, 89, 91–92; need for, 94; permission for, 67; in pharmaceutical industry, 93; in sugar industry, 71; in timber industry, 88; in transportation, 96
foreign management: of manufacturing, 94; of mining industry, 89, 90; need for, 94
foreign military relations, 300–301; with Britain, 300; with Canada, 300; with United States, 300
foreign ownership, 71–72; and economic problems, 71–72
foreign relations
  Belize: 280–86
  Guyana: 123–29
forestry
  Belize: land controlled by, 172–73; as percentage of gross domestic product, 240; products, export of, 174, 224, 240
  Guyana: 88; dispute over, with Suriname, 147–48; as foreign exchange earner, 88; foreign investment in, 88, 102; military support for, 136; production, 88; products, export of, 74, 88; rights, 127
forests, 33, 86; access to, 88; management of, 88
Fort George Hotel, 242
France: in British-Dutch war, 8; in Donor Support Group, 100; foreign investment from, 102; Guyana ruled by, 8; Netherlands occupied by, 8; settlements, 163; war of, with British, 8
French Guiana, 4
fuel: imports of, 99
Fuentes, Ydígoras, 183
Fuller, Herbert, 269
Fyffes International, 238

gangs
  Belize: 209
  Guyana: 143
Garifuna language, 172, 201
Garifuna people, xxiii, xxv, 157, 172; agriculture pioneered by, 173; distribution of, 200; emigration of, 169, 195, 196; occupations of, 208; origins of, 198; percentage of, in population, 198; religion of, 201, 202; reservations for, 169
garment industry, 241
Garvey, Marcus, 178
GATT. *See* General Agreement on Tariffs and Trade
GAWU. *See* Guyana Agricultural and General Workers' Union
GCE. *See* General Certificate of Education
GDF. *See* Guyana Defence Force
GDP. *See* gross domestic product
GEC. *See* Guyana Electricity Corporation
General Agreement on Tariffs and Trade (GATT), 245
General Certificate of Education (GCE), 56
General Workers' Union (GWU), 178, 234, 270, 274; cooperation of, with People's Committee, 275; membership in, 274
geography
  Belize: 161, 189–93; area, 189; boundaries, 189; cays, 161, 189; geology, 191; lagoons, 189; size, 189, 225, topography, 191–92

Guyana: 31–35; land area, 31; location, 31; zones, 31
Georgetown, 8, 38, 117; crime in, 133; population of, 38
Germany: in Donor Support Group, 100; exports to, 99, 238
Germany, Democratic Republic of (East Germany); trade agreement with, 21
Giant Resources, 92
GIWU. *See* Guiana Industrial Workers' Union
GLU. *See* Guyana Labour Union
GNP. *See* gross national product
Goa Declaration on International Security (1983), 323
Godolphin Treaty (1670), 163–64
gold
Belize: 192
Guyana: 91–92; discovery of, 10; exports of, 97, 98, 99; foreign investment in, 91–92, 102; location of, xix, 33; market value of, 92; mining of, 75; processing, 93; production, 91, 92; reserves, 89; smuggling of, 75, 76, 91
Golden Star Resources, 92
Goldson, Philip, xxvi, 180, 269, 271, 272, 277; jailed, 181
Goliath-Knight company, 90
Gombay, 275
Gordon, Minita, 255
government
Belize: xxv; expenditures, 233; health policy, 219, 220; Peace Corps volunteers in, 281; revenues, 233; schools run by, 211, 212
Guyana: 113–18; church opposition to, 122; control of economy, 72, 75; executive branch, 113–15; foreign exchange rationed by, 73, 75–76; governor under, 18; ministerial system under, 18; as percentage of gross domestic product, 74; relations of, with labor, 121; response to parallel economy, 77; spending, 62, 72, 73, 78
government, cooperative republic. *See* cooperative republic
government, first People's Progressive Party (1953), 18–19; British suspension of, xix, 18; controversial issues under, 18
government, interim (1953–57), 19
government, local
Belize: 263–4
Guyana: 116, 117
government, PNC/UF coalition (1964–68), 22
government, second People's Progressive Party (1957–61), 19–21
Government Gazette, 260, 279
Government Technical Institute, 58
governor
Belize: 251; powers of, 251, 253
Guyana: xix, 12, 18, 109–10, 111; elimination of, 24
governor general
Belize: 255–58; appointments by, 256–57, 261, 263; authority of, 255–56; as commander in chief, 298; qualifications of, 255; role of, 255; term of, 255
Guyana: 111
Granger, David, 139
grass roots class. *See* lower class
Great Depression
Belize: xxiv, 174–78, 226; Belize Estate and Produce Company in, 175
Guyana: 14
Greater Antilles: settlement of, 4
Greenridge, Carl, 78
Grenada, 18, 325; invasion of, 105, 124, 126, 128
gross domestic product (GDP)
Belize: agriculture, 231; construction, 242; current expenditures, 233; defense, 300; development expenditures, 233; fishing, 240; forestry, 224, 240; government revenues, 233; growth of, 228; telecommunications, 243; tourism, 231
Guyana: agriculture, 74; balance of payments, 101; budget deficit, 80; construction, 74; current account deficit, 80; debt payments arrears, 81; decline in, 67, 82; external debt, 74, 99; government, 74; growth of, 72; imports, 97; manufacturing, 74; mining, 74; service sector, 74; trade, 97; value of 67
gross national product (GNP)
Belize: 225;
Guyana: foreign investment as percentage, 71
Guatemala: attacks by, 295; constitution

of, 283; immigrants to Belize from, 195; relations of, with People's United Party, 181; relations with, 282–84, 285; territorial claim of, to Belize, xxiv, xxvi, 157, 181–84, 226, 249, 253, 282–84, 291, 293, 294–95
Guevara, Ernesto "Che," 21
Guiana: etymology of, 4
Guiana Agricultural Workers' Union, 21
Guiana Industrial Workers' Union (GIWU), 17; strikes by, 19, 22
Guyana Agricultural and General Workers Union (GAWU), 82, 121; political affiliations of, 82
Guyana Airports Limited, 96
Guyana Bar Association, 140
Guyana Business, 97
Guyana Chronicle, 122
Guyana Council of Churches, 51; conflict of, with Burnham government, 51–52; criticism by, of government, 51, 122, 140; opposition of, to political parties, 122
Guyana Defence Force (GDF), 133–40; Afro-Guyanese in, 133, 136; border security by, xx, 136; capabilities of, 136–37; civic-action role of, 136; commander in chief of, 136; connection of, to People's National Congress, 133; criteria for officers, 134; election fraud by, 118, 137–40; Indo-Guyanese purged from, 134; internal security by, 136; matériel for, 136; missions of, 133, 136, 140; noncommissioned officers in, 133–34; number of troops in, 133, 136; officers in, 133–34; organization of, 136–37, 140; pay and benefits in, 137; political role of, 133, 134–36, 137–40; protocol signed with Venezuelan Army, 147; purged, 139; restructuring of, 139; services in, 133; training, 134, 136; uniforms, ranks, and insignia, 137; women in, 136, 137
Guyana Defence Force Air Command, 133, 137
Guyana Defence Force Maritime Corps, 133, 137
Guyana Electricity Corporation (GEC), 80, 92; capacity of, 92; deterioration of, 92; generation by, 92; rehabilitation of, 93
Guyana Fisheries Limited, 88, 103
Guyana Fertility Survey, 37
Guyana Geology and Mines Commission, 92
Guyana Human Rights Association, 144, 145
Guyana Labour Union (GLU), 82
Guyana Manufacturing and Industrial Development Agency (Guymida), 102
Guyana Mining Enterprise Limited (Guymine), 74, 89; foreign management of, 90
Guyana Ministry of Agriculture, 58
Guyana Ministry of Education, Social Development, and Culture, 54; Education Department under, 54
Guyana Ministry of Higher Education, 54
Guyana Ministry of Labour, 58
Guyana National Guard, 133
Guyana National Service (*see also* Guyana Defence Force), 133, 140; Afro-Guyanese in, 140; avoidance of, 141; corps of, 140; created, 140; Indo-Guyanese in, 140–41; political indoctrination in, 141
Guyana National Service State Paper, 140
Guyana People's Militia, 133
Guyana Police Force, 142; intimidation by, of opposition, 133; Mounted Branch, 142; people killed by, 144; response of, to gangs, 143; role of, 133; Rural Constabulary, 142; shooting of workers by, 17; Special Constabulary, 142
Guyana Rice Milling and Marketing Authority, 86
Guyana Rice Producers' Association, 86
Guyana School of Agriculture, 58
Guyana Sugar Company (Guysuco), 74, 84, 85
Guyana Telecommunications Corporation, 97
Guyana Timbers, 102
Guyana United Sadr Islamic Anjuman, 49
Guyana Volunteer Force, 133
Guyana Youth Corps, 140
Guymida. *See* Guyana Manufacturing and Industrial Development Agency
Guymine. *See* Guyana Mining Enterprise Limited
Guysuco. *See* Guyana Sugar Company
GWU. *See* General Workers' Union

Hallelujah Church, 48
Heads of Agreement (1981), 184; contents of, 283; opposition to, 275–76, 283
Heads of Government Conference, 329–30, 334
health (*see also* medicine)
Belize: 218–20; government policy on, 219, 220
Guyana: 60–62; expenditures, 62; services, 61–62
health care
Belize: access to, 217, 219; distribution of, 219; quality of, 225
Guyana: access to, 62; facilities, 61, 62; military support for, 136; national insurance for, 62; right to, 112; in rural areas, 62
Hererra Campíns, Luis, 125
High Court, 115, 144–45; jurisdiction of, 116
Hill, David (*see also* Washington, Edward), 50, 142
Hill Bank, 298
Hinduism, 47, 48–49, 202; festivals of, 49; orthodox, 49; percentage of followers in population, xx, 47; political pressures on, 52; political role of, 122, 123; reform, 49; rituals in, 48; status of, 48; Vaishavite, 48
Hoare family, 175–76
Holi, 49
Homestake Mining, 92
Hondo River, 189
Honduran Independence Party, 271
Honduras; immigrants to Belize from, 195
Hong Kong: investment from, 342
hospitals, 219
Hotel Training School, 333
House of Assembly, 110
House of Israel, 50, 142–43; activities of, 50, 51, 142–43; number of members in, 142; and People's National Congress, 50, 122, 142
House of Representatives, 253; elections to, 266; members of, 259; quorum in, 259; Speaker of, 259
housing: access to, 217
Hoyte, Hugh Desmond, 3, 112, 121; as executive president, xxi, 27, 109, 143; visit of, to United States, 28
Hoyte administration (1985–93), 27; economy under, 67, 78, 120; elections under, 118; foreign policy under, 28, 123, 124, 128, 129; House of Israel under, 50; human rights under, 144; People's National Congress under, 119–20; political reforms in, 27–28
human rights: abuses, 143–44; under Hoyte, 144
Hummingbird Highway, 242, 243, 282
Hungary: trade agreement with, 21
Hunt Oil, 103
hurricanes: of 1931, 175, 193, 251; Greta, 193; Hattie, 193; Janet, 193
Hyde, Evan X., 280
hydrology
Belize: 191–92
Guyana: 34

Ibo people, 166
Id al Adha, 49
Id al Fitr, 49
IDB. *See* Inter-American Development Bank
IMET. *See* International Military Education and Training
IMF. International Monetary Fund
immigrants: illegal, 302–3; occupations of, 210, 226
Imperial Conference: of 1926, 321; of 1932, 321
imports
Belize: 227; under colonial rule, 166; of food, 173
Guyana: 71, 99; effect of foreign exchange restrictions on, 76; illegal, 73; as percentage of gross domestic product, 97; restrictions lifted, 79; value of, 99
income: average, 217; distribution, 223, 225
Income Tax Act (1990), 232
indentured laborers, 31, 40; and education, 52, 59; from India, xviii, 10, 40; recruiting of, 40
indentured service, 10; abolished, 13, 70; terms of, 40
independence
Belize: achievement of, xxiv, 184, 249, 295; demands for, 183, 294; influences on, 212; obstacles to, xxiv, 181, 283; origins of movement for, 178; recognition of, 182; statements of case for, 183; transition to, 181–84

Guyana: 3, 111–12; date set for, 23
India: in Commonwealth of Nations, 322; indentured workers imported from, xviii, 10, 40; independence of, 322
Indians. *See* East Indians
indigenous people. *See* Amerindians; Maya people
Indo-Guyanese culture, 14, 46–47; caste in, 41, 46; education in, 58–59; family in, 47; intimidation of, by military, 133; men in, 47; religion in, 50; retention of, 41; weddings in, 46; women in, 47
Indo-Guyanese people, 3, 17, 41; acculturation of, 43; under British rule, 52; British values of, 44; conflicts of, with Afro-Guyanese, 3, 70; education of, 52; emigration of, 40; as farmers, 70; gang attacks on, 143; geographic distribution of, 43; as indentured workers, 41; in lower class, 42; occupations of, 14; as percentage of population, xx, 37; in professional class, 41; purged from officer corps, 134; religion of, 47; in rural areas, 38; social distribution of, 43; as teachers, 55
Industrial Development Unit, 324
Industrial Programming Scheme, 333
Industrial Training Centre, 58
industry
  Belize: 240–42
  Guyana: 92–94
infant mortality, 35–36, 61
inflation
  Belize: rate of, 228–29, 229
  Guyana: 75
infrastructure
  Belize: 245; lack of, 242
  Guyana: 77–78; deterioration of, 27, 67, 68, 86; foreign investment in, 102; lack of basic, 77; loans for, 100; need for investment in, 77, 94
Institute of Commonwealth Studies, 324
Institute of Education, 58
insurrection of 1969, 23, 136, 145–46
Intelsat. *See* International Telecommunications Satellite Corporation
Inter-American Development Bank (IDB), 93, 234, 340
Inter-American Regional Organization of Workers (Organización Regional Interamericana de Trabajadores—ORIT), 274
interior highlands, xix, 31, 33–34, 84; attempts to populate, 140; mountains in, 33; savannah in, 33–34
Internal Revenue Service Code, Section 936, 104, 340
internal security, 301–7
International Confederation of Free Trade Unions, 235, 274
International Development Association (IDA), 88
International Military Education and Training (IMET), 300
International Monetary Fund (IMF)
  Belize: 341; economic stabilization plan, 268; presence of, 273; standby arrangement with, 228; special drawing rights, 228
  Guyana: economic recovery program of, xxi, 68, 74, 81; loan from, 99, 100
international reserves, 228
International Telecommunications Satellite Corporation (Intelsat), 243
International Trade Commission, 340
investment
  Belize: 231–32
  Guyana: 79
Iraq, 286
irrigation: deterioration of, 86; in Mayan civilization, 158; and village layout, 38
Isaiah Morter Harambe Association, 278
Islam, 47, 48, 49; holidays of, 49; orthodox, 49; percentage of followers in population, xx, 41, 47; political pressures on, 52; reform, 49; status of, 48
Islam, Sunni, 49
Itzá people, 163

Jagan, Cheddi, xviii, 3, 20; attempt by, to resolve conflict with Burnham, 25; background of, 16; church opposition to, 122; conflict of, with Burnham, 15–16, 18–19; education of, 16; in election of 1992, xxi–xxii; as executive president, xxii; People's Progressive Party founded by, 17, 120; as prime minister, xviii, xix, 21–22, 110, 111; veto by, of participation in West Indies Federation, 20, 128
Jagan, Janet Rosenberg, 16; political office held by, 17; political roles of, 123
Jamaica: Belize Defence Force deployed to, 300; conquered by Britain, 163
Japan: aid from, 325, 340; exports to, 99; investment by, 97, 102

Jehovah's Witnesses, 48, 278
Jessell Securities, 71, 72
Jesuits: influence of, 212, 214, 277
Joint Consultative Group, 331
Jones, Jim (*see also* People's Temple of Christ), xx, 25-26, 50
Jonestown massacre (*see also* People's Temple of Christ), xx, 25, 26, 50-51
judges
  Belize: appointment of, 261, 305; types of, 261-62
  Guyana: appointment of, 116
Judicial Committee of the Privy Council in London, 262, 306
judicial officers, 115-16; tenure of, 115-16
Judicial Service Commission, 116
judiciary
  Belize: 261-62; appointments to, 261
  Guyana: 115-16, 144-45; courts in, under Dutch rule, 8

Kaieteur Falls, 34
Kaieteur Plateau, 33, 34
Kanuku Mountains, 33, 34
Kekchí Maya people, 171, 198
kidnapping, 302
King, Sydney, 19
Kinich Ahau, 159
Koama, Ohena, 144
Kuru Kuru Cooperative College, 58
Kwakwani: aluminum mines at, 90
Kwayana, Eusi, 144

labor
  Belize: 234-35; force, 234; shortage of, 234; unrest, xxiv, 294
  Guyana: 82-84; conditions, 176; reforms, 178; relations of, with government, 121; shortage, 6; unrest, 14, 22, 111
labor movement, 180; and job-related issues, 275; as political force, 275
labor unions
  Belize: 274-76; legalized, xxiv, 178
  Guyana: xviii; connection of, to political parties, 82, 121; role of, in anticolonial movement, 83; role of, in nationalization, 83
Labour Amendment Act (1984), 121
Labourers and Unemployed Association (LUA), 177, 274; in independence movement, 178
Labour Party, 16
Labour Relations Act (1953), 19, 110
Labour Relations Bill (1964), 21-22
Lachmansingh, J.B., 19
Ladyville Barracks, 300
lagoons, 189, 191
Lamanai, 159-60, 161; excavation of, 161
land
  Belize: arable, 226; ownership of, 173
  Guyana: arable, 84; area, 31, 84; covered in forest, 86; distribution of, 40; reclamation, xviii, xix, 3, 7, 33, 69; tenure, 115
language (*see also under individual languages*), 200-1; and social stratification, 201
Latin America: education in, 217; support by, for Belize's independence, 283
Latin America Integration Association, 328
leader of the opposition, 257
League of Coloured People, 18
League of Nations, 321
Legislative Assembly
  Belize: 250-51; established, 170, 252; members of, 170, 250-51, 252; replaced, 251; surrendered, 250
  Guyana: 21, 110
Legislative Council
  Belize: 172, 251; agitation for elective, 174; elections for, 176, 251; members of, 173-74, 251; powers of, 251; replaced, 252
  Guyana: 14, 19, 110; elections for, 110; membership in, 15
legislature
  Belize: 249, 258-61; bills in, 260
  Guyana: 110, 115; under constitution of 1961, 21; members of, 115; minority leader in, 115; powers of, 115
Lend-Lease Act (1941), 15
Lesser Antilles: abandonment of, 7; settlement of, 4
Lethem, Sir Gordon, 15
Leucadia company, 93
Lewis, Arthur, 328
Liberal Party, 272
lieutenant governor, 172, 251

life expectancy
- Belize: 218, 225
- Guyana: 61

Lilian Dewar College of Education, 58
limestone, 192
Linden, 117; aluminum mines at, 90; population of, 38
Lindo, Dean, 272
literacy rate, xx, 52, 58
livestock, 74, 85, 88
living costs, 227
living standards
- Belize: 217–22, 223, 225; in Guyana, 27
- Guyana: 27

logwood, xxiii, 223, 224; decline of, 224; exports of, 223; harvesting of, 163, 165
Lomé Convention, 85, 235, 238, 322, 334
London and Scottish Marine Oil Company, 103
London Convention (1814),10
London Missionary Society, 52
Longchamps (*see also* Georgetown), 8
lower class
- Belize: 204, 208–10; education of, 208, 215, 216; ethnic composition of, 208; households, 209; members of, 208; occupations of, 208, 210; rural, 210; unemployment among, 209; women in, 209
- Guyana: Amerindians in, 42

Low German, 201
LUA. *See* Labourers and Unemployed Association
Lubaantún, 159
Luyt, Richard, 133

McLean, Norman, 139
Macusi tribe, 42
Madeira, 41
magistrate's court
- Belize: 261, 306
- Guyana: 115, 116, 144–45

magistrates, 261
mahogany, 223; depletion of, 174, 224; exports of, 173, 174, 175, 224; harvesting of, xxiii, 165, 167; processing, 167; production, xxiv, 174, 176; trade, decline of, xxiv, 174; workers' rebellion, 177, 294
Major, John, 245
malaria, 60, 218
Malaysia: investment by, 88
malnutrition, 60; of prisoners, 145
Malvinas. *See* Falkland Islands
Manatee Hills, 191
Manche people, 161; displaced by Spanish conquerors, 162
Manpower Citizens Association (MPCA), 16, 121
manufactured products: exports of, 97
manufacturing
- Belize: 241; protections, 241
- Guyana: 75, 93–94; conditions for development of, 94; employment in, 82; foreign investment in, 93–94, 102; as percentage of gross domestic product, 74; privatization of, 93, 94; products, 93

Mao Zedong, 20
marijuana, 209; efforts to eradicate, 302; production, 230, 291, 302
marriage
- Belize: in elite class, 205; across ethnic boundaries,210
- Guyana: age for, 36; ceremonies, 46, 47; common-law, 46, 47; durability of, 46; first, 46; forbidden to slaves, 46; interethnic, 42, 43; women in, 36

martial law (Belize), 294
Masters and Servants Act (1883), 176, 178
matériel: army, 136; from Britain, 136; from the Soviet Union, 136; from the United States, 136
Maya Mountains, 191
Mayan civilization, xxii–xxiii, 157–61; agriculture in, 158; archaeology of, 158, 159; architecture of, 159; art of, 158, 159; breakdown of, 161; calendrical system of, 158; distinguishing features of, 158–59; economy of, 158; emergence of, 158; occupations of, 158; Spanish conquest of, 161–63
Mayan dialects, 201
Maya people, xxiii, xxv, 157, 171; agriculture pioneered by, 173, 240; attacks by, on British, 171, 293; distribution of, 200; identification as, 202; religion of, 201, 202; reservations for, 169, 293; resettlement of, 171, 176, 293; resistance by, to British, 170
media, 122
Melbourne Declaration (1981), 323

Melhado, Henry I., 174
Mennonites, 198, 200; agriculture by, 240; exemptions for, 264
merchant class, 172
Mestizo people, xxv, 157, 171, 267; agriculture pioneered by, 173; culture of, 171; distribution of, 198, 200; in elite class, 205; identification as, 202–4; immigration of, 196; occupations of, 206–8; physical features of, 197–98; power of, 210; religion of, 201, 202, 208
Methodist Church, 48, 201; missionaries of, 167; schools of, 214
Mexico: aid from, 340; Belize Defence Force deployed to, 300; border with Belize, 293; claim to Belize by, 182; electricity from, to Belize, 241; immigrants to Belize from, 195–96; recognition of Belize's independence, 182; relations with, 285; support for Belize's independence, 183, 283
Michigan Partners, 212
middle class
  Belize: xvii, 204; Afrocentric cultural consciousness in, 208; British cultural influence on, 268; education of, 206, 210, 216; emigration by, 206; members of, 206; religion in, 208
  Guyana: xvii, 12; Afro-Guyanese in, 17, 24; British values of, 44; education of, 52–54, 55; emigration of, 40; Portuguese in, 41; pressure from, for reform, 12; reaction of, to Burnham, 24; respect for, 58
Middle East, 286
migration (*see also* emigration)
  Belize: 195–96; of Central Americans to, 189, 211; destinations for, 195; impact of, on ethnic balance, 198; urban, 210
  Guyana: 40
military aid, 281
military history (Belize), 292–95
militia, 292
minerals
  Belize: 192
  Guyana, 93
mining
  Belize: 240–41
  Guyana: 38, 74, 89–92; employment in, 82; foreign investment in, 89, 102; foreign management of, 89; military support for, 136; as percentage of gross domestic product, 74
ministerial system, 18
ministers
  Belize: 257
  Guyana: 115
Mirror, 122
missionaries, 42, 50, 162, 201; attempts to convert Mayans, 162; attempts to suppress African culture, 167; Protestant, 278
Misuse of Drugs Act (1990), 306–7
Monetary Authority (Belize), 244
money laundering, 230
Monroe Doctrine, 11, 170
Mons Office Cadet Training School, 134
Mopán Maya people, 161, 171, 198
Moravian Church, 48
Morgan, Carl, 139
Mormons, 278
mortality, 7
Mosquito Coast (Costa de Mosquitos), 165
Mountain Pine Ridge, 191, 298
mountains, 33
Mount Roraima, 33
Moyne, Lord, 14
Moyne Commission, 14; directives of, 14
MPCA. *See* Manpower Citizens Association
Mulford, David, 101
municipal councils, 263; elections for, 263; role of, 263
Multi-fibre Arrangement, 235, 241, 338
Musa, Said, 270, 284, 286
Muslims (*see also* Islam), 122

Napoleonic Wars, 8
National Alliance for Belizean Rights, xxvi
National Assembly
  Belize: 249; elections, 258; established, 253; members' qualifications, 258; term of, 258
  Guyana: voting for, 118
National Congress of Local Democratic Organs, 116, 117
National Democratic Front, 120
National Democratic Party (NDP), 18

National Drug Abuse Control Council, 306
National Garifuna Council, 278
National Guard Service, 141; creation of, 141; mission of, 141; number of personnel in, 141
National Independence Party, 271
National Insurance Board, 62
nationalization, 72, 112; advocated by Jagan, 20; under Burnham, xx, 112, 113, 124; ended, 79, 102; of foreign holdings, 20–21, 67; role of labor unions in, 83
National Newsmagazine, 279
National Party, 181; founded, 271
National Security Act, 139, 145
National Trades Union Congress of Belize, 235, 274
native Americans. *See* Amerindians
Natives First campaign, 179
natural resources, 192
Nazarene Church, 48
NDP. *See* National Democratic Party
Nestlé, 237
Netherlands (*see also under Dutch*): occupied by French, 8; settlers from, 69; war of, with British, 8
New Amsterdam, 38, 117; population of, 38; rainfall in, 35
New Delhi Statement on Economic Action (1983), 323
New Nation, 122
New River, 192
New River Triangle: dispute over, 147
newspapers (*see also* journalists; media)
    Belize: 279
    Guyana: 28, 122
New Zealand: in Commonwealth of Nations, 321
Nicaragua: support by, for Belize's independence, 183
Nimli Punit, 159
Nisshan Suissan company, 103
Nonaligned Movement (NAM), 129
    Belize: as member of, 286; Belize's case for independence presented to, 183, 283
    Guyana: as member of, 24; support by, for Belize's independence, xxiv, 183
nonalignment, 123
Norsk Hydro company, 90
North American Free Trade Agreement, 237, 245
North Korea: physicans from, 62
Northern Telecommunications, 97
Norway: investment of, in mining, 89, 90
nurses, 62

OAS. *See* Organization of American States
Obeah, 50
occupations: of immigrants, 210
Office of the United States Trade Representative, 340
oil (*see also* petroleum)
    Belize: imports of, 241
    Guyana: imports of, 99, 100
Oils and Fats Agreement, 331, 332
Old River, 192
OPIC. *See* Overseas Private Investment Corporation
Orange Walk: courts in, 306; East Indians in, 199; street vendors in, 196; violence in, 209
Orange Walk District, 193, 263; Maya in, 200; Mennonites in, 200; Mestizos in, 198; religion of, 202; Spanish language in, 200–201
Organisation of Eastern Caribbean States, 325, 329
Organización Regional Interamericana de Trabajadores. *See* Inter-American Regional Organization of Workers
Organization of American States (OAS), 284, 337; application for membership in, 125, 127; support by, for Belize's independence, xxiv, 283; support by, for Guatemala's claim to Belize, 282
Orinoco River, 10, 11
ORIT. *See* Inter-American Regional Organization of Workers
Overseas Private Investment Corporation (OPIC), 104, 340

PAC. *See* Political Affairs Committee
PAC Bulletin, 16
Pakaraima Mountains, 33
Pakistan: in Commonwealth of Nations, 322; independence of, 322

Panama: support by, for Belize's independence, 183
Pan American Health Organization, 218
Paranapanema, 92
Patamona tribe, 42
Patriotic Coalition for Democracy (PCD), 120
PCD. *See* Patriotic Coalition for Democracy
Peace Corps, 281, 340; and education, 212, 214; volunteers in Belize, 200, 273, 281
peasant class, 9
Pembroke Hall, 224
Peñaloza, Carlos, 147
pensions, 62
Pentecostal Church, 48, 201
People's Committee: cooperation of, with General Workers' Union, 275; formed, 180, 270
People's Democratic Movement, 120
People's Development Movement, 272
People's Militia, 141; creation of, 141; mission of, 141; number of personnel in, 141; organization of, 141; political indoctrination in, 141; recruitment for, 141; training for, 141; uniforms of, 141
People's National Committee, 178–79
People's National Congress (PNC), 109, 119–20; destabilization campaign by, 21–22; founded, 15, 20, 119; gangs sponsored by, 143; Hindus in, 123; and House of Israel, 50, 142; under Hoyte, 27, 119; ideology of, 119–20; labor unions connected to, 82, 121; loyalty to, 118, 133, 134–36, 145; Muslims in, 123; in 1961 elections, 21; in 1964 elections, 22; in 1968 elections, 24, 111; in 1980 elections, 27; in 1985 elections, 27; power of, 111, 113; publications of, 122; support for, 52
People's Progressive Party (PPP), xviii, 120; Afro-Guyanese abandonment of, 20; British aversion to, 17–18; church opposition to, 122; coalition government of, xxii; demonstrations against, 21; founded, 15, 17; labor unions connected to, 82; in 1953 elections, 110; in 1957 elections, 20; in 1961 elections, 21; in 1968 elections, 24; in 1980 elections, 27; in 1985 elections, 27; in 1992 elections, xxi–xxii; opposition to, 51; platform of, xxi–xxii, 20; publications of, 122; reform program of, 18; schism in, 18–19, 20
People's Pulse, 279
People's Republican Party, 178
People's Temple of Christ (*see also* Jones, Jim; Jonestown massacre), xx, 25–26; allegations of abuse at, 51; government view of, 26
People's United Party (PUP), xxvi, 178, 249, 269–271; business support for, 276–77; cabinet under, 260; defeat of, in 1984 election, 267, 272; dispute with UDP, 301–2; dissatisfaction with, 270; divisions in, 270, 275; economy under, 228, 271; education under, 212; in election of 1989, 267, 268; formed, xxiv, 180; ideology of, 271, 284; and independence, 253; leadership of, 270–71; orientation of, to Central America, 268–69; origins of, 270; relations with Guatemala, 181; relations with United States, 280; weaknesses in, 266–67, 272; wings of, 270–71
Persian Gulf War, 286
Petrojam, 237
petroleum (*see also* oil)
  Belize: dependence of, on imported, 192; exploration for, 192, 241
  Guyana: exploration for, 103; price controls on, 79
pharmaceutical industry, 93; foreign investment in, 102
Philip Goldson international Airport, 243
physicians
  Belize: 219
  Guyana, 62
Pierce, Franklin, 170
Pilgrim, Ulric, 139
Pinzón, Martín, 162
piracy, xxiii, 162, 163, 223; suppression of, 292; treaty to suppress, 163
Placer Dome, 92
plantation agriculture, 166; efforts to develop, 714
Plantation Ruimveldt, 13
planters: political power of, 11; problems of, with Dutch West India Company, 7–8; resistance of, to constitutional reform, 12
plantocracy
  Belize: xvii, 166, 172
  Guyana: xvii, 9
PNC. *See* People's National Congress

polder system, 7
Police Special Force, 304
Police Training School, 304
Political Affairs Committee (PAC), 16
political: demonstrations, 50, 291; reform, 12; structures in Belize, 249-55; system, 225; violence, 26, 111
political parties (*see also under individual parties*)
  Belize: 250, 269-274
  Guyana: xviii, 119-20; development of, 15-18; labor unions connected to, 82
political roles: of business community, 276; of Chamber of Commerce and Industry, 276; of Guyana Defence Force, 133, 134-36, 137-40; of religious groups, 122-23, 276-78
politics: racial polarization of, 16; and religion, 51-52, 277
Pope, Ronald, 133
population (*see also* population statistics)
  Belize: 193-96; age distribution, 194-95; defense force as percentage of, 297; density, 193, 194, 226; distribution of, 193-94, 225; Garifuna as percentage of, 198; gender ratio, 194; rural, 193, 225; of immigrants, 195; in 1980, 193; percentage of, in Belize City, 193; percentage of, in Belize District, 193; percentage of Catholics in, 202
  Guyana: 35-40; Afro-Guyanese as percentage of, xx, 37; age distribution in, 35; crowding of, 60; density, 37; distribution of, xix, 31, 37-38; distribution of religion in, 47; ethnic distribution in, 37; of Georgetown, 38; Indo-Guyanese as percentage of, xx, 37; of Linden, 38; of native Americans, 6; of New Amsterdam, 38; in 1990, 35; rural, 37; of slaves, 6; urban, 38
population statistics
  Belize: birth rate, 195; death rate, 195, 218; fertility rate, 195; infant mortality rate, 195, 218; life expectancy, 218, 225; rate of increase, 195
  Guyana: birth rate, 35; death rate, 35-36; fertility rate, 36-37; growth rate, 35, 37; infant mortality rate, 35-36, 61; life expectancy, 61; mortality rate, 7
ports
  Belize: 238, 243
  Guyana: 102
Portugal: indentured servants recruited from, 40, 41
Portuguese language, 42
Portuguese people, xviii, 41; acculturation of, 43; cooperation of, with other ethnic groups, 12; discrimination against, 12, 41; as indentured workers, 41, 70; occupations of, 41; as percentage of population, 37; religion of, 48; as sugar plantation workers, 10
Potaro River, 34
PPP. *See* People's Progressive Party
PPP-Civil coalition, xxii; goals of, xxii
Presbyterian Church, 48
president (*see also* executive branch; executive president), 24, 111; position abolished, 26
press (*see also* media; newspapers); freedom of, 122
Price, Clarence, 134, 139
Price, George Cadle, 179, 180, 181, 183, 249, 269, 279, 284; characteristics of, 270; economy under, 233; ethnicity of, 267; as leader of People's United Party, 266, 267, 268-69, 270; orientation of, to Central America, 268-69, 272; popularity of, 270; as prime minister, xxv, xxvi, 283
Price Barracks, 298
price controls, 68, 79
primary products, 71; processing of, 75
prime minister
  Belize: 249; appointment of, 256-57; as defense minister, 298
  Guyana: 115; under constitution of 1961, 21, 110-11
prisoners, 145
prison system, 145
private investment: encouraged, 120
privatization, 68; of bauxite industry, 80; of manufacturing, 93-94; of sugar industry, 80
productivity, 81; losses in, 83
professional class, 41
Project Concern, 218
Project Hope, 218, 278
Protestantism (*see also under individual*

denominations), 171; ethnic affiliations with, 171, 202, 208; missionaries, 201; percentage of followers in population, 47
Protocol of Port-of-Spain (1970), 125, 147
Public Meeting, 166, 249, 250; participation in, 250
public-sector deficit, 80; attempts to cut, 80; as percentage of gross domestic product, 80
public services
Belize: 262–63; employees, 262–63, 301
Guyana: deterioration of, 27
Public Services Commission, 262, 305; powers of, 262
Public Service Union, 234, 275
Puerto Rico, 339
Punta Gorda, 169; courts in, 306; municipal government of, 263; troops stationed at, 298, 299
PUP. *See* People's United Party

Queen's College, 54

radical nationalists, 178, 179
radio
Belize: 243
Guyana: 97
RAF. *See* Royal Air Force
Ramada Royal Reef Hotel, 242
Rastafarianism, 48, 202
Reagan, Ronald, 124, 337
reexport business, 228
Reform Association, 12
Reform Club, 12
Regional Democratic Council, 116, 117
Regional Food and Nutrition Strategy, 333
regional integration, 104–5, 334, 335; progress toward, 329
Regional Shipping Council, 328, 331, 333
regions, 117
religion (*see also under individual sects*)
Belize: 201–2; and education, 201; and ethnicity, 201; in middle class, 208; syncretic, 201
Guyana: 47–52; distribution of, in population, 47; importance of, for marriage, 46; and politics, 51–52
religious cults, 50–51
remittances from expatriates
Belize: 195, 234
Guyana: 67, 76, 77
Reporter, 279
Representation of the People Ordinance, 265
Republic Day, 49
Reynolds Bauxite Company, 71, 72, 90
Reynolds Metals Company, 71
rice, 84; area under cultivation, 86; decline in exports of, 14; decline in production of, 67, 73, 74, 86; exports of, 74, 86; farming, 42, 70; in Great Depression, 14; imports of, 74; killed by plant diseases, 84; price controls on, 79; problems with, 86; processing, 75, 93; production, xviii, 86; shortages, xxi, 27, 74; smuggling of, 76
Richardson, Leigh, 180; jailed, 181
Ridley, Nicholas, 254
riots
Belize: 176–77; against Heads of Agreement, 283, 294–95; labor, 176, 294
Guyana: xix, xxii, 13, 14; against People's Progressive Party administration, 21
rivers
Belize: 192, 219
Guyana: 34
roads
Belize: 243
Guyana: construction of, 127; need for improvement of, 77; network of, 96
Robertson Group, 92
Rodney, Donald, 26
Rodney, Walter, 26; arrested, 26; assassinated, 26, 144
Rogers, C.L.B., 254
Roman Catholic Church
Belize: 205; ethnic distribution of, 201; influence of, 277; membership in, 48, 208; percentage of followers in population, 47, 202; political role of, 277; publications of, 2800; school system controlled by, 201, 205
Guyana: 41, 171; opposition of, to People's Progressive Party, 51; publications of, 122; role of, 51; support of, for United Force, 51
roots class. *See* lower class

Rosenberg, Janet. *See* Jagan, Janet Rosenberg
Royal Air Force (RAF), 291
Royal Bank of Canada, 94
Royal Military Academy (Sandhurst), 134
Ruimveldt Riots (1905), 13
Rules of Origin, 331, 332
Rupununi rebellion, 23–24, 146; Venezuela's role in, 146
Rupununi River, 34
Rupununi Savannah, 33; Amerindian tribes in, 42; rainfall in, 35
rural areas
  Belize: 209; Central American immigrants in, 193; lower class in, 209–10; population in, 225; population growth in, 193; schools in, 209–10
  Guyana: health care in, 62; Indo-Guyanese in, 38; malnutrition in, 60; population in, 37
Ryan, Leo, 26, 51

Sahlman Seafoods, 103
Saint George's Cay, 293
Saint John's College: graduates of, in politics, 179, 269, 277
Salahuddin, Salim, 121
Salamanca de Bacalar, 162
San Ignacio, 263; courts in, 306
sanitation, 60, 61
San Jose, 176
San Pedro, 263
Sarstoon River, 189
Sataur, Raymond, 134
Schomburg, Robert Hermann, 10
schools
  Belize: 210, 213–14; British model for, 214; degrees from, 214; enrollments in, 211, 215–16, 225; government control of, 211, 212; graduates, 211; Jesuit influence on, 214; levels in, 214; number of, 211; Peace Corps volunteers in, 281; secondary, 214
  Guyana: attendance, 54, 55, 56, 58; church, 51; entrance examinations for, 55–56; government control of, 51, 54–55; grades, 55; number of, 55, 56; number of years in, 52; nursery, 55; primary, 52, 55; private, 52, 54–55; public, 52; secondary, 55–56; religious, 54–55; teacher-training, 52; trade, 56, 58, 59
seawalls, xviii, 77
Secondary School Entrance Examination (SSEE), 55–56
Secondary Schools Proficiency Examination, 56
Security and Intelligence Service (SIS) (Belize), 268, 301; missions of, 301; opposition to, 301
Security and Intelligence Service Act (1987), 302
self-reliance, 25
self-rule (Belize), 253
Senate
  Belize: members of, 260; powers of, 253; President of, 259
  Guyana: 21, 110
Serrano Elías, Jorge, xxvi, 284
service sector, 94–97; employment in, 82; as percentage of gross domestic product, 74
Settlement of Belize in the Bay of Honduras, 157, 170, 249, 292; laws of, 164–65; self-rule of, 249; superintendent of, 165
Seventh-Day Adventist Church, 48, 201, 278
sewage systems, 219
Shahabbuddeen, Mohammed, 112
shamans, 50
Sharper, 168
shipping, 102
Shoman, Assad, 270
shrimp: catch, 88; exports, 88, 97, 98; foreign investment in, 102, 103; production, 88; smuggling of, 76
Sibun River, 192
Singh, J.B., 16
Singh, Joe, 147
SIS. *See* Security and Intelligence Service (SIS)
slavery, 3, 40, 157; abolished, xviii, 9, 40, 168; ramifications of abolition of, 9
slaves, xvii, xviii, 6–7, 166; culture of, 166–67; division of labor among, 167; domestic, 167; emancipation of, 3, 69, 250; escape by, 168; importation of, 6; marriage forbidden to, 46; in militia, 292, 293; mortality rate of, 7;

oppression of, 167–68; population of, 6, 69, 166; rebellions by, 7, 168; sources of, 166; on sugar plantations, 31; tax on, 8; trade, abolished, 9; working conditions for, 7
Smith, John, 181
smuggling, 77; by European powers, 163; of diamonds, 75, 76; of gold, 75, 76
Soberanis Gómez, Antonio, 177, 274
social security
Belize: 220
Guyana: 62
society, Belizean: dynamics of, 210–11; structure of, 204–10
Society for the Promotion of Education and Research, 278–79
soldiers: riots by, 294
Southern Christian Union, 275
South Korea: investment by, 88, 342
Soviet Union: relations with, 123, 129
Spain: attacks by, on British settlers, xxiii, 164, 165–66, 292, 293; rivalry of, with Britain, 157, 163–64, 292
Spanish conquest, xvii; of Greater Antilles, 4; of Mayan societies, 161–64; resistance to, 162
Spanish language, 171, 172, 200
Spearhead, 279
Special Service Unit (SSU) (Guyana): ethnic balance within, 134; origins of, 133; recruiting for, 134
Sri Lanka, 325; in Commonwealth of Nations, 322; independence of, 322
SSEE. *See* Secondary School Entrance Examination
Stabroek (*see also* Georgetown), 8
Stabroek News, 122
Stalin, Josef, 20
Standing Committee of Foreign Ministers of Caricom, 334
Standing Committees of Ministers, 331
Stann Creek, 169
Stann Creek District, 193, 263; agriculture in, 237; Garifuna in, 200; Mayans in, 200; Mestizos in, 200
State Council, 110
state enterprises, 77
state of emergency
Belize: of 1981, 184
Guyana: in 1963, 111; of 1964, 22; of 1991, 118
Statute of Westminster (1931), 321, 322
Stephens, John, 169
strategic setting, 292–95
strikes
Belize: 176–77, 291, 301; against Heads of Agreement, 275–76
Guyana: 84; breaking of, 143; general, of 1964, 21–22; by Guiana Industrial Workers' Union, 19, 22; of 1905, 13; by sugar workers,22, 25
structural adjustment program (SAP), 229
students: number of, 56; service of, in Guyana National Service, 140–41
suffrage
Belize: extension of, xxiv, 252; restrictions on, 177, 180
Guyana: for Afro-Guyanese, 12; under constitution of 1980, 118; extent of, xviii, 18, 110; qualifications for, 15; for women, 14
sugar
Belize:
223, 224, 236–37; exports of, 227, 231, 236, 245; foreign investment in, 224; mills, 237; prices, xxv, 223, 227–28, 245; production, xxiv, 224, 236–37; quotas, 228, 235, 341; revival of, 229
Guyana: 3, 7, 84–86, 97; decline in demand for, 73; decline in exports of, 14; decline in production of, 67, 73, 74; exports of, 74, 84, 85, 97,98, 129; as foreign exchange source, 85; foreign investment in, 102; in Great Depression, 14; imports of, 74; killed by plant diseases, 84; price controls on, 79; prices of, 72, 85; processing, xviii, 75, 93; shortages, xxi, 27, 74; smuggling of, 76
sugar industry, 72; employment in, 71; energy for, 93; foreign investment in, 71; labor unions in, 82; nationalization of, 21, 84, 124; privatization of, 80; restructuring of, 85
sugar plantations, xviii, 31; canals in, 34; Chinese workers on, 10; departure of Afro-Guyanese from, 9–10; drainage networks in, 34, 38, 69; East Indian workers on, 10; indentured laborers on, 10, 31, 70; labor on, 43; labor shortages on, 9–10; land reclaimed for, 69; number of, 69; Portuguese workers on, 10; slaves on, 31, 69

sugar production, 71, 84; costs, 85; decline in, 25; problems in, 84–85
Sugar Protocol, 235
sugar workers: organization of, 21; strikes by, 22, 25
Summary Jurisdiction Court, 261, 306
Sunnatival Jamaat Islam, 49
superintendent of Belize, 250, 251; as commander in chief, 292
Supreme Congress of the People, 115, 116
Supreme Court
Belize: 291, 305
Guyana: 115, 144–45
Suriname, 4; border problems with, 123, 127, 147–48; fishing dispute with, 147–48; Guyanese living in, 127; relations with, 127
swamps, 33, 34

Taiwan: Belize's relations with, 286
Tate & Lyle company, 85, 224
taxes
Belize: under colonial rule, 166, 293
Guyana: 80, 94; evasion of, 77
teachers, 58; Afro-Guyanese as, 55; conditions for, 55; Indo-Guyanese as, 55; ratio of, to pupils, 55, 56; training of, 52, 58
Tecno Bago company, 93
Teekah, Vincent, 26, 144
Tele Network, 97
telephones
Belize: 243
Guyana: 97
television
Belize: 243
Guyana: 97
textiles, 97
Thomas, Clive, 75, 76
Thomas Lands School, 55
timber, 38; exports of, 97; foreign investment in, 88; processing, 93; production, 88
Timehri Airport: constructed, 15; development of, 96; military training at, 134
Tipu: autonomy of, 163; conquered by Spanish, 162; rebellion of, 162
tobacco: export of, 6
Toledo District, 193, 263; Central American immigrants in, 196; Garifuna in, 200; infant mortality in, 218; Mennonites in, 200; Mestizos in, 200; population density in, 194
Toledo Maya Cultural Council, 278
Torrijos, Omar, 184
Total oil company, 103
tourism
Belize: 229, 242, 303; arrivals, 242; constraints on, 242; receipts, 242
Guyana: and economy, 76; foreign investment encouraged in, 102; as percentage of gross domestic product, 231
TPC. Tropical Produce Company
trade (*see also* exports; imports)
Belize: 228; patterns, 236; preferential agreements, 235, 236
Guyana: 97–9; agreements, 21; balance. *See* balance of trade; as percentage of gross domestic product, 97; liberalized regulations for, 68
Trades Union Congress (TUC), 82, 121; elections, 121; political affiliations of, 82, 121; reform, 121–22
Trades Union Ordinance (1921), 13
trade union movement, 13; encouraged, 14
trade unions
Belize: 250; rights of, 301
Guyana: 120–22
transportation
Belize: 243
Guyana: 96; air service, 96; need for investment in, 77; problems with, 96; roads, 96
Treaty of Chaguaramas, 329, 334
Treaty of Dickenson Bay, 328
Treaty of Munster (1648), 6
Treaty of Paris (1763), 164
Treaty of Saint John's, 328
Treaty of Versailles (1783), 164, 292
treaty to suppress piracy (1667), 163
Trinidad, 18
Trinidad and Tobago: debt to, 99, 105; in Donor Support Group, 100; foreign investment from, 102; imports from, 99, 100; petroleum exploration by, 103
Trinidad Citrus Association, 237
Tropical Produce Company (TPC), 240
Turton, Robert S., 174, 176, 177

Ubico, Jorge, 182
UCB. *See* University College of Belize:
UF. *See* United Force

Unemployed Brigade, 177
unemployment
Belize: 209, 234, 294
Guyana: 17, 71, 82
UNICEF. *See* United Nations Children's Fund
Union of South Africa: in Commonwealth of Nations, 321
United Colony of Demerara and Essequibo: British takeover of, 8; formed, 8
United Democratic Party, xxvi, 20, 249, 271–73; business support for, 276–77; disputes with People's United Party, 301–2; in election of 1984, 213, 267, 272; in election of 1989, 267, 268, 273; in election of 1993, xxvi; formed, 272; and independence, 253; internal problems of, 268, 272, 273; publications of, 280; relations of, with United States, 281; Roman Catholic influence on, 277
United Farmers' and Workers' Party, 18
United Force (UF), xxii, 21, 120, 123; destabilization campaign by, 21–22; in 1961 elections, 21; in 1964 elections, 22; in 1968 elections, 24; in 1980 elections, 27; in 1985 elections, 27; support for, 51
United Fruit, 238
United General Workers' Union, 275
United National Party, 18
United Nations: Belize as member of, 286; Belize's case for independence presented to, 183, 283; resolution passed demanding Belize's independence, 184
United Nations Children's Fund (UNICEF), 218
United Nations High Commissioner for Refugees, 303
United Nations International Labour Organisation, 220
United States, 325; aid to Belize, 212, 234, 280, 281; aid to Guyana, 101, 104, 124; as arbitrator in border disputes, 10–11, 183, 282; Belizean population in, 195; Development Assistance program, 281; in Donor Support Group, 100; Economic Support Funds, 281; economic ties of, with Belize, 226; education in, 205, 217; emigration to, 38, 189, 193, 195, 206; expatriates in Belize, 200; exports to, 85, 97–98, 237; foreign policy objectives, 280; Hoyte's visit to, 28; and independence of Belize, 283; imports from, 227, 344; influence of, on Belize, 208, 210, 212; intervention in Grenada, 105, 124, 126, 128; investment from, 70, 92, 97, 102, 280, 342–43; investment of, in mining, 89; military assistance from, 280, 281, 300, 302; military training in, 298, 300; missionaries from, 201; orientation toward, 277, 280; reduction of role of, 271; relations with Belize, 280–81; relations with Guyana, 123–24; trade quotas, 228, 235, 237; trade with, 236, 238, 343
United States Agency for International Development (AID), 104, 214, 234, 340; objectives of, 280–81; presence of, 273; role of, 281
United States Association of Junior Colleges, 214
United States Department of Agriculture, 340
United States Department of Commerce, 340, 342
United States Department of Labor, 340
United States Department of State, 82, 144
United States Department of Transportation, 340
United States Drug Enforcement Agency, 230
United States Tariff Schedule 807 program, 235, 241, 341, 344
Universal Negro Improvement Association, 178
University College of Belize (UCB), 213; nationalized, 271
University of Guyana, 26, 56, 140, 331; degrees awarded, 56; enrollment, 56; established, 54; Extramural Department, 58; faculties in, 56; teacher training in, 58
University of the West Indies, 214, 328, 331, 333
Upper Demerara Forestry Project, 88
urban areas
Belize: health care in, 219; schools in, 209–10, 215
Guyana: 38; Afro-Guyanese in, 38, 40; British values in, 44; Chinese in, 42; population in, 38
Uring, Nathaniel, 164

Varig airlines, 96
Venalum company, 90
Venezuela, 340; aid to Rupununi secession, 146; Ankoko Island seized by, 23, 145–46; army, 147; border dispute of, with Guyana, xx, 10–11, 23, 112, 123, 125, 145; in Donor Support Group, 100; imports from, 99, 100; relations of, with Britain, 10; relations of, with Guyana, 125–27, 147; territorial waters extended by, 146
vice president, 115
Victoria Peak, 191
villages
  Belize: government of, 263
  Guyana: layout of, 37–38; size of, 37
VITA. *See* Volunteers in Technical Assistance
Voice of America, 243, 273
Volunteer Guard, 296; deployment of, 299; enlistment in, 297
Volunteers in Technical Assistance (VITA), 278
voter qualifications: in Belize, 178, 251; in Guyana, 12
voting
  Belize: 251, 266; protocols, 265–66; rights, 265; by women, 251
  Guyana: 12; ethnic divisions in, xix; reform of, 27–28

wage: increases, 83, 94; minimum, 67; strikes, 13, 83
Waiwai tribe, 42
Wallace, Peter, 163
Wapisiana tribe, 42
war, 163
Warao people, 42
Washington, Edward ("Rabbi") (*see also* Hill, David), 50, 142; arrested, 143
water
  Belize: sources of, 219
  Guyana: access to potable, 61; shortages, 27; system, need for investment in, 77
waterfalls, 34
welfare
  Belize: 218–20
  Guyana: 61–62
West India Committee, 12
West India Association of Glasgow, 12
West Indians: as indentured laborers, 70
West Indies: education in, 205, 217
West Indies Federation, 180; Belize's resistance to joining, 226, 227, 268–69, 270, 284; demise of, 328; problems with, 328; Jagan's veto of participation in, 20, 128
West Indies Shipping Corporation, 333
West Indies States Association, 329
White Paper on the Proposed Terms for the Independence of Belize, 253
white sand belt, xix, 31, 33, 84
women
  Belize: emigration by, 194; as household heads, 209; as police, 304; and politics, 264; as soldiers, 297; unemployment of, 209; voting rights of, 178, 251; in work force, 234
  Guyana: maternity leave for, 62; in military, 136, 137; rights of, 112, 123; use of birth control by, 37
women, Afro-Guyanese: family role of, 46; fertility rate of, 36
women, Indo-Guyanese: family role of, 47; fertility rate of, 36; in Guyana National Service, 140–41; marriage of, 36; suffrage for, 14
Women Against Violence, 278
Women's Affairs Bureau, 123
women's associations, 123, 278
workers
  Belize: demands of, 177; rights, 342; riots by, 294
  Guyana: commuting costs for, 96; conditions for, 83; demonstrations by, 17; effect of economic reform on, 83; shooting of, 17
Workers' Education Unit, 58
work force: percentage of, employed in fishing industry, 88; percentage of, employed in sugar industry, 71
working class
  Belize: 180, 204; education of, 206, 216; emigration by, 206; independence movement in, 178; members of, 206
  Guyana: 12; Afro-Guyanese in, 17; political grievances of, 13; riots by, 13
Working People's Alliance (WPA), xxii,

120; demonstration by, 144; founded, 25; government violence against, 26; in 1980 elections, 27; in 1985 elections, 27
World Atlas, 225
World Bank, 225, 341; aid from, 88; debt to, 99, 100; economic recovery program of, xxi, 81
World Federation of Trade Unions, 275
World Health Organization (WHO), 218
World War I, 13, 294
World War II, 15
Worrell, DeLisle, 71
WPA. *See* Working People's Alliance
Wrigley, 174

Xunantunich, 159, 161; excavation of, 161

Yalbac, 176
Yalbac Hills, 171, 191
Yaum an Nabi, 49
Young Socialist Movement (YSM), 142; number of personnel in, 142; training for, 142
YSM. *See* Young Socialist Movement
Yucatán Platform, 191
Yucatecan people, 198

Published Country Studies

(Area Handbook Series)

550-65	Afghanistan	550-87	Greece
550-98	Albania	550-78	Guatemala
550-44	Algeria	550-174	Guinea
550-59	Angola	550-82	Guyana and Belize
550-73	Argentina	550-151	Honduras
550-169	Australia	550-165	Hungary
550-176	Austria	550-21	India
550-175	Bangladesh	550-154	Indian Ocean
550-170	Belgium	550-39	Indonesia
550-66	Bolivia	550-68	Iran
550-20	Brazil	550-31	Iraq
550-168	Bulgaria	550-25	Israel
550-61	Burma	550-182	Italy
550-50	Cambodia	550-30	Japan
550-166	Cameroon	550-34	Jordan
550-159	Chad	550-56	Kenya
550-77	Chile	550-81	Korea, North
550-60	China	550-41	Korea, South
550-26	Colombia	550-58	Laos
550-33	Commonwealth Caribbean, Islands of the	550-24	Lebanon
550-91	Congo	550-38	Liberia
550-90	Costa Rica	550-85	Libya
550-69	Côte d'Ivoire (Ivory Coast)	550-172	Malawi
550-152	Cuba	550-45	Malaysia
550-22	Cyprus	550-161	Mauritania
550-158	Czechoslovakia	550-79	Mexico
550-36	Dominican Republic and Haiti	550-76	Mongolia
550-52	Ecuador	550-49	Morocco
550-43	Egypt	550-64	Mozambique
550-150	El Salvador	550-35	Nepal and Bhutan
550-28	Ethiopia	550-88	Nicaragua
550-167	Finland	550-157	Nigeria
550-155	Germany, East	550-94	Oceania
550-173	Germany, Fed. Rep. of	550-48	Pakistan
550-153	Ghana	550-46	Panama

550-156	Paraguay	550-53	Thailand
550-185	Persian Gulf States	550-89	Tunisia
550-42	Peru	550-80	Turkey
550-72	Philippines	550-74	Uganda
550-162	Poland	550-97	Uruguay
550-181	Portugal	550-71	Venezuela
550-160	Romania	550-32	Vietnam
550-37	Rwanda and Burundi	550-183	Yemens, The
550-51	Saudi Arabia	550-99	Yugoslavia
550-70	Senegal	550-67	Zaire
550-180	Sierra Leone	550-75	Zambia
550-184	Singapore	550-171	Zimbabwe
550-86	Somalia		
550-93	South Africa		
550-95	Soviet Union		
550-179	Spain		
550-96	Sri Lanka		
550-27	Sudan		
550-47	Syria		
550-62	Tanzania